*Mark Smith is Professor of Theology,
Saint Joseph's University, Philadelphia,
Pennsylvania.*

JOURNAL FOR THE STUDY OF THE OLD TESTAMENT SUPPLEMENT SERIES
239

Sheffield Academic Press

The Pilgrimage Pattern
in Exodus

Mark S. Smith

with contributions by
Elizabeth M. Bloch-Smith

Journal for the Study of the Old Testament
Supplement Series 239

To my mother,
Mary Elizabeth Reichert Smith
(1922–1982)

For now we see in a mirror dimly,
but then face to face.
Now I know in part;
then I shall understand fully,
even as I have been fully understood.
So faith, hope, love abide, these three;
but the greatest of these is love.

1 Corinthians 13.12-13

Copyright © 1997 Sheffield Academic Press

Published by
Sheffield Academic Press Ltd
Mansion House
19 Kingfield Road
Sheffield S11 9AS
England

Typeset by Sheffield Academic Press
and
Printed on acid-free paper in Great Britain
by Bookcraft Ltd
Midsomer Norton, Bath

British Library Cataloguing in Publication Data

A catalogue record for this book is available
from the British Library

ISBN 1-85075-652-X

CONTENTS

PART I
LITURGICAL LIFE IN ANCIENT ISRAEL

ACKNOWLEDGMENTS

Like the Israelites' journeys in the wilderness in the books of Exodus and Numbers, this work proceeded in stages. The first was my reflections on the poem in Exodus 15 presented to my wife's family on the occasion of Passover in 1992. I thank my in-laws, Sonia and Ted Bloch, for their interest and support for this project. I initially unveiled my proposal for the literary arrangement of the priestly redaction of Exodus to Rabbi Dr Benjamin Scolnic who contributed a number of points. His comments and reflections graced the spring and summer of 1992. Since then Ben Scolnic and I have exchanged ideas in our on-going quest to unlock the Pentateuch. Professors Christopher Seitz and William Propp offered their criticisms and comments on an initial draft of Part II. I am grateful to Chris Seitz for many acts of kindness. Our many years together, both as students and teachers, have often made me rethink the place of theology in biblical studies and the place of the Bible in theological studies. A co-student from days of old at Harvard, Professor Propp is preparing the Anchor Bible volume for the book of Exodus, and Part II benefited from his advice. I have also had the opportunity to discuss some of the problems with Dr Aaron Schart during the 1992–93 academic year. Since then I have had occasion to discuss a number of questions involving priestly material with Professors Avi Hurvitz, Israel Knohl and Baruch Levine, and I thank all three of them for their kindness and generosity. In the fall of 1995 Dr Herb Levine and I enjoyed surveying together the modern history of Pentateuchal scholarship. Dr Levine also offered a critical assessment of the manuscript. As a result, I have altered the force of some arguments, amplified the presentation at some points and made smaller changes. I am very grateful to Dr Levine who has understood this work so well.

The Introduction was presented before the colloquium of Saint Joseph's Department of Theology in September of 1995. Professor Paul Aspan made many suggestions for improving section two, and Professors David Carpenter, Millie Feske and Steve Long raised a number of questions that they thought I should address further in section three. Based on their suggestions I have made many changes and additions to these sections. The members of the theology department have supported my work and spurred further thought on the place of specialized studies in the wider arena of theological reflection. Chapters 1 through 3 are derived from my notes for my Psalms class at Saint Joseph's University which I have taught a number of times over the past three years. I am heartfully grateful to all the students who have worked through this material with me. Constantly they remind me of the humble truth spoken by Origen at the beginning of his first homily on Exodus: 'it is important to recognize that there is knowledge of these words beyond our power'.[1] The excursus to Chapter 2 was presented first at Saint Vincent's College in Latrobe, Pennsylvania in February, 1995 (kindly hosted by Professor Elliott Maloney, OSB) and the national meeting of the Society of Biblical Literature held in Philadelphia in November, 1995. I am grateful to Richard J. Clifford, SJ, for offering several helpful suggestions to this chapter.

Chapter 6, as well as several details from Chapters 7 through 9, were presented before the Colloquium for Biblical Research held at Union Theological Seminary of Richmond in August of 1992 and before the Biblical Theology group at the Catholic Biblical Association held in Atchison, Kansas, in August of 1993. My presentation before these two groups provided many necessary additions and corrections as well as further thought. I am especially grateful to Professors S. Dean McBride, Richard J. Clifford, SJ and Thomas Dozeman for their insightful comments and criticisms. Chapter 6 was improved in the process of submitting it to the *Catholic Biblical Quarterly* which published it in 1996.

Chapter 10 was presented in part before the Biblical Theology group at the Catholic Biblical Association in August, 1995. Chapter 11 was submitted to a volume honoring and engaging the work of Brevard S. Childs, my former teacher and colleague.

I reserve a word of thanks to a number of my teachers. My first university teacher of Old Testament/Hebrew Bible was Dr Peter Kearney at Catholic University. Since my days at Catholic University, Peter Kearney has encouraged me. In graduate school I read Exodus with

---

1. Origen, *Homilies on Genesis and Exodus* (trans. R.E. Heine; Washington: The Catholic University of America Press, 1982), p. 228.

Professors Frank M. Cross, Aloysius Fitzgerald, and Dr Kevin O'Connell, SJ. Finally, the influence of Professors Robert R. Wilson and Brevard Childs may be seen in the attempt to address the historical and theological dimensions of Exodus. I was fortunate to have such fine teachers, and this book is better for their lasting influence. Of course, all failings and errors remain my own.

I am very grateful to Sheffield Academic Press for accepting this book for publication, and in particular to Eric Christianson for shepherding this study to its completion.

Finally, no book of mine is written without the daily voices of my family. To my wife, Liz, I am especially indebted not only for her contributions to Chapter 2, but also for her abiding interest and help in so many issues relevant to Syro-Palestinian archaeology and the ancient Near East. Our children, Benjamin, Rachel and Shulamit, likewise provide me with so many intimations and expressions of life. Thanks to my family I always know that I am blessed. This knowledge also includes the great concern and support of my father, Donald E. Smith, my step-mother, Barbara Pindar Smith, and my siblings, Greg, Cecily, Annie, Ronnie, Teresa, Val, Jeff and Stephanie. It has been a great comfort to travel through life with so many who have known me so long and well. This book is dedicated to the memory of my mother who died fourteen years ago. Good as these years have been, they have been less as a result; such things do not change. Yet in my family's daily expressions of affection I glimpse again her presence.

Department of Theology, Saint Joseph's University
16 October 1996

ABBREVIATIONS

AB	Anchor Bible
ABD	D.N. Freedman (ed.), *Anchor Bible Dictionary*
ABRL	Anchor Bible Reference Library
AGJU	Arbeiten zur Geschichte des antiken Judentums und des Urchristentums
AJSL	*American Journal of Semitic Languages and Literatures*
AJS Review	
AnBib	Analecta biblica
ANET	J.B. Pritchard (ed.), *Ancient Near Eastern Texts*
AnOr	Analecta orientalia
AOAT	Alter Orient und Altes Testament
ASOR	American Schools of Oriental Research
BA	*Biblical Archaeologist*
BARev	*Biblical Archaeology Review*
BASOR	*Bulletin of the American Schools of Oriental Research*
BDB	F. Brown, S.R. Driver and C.A. Briggs, *Hebrew and English Lexicon of the Old Testament*
BETL	Bibliotheca ephemeridum theologicarum lovaniensium
BHS	*Biblia hebraica stuttgartensia*
BI	*Biblical Interpretation*
Bib	*Biblica*
BibOr	Biblica et orientalia
BJRL	*Bulletin of the John Rylands University Library of Manchester*
BJS	Brown Judaic Studies
BO	*Bibliotheca orientalis*
BT	*The Bible Translator*
BWANT	Beiträge zur Wissenschaft vom Alten und Neuen Testament
BZAW	Beihefte zur *ZAW*
CAD	*The Assyrian Dictionary of the Oriental Institute of the University of Chicago*
CahRB	Cahiers de la Revue biblique
CB	*Cultura bíblica*
CBQ	*Catholic Biblical Quarterly*
CBQMS	*Catholic Biblical Quarterly*, Monograph Series
ConBOT	Coniectanea biblica, Old Testament
CRINT	Compendia rerum iudaicarum ad Novum Testamentum
DDD	*Dictionary of Deities and Demons in the Bible*
DJD	Discoveries in the Judaean Desert
DSS	Dead Sea Scrolls

EncJud	*Encyclopaedia Judaica*
ErIsr	*Eretz Israel*
ETL	*Ephemerides theologicae lovanienses*
FRLANT	Forschungen zur Religion und Literatur des Alten und Neuen Testaments
GBH	P. Joüon, *A Grammar of Biblical Hebrew* (trans. and rev. T. Muraoka; Subsidia biblica, 14.1.2; Roma: Editrice Pontificio Istituto Biblico, 1991)
HAR	*Hebrew Annual Review*
HAT	Handbuch zum Alten Testament
HDR	Harvard Dissertations in Religion
HSM	Harvard Semitic Monographs
HSS	Harvard Semitic Studies
HTR	*Harvard Theological Review*
HUCA	*Hebrew Union College Annual*
ICC	International Critical Commentary
Int	*Interpretation*
JAAR	*Journal of the American Academy of Religion*
JANESCU	*Journal of the Ancient Near Eastern Society of Columbia University*
JAOS	*Journal of the American Oriental Society*
JBL	*Journal of Biblical Literature*
JEOL	*Jaarbericht. . . ex oriente lux*
JJS	*Journal of Jewish Studies*
JNES	*Journal of Near Eastern Studies*
JPS	Jewish Publication Society
JQR	*Jewish Quarterly Review*
JSJ	*Journal for the Study of Judaism in the Persian, Hellenistic and Roman Period*
JSNT	*Journal for the Study of the New Testament*
JSOT	*Journal for the Study of the Old Testament*
JSOTSup	*Journal for the Study of the Old Testament*, Supplement Series
JSS	*Journal of Semitic Studies*
KHAT	Kurzer Hand-Commentar zum Alten Testament
KTU	The Cuneiform Alphabetic Texts from Ugarit, Ras ibn Hani, and Other Places
LAB	*Liber Antiquitatum Biblicarum*
LD	Lectio divina
Leš	*Lešonénu*
MARI	*Mari Annales des Recherches Interdisciplinaires*
NCB	New Century Bible
NJBC	New Jerome Biblical Commentary
NJPS	Tanakh. The Holy Scriptures: The New JPS Translation according to the Traditional Hebrew Text
NovTSup	*Novum Testamentum* Supplements
OBO	Orbis biblicus et orientalis
OTG	Old Testament Guides
OTL	Old Testament Library

OTP	*Old Testament Pseudepigrapha*
OTS	*Oudtestamentische Studiën*
PEQ	*Palestine Exploration Quarterly*
RB	*Revue biblique*
RHR	*Revue de l'histoire des religions*
RSV	Revised Standard Version
SBLDS	SBL Dissertation Series
SBLMS	SBL Monograph Series
SBLSBS	SBL Sources for Biblical Study
SBLSCS	SBL Septuagint and Cognate Studies
SBS	Stuttgarter Bibelstudien
Sem	*Semitica*
SJOT	*Scandinavian Journal of the Old Testament*
SJT	*Scottish Journal of Theology*
SOTSMS	Society for Old Testament Study Monograph Series
TA	*Tel Aviv*
TynBul	*Tyndale Bulletin*
UF	*Ugarit-Forschungen*
VT	*Vetus Testamentum*
VTSup	*Vetus Testamentum*, Supplements
WO	*Die Welt des Orients*
WUNT	Wissenschaftliche Untersuchungen zum Neuen Testament
ZAW	*Zeitschrift für die alttestamentliche Wissenschaft*

INTRODUCTION

1. *Presuppositions*

This study originated in two concerns which have occupied my attention
since the early 1990s. At that time I began to think about the character
of lawin Exodus as well as the literary framework andtheological concepts which Israelite redactional activity brought to this biblical book.
Law in biblical texts is hardly monolithic, and even within a single book
such as Exodus, readers are witnesses to its conceptual transformations.
The literary and theological result of redactional activity is a question
which has faced biblical scholars especially in the last two decades. Biblical interpreters over the past 150 years have been adroit at dividing
biblical books into sources and redactions, but we have been less interested in addressing the resulting literary-theological product. The processes of accumulation and redaction were hardly haphazard, but they
bear the marks of the ancients' literary traditions and theological concerns. Moreover, they witness to more than the redactors' viewpoints;
they issued in original works of great literary character and theological
purpose. This volume is largely a synthetic effort aimed at bringing to
bear on Exodus these twin concerns of the conceptualization of law and
the literary-theological product of redaction. The point of departure
for this investigation is the priestly arrangement of Exodus, the role of
pilgrimage in organizing the book, and the view of law that emerges
from this conceptual organization. The larger pattern or paradigm underlying the priestly presentation of covenant law in Exodus is pilgrimage. This liturgical journey in Israel was used as a literary pattern
to tell Israel's story in a number of biblical texts, including Exodus.
The literary product represented by the book's priestly formation is
rich in its accumulated senses of law. Perhaps most important of all
these senses, law belongs with narrative and vice-versa. The two provide identity and meaning for one another.

Part I surveys pilgrimage in ancient Israel, with an eye to pilgrimage
features in the book of Exodus. In order to appreciate the pattern of

pilgrimage in Exodus, it is necessary to lay out the major features of pilgrimage in ancient Israel, namely sacred journey and arrival to the temple, with the prayers and sacrifices which ensue. At several points along the way, these chapters discuss the relevant information about pilgrimage used in the book of Exodus. Indeed, Part I provides more than the formal groundwork for the analysis of Exodus in Part II; Part I also anticipates the discussion there at many points. As a result, Part I illustrates the cultic sensibility of the book of Exodus.

Part II of this work shows how the priestly redaction of Exodus modelled the literary arrangement of the book on the pattern of pilgrimage. The priestly arrangement of Exodus created a picture of Moses and Israel, first separately and then jointly, as pilgrims who journey to the mountain of God where they received their call and commission in liturgical fashion. The association of law and liturgy was hardly original with the priestly redaction of Exodus. The teaching of torah is evident in liturgical contexts, for example in texts such as Psalms 50 and 81. In turn, liturgical themes are sounded in priestly narrative pieces and redactional touches as well as the massive sections of instructional literature in Exodus. With the priestly redaction of Exodus this interrelation reaches its apex: liturgy and law came together as a single whole thanks largely to the priestly arrangment of the book. Because of these various interrelations, it may be said that law is integrally related to liturgy.

Part III offers some broader reflections on Exodus, especially on law in the book and its place in the larger context of the Pentateuch. At the very outset, it is important to clarify the meaning of the word 'law' in its biblical context. The Hebrew term is spelled sometimes torah, or Torah when used for the first five books of the Bible (the comparable Christian term is Pentateuch). This study sometimes uses תורה (except when referring to the first five books as the Torah or Pentateuch). While תורה is commonly translated 'law' in English, the word is understood etymologically and in many cases contextually as 'teaching' or 'instruction',[1] and this nuance applies to Exodus and the

---

1. For תורה, see BDB, p. 435; G. Östborn, *Tora in the Old Testament: A Semantic Study* (Lund: Håkan Ohlssons Boktryckeri, 1945); H. Gese, 'The Law', in *Essays on Biblical Theology* (trans. K. Crim; Minneapolis: Augsburg, 1981), pp. 60-92; J. Jensen, *The Use of Tôrâ by Isaiah: His Debate with the Wisdom Literature* (CBQMS, 3; Washington: Catholic Biblical Association, 1973), pp. 3-27; J.D. Levenson, 'The Sources of Torah: Psalm 119 and the Modes of Revelation in

Pentateuch as a whole. Law shows different understandings in Exodus which reflect different usages in ancient Israel. As a consequence, biblical law is to be seen in the context of a living, dynamic liturgical tradition. While the subsequent demonization of 'the Law' as a dead letter in Christian tradition seems to have passed from most theological discourse, the positive place of biblical law in Christian theology remains to be worked out. Most Christian professors of Old Testament are no longer hostile to Old Testament law as in ages past, but there remains the task of how Christians will address it in a constructive manner instead of simply passing over it in silence. It is my hope that this work will help make a contribution to future, theological discussions of law by examining it within some of its ancient contexts in Exodus. Part III examines the effect which the cumulative priestly redaction had on the understanding of 'law'.

Before formally beginning the study of Israel's pilgrimage celebrations and how they relate to the priestly arrangement of Exodus, it may be helpful to explain what led to this work and then to lay out the course of this study in greater detail. In the past authors have written long volumes on biblical matters without shedding any light on their personal presuppositions. In matters of theology this no longer seems desirable. Critical interpreters have raised the issue: 'How are we as critics implicated in our own social texts?' This question[2] is especially challenging to students of the Bible who have a confessional commitment, as it sometimes appears impossible to avoid, even with the greatest of effort, the interpretative stance expressed so well by L. Cormie: 'We see our lives in the Bible and the Bible in our lives'.[3] At times, it seems that the best we interpreters can do is to try to understand the ancient character of biblical texts and avoid using the Bible as a distorting mirror for our prejudices.[4] While cognizant of this state of

Second Temple Judaism', in P.D. Miller, Jr, P.D. Hanson and S.D. McBride (eds.), *Ancient Israelite Religion: Essays in Honor of Frank Moore Cross* (Philadelphia: Fortress Press, 1987), esp. p. 561.

2. So posed by R. Fraden, 'Response to Professor Carolyn Porter', *New Literary Criticism* 21.2 (1990), p. 277. See also C. Porter, 'Response to Rena Fraden', *New Literary Criticism* 21.2 (1990), pp. 279-81.

3. L. Cormie, 'Revolutions in Reading the Bible', in D. Jobling, P.L. Day and G.T. Sheppard (eds.), *The Bible and the Politics of Exegesis: Essays in Honor of Norman K. Gottwald on his Sixty-Fifth Birthday* (Cleveland: Pilgrim Press, 1991), p. 173.

4. Politically oriented critics espouse a more far-reaching goal to affect, if not to

affairs, reading into the text either ideas or meanings which are not in the text (eisegesis) remains. Fortunately, one scholar's eisegetical readings may be countered or constrained by the readings of other commentators. Yet, as every generation of scholarship makes its contributions, it is inevitable that each one also adds its own prejudices which later generations need to expose.

Despite these difficulties it is evident that many modern critical scholars have made many of their insights precisely because of the post-Enlightenment and denominational backgrounds which they bring to the text. Biblical scholars generally call for an awareness of one's background in order to avoid 'eisegesis', that is, reading into the text one's own ideas and agenda. With all its dangers, readings generated by denominational and personal backgrounds are not only inevitable, but also appropriate insofar as theological reflection on Scripture involves a person's theological convictions. Cardinal Jean-Marie Lustiger, a Jewish holocaust survivor, expresses the personal dimension of the theological task in honoring the life and work of Elie Wiesel:

> This unimaginable ordeal of faith is part and parcel of the struggle of faith. This is what Elie Wiesel ceaselessly keeps telling us, ever since he recovered the ability to speak the Word. To be a theologian is to chart this path and to struggle continually with God's incomprehensible love for his forsaken and distressed people.[5]

I believe that a Jewish feeling for law may advance Christian sensibilities for legal material in the Pentateuch and may serve as a deterrent against anti-Semitism found not only in some older Christian theologies of law, but also among contemporary Christians without their awareness. This personal perspective is informed by the circumstances of my life. I live, work and to an extent, identify, with two religious worlds related at their ancient roots and parallel in some areas (especially tradition and liturgy), but whose present horizons and sensibilities rarely coincide. I am a Roman Catholic from birth and faith, now teaching at Saint Joseph's University in Philadelphia. I also taught for two years at Saint Paul Seminary in Saint Paul, Minnesota (now the

transform, the world. See, for example, Cormie, 'Revolutions in Reading the Bible', p. 192. The goals are not only admirable, but also necessary, and they may serve as an important negative constraint on interpretation. How they function as positive criteria for biblical interpretation is not clear methodologically.

5.   J.-M. Lustiger, 'The Absence of God? The Presence of God? A Meditation in Three Parts on Night', *America* (November 19, 1988), p. 402.

Divinity School of the University of Saint Thomas). I was a student for sixteen years at Catholic institutions, including Saint Anselm's Abbey School and the Catholic University of America, both in Washington, DC. My wife and children are Jewish by birth and observance. We have attended services and maintained a kosher household for our fourteen plus years of family life. In addition, three years of research and travel in Israel included two terms at the Hebrew University. If it can be said that by the way people live their lives and raise their children, they indicate how they have chosen their destiny, then I envision my destiny as two-fold, entwined and perhaps emblematic of the joint journey for which I would imagine and hope Judaism and Christianity are destined. This theme, expressed by Cardinal Lustiger in a number of his writings, is a way of life for me. Both of these religious traditions inform this study. (By the same token I make no claims either to speak for the Jewish community or to provide a sufficient discussion of תורה in Judaism.) The appreciation for priesthood is at home in my Catholic upbringing, and my appreciation for Jewish law has come slowly over these years. At the heart of both Catholic and Jewish traditions stands a real sensibility both for liturgy and community.[6] For both traditions, freedom is not a matter of merely private, individual choice; freedom is achieved by participation in community, as it lives, shares and expresses life through celebration and shared norms.

The same may be said of the Pentateuch (Torah): the books of the Torah, especially in their priestly materials and redaction, grew out of a priestly liturgical life and in turn created a priestly vision of liturgical life for Israel. As noted above, the liturgical life expressed in the priestly literature of the Pentateuch and the Psalms derives from a single social matrix, the liturgical life of the temple.[7] The priestly narra-

---

6. The liturgy of the Mass continues to stand at the center of Catholic life and identity, but today the Catholic communitarian spirit may not be as evident in American culture as it once was. Yet note the comments of cultural critic and Roman Catholic, Richard Rodriguez; 'Two pronouns war within me—the American 'I' and the Catholic 'we'. Sometimes the tension is creative. There are other times when I feel Catholicism urging me toward a grammar and understandings that are un-American.' (P. Crowly, 'An Ancient Catholic: An Interview with Richard Rodriguez', *America* 173.8 [September 23, 1995], p. 9). For an appreciation of the Catholic communitarian tradition, see D. Hollenbach, SJ, 'The Catholic University and the Common Good', *Current Issues in Catholic Higher Education* 16.1 (1995), pp. 3-15 (reference courtesy of Nicholas Rashford, SJ).

7. See H.J. Levine, *Sing unto God a New Song: A Contemporary Reading of*

tive and redaction of the book of Exodus were informed by liturgical themes such as pilgrimage. תורה is not lifeless legalism, as Christianity has viewed it at times.[8] Torah covers not only laws in the legal sense, but also priestly instructional literature, poems, stories and many other genres. This 'law' was a dynamically developing body of religious literature. Apart from illustrating some of the failings of traditional Christian polemics aimed against 'the Law',[9] this volume may indicate the difficulty underlying the dichotomy made between 'the Law' and 'the Gospel' and the descendant dichotomy between law(s) and narrative. The study of Exodus in this work suggests that the contrast between 'the Law' and 'the Gospel' and the descendant dichotomy between law(s) and narrative[10] are inadequate as historical categories for the book. Indeed, they distort both the book's historical development and its theology as embodied in the book's priestly redaction.

This study would also call into question a possibly related dichotomy which presently informs discussions of biblical theology. In their

the Psalms (Indiana Studies in Biblical Literature; Bloomington: Indiana University Press, 1995), esp. pp. 32-35. Perhaps by beginning with the prophetic critique rather than the liturgical context, this dimension is understated in the otherwise helpful study of F. Crüsemann, *Die Tora: Theologie und Sozialgeschichte des alttestamentlichen Gesetzes* (Munich: Chr. Kaiser Verlag, 1992). For further connections between psalms and Pentateuch, see section 4 below. This point adds to the well-known point that many narratives in Exodus, priestly and otherwise, reflect liturgical themes. On this point, see for example, the famous study of W. Beyerlin, *Origins and History of the Oldest Sinaitic Traditions* (trans. S. Rudman; Oxford: Basil Blackwell, 1965).

8. For a fine attempt to demonstrate this point from the Jewish side, see R. Brooks, *The Spirit of the Ten Commandments: Shattering the Myth of Rabbinic Legalism* (San Francisco: Harper & Row, 1990), esp. pp. 14-7. My thanks go to Professor Paul Flesher for bringing this book to my attention. To be sure, Christians, biblical scholars and theologians have made important advances in their attitudes towards Torah. For example, see the many fine essays on Torah in E. Blum, C. Macholz and E.K. Stegemann (eds.), *Die hebräische Bibel und ihre zweifache Nachgeschichte: Festschrift für Rolf Rendtorff zum 65. Geburtstag* ((Neukirchen–Vluyn: Neukirchener Verlag, 1990).

9. See Crüsemann, *Die Tora*, pp. 7-10, 423-25.

10. Or, in the terms of J.D. Levenson, '*mythos*' to '*ethos*' or vice-versa. See Levenson, 'The Theologies of Commandment in Biblical Times', *HTR* 73 (1980), p. 19; *idem*, 'The Sources of Torah', p. 569. See also J.D. Levenson, *The Hebrew Bible, the Old Testament, and Historical Criticism: Jews and Christians in Biblical Studies* (Louisville, KY: Westminster/John Knox Press, 1993), p. 40.

attempts to find a successor to 'history', some scholars champion the label, 'story'.[11] This shift from 'history' to 'story' is understandable. The narrative materials in the Pentateuch and the so-called historical books do not comply with the modern canons of history, but of historiography.[12] On this basis, 'story' would therefore seem to be a better label, but this category has its limitations as well.[13] 'Story' does not accommodate the large sections of Pentateuchal laws and priestly instruction. Moreover, 'story' appears to be an intellectual category descendant from gospel and 'mythos', to use Levenson's term. The problem is not simply that 'story' sets legal and priestly instructional material to the side. Rather, it cannot account for the profound relationship between story and laws and priestly instructional literature in a book like Exodus. It will not do to make the counter-claim that while legal material is important in Exodus, ultimately the legal material appears in a narrative framework and may be subsumed under the larger category of narrative. Exodus does not subordinate story or the various legal and priestly materials to one another; instead, they depend on one another for their theological intelligibility.

The same point may be made on historical grounds. At several points in this study, it is evident that an old relationship between תורה ('law, instruction, teaching') and story affected the development of Exodus, and the two interpenetrate one another issuing in the whole book as תורה. This creation served historically as a source for teaching intended for all generations. If any single category could subsume the diversity of materials only within the book of Exodus, it might be teaching.[14] For Exodus this teaching is a source of life in creating not

11. See J. Barr, *The Bible in the Modern World* (New York: Harper, 1973), p. 55; *idem*, *The Scope and Authority of the Bible* (Philadelphia: Westminster Press, 1980), p. 5. Cited and discussed in J.J. Collins, 'Is a Critical Biblical Theology Possible?', in W.H. Propp, B. Halpern and D.N. Freedman (eds.), *The Hebrew Bible and its Interpreters* (Winona Lake, IN: Eisenbrauns, 1990), p. 10. See also Collins, 'The "Historical Character" of the Old Testament in Recent Biblical Theology', *CBQ* 44 (1979), pp. 185-204.
12. See Collins, 'Is a Critical Biblical Theology Possible?', p. 11.
13. For other criticisms, see B.S. Childs, *Biblical Theology of the Old and New Testaments: Theological Reflection on the Christian Bible* (Minneapolis: Fortress Press, 1992), pp. 18-20, 664; Collins, 'Is a Critical Biblical Theology Possible?', p. 10.
14. By this remark, however, I do not mean to privilege the Torah (i.e., the Pentateuch) over other parts of the Bible, which is the effect of arguments made by

only boundaries to demarcate community, but also internal direction to create community. Teaching over the past few years, I have been made aware of how 'anti-Law' attitudes are so woven into the fabric of Christian religious culture in the United States that students are often unaware that these attitudes are part of their mental world. In part, a deterrent against this situation will be achieved only when Christians realize that even New Testament attitudes toward Jewish law are much more complex than often assumed and do not generally support the idea of law as a lifeless legalism.

2. *Law and the New Testament*

Even a brief sketch will indicate the wide diversity of views of law in the New Testament. New Testament expressions about law range from Matthew's positive expressions about Law (Mt. 5.17-20) to the more negative Pauline evaluation (e.g. Gal. 3.19-29, 4.1-7).[15] The positive

O. Kaiser and N. Sarna. This is not to deny the importance of תורה ('teaching') outside of the Pentateuch (discussed by Kaiser), or the theme of תורה noted at significant junctures in the Jewish canon (so Sarna). See Kaiser, 'The Law as the Center of the Hebrew Bible', in M. Fishbane and E. Tov with W.W. Fields (eds.), *'Sha'arei Talmon': Studies in the Bible, Qumran, and the Ancient Near East Presented to Shemaryahu Talmon* (Winona Lake, IN: Eisenbrauns, 1992), pp. 93-103; Sarna, *Songs of the Heart: An Introduction to the Book of Psalms* (New York: Schocken Books, 1993), pp. 27-28. At the other extreme, it remains an important task to root out the scholarly anti-Semitism hiding behind criticisms of 'the Law', post-exilic Judaism or other 'scholarly' constructs. For a recent discussion of this tradition from de Wette to von Rad, see R. Rendtorff, 'The Image of Postexilic Israel in German Bible Scholarship', in Fishbane and Tov with Fields (eds.), *'Sha'arei Talmon'*, pp. 165-73. It is to be observed that W. Vatke was a notable exception from whom Wellhausen could have, but did not, learn. Vatke stands as an important reminder that nineteenth-century German Old Testament scholarship was hardly uniform. On Vatke's rejection of de Wette's view of the degeneration of Israelite religion after the exile, see J.W. Rogerson, *W.M.L. de Wette. Founder of Modern Biblical Criticism: An Intellectual Biography* (JSOTSup, 126; Sheffield: JSOT Press, 1992), p. 250. Scholarly anti-Semitism in descriptions of 'the Law' and post-exilic Judaism is now better understood and rejected, but more recently this scholarly tradition seems to have found refuge in 'scholarly' descriptions of earlier periods. See G.E. Mendenhall, *The Tenth Generation: The Origins of the Biblical Tradition* (Baltimore: The Johns Hopkins University Press, 1973), p. 226.

15. For general treatments of law in the Roman world, see E.P. Sanders, *The Jewish Law from Jesus to the Mishnah* (London: SCM Press; Philadelphia: Trinity,

accents certainly include the famous passage from the Sermon on the Mount (Mt. 5.18). Jesus is quoted as proclaiming:

> For truly I say to you, till heaven and earth pass away, not an iota, not a
> dot, will pass from the law until all is accomplished.

This verse 'asserts the permanence of the law while the physical universe lasts'.[16] Mt. 23.2-3 depicts Jesus advocating obedience to the scribes and the Pharisees, who 'sit in the chair of Moses'.[17] Parenthetically, it should be noted that Matthew contains severe criticisms of the Pharisees that teach an important lesson for a Christian biblical theology of law: an understanding of Law in New Testament sources need not be tied to their criticisms of the Pharisees. The increasing level of conflict with Jewish authorities in the Gospels seems to reflect ongoing Christian difficulties with them. While Mark shows conflict with the Jewish authorities (Mk 2–7), this Gospel shows a constructive and positive dialogue about the Law between Jesus and 'one of the scribes' (Mk 12.28-34), with Jesus quoting from the Law. In contrast, Matthew describes the same exchange with less equanimity (Mt. 22.34-40) and proceeds to greater conflict (22.41-46; 23.1-36; cf. 15.1-20; 21.23-27). Despite these tensions, it is important to note that in both Gospels, Jesus is concerned with teaching the divine law to his disciples and the people. What is to be underscored here is that the argument between Jesus and the authorities is not over a rejection of divine law, but over what constitutes divine law. Jesus, for example, seems to reject Pharasaic oral law in Mark 7, but he quotes the Sinai law and he shares the common Jewish acceptance of this law.

1990); and the essays in P. Richardson and S. Westerholm, *Law in Religious Communities in the Roman Period: The Debate over* Torah *and* nomos *in Post-Biblical Judaism and Early Christianity* (Studies in Christianity and Judaism, 4; Waterloo, ON: Wilfred Laurier University Press, 1991). See also the brief survey with bibliography in Sanders, 'Law in Judaism of the New Testament Period', *ABD*, IV, pp. 254b-65a. For an introduction to the problem of the understanding of *tôrâ* by *nomos* in the Graeco-Roman period, see A.F. Segal, 'Torah and *nomos* in Recently Scholarly Discussion', *Studies in Religion/Sciences Religieuses* 13 (1984), pp. 19-28 (reprinted in Segal, *The Other Judaisms of Late Antiquity* [BJS, 127; Atlanta: Scholars Press, 1987], pp. 131-45). On this point see also Segal, *Paul the Convert: The Apostolate and Apostasy of Saul the Pharisee* (New Haven, Yale University Press, 1990), p. 260.

16. B. Viviano, 'Matthew', *NJBC*, II, p. 641b.
17. So Levenson, *The Hebrew Bible*, p. 6.

Like Matthew, Luke held a positive regard for תורה. Like Mt. 5.18, Lk. 16.17 contains the saying of Jesus: 'But it is easier for heaven and earth to pass away than for one dot of the law to become void'.[18] Luke's views are expressed also through his historiography in the book of Acts. On the question of whether Jewish observance includes circumcision, the 'Jerusalem conference' as recorded in Acts reflects Luke's attitude toward Law. Luke offers a compromise between the Jewish Christians who insist on תורה observance (i.e. 'the believers who belonged to the party of the Pharisees' in Acts 15.5) and Paul's general rejection of it:

> Luke's Paul agrees with the authentic Pauline letters in saying that the law is good but does not offer a way to salvation (Acts 15.10; 13.39). Luke says that the gentiles should not be required to keep the *burdensome* parts of the Law (Acts 15.10, 28). Paul himself denies any motivation of ease. . . . Possibly, Luke was writing to effect a compromise position in a church that still contained an active and vibrant Jewish Christian community. . . . Luke's Paul does not say that Jews have misunderstood the law since the arrival of Christ, and there is no criticism in Luke of the Jewish desire to be justified by the law.[19]

> According to Acts, much of the church accepted that gentile Christians do not need circumcision. So Paul hardly invented or singlehandedly promulgated the idea.[20]

Luke seems to stand with the church leadership of Peter and James who do not agree with either Paul or the most traditional Jewish Christians. Luke and the leadership of Peter and James eventually accommodated the Gentiles with respect to circumcision and partly in regard to dietary laws.[21] Therefore, the Law continues to hold a role within the economy of salvation for Luke.[22] Like Matthew, Luke upholds the positive and constructive role of תורה in the spiritual life of Jewish Christians.

---

18. Unlike the form of the saying in Matthew, the form in Luke lacks the addendum, 'until all is accomplished'. See S.G. Wilson, *Luke and the Law* (Cambridge: Cambridge University Press, 1983), p. 13.

19. Segal, *Paul the Convert*, p. 146. Segal's italics.

20. Segal, *Paul the Convert*, p. 181.

21. Segal, *Paul the Convert*, p. 214. For further details of Luke's particular compromise view, see also J. Jervell, 'The Law in Luke–Acts', in his *Luke and the People of God: A New Look at Luke–Acts* (Minneapolis: Augsburg, 1972), pp. 133-51 (reference courtesy of Professor Paul Aspan).

22. Jervell, 'The Law in Luke–Acts', p. 147. See also Segal, *Paul the Convert*, p. 275.

When discussing the matter of Jewish Law and Christianity, the figure of Paul looms above the other New Testament authors not only because his views gradually dominated mainstream Christian theology, but also because he returns to the topic so often and in such a personal way.[23] Paul's theology on many issues is complex and even one of them cannot be done justice in such a short compass. Rather, only a short and simplified summary of Paul's views on Jewish תורה-observance is offered here. Paul is well-known for his rejection of the normative character of Jewish תורה, but it needs to be said at the outset that his view is complicated and many scholars do not regard it as consistent or systematic.[24]

23. The recent literature on Paul and the Law is immense. Important studies include (by year): H. Hübner, *Das Gesetz bei Paulus: Ein Beitrag zum Werden der paulinischen Theologie* (FRLANT, 119; Göttingen: Vandenhoeck & Ruprecht, 1978); E.P. Sanders, *Paul, the Law and the Jewish People* (Philadelphia: Fortress Press, 1983); H. Räisänen, 'Paul's Theological Difficulties with the Law', *JSNT* 3 (1980), pp. 301-20, and 'Legalism and Salvation by the Law', in S. Pedersen (ed.), *Die paulinische Literatur und Theologie. Skandinavische Beiträge* (Teologiske Studier, 7; Göttingen: Vandenhoeck & Ruprecht, 1980), pp. 63-83, reprinted in *The Torah and Christ: Essays in German and English on the Problem of the Law in Early Christianity* (Publications of the Finnish Exegetical Society, 45; Helsinki: Finnish Exegetical Society, 1986), pp. 3-24, 25-54 (cited here); Räisänen, *Paul and the Law* (WUNT, 29; Tübingen: Mohr–Siebeck, 1983); B.L. Martin, *Christ and the Law in Paul* (NovTSup, 62; Leiden: Brill, 1989); P. von der Osten-Sacken, *Die Heiligkeit der Tora: Studien zum Gesetz bei Paulus* (Munich: Chr. Kaiser Verlag, 1989); F. Thielman, *From Plight to Solution: A Jewish Framework for Understanding Paul's View of the Law in Galatians and Romans* (NovTSup, 61; Leiden: Brill, 1989); Segal, *Paul the Convert*; P.J. Tomson, *Paul and the Jewish Law: Halakha and the Letters of the Apostle to the Gentiles* (CRINT, 3; Jewish Traditions in Early Christian Literature I; Assen: Van Gorcum; Philadelphia: Fortress Press, 1990).

24. A succinct discussion of the difficulties of Paul's thought on law generally (and not only on Jewish Torah-observance) appears in Räisänen (*The Torah and Christ*, pp. 3-24). See the list of contradictions alleged by Räisänen (*The Torah and Christ*, pp. 8-9). Räisänen rejects a dialectical or paradoxical approach to Paul to resolve these apparent contradictions, since Christian scholars would not allow the same approach to the Dead Sea Scrolls or the Quran. Räisänen (*The Torah and Christ*, p. 3) shows a very critical assessment of Paul's thought: 'I wish to argue that Paul's thought is the real problem, rather than being the obvious solution to theological problems concerning the law. Paul had vast difficulties with the law, not on the existential level in his pre-Christian life, as older generations used to think, but as a Christian, on the theoretical theological level.' The difficulty may be on both levels. Cf. Segal's renewed emphasis on the experiential level expressed in Paul's theology

On the one hand, Paul upholds the positive character of the תורה, as it came from God. E.P. Sanders comments on Paul's reference to the Jews in Rom. 10.2:

> In recent years scholars have rightly been concerned to correct the view that Judaism was 'legalistic' in the pejorative sense, and this has led to the emphasis that *tôrâ* and *nomos* mean not only 'law' but also 'grace'. When this emphasis is accepted, the characterization of 1st-century Jews as being 'zealous for the law' (Rom. 10.2) means not that they sought meritorious achievement and thereby became self-righteous, but rather that they lived faithfully within the covenant which was given by God's grace.[25]

On the other hand, תורה-observance is not the means to salvation, but functions to indicate sin to those who observe it. Paul ultimately stresses the law as an instrument not of salvation, but of knowledge of sin (Rom. 3.19). Paul's concluding sentence to Rom. 7.9-12 may seem to lead in one direction: 'The law is holy, and the commandment is holy and just and good' (Rom. 7.12).[26] Yet even here the law has an educative function of indicating sin (7.13).[27] In sum, Paul treats תורה not on its own terms, but in its twin relationship with the Christian gospel.

Paul proclaims the gospel of Christ for Jews and non-Jews alike, but he is not always consistent in his treatment of the Jews and תורה. According to Sanders, 'Romans 2 repeatedly holds out the possibility of righteousness by the law as a real one'.[28] The positive judgment described in vv. 6-7 does not discriminate Jews from non-Jews:

of law in his *Paul the Convert*. Other Pauline scholars argue for the lack of contradiction in Paul's thought on *nomos* (see, for example, Martin, *Christ and the Law in Paul*). This debate is well beyond the scope of this study.

25. Sanders, 'Law in Judaism', p. 255a.

26. Segal, *Paul the Convert*, p. 226. Segal takes this passage as a personal statement on Paul's part, that at some point after becoming a Christian he felt the attraction of observing ceremonial Torah, but unlike other Jewish Christians he rejected it as antithetical to his Christian faith.

27. Räisänen (*The Torah and Christ*, p. 19) shows a very critical assessment of Paul's thought on the negative function of law: 'I find it hard to agree with those who value this negative assessment of law as a contribution of theological genius. I cannot help seeing it as another instance of artificial theorizing, the result of which is dictated by a priori considerations: Christ is the only way to salvation; therefore the law cannot be one; therefore another purpose must be found for the law, and a negative one at that.'

28. Sanders, *Paul, the Law, and the Jewish People*, p. 35.

> For he will render to every man according to his works: to those who by
> patience in well-doing seek for glory and honor and immortality, he will
> give eternal life;

whereas v. 25 speaks specifically to the Jewish people:

> Circumcision indeed is of value if you obey the law. . . For he is not a
> real Jew who is one outwardly, nor is true circumcision something exter-
> nal and physical. He is a Jew who is one inwardly, and real circumcision
> is a matter of the heart, spiritual and not literal.

Here Paul does not deny the value of physical circumcision, but affirms
its full realization only through interior religious conviction.

Paul provides statements which stand in tension with his own
theology on both theoretical and practical levels. Despite the general
thrust in Romans 2–3 and 9–11, Paul asserts that all—which would
include the Jewish people—will be saved (Rom. 11.32). In some of the
cases involved there is no clear declaration that this will take place as
a consequence of conversion. Sanders emphasizes the specific thematic
contexts for Paul's expressions that all will be saved:

> When Paul thought of those who reject the gospel, he considered them
> 'lost' or 'being destroyed' (see 2 Cor. 2.16; 4.3). When he thought of
> God's intention and the greatness of his mercy, he would say all would be
> saved (1 Cor. 15.22; 15.28; Rom. 11.32, 36).[29]

Despite his own theology, Paul offered accommodation to the Jewish-
Christian community on the practical level in circumcizing Timothy
(1 Cor. 7.17-20).[30] Within Paul's own thought and actions, a tension
existed over the relations of the Jewish people and its תורה to the
Christian community and its gospel.

The variety of formulations in Paul's theology of law has been recently ascribed to the personal character of his letters, which are not to
be regarded as systematic treatises. Rather, Paul's new understanding
of תורה resulted from his personal experience of conversion and
ministry.[31] Paul's experience necessitated a significant reorientation of
his religious convictions. The most notable of these was Paul's new

---

29. Sanders, *Paul, the Law, and the Jewish People*, p. 57 n. 63. See also Segal,
Paul the Convert, p. 280.

30. Segal, *Paul the Convert*, pp. 218-19, 242-43.

31. The precise background of Paul's Judaism remains a matter of great discussion. J.A. Fitzmyer argues that some of Paul's writings show greater contact with the
literature of Qumran than with rabbinic sources. See Fitzmyer, *According to Paul:
Studies in the Theology of the Apostle* (Mahwah, NJ: Paulist Press, 1993), pp. 18-35.

understanding of the value of Law in the drama of salvation. So A.F. Segal comments:

> Instead of trying to define Paul's new faith and the nature of his audience, most exegetes of Paul have pursued the implicit contrast between law and faith, supposing that since Paul believes that Jesus was the messiah, the law must be wrong. Such a tack is mistaken in two respects: (1) Paul does not say here that Torah is wrong; rather he asserts that its meaning is different from what he thought at first and that properly performing Torah is an all or nothing proposition; (2) he is not pursuing an intellectual argument about the value of abstract concepts; rather, he is exegeting a passage from the perspective of conversion, hence his justification and anticipated salvation. He is trying to legitimate a new concept of gentile community. Further, he is trying to show that those who have faith can also count themselves as part of the covenant relationship with Abraham.[32]

Paul does not discredit the Law, but in the aftermath of his 'Damascus experience', he understands the Law's place in a wider horizon of salvation. In his comments on Galatians 2, Segal explains this point more fully:

> For Paul, something critical happened to Torah, based on Christ's saving death. Paul knows that Torah must still somehow be true, because it comes from God and is necessary for understanding the meaning of Christ's mission and victory. He posits the idea, however, that the *complete* Torah law need not be the standard of righteousness, at least for the gentiles.[33]

Paul's post-conversion apocalyptic world-view stipulates that the complete תורה, while revelatory, cannot serve as a levee of righteousness against the pervasive power of sin.

3. *Toward a Christian Theology of Biblical Law*

Paul's experience led to a relativizing of law, but it did not issue in a clear Christian definition or understanding of it. For Paul, law remained a theological question, one which Christianity has never fully resolved for itself. Since this lack of resolution continues today, Christian theologians in this era of ecumenical understanding have an unparalleled opportunity at hand: it is imperative to transform biblical law into a positive resource for exploring Christian identity. The

32. Segal, *Paul the Convert*, p. 121.
33. Segal, *Paul the Convert*, p. 130. Segal's italics.

present Christian theological task of addressing differs from either Paul's or Matthew's because the present setting is not Paul's or Matthew's. Paul proclaimed the gospel of a Jewish sect to an audience that at once included Jews and non-Jews. Matthew addressed a Jewish-Christian community. Both writers were Jews often writing for Jewish-Christian audiences. Indeed, most, if not all, New Testament authors were Jewish.[34]

Unlike Paul, Matthew and the other New Testament writers, the vast majority of contemporary Christians are not Jews struggling to understand the relationship between their ancient heritage and their new Christian faith. Similarly, the modern theological quest differs from the stance of Jesus. Jesus' critique of Pharisaic traditions represents an inner-Jewish debate. No Christian view of law can be predicated on Jesus' assessment of Pharisaic rulings for two reasons. Two thousand years of Jewish life according to the joy of תורה cannot be judged by Christian outsiders based on first-century Jewish-Christian assessments. Indeed, any contemporary Christian viewpoint premised on Jesus' views would represent an outsider's denigration of another religion. At the close of the second millennium Christians are not in a position to define themselves or their gospel in relation to a faith, tradition and תורה-centered practice not only distinctly different from Christianity, but also alien to it. Furthermore, we Gentile Christians stand at a significant theological distance from our own New Testament because it is largely a series of works written by Jews for Jews. The Jewish theological foundations of the early Church differ radically from the fundamental theological frameworks of the church 'fathers', the medieval schoolmen and mystics, the reformers, and twentieth-century Christians. As much as we might celebrate and emulate the early Church, we are not the early Church. Rather, the early Church is mediated to us by a tradition which largely lost touch with its own Jewish character and then denigrated it.

The modern theological task then is not to select the New Testament view which suits one's theological prejudices, whether 'liberal', 'conservative' or otherwise. Instead, the initial theological task involves challenging Christian viewpoints on law that are lacking in biblical

34. According to E.E. Ellis, all New Testament authors were Jewish. See Ellis, *The Old Testament in Early Christianity: Canon and Interpretation in the Light of Modern Research* (WUNT, 54; Tübingen: Mohr–Siebeck, 1991), p. 121. On this point Luke is debated, however.

warrant. This is not a new problem that only the vicissitudes of an ecumenical era have brought to the fore, although this is not to deny the role that such a new situation presents, especially after the murder of six million Jews in the Holocaust. Thomas Aquinas addressed the question of biblical law in questions 98-107 of his *Summa Theologica*.[35] His treatment shows a comprehensivness and consideration of various sides of the issue, including the recognition that Jesus was a teacher of traditional law. In the end, however, little was achieved in coming to a Christian theology of Old Testament law: biblical law remains marginal at best, subordinated and muted by the 'New Law' of Jesus.

On Old Testament law, John Calvin represents an advance over Thomas. Following Calvin, the Reformed tradition developed three uses of the law: (1) to serve to show God's righteousness and to convict people of their sin and unrighteousness (*usus elenchticus* or *theologicus*); (2) to restrain people from sin (*usus politicus*); and (3) to instruct believers as to the divine will (*usus in renatis* or *usus didacticus*).[36] In the third use contemporary Christian theology may discover a thoughtful approach to Old Testament law, one with a potential for Christian-Jewish dialogue. The third use may be understood as a means to sanctification.[37] The third use, which Calvin considered the most important of the three, provides a truly positive role for law and comes closer to the primary biblical understanding of observing torah. The book of Leviticus as well as other priestly material in the Pentateuch has the holiness of the people as its central theme: 'You shall be holy, For I, the Lord your God, am holy' (Lev. 19.2 NJPS; cf. 20.7, 8). In contrast, the negative function of law to convict and condemn

35. See the convenient edition of *Summa Theologica: Complete English Edition in Five Volumes* (trans. Fathers of the English Dominican Province; Westminster, MD: Christian Classics, 1948), II, pp. 1025-113.

36. For Calvin's discussion of the three uses of the law, see *Institutes of the Christian Religion*, 2.7.6-12. For a translation, see *Calvin: Institutes of Christian Religion* (ed. J.T. McNeill; 2 vols.; The Library of Christian Classics, 20; Philadelphia: Westminster Press, 1960), I, pp. 354-61. For discussion of the three uses in Calvin, see I.J. Hesselink, *Calvin's Concept of the Law* (Allison Park, PA: Pickwick Publications, 1992), pp. 217-76 (reference courtesy of Dr David Little). For a general discussion of the uses of the law in Calvinist, Lutheran and Methodist traditions, see D.S. Long, *Living the Discipline: United Methodist Theological Reflections on War, Civilization, and Holiness* (Grand Rapid: Eerdmans, 1992), pp. 88-94.

37. Calvin, *Institutes of the Christian Religion*, 2.7.13.

people of their unrighteousness is not a particular biblical or post-biblical Jewish topos.[38] (Perhaps, then, it is no accident that Calvin cites no Old Testament passages in his treatment of the first two uses of the law.) By this point I do not mean to imply that divine judgment is absent from the Bible; on the contrary. Yet while judgment is an important biblical theme, in the Hebrew Bible it is the absence of law or disregard for it (Pss. 1.6; 119.85, 150; 11QPs^a 18.13) and not the law itself which functions to condemn. The purpose of torah is to restore Israelites (Ps. 19.8) and to enlighten them (cf. Pss. 19.9; 119.18).

The biblical theme of law as a means of sanctification may provide Christianity and Judaism with some common ground.[39] Yet even here some further nuancing is necessary. For both Thomas and Calvin, the positive use of Old Testament law excluded what Thomas called Old Testament 'ceremonial law', what we have called 'priestly instructional literature' (following C. Cohen), the material which constitutes the vast bulk of the Sinai covenant. This distinction is an old one in Christian theology, found, for example, in the second century letter to Diognetus[40] and the *Apostolic Constitutions*.[41] The trend to distinguish between the Ten Commandments and the 'ceremonial law' was perhaps inspired by the perceived theological needs to move away from the ritual practice of at least some forms of Jewish Christianity and (or?) to assert the general supremacy of Christianity over Judaism. This theological distinction was invoked in appeals made to faithful Jewish Christians. One passage in the *Apostolic Constitutions* addressed ritually observant Jewish Christians in precisely this manner: 'we exhort you in the Lord to abstain from your old conversation, vain bonds,

38. See Brooks, *The Spirit of the Ten Commandments*, esp. p. 18.

39. For law as a means to sanctification in rabbinic thought, see Brooks, *The Spirit of the Ten Commandments*, p. 18.

40. See *Early Christian Fathers* (trans. and ed. C.C. Richardson; The Library of Christian Classics, 1; Philadelphia: Westminster Press, 1953), p. 216. Compare the letter of Ignatius of Antioch to the Magnesians in *Early Christian Fathers*, p. 96. See also the view in Ptolemy's letter to Flora, a Valentinian gnostic text. See B. Layton (ed.), *The Gnostic Scriptures* (Garden City, NY: Doubleday, 1987), pp. 308-15.

41. *Apostolic Constitutions* 1.2.6; 6.4.18-25. See J. Donaldson, *The Apostolic Constitutions* (Ante-Nicene Christian Library, 17; Edinburgh: T. & T. Clark, 1870), pp. 20-21, 162-70.

separations, observances, distinctions of meats, and daily washings'.[42] One Jewish-Christian view of the debate is represented in the Pseudo-Clementines: 'In all circumstances good works are needed; but if a man has been considered worthy to know both teachers [Moses and Jesus] as heralds of a single doctrine, then that man is counted rich in God...'[43] As Justin's *Dialogue with Trypho* (47-48) indicates, this position was hardly the extreme one among Jewish-Christian communities, some of which required observance of the Mosaic Law for Christian salvation.[44]

Despite the theological alternatives urged within early Jewish Christianity, the distinction drawn between the Ten Commandments and the 'ceremonial' law remained a major theological approach to the Law through the Reformation.[45] (Later Catholic theology as well as more recent Protestant thinkers such as Karl Barth largely maintained this distinction.) In citing this historical discussion, I am not advocating that Christians should adopt Jewish 'ritual practices', as if such

42. *Apostolic Constitutions* 1.4.18. See Donaldson, *The Apostolic Constitutions*, pp. 162-63.

43. Pseudo-Clementines, H VIII, I, 7.5. For translation, see J. Irmscher, 'The Pseudo-Clementines', in E. Hennecke, *New Testament Apocrypha* (ed. W. Schneemelcher; trans. R.M. Wilson; 2 vols.; Philadelphia: Westminster Press, 1965), II, p. 564. This passage (H VIII, I, 5.3-7.5) accords comparable status to Moses for Jews and Jesus for Christians. For a recent study on the Jewish-Christian background of this composite text, see F.S. Jones, *An Ancient Jewish Christian Source on the History of Christianity: Pseudo-Clementine Recognitions 1.27-71* (Atlanta: Scholars Press, 1994). Epiphanius (*Pan.* pp. 30, 15) noted the use of this text by Jewish Christians. See the discussion in J.A. Fitzmyer, 'The Qumran Scrolls, the Ebionites and their Literature', in *idem*, *Essays on the Semitic Background of the New Testament* (SBLSBS, 5; Missoula, MT: Society of Biblical Literature/Scholars Press, 1974), pp. 447-53. The surviving early Church literature mentions several differing theological positions held by various Jewish-Christian communities, indicating that 'Jewish Christianity' was hardly a monolithic entity on various practices. Unfortunately, little of the literature authored by various Jewish-Christian communities survives.

44. See the primary sources cited in Fitzmyer, *Essays on the Semitic Background of the New Testament*, p. 440; see also H. Küng, 'Jewish Christianity and its Significance for Eucumenism Today', in A.B. Beck *et al.* (eds.), *Fortunate the Eyes That See: Essays in Honor of David Noel Freedman in Celebration of his Seventieth Birthday* (Grand Rapids: Eerdmans, 1995), pp. 584-600.

45. Note the rabbinic tendency in many texts not to privilege the Ten Commandments. See R. Brooks, *The Spirit of the Ten Commandments*.

adoption were the only alternative.[46] Instead, Christians should read
this biblical material seriously and develop a theology accordingly, just
as Christians believe that they take the Ten Commandments seriously.
Christians are quick to claim the Ten Commandments for themselves
as the pre-eminent Sinai law (it is the only Old Testament law which
students in my courses at Saint Joseph's have ever heard of). While the
Ten Commandments in Exodus 20 hold the pre-eminent position in
the Sinai law and are framed by theophanies as well, the 'ceremonial
law' as well as the Covenant Code are placed precisely so that they
cannot be separated from the Ten Commandments. They, too, are 'as
scriptural' as the Ten Commandments and warrant the attention of
Christian theology. Furthermore, the Ten Commandments contain
some 'ceremonial' law such as the observance of the Sabbath, which
shows that the strict distinction between them and ritual laws is spe-
cious. Despite their thorough and thoughtful approaches to Old Testament law, neither Thomas nor Calvin resolved the issues in a theologically satisfactory manner that recognizes the 'ceremonial' law's
full status as Scripture. It, too, has a place in understanding Christian
sanctification.

Toward a Christian theology of Old Testament law, a negative
critique and a constructive observation may be made. As a negative
critique, it is not possible to sanction the major accent of Paul's view
of תורה-observance, as it is normative for neither the Old Testament
nor Judaism of his time. Among his contemporaries, Paul's view was
unique, according to Segal: 'No other Jews in the first century distinguish faith and law in the way Paul does'.[47] H. Räisänen is more
radical in his criticism of the use of Pauline theology:

46. In his opening remarks to his first homily on Leviticus, Origen presents a
literal adoption of such practices as the alternative to allegory or taking language
figuratively. See Origen, *Homilies on Leviticus 1–16* (trans. G.W. Barkley; Washington: The Catholic University of America Press, 1990), pp. 29-30. Such an approach is no more the case for Christians than for Jews who no longer have the
Tabernacle described in the book of Exodus or the priesthood mentioned in
Leviticus.

47. Segal, *Paul the Convert*, p. 128. For further differences between Paul and
Judaism contemporary to him, see T. Laato, *Paul and Judaism: An Anthropological
Approach* (Atlanta: Scholars Press, 1995); E.J. Christiansen, *The Covenant in
Judaism and Paul: A Study of Ritual Boundaries as Identity Markers* (AGJU, 27;
Leiden: Brill, 1995).

> Christian theologians engaged in a dialogue with Judaism ought to realize
> that Paul's theology presents, above all, a dilemma for the Christian
> side. . . No discussion of Christianity's relation to the parent religion
> should be based on an uncritical acceptance of Paul's statements con-
> cerning Judaism.[48]

This point applies to Christian theology of law as well. Paul echoes
Jeremiah 31's extolling the circumcision of the heart as a higher ideal,
but for Jeremiah 31 this ideal does not replace the covenant of circumcision; it does not mean that the covenant was not first and foremost
physical. The covenant of circumcision did not include conditions dependent on interior attitude. It is a covenant with the God of the Israelite people, and it is for eternity (Gen. 17.1-14, esp. v. 14). The biblical
view of the Jewish people necessarily involves physical descent and
circumcision, and no argument to the contrary can change this fact.

As a positive observation, a Christian biblical theology of law
should perhaps begin with the viewpoint shared by all of the New
Testament witnesses: the Law was a positive divine creation which
linked Israel and its deity in an eternal covenant. The New Testament
witnesses are not unanimous in the view that Sinai covenant was
abrogated by the covenant through Jesus the Christ. While Mark and
John[49] may be read in this manner, Matthew and Luke do not endorse
this view, and Paul is equivocal. Indeed, even Paul does not clearly
express a negative view of the Law in either general or abstract terms.
A critical Christian theology of biblical law would ultimately require
a dialectic among the various views toward Law, not only in the New
Testament, but also in the Hebrew Bible/Old Testament. While the
New Testament provides some parameters for a theology of Law, it
does not indicate the endpoint of such a theology. The Christian claim
that both Testaments constitute the Christian Bible warrants reclaim-
ing the diversity of perspectives in the Old Testament not reflected in
the New.

If the Old Testament is to be a Christian book, then its theology of
laws and law requires a positive and constructive approach. The view
of law propounded in the priestly tradition in Exodus warrants a place
in a Christian biblical theology. On the basis of the book of Exodus, a
Christian theology that accounts sufficiently for its Old Testament heritage may consider and appropriate the notion that law is the occasion

---

48. Räisänen, *The Torah and Christ*, p. 53.
49. See especially the reaction to Jesus' teaching in Jn 6.66.

for freedom. The priestly level of the book of Exodus serves as an appropriate beginning-point for understanding one Old Testament evaluation of law and laws as a source for freedom. Freedom from Egypt was completed with the law of Sinai.[50] The priestly gloss to Exod. 29.46 conveys this view of the Sinai covenant as the purpose for the Exodus: 'And they shall know that I am the Lord their God, who brought them forth from the land of Egypt that I might dwell among them' (see also Lev. 22.32-33; Num. 15.41). For the priestly tradition, the reason for the escape from Egypt was a freedom grounded in the covenantal relationship between Yahweh and Israel and mediated by the cultic laws delivered at Sinai. In the priestly theology of the book of Exodus, the freedom of the Exodus was completed with the laws of Sinai, and this view deserves its own place in any Christian theology of law that calls itself biblical.[51]

While Paul's theology belongs to Christian tradition, so does the book of Exodus, and it may be questioned whether Exodus as mediated by New Testament readings is a theologically sufficient avenue for Christian appropriation of the book and its message. Christians are called to struggle with the meaning not only of the life and mission of Jesus as the Christ and his relation to his people, but also the divine choice of the Jewish people to which Jesus was born and through which Christians know their divine election. A full Christian view of the two Testaments, the Old and the New, calls for a critical Christian reconsideration of the Law. The modern Christian quest to understand Law in Judaism is as vital to contemporary Christian self-understanding as it was for Paul or Matthew, but for the opposite reason. Unlike

50. So J.D. Levenson, 'Liberation Theology and the Exodus', *Mainstream* 35.7 (1989), pp. 30-36. The National Conference of Catholic Bishops has similarly stressed that the exodus from Egypt is not simply freedom from constraint, but freedom for participation in the shared life of a people as community. See National Conference of Catholic Bishops, *Economic Justice for All: Pastoral Letter on Catholic Social Teaching and the U.S. Economy* (Washington: United States Catholic Conference, 1986), n. 36 (cited and discussed in Hollenbach, 'The Catholic University and the Common Good', p. 8).

51. According to Levenson, Paul replicates this view of law in his vision of the law of Christ, that Christians move from the slavery of sin to the freedom won by the servitude of righteousness (Rom. 6.17-18): 'You, who once were slaves of sin, have yielded whole-hearted obedience to the pattern of teaching to which you were made subject, and, emancipated from sin, have become slaves of righteousness'. See Levenson, *The Hebrew Bible*, p. 149.

Paul or Matthew, Christianity generally has little experience of, and therefore concept of, Judaism. Rather, the paradigm might at this time be reversed: Christianity stands in a position to assess only itself and its attitude toward the Law. If the place and role of Judaism vis-à-vis the Christian economy of salvation remained a mystery for Paul at the end of his discourse in Romans 9–11, so it remains for Christianity today.

What the theological debate in New Testament sources generally fails to mention is the positive contribution of law in creating community. The Christian discussion represented in most New Testament witnesses seems to accept the extent to which Jewish law is either a burden or indicator of how humans fall short in following divine directives. However, both the book of Exodus as well as my limited experience of Judaism points in another direction altogether: law creates boundaries around community (that are hardly impermeable by contact with others outside this community) and they also create identity within community. In their own self-understanding Christians tend to begin with faith and then act accordingly. Judaism tends to begin with community as the locus of practice and faith, and the practices within community lead to further faith. When I ask my students at Saint Joseph's University how to define Christianity, they usually provide me with a list of beliefs. When I ask them what they know about Judaism, they supply me with another list of beliefs. Christian sensibilities about self-definition and experience are not the same for Jews. 'The Law' provides for a community way of life which produces the space and orientation for Jews to make a turn and return (תשובה) to God and to inspire them to acts of religious mercy (צדקה) for others. תורה also requires members to take responsibility for one another within a larger network of mutual interdependence.[52] It was not an individual Israelite who was called at Mount Sinai, but all the community of Israel. Under the direction of rabbinic tradition many Jews live out aspects of Old Testament law, such as sabbath observance and keeping kosher homes (כשרות). Other aspects of Old Testament law, such as sacrifices and the priesthood, ceased with the destruction of the Temple in 70 CE,[53] but lived on in transmuted forms in Jewish liturgy and prayer. To judge from the example provided by Jewish tradition,

52. So as I am reminded by E.L. Greenstein in his piece, 'Beyond the Sovereign Self', which appeared in *The Jerusalem Report* (February 9, 1995), p. 45.
53. All dates given in this book are BCE, unless otherwise noted.

the question before Christians is not necessarily a requirement to practice the laws as laid out in the Old Testament, but how to incorporate them in our reflections and language in order to advance our sanctification. The early Church did this in interpreting Jesus' life and death; the church should now emulate its first-century Jewish forbears in taking 'ceremonial law' seriously.

The Christian notion of 'the Law' itself remains something of an impediment, but even here Christians' own experience might also lead us to recognize the positive functions that law plays in our lives. Secular laws provide norms for the limits of acceptable behavior in our society and so people benefit from laws and their maintenance. The American Constitution, the charter document of the United States, provides not only for the development of laws; it is also a statement of American identity. Despite the great diversity of their ancestral homelands, Americans look back to the period of the revolutionary war and the new nation that emerged from that conflict. The Constitution embodies this early history with which all Americans may identify. Similarly, the Sinai law is the charter document of the Israelite community. It provides for the development of laws, but more fundamentally it provides an expression for Israelite identity and for the norms for continuing and living out that identity. The relationship between the two may be more than a matter of analogy. S. Levinson in his book, *Constitutional Faith*, has argued that the founders of the United States as well as many members of the Supreme Court were familiar with the Bible.[54] They used biblical language and it was part of their mental landscape. As a result, it has been argued that the tradition of making and interpreting law in this country was shaped by biblical concepts and content. In any case, through their American citizenship Christians in this country may fathom and feel the value of Israelite and later Jewish Law as a living legacy and entity, which in turn generates identity.

A positive sense of law may come to Christians from another direction as well. Christians look upon the traditions of their own churches with a sense of pride. Those traditions express something of our own identity, and the norms in our communities may be perceived as ways of living out the call and commission which our founders felt and experienced so deeply. Churches develop norms (such as church rules

54. S. Levinson, *Constitutional Faith* (Princeton, NJ: Princeton University, 1988).

and canon law) to extend the values expressed in the Bible and subsequent Christian tradition. While church norms in themselves do not hold biblical status, they form a core of teaching that help churches to function. Churches develop these norms in order to address ongoing issues. Biblical law likewise reflects ongoing challenges which Israelites had to face. Law, whether in churches or in the Bible, is not a dead letter vacuous of any spiritual meaning. On the contrary, it represents the ongoing, living repository of wisdom emerging from new challenges facing the Israelite communities or the churches. So here again Christians have something in their experience that can give them a feel for biblical Law as the accumulation of early traditions which express Israelite and later Jewish identity in the midst of ongoing issues.

There is a third basis for a Christian appreciation of law, and of the three it is the most theologically compelling. In the previous section on law in the New Testament it was evident that the 'founder' of Christianity understood and taught the divine law to his disciples. In the task to recover biblical law, Christians have no better antecedent than Jesus Christ. Christians may not be predisposed to appreciate biblical law, but this condition may be due more to the age in which we live rather than any theological reason. Nowadays freedom is viewed as the absence of constraints upon individuals and tolerance of others, or in other words, doing what you want as long as it does not hurt others. To many people law by definition seems to increase constraints and is therefore antithetical to freedom. Yet both the American Constitution and biblical Law use laws to construct norms to protect their communities and to provide them with a kind of space and identity to foster mutual interdependence among members. Whether people want to recognize it or not, laws provide them with a basis for liberty. To repeat the biblical view, freedom is not merely a matter of private, individual choice; it is achieved by participation in communities that live, share and express life through celebration and shared norms. In sum, Christians have no reason to continue to demonize or ignore biblical law as a theological resource, especially as such a stance results in ignoring a large part of our own canon.

Christians have a number of positive theological avenues open for exploring law.[55] Above I mentioned the positive function of law as a

---

55. See the approach of F.J. van Beek, SJ, *Loving Torah More than God? Toward a Catholic Appreciation of Judaism* (Chicago: Loyola Press, 1989).

means toward sanctification. Or, in more general terms, תורה might
be understood perhaps as the gospel to the Jewish people which leads
to life with God. Or, to reverse the order, the gospel is the Law of
Christianity. (Thomas Aquinas devoted question 106 of his *Summa
Theologica* to 'the Law of the Gospel',[56] and John Wesley saw 'no
contrariety at all between the law and the gospel'.[57]) Another approach might be to reverse the traditional Christian idea of the economy of salvation vis-à-vis Judaism. Instead of viewing Judaism as
prologue to and then superseded by Christianity, Christianity emerged
as a Jewish phenomenon and stands within the Jewish economy of
salvation first described in the Torah. Christians may appreciate the
practice of reading and preaching תורה as the Jewish parallel to proclaiming the Word. Passover might be seen to bear a kind of sacra-
mental character that identifies the ancient and modern reality of
exodus through the experience of the seder, one which Christians can
appreciate further, though if only at a distance. (In turn, Jews might
appreciate Catholic and Orthodox understandings of priesthood, but it
is up to the Jewish community from its own side to seize upon such
possibilities.) Similarly, both religions may share the different transformations that sacrifice has taken in their traditions. It will be necessary to learn and inculcate understanding of the parallel yet different
concepts, practices and horizons.[58] Christian assimilation of such facts
has been and will continue to represent a great step forward, requisite
to further advance in mutual understanding.

An older Christian way into the Pentateuch was to retell the story in
Christian terms. To cite only one example, this approach appears in
Irenaeus' *Proof of Apostolic Preaching*,[59] which relates the ancient
events largely with a christological viewpoint. Accordingly, the Christian recovery of biblical תורה requires a return to reading, learning

56. *Summa Theologica* 2.1103-108 (reference courtesy of Professor D. Stephen
Long).

57. Wesley, 'Sermon on the Mount V', *Sermons*. Vols. 1–4 of *The Works of
John Wesley* (ed. A.C. Outler; Nashville: Abingdon Press, 1984–87), I, p. 568
(cited in Long, *Living the Discipline*, p. 89).

58. A fine recent example is the insightful book of Levenson, *The Death and
Resurrection of the Beloved Son: The Transformation of Child Sacrifice in Judaism
and Christianity* (New Haven: Yale University Press, 1993).

59. St Irenaeus, *Proof of the Apostolic Preaching* (ed. J.P. Smith; Ancient
Christian Writers, 16; New York: Newman, 1952), pp. 54-67.

and retelling the text. J.D. Levenson contrasts the Jewish and Christian attitudes toward Pentateuchal legal texts and their theologies: Judaism retains a high esteem and attention to the texts and their theologies, while Christianity separates the theology of legal texts from the texts themselves and thereby escapes a positive appropriation of the latter.[60] But what would a greater Christian appropriation of the textual specifics of Pentateuchal law involve? How could Christian theology and practice accomplish such a task in accordance with its tradition, identity and mission? A chief means involves reading and reflecting deliberately on these texts. Judaism reads the Torah on either an annual or tri-annual basis, and it serves as the basis for ongoing reflection. Christianity need not replicate this level of reading, but it would be a great advance to insist on the regular readings of these materials in the lectionary[61] and apart from it, to ask Christian laity and leadership alike to read and experience the specific temple and sacrificial languages that Christianity long ago appropriated from Pentateuchal law, in order to enter into a deeper understanding of the life and death of Jesus Christ. Similarly, Christian theologians should study these texts and use them and other texts from the Old Testament rather than New Testament texts as the beginning-points for systematic reflection.[62] Furthermore, Christians should study the Pentateuch as a part of the Christian canon. In the wake of the encyclical *Divino Afflante Spiritu*

60. Levenson, *The Hebrew Bible*, pp. 53-54. This situation may be related to the Christian championing of 'the spirit of the law' as opposed to 'the letter of the law'.

61. J.M. Ford has suggested that at least some of final lectionary readings on Sundays should come from the Old Testament instead of the New Testament Gospels so as to suggest to Catholic audiences that the Old Testament offers an authentic witness without need of fulfillment or explanation from a New Testament passage. See Ford, 'The New Covenant, Jesus, and Canonization', in R. Brooks and J.J. Collins (eds.), *Hebrew Bible or Old Testament? Studying the Bible in Judaism and Christianity* (Christianity and Judaism in Antiquity, 5; Notre Dame: University of Notre Dame Press, 1990), p. 39.

62. It is commonplace to insist on Jesus' Jewishness in the dialogue between Christians and Jews, but what does Jesus' Jewishness truly mean to most Christians? It is not too great a burden for theologians to reckon with the specifics of Jesus' Judaism and its biblical background, especially in view of newer studies of the life of Jesus. See especially J.P. Meier, *A Marginal Jew: Rethinking the Historical Jesus* (ABRL; New York: Doubleday, 1991); *idem, A Marginal Jew*. II. *Rethinking the Historical Jesus: Mentor, Message, and Miracles* (ABRL; New York: Doubleday, 1995). The third volume is in preparation.

in 1942, the Second Vatican Council helped to initiate a massive revolution in the Catholic laity's appreciation of both biblical studies and the early Church writers.[63] In many respects Christian reading, study and reflection on many areas of the Old Testament, most especially the 'legal sections' of the Torah, await this revolution.[64] With it will come temptations to 'Christianize' the Old Testament or to 'de-Judaize' it, but it may be hoped that the historical-critical method will help to restrain such tendencies. Instead, Christians may inquire as to how their Old Testament witnesses to the God of the New Testament without imputing a specifically christological perspective.[65]

The Christian scholar of Bible, R. Rendtorff, has faced the implications of these questions. Rendtorff remarks:

> Christianity has lost its Jewish dimension, or at least lost the consciousness of its Jewish dimension. I believe that the discussion around the question of biblical theology makes this loss visible. Christians always want to define their difference from Judaism instead of rethinking their close relations to the religion they grew out of. Therefore I believe that even biblical theology could provide an important contribution to the recovery of the Jewish origins of Christianity, not only as an element of the past but as an important ingredient of the present self-definition of Christian existence.[66]

63. See *Dei Verbum in The Documents of Vatican II* (ed. W.M. Abbott; New York: America Press, 1966), pp. 111-28. See especially paragraphs 7, 8 and 12.

64. In the meantime, see E.J. Fisher and L. Klenicki (eds.), *In Our Time: The Flowering of the Jewish-Catholic Dialogue* (New York: Paulist Press, 1990).

65. Levenson overstates the case that Christians interpreters must necessarily interpret the Old Testament from a christocentric perspective. See his essay 'Theological Consensus or Historicist Evasion? Jews and Christians in Biblical Studies', in Brooks and Collins (eds.), *Hebrew Bible or Old Testament?*, pp. 109-45. With R.E. Murphy, I would say that Christians will sometimes read the Old Testament from a christocentric perspective and at many other times they will not. There are more Christian ways to think and believe christologically without claiming Jesus as the fulfillment of Old Testament 'promises'. See Murphy, 'Old Testament/ *Tanakh*— Canon and Interpretation', in Brooks and Collins (eds.), *Hebrew Bible or Old Testament?*, pp. 11-29. I would also dispute Levenson's point that biblical interpreters necessarily have to drop their confessional commitments and identities in pursuing biblical research in an ecumenical context. For example, the national meetings of the Catholic Biblical Association of America hardly require the bracketing of confessional commitments, including those of non-Catholics.

66. Rendtorff, 'Old Testament Theology, Tanakh Theology, or Biblical Theology? Reflections in an Ecumenical Context', *Bib* 73 (1992), p. 451. Rendtorff takes

Though largely non-Jews alien to Judaism, modern Christians may look to their tradition's Jewish origins, and, to echo Rendtorff's sentiment, behold something of their forgotten religious identity.

Beyond these important measures, there is a further goal. A new Jerusalem which holds Jews and Christians together in a common vocation will be rebuilt someday. What is called for is some real sense of shared community that at the same time protects the present individual identity of both communities. Our ancient origins were one, and it may be that our future destiny is to be one; we both came from Abraham and Sarah; we both await the Messiah. Given that ritual brings each community together to celebrate the biblical Word including Torah (Pentateuch), and given the ritual or liturgical character of so much biblical תורה, it might be through ritual that the two communities can not only acknowledge their differences, but also live with those differences together. We already have sabbaths and holidays with common historical roots. We can study the ancient texts that we share in common and we can share the parallel spiritualities that our communities have. We have comparable ritual sensibilities. These might serve as beginning points capable of further pursuit.

Whatever form such an endeavor takes, we have to keep our eyes open to the grave difficulties that it will involve. The nexus, ritual or otherwise, would constitute a supreme challenge for at least two reasons. The different Christian denominations have hardly resolved their many differences. To be sure, much progress has been made, but it has been commonly observed that the heyday of such efforts seems to have passed. In view of such problems, a comparable Christian-Jewish effort seems unfeasible at the outset. Furthermore, American culture at least in its urban areas (where the majority of Americans live) is rapidly moving away from religious rituals celebrated by well-formed communities.[67] Mary Douglas has emphasized how religious ritual is

his cue from N. Lohfink's *Das Jüdische am Christentum: Die verlorene Dimension* (Freiburg: Herder, 1987). To be noted also is Lohfink's attempt to wrestle with the problem of biblical positive and negative views of law in both Testaments (for one negative passage in the Hebrew Bible, see Ezek. 20.25). See Lohfink, *The Inerrancy of Scripture and Other Essays* (Berkeley, CA: Bibal, 1992), pp. 103-19. See also J. Blenkinsopp, 'Old Testament Theology and the Jewish–Christian Connection', *JSOT* 28 (1984), pp. 3-15.

67. According to Mary Douglas, secularism is not simply a modern Western phenomenon; it is found also in traditional tribal societies. See Douglas, *Natural*

an increasingly precarious basis for experiencing meaning for West-erners.[68] The rule of the day seems to be either religious rituals of increasing anonymity or secular rituals of anonymity, where we pass but do not meet, whether in Masses where participating Catholics are all too often strangers to one another, or in malls, the internet or other centers of unsustained and relatively impersonal contact. Americans have already become highly deracinated from communities where work, play, residence and worship by the same persons take place. Many middle-class Christians can work in one area, socialize in a second, reside in a third and go to church in a fourth. Even some Christians' ability to 're-racinate' by combining two or three of these spheres of life in a single geographical area does not re-constitute com-munity in any traditional sense. Despite these difficulties, American Christians still need guidelines to live their complicated lives and they need community, they need to 're-racinate' in order to 'be in Christ'. Despite these obstacles, some sort of joint vocation between Jews and Christians seems called for to achieve deep understanding between these religious communities. It is perhaps premature, however, to call for shared ritual or some interaction involving comparable risk in the face of so many centuries of Christian anti-Semitism and the relatively shorter period of constructive engagement since the Second Vatican Council, not to mention the even shorter period since the papal recognition of the state of Israel. Each party will desire to inform the other how it wishes to be called and known, and what things it wishes to share. The suggestion here may seem to be but a dream, but as Mt. 5.18 says, the law will not pass away until all has been accomplished.

4. *This Study*

This study does not aim to break through the debate about law in the New Testament nor to provide a full Christian systematic of Old

Symbols: Explorations in Cosmology (New York: Vintage Books, 1973), p. 360 (reference courtesy of Professor David Carpenter). If she is correct, then the chal-lenge posed by secularism is correspondingly complex.

68. Douglas, *Natural Symbols*, pp. 19-58, esp. p. 25. Such a problem is to be expected in American culture, because in Douglas's view 'when the social group grips its members in tight communal bonds, the religion is ritualist; when this grip is relaxed, ritualism declines. . . the most important determinant of ritualism is the experience of closed social groups' (pp. 32, 33).

Testament law. Nor am I offering a general treatment about תורה as instruction. Instead, I wish to raise the issue of law prominently at the outset of this work in order to focus attention on the importance of legal material in the Pentateuch for Christians. Although the era of accusing Jews or Judaism of legalism seems to have passed, Christians' capacity to address the legal material in the Pentateuch as their own has not enjoyed a corresponding advance. As a piece of research, this work investigates the features and form of pilgrimage in Exodus which grew out of the priestly arrangement of the book, but this also represents an exploration for me of how a Christian scholar can begin to address material in the Pentateuch which is passed over sometimes all too quickly in surveys of the Old Testament. Through this study, Christian readers may witness the vital relations of law and liturgical life in ancient Israel's history and in one of the books of 'the Law', namely Exodus. This volume describes for readers the relations between liturgy and law in ancient Israel. From Israelite liturgy springs both the prayer of the psalms and the priestly instructional literature that constitutes the bulk of what is known as 'the Law' that Yahweh gave to the Israelites through Moses on Mount Sinai. Prayer and law are both dynamic expressions of Israelite faith and practice, and it is impossible to appreciate the one without the other. For Jewish readers, this study offers the hope that Christians such as myself are not interested in them or their Scriptures only in order to reintroduce a covert agenda of intellectual or religious conversion. Instead, such studies may offer some sign of hope for religious respect and cooperation in the area of biblical studies.

If theology can be said to be reflection on experience, then priestly theology in Pentateuchal narrative and redaction represents reflection on cultic experience. Put differently, priestly reflection on experience in the Jerusalem temple helped to produce the Pentateuchal portrait of pilgrimage to Mount Sinai and Israel's liturgical celebration there. In a sense, Part I of this study begins a journey from Jerusalem to Mount Sinai described in Parts II and III. Readers will not find here a study of particular priestly terminology, procedures, vocabulary or priestly instructional literature.[69] This study, however, stresses the teaching

---

69. For these matters readers may consult the summary of J. Milgrom, *Leviticus 1–16* (AB, 3; New York: Doubleday, 1991), pp. 3-51. For a listing of Milgrom's detailed studies from 1955 up through 1994, see D.P. Wright, D.N. Freedman and A. Hurvitz (eds.), *Pomegranates and Golden Bells: Studies in Biblical, Jewish, and*

which the priesthood wished to convey generally to ancient Israelites through the liturgical sensibilities and forms imprinted on the arrangement of law, priestly instructional literature and narrative in Exodus. Israelites received an education in making the pilgrimages to Jerusalem, and in turn, the priesthood further reinforced this religious inculcation by envisioning the ancient foundational events surrounding Mount Sinai in Exodus and the other books of the Pentateuch in terms of the people's traditions of pilgrimage.

Part I surveys the liturgical experience centered on Jerusalem. Chapter 1 describes the pilgrimage feasts and the journey. Chapter 2 investigates the many sides of Jerusalem. The power of the capital had many facets, at once religious, political, economic and social. At the heart of the pilgrimage experience was the Temple and its sacrificial liturgy. While little is known of actual liturgy or liturgical practices, bits and pieces are preserved in the Bible, and these provide some insight into the liturgical sensibilities of ancient Israelites. In order to augment the meager biblical resources on some topics in Part I, such as the pilgrimage feasts, I have added material from the Mishnah. The treatments on pilgrimage and the Temple and its symbolism have also benefitted from the archaeological information, discussed in the contributions made by Dr Elizabeth M. Bloch-Smith. Chapter 3 selectively describes human communication in sacrificial liturgy. Prayers, postures and gestures, and sacrifices formed three aspects of a single system of Israel's communication with God. Chapter 4 steps back from the historical description of pilgrimage in Israel in order to show the impact of pilgrimage on biblical literature. Israel used the pilgrimage pattern to describe its distant past, its present experience of God and its future hopes. This chapter introduces the argument that Exodus was one biblical book that shows the impact of the pilgrimage pattern on its overall arrangement.

Readers will not find in Part I a treatment of every scholarly theory pertaining to aspects of pilgrimage and pilgrimage feasts, Jerusalem or the Temple. Instead, Part I draws many examples of Israelite liturgy from Exodus in order to illustrate how cultically charged it is. Connections between Israel's liturgical life and the book of Exodus have

Near Eastern Ritual, Law, and Literature in Honor of Jacob Milgrom (Winona Lake, IN: Eisenbrauns, 1995), pp. xiii-xxv. For a non-technical treatment of priestly theology, see R.D. Nelson, *Raising Up a Faithful Priest: Community and Priesthood in Biblical Theology* (Louisville, KY: Westminster/John Knox Press, 1993).

been noted in details, such as the comparison between the tabernacles described in Exodus and the temple in Jerusalem and the correlation between prayer and sacrifice in Exodus on the one hand, and in the Psalms and other biblical books on the other hand.[70] Similarly, the sermonic style known from various psalms of instruction may be reflected in various speeches of Moses in the Pentateuch.[71] However, the depth of the connections, especially as they inform the priestly narrative and redaction in the book, has not been adequately appreciated up to this point. In a number of cases, Part I anticipates the more developed discussions of the impact of pilgrimage and liturgy on Exodus discussed in Part II. Part I also provides some background information on the priestly theology discussed in Parts II and III.

Part II is devoted to the priestly redaction of Exodus as a literary and theological product. Chapter 5 reviews several scholarly approaches to the book of Exodus and locates the approach of this study within the larger scholarly discussion. Readers uninterested in the modern scholarly debates can afford to skip this chapter, since Chapter 6 briefly provides some context for this study of Exodus. Chapter 6 lays out the basic proposal for the priestly arrangement. The priestly arrangement of Exodus describes the journey of Moses, first alone and then with the Israelites, to the holy mountain where they would receive their call and commission in the presence of Yahweh. Pilgrimage supplied the priestly redaction of Exodus with a ready model in order to understand the journey to, and call and commission at, the divine mountain. Chapter 7 discusses the first three sections of the arrangement. Some of the redactional and literary dynamics between the second and third sections (Exod. 3.1–6.1 and 6.2–14.31) are presented. This chapter also discusses how the first three sections of the book (Exod. 1.1–13.16) correspond in some general ways to the last three sections of the book (Exod. 15.22–40.38). Chapter 8 is concerned with the middle section of the book, the poem of Exodus 15. The poem represents not only a general middle point of Exodus. Rather, for the poem in its present setting, the first part (vv. 1-12) refers to the preceding events of the book while the second part (vv. 13-18)

---

70. See most recently H.J. Levine, *Sing unto God a New Song*, esp. pp. 41-45.

71. See the discussion of Psalms 50 and 81 below in Chapter 1, section 2. To cite another good example (brought to my attention by Dr H.J. Levine), Psalm 95 puts into the mouth of a cultic mediator the quoted divine words that warn its audience not to be stubborn as on the day of Meribah and Massah.

refers to the events in the remainder of Exodus. The poem plays a new role in the book's redaction and structure. More specifically, the poem occupies the fulcrum-point of the book linking the preceding and following sections. Chapter 9 addresses the last three sections of the book in Exod. 15.22–40.38. This chapter treats some further connections between chs. 1–2 (A) and 15.22–18.27 (A′). A number of redactional and thematic features linking chs. 19–32 (B′ i) and 33–40 (B′ i′) are noted. The discussion ends by observing some critical relations between these two sections and Exod. 3.1–6.1 (B i) and Exod. 6.2–14.31 (B i′).

Part II shows the impact that liturgy had made on both priestly and non-priestly texts prior to the priestly redaction. Liturgical influence stands at many different points in the book's narrative and at many different levels in its development. The priestly redaction in turn developed the arrangement of the book in order to depict the holy, liturgical life that Israel was destined to live. That the priestly redaction issued in a literary arrangement is evident from the discussion in Part II. Whether this arrangement was planned at any particular redactional level cannot be proven. It may be that this arrangement reflects what Martin Noth called 'unexpected narrative connections and theological insights'[72] derived from the accumulation of priestly redactional activity. Or, in E. Blum's terminology, the present formulation of Exodus is due to 'K^P', or a priestly composition after which there is no evident thorough-going redaction.[73] (This is not to preclude further redactional touches designed to link larger units such as the Hexateuch, but the question is beyond the scope of this study.) I am aware of the possibility that the arrangement offered here may be due in large measure to the way in which I have posed the issues. I have tried to hedge against this methodological problem by appealing to priestly redactional material and themes throughout the study, but such an attempt at a critical analysis may fail; I leave it to readers to

72. M. Noth, *A History of Pentateuchal Traditions* (trans. with introduction by B.W. Anderson; repr. of 1972 English edition; Atlanta: Scholars Press, 1981), p. 250.

73. E. Blum, 'Israël à la montagne de Dieu: Remarques sur Ex 19-24; 32–34 et sur le contexte littéraire et historique de sa composition', in A. de Pury (ed.), *Le Pentateuque en question: Les origines et la composition des cinq premiers livres de la Bible à la lumière de recherches récentes* (MDB, 19; Geneva: Labor et Fides, 2nd edn, 1989), pp. 271-95, and 'Débat sur la contribution de E. Blum', pp. 297-300.

decide. Yet even if this is so, the connections and insights, to echo Noth's turn of phrase, remain nonetheless, and they offer a productive literary and theological reading of Exodus.

Part III recapitulates many of the general points made in Part II and offers a wider context for discussing Exodus. Chapter 10 steps back from the redactional details provided in Chapters 6 through 9 in order to provide an overview of the theology of the priestly redaction and the notions of law that inform Exodus. Chapter 10 explores different concepts of law or תורה in the book of Exodus as well as the historical background of these ideas in order to help understand the message of the book. Law in Exodus is not simply a matter of definition or usage. The priestly redaction further contributed toward the understanding of law by producing, again to advert to Noth, 'unexpected narrative connections and theological insights'.[74] While some of these connections and insights may not have been intended by the priestly redaction, they are perceptible thanks to it; such connections and insights are recognized and drawn into the discussion of law in the larger context of the whole book of Exodus. The notion that all of Exodus constitutes part of the Torah is not attested clearly in any passage in the book. Rather, Exodus shows this notion only by virtue of its place in the canon.

Chapter 11 ends this work with an analysis of Exodus within the larger context of the Pentateuch, in particular the redactional relations between Exodus and Numbers. The redactional relations between the two books stand at a higher level of generalization than the specific arrangement described for Exodus in Chapter 6. The absence of a more refined correlation between Exodus and Numbers in the priestly redaction lies, in my mind, in the constraints placed on the redaction by the material in Numbers 27–36 and by the additional theme of Moses' journey to the mountain in Exodus 1–2. Furthermore, Numbers not only looks back to Exodus, but it also looks forward to the land. Indeed, some correlations between the books mark progressions forward: in Exodus toward Sinai, in Numbers toward the land. Complete symmetry on the more detailed level was subordinated in the overall scheme of the Pentateuch. Or, to cite the insightful intuition of R. Rendtorff, 'the theological arrangement of the individual units within the Pentateuch cannot be equated with the arrangement of the

---

74. Noth, *A History of Pentateuchal Traditions*, p. 250.

Pentateuch as a whole'.[75] Apart from the specific design of Exodus described in Part Two, this biblical book shares with Numbers some very specific linkages involving sacred time and space which create a defining and definitive priestly identity for ancient Israel. Chapter 11 closes with a brief consideration of the implications that geographical and chronological notices hold for understanding the formation of the Pentateuch. While such a broad topic as this one deserves considerably greater analysis, it is important to note, if only briefly, the impact of Israel's liturgical tradition on the Pentateuch's formation.

This Introduction has been designed to introduce you to this book and to my interests and motivations in writing it. These personal concerns do not constitute the subject of the book, but my discussion has served to indicate its background, and I therefore adopted a personal style in keeping with this goal. The study which follows is a technical one, following the custom of the scholarly community. My task often involves presenting the state of scholarly discussion on many specific points and then adjudicating such discussion to the best of my ability and judgment. For me, it is necessary to take this trouble out of deep respect for scholars whose own research has advanced my own. Readers uninterested in these matters may reduce the difficulty of reading by ignoring the footnotes. In a work of synthesis such as this one, it is impossible not to let the voices of predecessors in this work be heard. In the end, it is my hope that readers will see the vision of the priestly redaction of Exodus and the Pentateuch: a portrait of Israel's holy life making pilgrimage to and sojourning with God, created not only through the content of stories and teaching, but also by the way these materials were arranged. Theological perspectives informed the process of composition and resulted in a literary masterpiece that could instill in readers a vision of the Holy God of Israel and a way of life that has lasted millennia.

---

75. R. Rendtorff, *The Problem of the Process of Transmission in the Pentateuch* (trans. J.J. Scullion; JSOTSup, 89; Sheffield: JSOT Press, 1990 [published originally as BZAW, 147; Berlin: de Gruyter, 1976]), p. 95.

Part I

LITURGICAL LIFE IN ANCIENT ISRAEL

'When will I go and see the face of God?'
Psalm 42.3

Chapter 1

PILGRIMAGE TO JERUSALEM

Pilgrimage feasts in the Bible have served for centuries as models for pilgrims worldwide.[1] Through the Bible, especially the psalms, the pilgrims of ancient Israel express experience and perspectives central to the traditional spirituality of the Church and the image of the Church as a pilgrim people. The Bible contains many allusions to pilgrimage customs, practices and liturgies, but the information is scattered and requires a considerable amount of reconstruction on the part of scholars. Extra-biblical sources on pilgrimage are considerably more meager than those in the Bible. Pilgrimage is rarely mentioned in ancient Near Eastern sources outside the Bible.[2] The pilgrimage centers, such as 'the amphictyonic shrines like Nippur and Tuttul... in earlier times' and 'Harran in the seventh to sixth-centuries BCE', are notable

---

1. On pilgrimage in ancient Israel, see A. Causse, *La vision de la nouvelle Jérusalem (Esaie LX) et la signification sociologique des assemblées de fête et des pèlerinages dans l'Orient sémitique* (Paris: Geuthner, 1939); H.J. Kraus, *Worship in Israel: A Cultic History of the Old Testament* (trans. G. Buswell; Richmond, VA: John Knox, 1965), pp. 208-18; R. Hendel, 'Sacrifice as a Cultural System', *ZAW* 101 (1989), pp. 374-78; M.S. Smith, 'The Psalms as a Book for Pilgrims', *Int* 46 (1992), pp. 156-66; H.J. Levine, *Sing unto God a New Song*, pp. 73-78. For rabbinic sources on pilgrimages, see S. Safrai, *Die Wallfahrt im Zeitalter des zweiten Tempels* (Neukirchen-Vluyn: Neukirchener Verlag, 1981); and J. Tabori, *Jewish Festivals in the Time of the Mishna and Talmud* (Jerusalem: Magnes, 1995), esp. pp. 48-51 (Heb.). See also the summary in S. Safrai, 'The Temple', in S. Safrai and M. Stern (eds.), *The Jewish People in the First Century: Historical Geography, Political History, Social, Cultural and Religious Life and Institutions* (Van Gorcum; Philadelphia: Fortress Press, 1987), II, pp. 898-904.

2. So J.N. Postgate, 'In Search of the First Empires', *BASOR* 293 (1994), p. 8 (reference courtesy of Dr Gary Beckman). An inquiry was posted on the following internet address: ane@oi.uchicago.edu. This turned up little further information apart from considerably later Egyptian sources.

exceptions. In Israel the ingredients of the pilgrimage feasts included deep religiosity, the recollection of the national story, economic fervor, geographical specificity, and a political dimension (namely in support of the Jerusalem monarchy).[3]

The political importance of pilgrimage feasts is not to be underestimated, and it may be specified further by locating the tradition of national pilgrimages within the larger societal context of Israel's patriarchal society.[4] Family ties tended to concentrate power locally while the creation of a national capital and the construction of a national shrine, such as the Jerusalem temple, concentrated power in the hands of the reigning dynasty. The national shrine stood under the aegis and authority of the monarchy, while regional popular cults and the local veneration of the deceased ancestors distanced religious authority from the reach of the monarchy. Saints whose powers assumed legendary proportions in life were, for example, the objects of special devotion in death, including pilgrimage. The Elijah and Elisha cycles suggest that these men were not simply prophets (although biblical historiography[5] conforms them generally to this picture), but also classic holy men whose deeds in life and death attracted the attention of the multitudes who travelled to their tombs to seek help in health and other areas of popular concern. The miracles of biblical holy men extended beyond their lifetimes. When a band of marauding Moabites attacked a funeral procession, the corpse was conveniently thrown into Elisha's

---

3.   Cf. the formulation of S. Safrai, 'Religion in Everyday Life', in Safrai and Stern (eds.), *The Jewish People in the First Century*, II, p. 809.

4.   The best article on the Israelite family remains L.E. Stager, 'The Archaeology of the Family', *BASOR* 260 (1985), pp. 1-35. For a discussion of the family within the context of law, see R. Westbrook, *Property and the Law in Biblical Law* (JSOTSup, 113; Sheffield: JSOT Press, 1991). On family and religion, see also the important works of R. Albertz, *Persönliche Frömmigkeit und offizielle Religion* (Stuttgart: Calwer Verlag, 1978); and K. van der Toorn, *From her Cradle to her Grave: The Role of Religion in the Life of the Israelite and the Babylonian Woman* (trans. S.J. Denning-Bolle; Biblical Seminar, 23; Sheffield: JSOT Press, 1994); *idem, Family Religion in Babylonia, Syria and Israel: Continuity and Change in the Forms of Religious Life* (Studies in the History and Culture of the Ancient Near East, 7; Leiden: Brill, 1996).

5.   For this material, see A. Rofé, *The Prophetical Stories: The Narratives about the Prophets in the Hebrew Bible: Their Literary Types and History* (Jerusalem: Magnes, 1988); and the essays in R.B. Coote (ed.), *Elijah and Elisha in Socioliterary Perspective* (Semeia, 22; Atlanta: Scholars Press, 1992).

tomb.[6] When the corpse touched Elisha's bones, the dead man miraculously revived (2 Kgs 13.20-21). Biblical recollection of the tombs of Rachel, the patriarchs and other luminaries may represent further evidence of regional cults paid to the famous dead. E.B. Reeves's study of the cult of the dead saints in modern Egyptian society, their popular following and the pilgrimage feasts centered on their burial sites[7] may provide some helpful analogues to the biblical phenomenon of the biblical holy men Elijah and Elisha, their bands of disciples and the cultic devotion paid to them after their deaths.

The family was another repository of traditional religious customs resistant to the advances of monarchic power. The long continuity of family beliefs and customs, especially associated with the dead, is evident in the archaeological record presented in the study of E.M. Bloch-Smith.[8] Her research suggests widespread devotion to deceased ancestors, including providing them with food. Just as the royal cults of Yahweh functioned to reinforce human kingship and power emanating from the capital to the countryside, so the family cult of the ancestors reinforced power within the family.[9] T.J. Lewis remarks in a similar vein: 'Such clan solidarity was strengthened and promoted through cults of the dead in ancient Israel'.[10] Lewis also argues that 'the inher-

6. See E.M. Bloch-Smith, *Judahite Burial Practices and Beliefs about the Dead* (JSOTSup, 123; Sheffield: JSOT Press, 1992), pp. 122, 127.

7. E.B. Reeves, *The Hidden Government: Ritual, Clientalism, and Legitimation in Northern Egypt* (Salt Lake City: University of Utah Press, 1990).

8. Bloch-Smith, *Judahite Burial Practices and Beliefs about the Dead*, pp. 103-108; *idem*, 'The Cult of the Dead in Judah: Interpreting the Material Remains', *JBL* 111 (1992), pp. 213-24. For studies of the literary evidence (in addition to studies cited below), see T.J. Lewis, *The Cults of the Dead in Ancient Israel and Ugarit* (HSM, 39; Atlanta: Scholars Press, 1989); K. Spronk, *Beatific Afterlife in Ancient Israel and in the Ancient Near East* (AOAT, 219; Kevelaer: Butzon & Bercker; Neukirchen–Vluyn: Neukirchener Verlag, 1986). See also B. Schmidt, *Israel's Beneficent Dead: Ancestor Cult and Necromancy in Ancient Israelite Religion and Tradition* (repr. Winona Lake, IN: Eisenbrauns, 1995); and a book by H. Niehr in preparation.

9. So B. Halpern, '"Brisker Pipes than Poetry": The Development of Israelite Monotheism', in J. Neusner, B.A. Levine and E.S. Frerichs (eds.), *Judaic Perspectives on Ancient Israel* (Philadelphia: Fortress Press, 1987), p. 89; *idem*, 'Jerusalem and the Lineages in the Seventh Century BCE: Kinship and the Rise of Individual Moral Liability', in B. Halpern and D.W. Hobson (eds.), *Law and Ideology in Monarchic Israel* (JSOTSup, 124; Sheffield: JSOT Press, 1991), pp. 71, 73.

10. Lewis, 'The Ancestral Estate (נחלת אלהים) in 2 Samuel 14.16', *JBL* 110 (1991), p. 608.

itance of gods/God' (נחלת אלהים) in 2 Sam. 14.16 refers to the ancestral estate, that is, the inheritance of the 'gods', that is the ancestors, a meaning of the word of אלהים which appears also in 1 Sam. 28.13 and Isa. 8.19-20.[11] If נחלת אלהים served as a general designation in early Israelite society, it would suggest that Israelite social structure as expressed through familial patrimony was integrally related to the religious devotion accorded the family ancestors. Family religion held traditions of its own apart from, and in many respects parallel to, national expressions of power.[12] It has been remarked that pilgrimage breaks down the importance of family ties in favor of more general societal ties.[13] In the context of monarchic Israel, pilgrimages to major national sites, such as Jerusalem, Dan and Bethel, would have functioned to subordinate family or regional ties in favor of the larger political ties championed by the sponsors of these cult-sites, namely the southern and northern kings. Indeed, the history of some pilgrimage feasts themselves may have reflected a change from family or regional cult to national cult.[14] The record of the national cult as presented in the Psalms may reflect the tension between family/clan and national/royal cults. The Psalms make very little explicit mention of family cult, and the little there is, is presented in a negative manner. For example, while Psalm 49 is indicative of many burial practices and beliefs about the dead, it presents these phenomena in a negative fashion.[15]

11. Lewis, 'The Ancestral Estate', pp. 597-612.

12. See M. Weinfeld, 'Zion and Jerusalem as Religious and Political Capital: Ideology and Utopia', in R.E. Freedman (ed.), *The Poet and the Historian: Essays in Literary and Historical Biblical Criticism* (HSS, 26; Chico, CA: Scholars Press, 1983), pp. 75-115.

13. Reeves, *The Hidden Government*, p. 154.

14. So for 'Unleavened Bread', see A. Cooper and B.R. Goldstein, 'Exodus and *Maṣṣôt* in History and Tradition', *MAARAV* 8 (1992), pp. 15-37. As Dr E.M. Bloch-Smith informs me, this view is anticipated by J. Morgenstern, *Rites of Birth, Marriage, Death and Kindred Occasions among the Semites* (Cincinnati: Hebrew Union College Press, 1966), pp. 166-78.

15. See N.J. Tromp, *Primitive Conceptions of Death and the Nether World in the Old Testament* (BibOr, 21; Rome: Pontifical Biblical Institute, 1969), pp. 69, 120-21; M.S. Smith, 'The Invocation of Deceased Ancestors in Psalm 49.12c', *JBL* 112 (1993), pp. 105-107.

1. *Going on Pilgrimage*

Pilgrimages would presumably begin with the gathering of pilgrims and their caravans in their home districts. This point marks the beginning of the holy experience of pilgrimage, a separation from the realm of the profane into the realm of the holy which increases in the progression toward the shrine.[16] This movement accordingly represents in the words of R. Gothóni, a specialist in comparative religion, 'a transformation journey'.[17] Or, as R.W. Frank comments in his study of pilgrimage in twelfth-century France: 'For all the climactic awareness of divine presence at the shrine, the pilgrims' own narratives told them that divine presence might be manifest along a whole spectrum: from the moment of beseeching through the whole pilgrimage experience. The sacral power that flowed mysteriously through the shrine flowed also along the pilgrim way.'[18] Accordingly, divine presence already meets and accompanies pilgrims en route to Jerusalem as an anticipation of the fuller experience of the divine that awaits them in the Temple (Ps. 43.3-4):

> Oh, send out Your light and Your truth,
> Let them lead me to Your holy hill
> And to Your dwelling!
> Then I will go to the altar of God,

16. On this point, see G.A. Anderson, *A Time to Mourn, A Time to Dance: The Expression of Grief and Joy in Israelite Religion* (University Park, PA: Pennsylvania State University Press, 1991), pp. 108-109. For further observations, see also the essays in B.N. Sargent-Baur (ed.), *Journeys Toward God: Pilgrimage and Crusade* (SMC, 30 Medieval Institute Publications; Kalamazoo, MI: Western Michigan University Press, 1992), especially R.W. Frank, Jr, 'Pilgrimage and Sacral Power', pp. 31-43. See also H.J. Levine, *Sing unto God a New Song*, pp. 73-78. These studies are indebted to the work of V. Turner. See especially 'Pilgrimages as Social Processes', in Turner's book, *Drama, Fields, and Metaphors: Symbolic Action in Human Society* (Ithaca, NY: Cornell University Press, 1974), pp. 166-230; and V. and E. Turner, *Image and Pilgrimage in Christian Culture: Anthropological Perspectives* (New York: Columbia University Press, 1978). For a helpful critique of Turner's views of pilgrimage, see R. Gothóni, 'Pilgrimage = Transformation Journey', in T. Ahlbäck (ed.), *The Problem of Ritual: Based on Papers Read at the Symposium on Religious Rites Held at Åbo, Finland on the 13th–16th of August 1991* (Scripta Instituti Donneriani Aboensis, 15; Stockholm: Almqvist & Wiksell, 1993), pp. 101-15.

17. Gothóni, 'Pilgrimage = Transformation Journey', pp. 101-15.

18. Frank, 'Pilgrimage and Sacral Power', pp. 33, 39.

To God, my exceeding joy;
And I will praise You with the lyre,
O God, my God.

This passage reflects the Israelite perception of divine accompaniment not only at the shrine, but already on the way. As Frank observes further,

> a sacral character inheres in the very act of pilgrimage. It is intermittent, it is nowhere near so pervasive as at the shrine, it is probably not perceived by all pilgrims, but it is always potentially present. The pilgrim travelled to and from the shrine in a kind of 'force field'.[19]

The divine characteristics of divine light and truth in Ps. 43.3 are not simply figurative, but express a heightened awareness from the beginning of the pilgrimage. The power of divine presence on the journey is perceived as proleptically related to the experience of presence in the shrine: the pilgrims not only journey to the shrine to meet Yahweh, but the divine power journeys out to pilgrims on their way to meet their deity at the shrine.

According to biblical texts pilgrimage meant an awareness of new joy and holiness. The pilgrimage festivals were joyous popular celebrations. 'I was glad when they said to me, "Let us go to the house of the Lord!"' begins Psalm 122. The prophecy of restoration of Jer. 31.6 likewise assumes the joy associated with the pilgrimage to Jerusalem (see also Hos. 2.13). Ps. 84.5-7 refers to the tradition of pilgrimage from the northern country of Israel down to Jerusalem:

Blessed are those whose strength is in You,
In whose heart are the highways to Zion.
As they go through the valley of Baca
They make it a place of springs;
The early rain also covers it with pools.
They go from strength to strength;
The God of Gods will be seen in Zion.

The fertility of rejuvenated nature surrounds them, since the early rains have fructified the earth. Each stop is a source of physical and spiritual strength, as they journey closer to Jerusalem. Nature serves as an external referent for the pilgrims' internal experience of divine presence.

The Bible does not provide information about the mechanics of pilgrimage. Post-biblical texts, including the Mishnah (*Bikk.* 3.2-5), offer

---

19. Frank, 'Pilgrimage and Sacral Power', pp. 33, 39.

a post-biblical description of how pilgrims travelled to the temple for one of the festivals (Booths or Sukkot, discussed below). Villagers would assemble in their towns and then go to the main town in the district for the night. On the next day they would journey with their offerings of fruits to the Temple in Jerusalem. Their procession would be headed up by an ox, with its horns overlaid with gold and its head adorned with a wreath of olive-leaves. According to Josephus, a three-day journey represents the amount of time necessary for a sixty-five mile journey from the south of Galilee to Jerusalem.[20] It is possible that the motif of the three-day journey in the wilderness to celebrate a feast to Yahweh in Exod. 3.18, 5.1 and 3 (cf. 8, 17) reflects the standard length for a pilgrimage journey. According to rabbinic tradition, millions gathered in Jerusalem for the festivals (*t. Pes*. 4.12; cf. *'Ab*. 5.8). Psalm 122.3-4 conveys the national center which Jerusalem represented: 'Jerusalem...to which the tribes go up, the tribes of the Lord'.

After gathering in Jerusalem, pilgrims would process to the Temple. Processions in Jerusalem were known in biblical times (Pss. 48.13-14; 68.24-27). According to the Mishnah, pilgrims would be met by the music of the flute until they reached the Temple Mount (*Bikk*. 3.2-5). Arriving in the Temple court, they were greeted by the Levites who are said to have sung Psalm 30. Processions (Pss. 42.5; 68.25-26) were proverbial for their joyful, musical celebration as in Isa. 30.29 (NJPS):

> For you there shall be singing
> As on a night when a festival is hallowed;
> There shall be rejoicing as when they march
> With flute, with timbrels, and with lyres
> To the Rock of Israel on the Mount of the Lord.

Similarly, Jer. 31.12-13 (NJPS) describes future pilgrimage in glowing terms:

> They shall come and shout on the heights of Zion,
> Radiant over the bounty of the Lord—
> Over new grain and wine and oil,
> And over sheep and cattle.
> They shall fare like a watered garden,
> They shall never languish again.

---

20. Cited in D.A. Dorsey, *The Roads and Highways of Ancient Israel* (Baltimore: The Johns Hopkins University Press, 1991), p. 12. For pilgrimage in Exodus, see especially the discussion of Chapter 11, section 1 below.

> Then shall maidens dance gaily,
> Young men and old alike,
> I will turn their mourning to joy,
> I will comfort them and cheer them in their grief.
> I will give the priests their fill of fatness,
> And My people shall enjoy My full bounty—declares the Lord.

The great number of animals of pilgrimage festivals was likewise pro-verbial: 'Like the flock for sacrifices, like the flock at Jerusalem dur-ing her appointed feasts, so shall the waste cities be filled with flocks of men' (Ezek. 37.38 RSV).

Communally pilgrimages were geared toward celebration and hym-nic praise of Yahweh. Yet pilgrimage festivals also provided opportu-nities for individuals to express their private concerns. During a visit to Shiloh on pilgrimage, Hannah addressed Yahweh in silent prayer in order to pray for a son (1 Sam. 1.10, 12-13). Furthermore, she made a vow to dedicate the divine gift of a son to Yahweh (1 Sam. 1.11). On her return to Shiloh she repaid the vow in the form of her son, Samuel (1 Sam. 1.19-23). Although the repayment of vows is other-wise unknown in the context of pilgrimage, Hannah's experience may not have been exceptional for most people, unlike royalty who might have other opportunities to make and repay vows at shrines.[21] This epi-sode in the life of Hannah may represent the sort of personal prayer and vows[22] that people might commit to Yahweh during pilgrimage. Such a background would then illuminate the poetic parallelism in Nah. 2.1:

> Celebrate your festivals, O Judah,
> Fulfill your vows.

The festivals provided the opportunity both to make and to fulfill per-sonal vows.

A religious aura surrounded pilgrimages, but the festivals also in-cluded what might be regarded as secular activities. (A strict division between the sacred and secular would represent, however, an anachro-nistic imposition on ancient Israelite pilgrimages, not to mention Israelite society more generally.) It is quite possible that the account

21. Cf. the story of King Keret in *KTU* 1.14 IV 34-43 who makes a vow to Asherah at her sanctuary while en route to besiege Udm.

22. On the payment of vows on pilgrimage feasts, see Frank, 'Pilgrimage and Sacral Power', pp. 33-39. For vows made at Israelite sanctuaries, see van der Toorn, *From her Cradle to her Grave*, p. 98.

in Judg. 21.19-23 assumes that young men and women could participate in courting rituals on the occasion of the pilgrimage festival. This
passage relates the horrific abduction of the 'girls of Shiloh' by Ben-
jaminites on the occasion of the fall harvest festival. Given later rabbinic reports of similar courtship activities on feast-days (*b. Ta'an.*
26b; 31a), it would seem that the biblical story draws on a known
courtship practice.[23] The pilgrimage feasts provided other arenas of
activity. It may be argued, as F.M. Cross has done, that 'Israel's pilgrimage festivals... took on many of the activities of fairs'.[24] In sum,
the festivals represented popular celebrations, at once religious, social,
economic and political.

2. The Pilgrimage Feasts

According to Exod. 23.14-17, 34.22-23 and Deut 16.16, pilgrimage
was to be made three times a year: the Feast of Unleavened Bread/
Passover in the spring; the late spring/early summer festival of Weeks,
seven weeks later; and Booths in the early autumn.[25] The three major
festivals were geared to the agricultural harvests. The festival calendars associate the three pilgrimage feasts with the different harvests:
Passover (פסח) was secondarily combined with Unleavened Bread
(מצות) at the time of the cereal (barley) harvest; Weeks (שבועת) occurred seven weeks later at the time of the wheat harvest; and the fall
festival of Booths (סכות) took place at the time of harvest of summer

23. The point and information are drawn from van der Toorn, *From her Cradle
to her Grave*, p. 57. See also van der Toorn, *Family Religion*, p. 295.

24. F.M. Cross, 'The Epic Traditions of Early Israel: Epic Narrative and the
Reconstruction of Early Israelite Tradition', in Freedman (ed.), *The Poet and the
Historian*, p. 17 n. 13.

25. For the complex historical issues involving the festival calendar, see I. Knohl,
'The Priestly Torah Versus the Holiness School: Sabbath and the Festivals', *HUCA*
58 (1987), pp. 65-117. This article was republished as chapter one in *The Sanctuary
of Silence: The Priestly Torah and the Holiness School* (Minneapolis: Fortress Press,
1995), pp. 8-45. See also B.R. Goldstein and A. Cooper, 'The Festivals of Israel
and Judah and the Literary History of the Pentateuch', *JAOS* 110 (1990), pp. 19-31;
for further references, see p. 20 n. 12. It is interesting to note that New Year's and
Yom Kippur (Day of Atonement) do not appear in these listings, but in Lev. 23.23
and 26 and Numbers 29, which, however, do not refer to any of the feasts as pilgrimage feasts; in the pre-exilic period New Year's and Yom Kippur may be primarily of priestly concern. The importance of these feasts especially New Year's for the
priestly redaction of Exodus is discussed in Chapter 12, sections 2 and 3.

fruit (Exod. 23.15-17; 34.18-26; Lev. 23.10-36; Deut. 16.13).[26] Each pilgrimage feast required tithes, sacrificial gifts, drawn from crops and livestock; this was the occasion of great joy (Isa. 9.2; 16.9-10). Each feast also associated a particular harvest with an event celebrated from Israel's tradition. Most of the information regarding the festival pilgrimages derives from post-biblical sources.

Passover/Unleavened Bread

Passover and the Feast of Unleavened Bread, though originally separate but contiguous feasts, came to be identified as a single complex feast celebrated around the time of the barley harvest in the spring.[27] A number of scholars believe that these feasts were originally domestic celebrations that were transformed into a national pilgrimage feast, perhaps during the late monarchy.[28] It is also thought that the celebration may have originated in the northern kingdom and was imported secondarily into the southern kingdom.[29] In biblical tradition, Unleavened Bread/Passover, understood as a single feast, was associated first and foremost with the exodus from slavery in Egypt. The Mishnah spells out how this pilgrimage feast was celebrated in Jerusalem, at least in later times (*m. Pes.* 5.5-10). After the court of the temple was filled with people, the gates to the court were closed. The shofar was blown. Each Israelite would slaughter his own offering and the priests would catch the blood in gold and silver vessels. Meanwhile, Psalms 113–18, known as the Hallel psalms (traditional psalms for pilgrimage),

---

26. For a fuller description of the agricultural background, see O. Borowski, 'Agriculture', *ABD*, I, pp. 95-98; *idem*, 'Harvests, Harvesting', *ABD*, III, pp. 63-64; *idem*, *Agriculture in Iron Age Israel* (Winona Lake, IN: Eisenbrauns, 1987).

27. R. de Vaux, *Ancient Israel* (2 vols; New York: McGraw–Hill, 1965), II, pp. 484-93.

28. For this development for the two feasts, see also B. Bokser, 'Unleavened Bread and Passover, Feasts of', *ABD*, VI, pp. 755-65, esp. p. 758. For Unleavened Bread, see also Cooper and Goldstein, 'Exodus and *Maṣṣôt* in History and Tradition', pp. 15-37.

29. In addition to the works cited in the previous note, see Y. Hoffman, 'A North Israelite Typological Myth and Judaean Historical Tradition', *VT* 39 (1989), pp. 169-82; K. van der Toorn, 'Migration and the Spread of Local Cults', in K. van Lerberghe and A. Schoors (eds.), *Immigration and Emigration within the Ancient Near East: Festschrift E. Lipiński* (OLA, 65; Leuven: Peeters, 1995), p. 373. On Exodus as a foundational story of the northern kingdom, see van der Toorn, *Family Religion*, pp. 287-315.

were sung. The priests were to take the sacrificial portions of the lamb for burnt offerings and return the rest to the people. After nightfall the people went out and roasted their offerings. The feast was accompanied by the consumption of a lamb, known from biblical sources (Exodus 12) and mishnaic texts (*m. Pes.* 2.8). According to some sources (*Jub.* 49.6; Mt. 26.27-30), the seder meal took place after the sacrifice.[30]

The ancient custom of the sacrifice of the lambs survives today in the Samaritan community which traces its origins to the northern kingdom of ancient Israel. Each year the Samaritan community gathers on Mount Gerizim near Shechem for a passover ceremony. In the New Testament, the occasion of the Passover coincides with Passion Week. According to the Synoptic Gospels, the Last Supper was a Passover meal (Mk 14.1-2, 2-17; Lk. 22.39, 47-54; Mt. 26.30, 47-50, 57; cf. Jn 13.1-2).[31] In the New Testament and Christian tradition, the passover lamb becomes a central image for Jesus as the sacrificial lamb, or more specifically the paschal lamb, who takes away the sins of the world (Jn 1.29; 19.36; 1 Cor. 5.7; 1 Pet. 1.19; Rev. 5.6, 12). The association between redemption and Passover also underlies the beautiful benediction that Rabbi Akiba prayed in ending the seder (*m. Pes.* 10.6):

> Therefore, O Lord our God and the God of our fathers, bring us in peace to the other set feasts and festivals which are coming to meet us, while we rejoice in the building-up of thy city and joyful in thy worship; and may we eat there of the sacrifices and of the Passover-offerings whose blood has reached with acceptance the wall of thy Altar, and let us praise thee for our redemption and for the ransoming of our soul. Blessed art thou, O Lord, who hast redeemed Israel.[32]

Feast of Weeks (Pentecost)
Although Weeks[33] was connected originally with the wheat harvest, in Judaism the feast became further associated with the gift of the Torah to Moses. While Exod. 19.1 makes no mention of the feast of Weeks,

30. Safrai, 'Religion in Everyday Life', p. 809.
31. For a discussion of whether or not the Last Supper fell on Passover, see J.A. Fitzmyer, *The Gospel According to Luke X–XXIV* (AB, 28A; Garden City, NY: Doubleday, 1985), pp. 1378-82. For Jn 13.1-2, see G.A. Yee, *Jewish Feasts and the Gospel of John* (Zacchaeus Studies: New Testament; Wilmington, DE: Michael Glazier, 1989), pp. 67-69.
32. H. Danby, *The Mishnah* (Oxford: Oxford University Press, 1974), p. 151.
33. De Vaux, *Ancient Israel*, II, pp. 493-95.

this verse dates the arrival of the Israelites at Mount Sinai to this holiday. The question is whether such a connection is likely to have been accidental or deliberate. Old Testament texts do not make an explicit connection between Weeks and the giving of the Torah. As the earliest reference for this connection has been thought to be in the Talmud (e.g. *b. Pes.* 68b), it has been held that this association is Pharisaic or rabbinic in origin (although allowance is made for an earlier date).[34] A few other pieces of evidence would suggest the late biblical period as the date for the connection.[35] M. Weinfeld notes the connection between Weeks and covenant-renewal in 2 Chron. 15.10-14.[36] The placement of the renewal of the Sinai covenant on the feast of Weeks is known in the intertestamental text of *Jub.* 6.17:

> Therefore, it is ordained and written in the heavenly tablets that they should observe the feast of Shebuot in this month, once per year, in order to renew the covenant in all (respects), year by year.[37]

34. L. Jacobs, 'Shavuot', *EncJud* 14, pp. 1320-21; Safrai, 'The Temple', p. 893.

35. M. Weinfeld has made perhaps the boldest claims for the antiquity of this connection. He suggests that Psalms 50 and 81 represent covenant renewal within the context of the pilgrimage feast of Weeks. See M. Weinfeld, 'The Uniqueness of the Decalogue and its Place in Jewish Tradition', in B.-Z. Segal (ed.), *The Ten Commandments in History and Tradition* (trans. G. Levi; Jerusalem: The Hebrew University, 1987), pp. 21-27. These psalms are speeches of a cultic mediator who quotes divine speech exhorting the faithful to follow Yahweh's teaching. In Ps. 81 the cultic mediator cites divine words to be obedient, citing the past witness of Joseph, the exodus and the Israelites' experience at the wilderness site of Meribah. (In this connection Ps. 95 should also be mentioned. This psalm likewise quotes divine speech exhorting the congregation not to be stubborn as on the day of Meribah and Massah.) Weinfeld argues that Pss. 50 and 81 quote the decalogue, and here Weinfeld follows in the work of A. Jepsen, 'Beiträge zur Auslegung und Geschichte des Dekalogs', *ZAW* 79 (1967), p. 303; A. Alt, *Essays on Old Testament History and Religion* (trans. R.A. Wilson; Garden City, NY: Doubleday, 1968), p. 168; G. von Rad, *The Problem of the Hexateuch and Other Essays* (trans. E.W.T. Dicken; Edinburgh/London: Oliver & Boyd, 1966), pp. 22-24; and W. Zimmerli, *I am Yahweh* (ed. W. Brueggemann; trans. D.W. Stott; Atlanta: John Knox, 1982), pp. 23-28. Yet it is difficult to confirm his theory for the festival behind these psalms since others scholars would place these psalms in the context of Booths (Sukkot). Therefore Weinfeld's argument for an older date for the connection is not firm. (It is quite possible that such preaching of Torah took place at all of the pilgrimage festivals, accented by the Torah narrative celebrated in the feast.)

36. Weinfeld, 'The Uniqueness of the Decalogue', p. 24.

37. *OTP*, II, p. 67; cited by Hendel, 'Sacrifice as a Cultural System', p. 373; Tabori, *Jewish Festivals*, p. 151.

Jubilees 6.19 likewise assumes the connection between Sinai and the feast: 'in your days the children of Israel forgot it until you renewed it for them on this mountain'. J.W. Milik argues that the Qumran community likewise commemorated their covenant on the feast of Weeks.[38] Here the evidence is less compelling than the references in *Jub*. 6.17 and 19. Milik cites 4Q267, frg. 18, col. 5, ll. 16-21 (completed by the parallel material from 4Q270, frg. 11, col. 2, ll. 11-15): 'The sons of Levi and the men of the camps will meet in the third month and will curse whoever tends to the right or to the left of the law'.[39] While the character or extent of the communal celebration of the Sinai covenant on Weeks is unclear in this passage, it may be said that it connects the date of Weeks with maintaining the law of the community. This association between Weeks and the Sinai covenant is paralleled also by the Christian feast of Pentecost, when the divine gift of the Spirit was given to the early Christian community in Jerusalem according to Acts 2.[40] The concept of the giving of the Spirit to the community through the Son at Pentecost seems to parallel Weeks' celebration of the giving of the Sinai covenant through Moses to the Israelite people. F.M. Cross remarks on the significance of Acts 2 for understanding the background of the attachment of the theme of Sinai to the feast of Weeks (Pentecost): 'It is intriguing to note that the entry into the new covenant at Qumrân also fell on Pentecost, as does the creation of the church, following old Jewish tradition going back to the priestly chronology [of Exod. 19.1-2]'.[41]

The pre-rabbinic evidence for the association between the Sinai covenant and Weeks would suggest a re-evaluation of the dating of the

38. J.W. Milik, *Ten Years of Discovery in the Wilderness of Judaea* (trans. J. Strugnell; Studies in Biblical Theology, 26; Naperville, IL: Allenson, 1959), p. 117; *idem*, 'Milkî-ṣedeq et Milkî-reša' dans les ancien écrit juifs et chrétiens', *JJS* 23 (1972), pp. 135-36. Milik is followed by Hendel, 'Sacrifice as a Cultural System', p. 373. See also Tabori, *Jewish Festivals*, p. 151.

39. F. García Martínez, *The Dead Sea Scrolls Translated: The Qumran Texts in English* (Leiden: Brill, 1994), pp. 57, 67.

40. See I.H. Marshall, 'The Significance of Pentecost', *SJT* 30 (1977), pp. 347-69; M.J. Olson, 'Pentecost', *ABD*, V, pp. 222-23. The Christian imagery of the Holy Spirit as fire may be grounded in the larger Jewish tradition. Olson compares Philo (*Dec.* 33): 'God created a sound on Sinai and changed it into fire'. For the comparison of the divine word with fire, see also Jer. 23.29.

41. F.M. Cross, *Canaanite Myth and Hebrew Epic: Essays in the History of the Religion of Israel* (Cambridge, MA: Harvard University Press, 1973), p. 312 n. 64.

arrival at Mount Sinai on Weeks in Exod. 19.1-2. The chronology is
hardly coincidental. Priestly chronological notices in Exodus and Numbers are not made casually. Instead, they reflect a schema correlating
the Pentateuchal event with Weeks.[42] In sum, these texts would push
back back the date of the connection to pre-rabbinic Judaism, more
specifically to the post-exilic period.

Booths (Sukkot)[43]

In both early and later texts Booths is the feast of the fruit harvest
associated with newly made wine and with dancing and joy (Judg. 9.27;
21.19, 20-21; Isa. 16.10; 2 Macc. 10.6; *m. Ta'an.* 4.8).[44] Eli's suspicion
that Hannah is drunk with wine makes sense in the context of the grape
harvest at the time of Sukkot and not the other two pilgrimage feasts
(1 Sam. 1.14-15).[45] In the late biblical apocalyptic text of Zech. 14.16,
all nations are to make pilgrimage to Jerusalem. Whoever refuses to
do so, will not receive the fall rain (except the Egyptians, who will
receive a different punishment because they have the Nile and do not
need the rain). As this passage indicates, Sukkot was not only time of
the harvest of fruit; it was also the crucial time for the rain, the expected blessing of the season (*LAB* 13.7[46]; *m. Ta'an.* 1.1-7). The rain
in due season was anticipated with anxiety (Job 29.23), and at the time
of Sukkot Israelites were to pray for its arrival (Zech. 10.1). If rain
failed to appear, it was interpreted as a divine curse which would occasion ever increasing public lamentation (Joel 2; *m. Ta'an.* 1-3[47]). The
cycle of life is entirely dependent on the rain: for Yahweh to give rain
is to provide life for crops and animals and therefore humans as well;

42. See Hendel, 'Sacrifice as a Cultural System', p. 373. G. von Rad (*The Problem of the Hexateuch*, pp. 34-35) entertains but rejects the theory that Exod. 19.1
reflects a late, priestly dating of Weeks. His alleged counter-evidence of Deut. 31.10-
11 may reflect, however, an alternative or earlier tradition. Contrary to the presupposition of von Rad's argument, the priestly tradition may have fixed this chronology
in Exod. 19.1 without concern for the other tradition, which in any case may not
have been current at the time of the priestly redaction of Exodus.
43. The feast is sometimes called 'Tabernacles', but this translation of הסכות is
inaccurate (see NJPS 193 n. c). The English word 'tabernacle' is better reserved for
BH משכן, described in Exodus 25–31 and 35–40 (see Chapter 11, section 3).
44. For a description of the feast, see de Vaux, *Ancient Israel*, II, pp. 495-502.
45. De Vaux, *Ancient Israel*, II, p. 496.
46. *OTP*, II, p. 321.
47. Danby, *The Mishnah*, pp. 194-99.

their sacrificial offerings therefore depend on the deity who provides the rains in the first place.

In later biblical tradition, Sukkot like the other pilgrimage feasts was associated with one of the national foundational events. Sukkot evoked the forty-year sojourn in the wilderness (Lev. 23.39-43; Neh. 8.13-18).[48] This feast was connected with shouts and trumpeting (Lev. 23.24), so often mentioned in the psalms describing divine kingship. *M. Sukk.* 2–5 (with parallel evidence in *Jub.* 16.30-31 and Pseudo-Philo, *LAB* 13.7) describe the celebration. People were to treat their booths as their main homes for the seven days of the feast. On the first night of the feast the Temple area was illuminated brightly by lamps and torches. Dancing took place in this light. Daily there was a procession around the altar; worshippers carried a branch in one hand and a piece of fruit in the other, and Psalm 118 was sung (*m. Sukk.* 3.9). According to *m. Sukk.* 3.8, Jerusalemites used to decorate the palm branches, called לולבים, with golden threads (the practice of waving לולבים has continued in Jewish celebration of Sukkot). The priests marched around the altar seven times. On the last day water was brought to the Temple from the Siloam pool and poured before the altar of burnt offerings. Horns and trumpets were blown at the great moments of the feast. In the New Testament the feast of Sukkot is mentioned only once explicitly; it is the feast which Jesus attended secretly after refusing to go publicly in John 7. The rivers of waters mentioned in Jn 7.37-39 may represent an allusion to the water-libation ritual during the feast.[49]

This ritual is known for *Sukkot* from mishnaic sources (*m. Shek.* 6.3; *Sukk.* 4.1, 9; *Zeb.* 6.2; *Midd.* 1.4, 2.6). Its roots appear to be biblical (1 Sam. 7.6; 1 Kgs 18.30-35).[50] In discussing the water libation, some mishnaic passages (e.g. *m. Midd.* 2.6) mention Rabbi Eliezer b. Jacob's

---

48. Was the sojourning of pilgrims in booths in Jerusalem (cf. Neh. 8.16) the inspiration for the association of this feast with the wilderness journey? See the end of Chapter 11, below.

49. For further discussion of the use of Booths imagery in John, see Yee, *Jewish Feasts*, pp. 77-82.

50. M. Delcor, 'Rites pour l'obtention de la pluie', *RHR* 178 (1970), pp. 117-32; H. Barstad, *The Religious Polemics of Amos: Studies in the Preaching of Amos ii 7B-8, iv 1-13, v 1-27, vi 4-7, viii 14* (VTSup, 34; Leiden: Brill, 1984), p. 72. Barstad would include 2 Sam. 23.16, Jer. 14–15 and possibly Lam. 2.19. See also possibly a metaphorical usage in Isa. 12.3.

citation of Ezek. 47.1-2. This passage refers to the old idea of the cosmic life-giving waters which flow from beneath the Jerusalem temple (see the following section). It may be that the idea of the waters' cosmic and life-giving properties underlie the ritual of the water-libation. The Talmud (*b. Ta'an.* 25b) remarks in a similar vein: 'When the libation of water takes place during the feast, one flood (תהום) says to the other: "Let your waters spring, I hear the voice of the two friends"'.[51] From this passage it might be inferred that the water libation ritual may have functioned as a gesture to accompany the prayers to induce rain.[52]

In an important and far-reaching treatment, S. Mowinckel used the psalms associated with rain to reconstruct a massive New Year-Sukkot festival.[53] Drawing on many psalms (Pss. 24, 47, 81,[54] 93–100, 118, 126, 132), Mowinckel reconstructed a 'New Year' feast connected to Sukkot.[55] This single festival celebrated a string of themes: creation and its renewal, Yahweh's enthronement over all creation and judgment of the nations, the revelation at Sinai and the making of the covenant,

---

51. See J.C. de Moor, *The Seasonal Pattern in the Ugaritic Myth of Ba'lu: According to the Version of Ilimilku* (AOAT, 16; Kevelaer: Butzon & Bercker; Neukirchen–Vluyn: Neukirchener Verlag, 1971), p. 108. Generally for the mishnaic evidence on the water-libation ritual, see Tabori, *Jewish Festivals*, pp. 198-200.

52. In 1 Sam. 7.6, the ritual is to induce God to come in the thunderstorm in order to fight on Israel's behalf, as indicated by v. 10.

53. S. Mowinckel, *The Psalms in Israel's Worship* (2 vols.; repr. of 1962 English original; trans. D.R. Ap-Thomas; Biblical Seminar, 14; Sheffield: JSOT Press, 1992), I, pp. 106-92. The notion of such a New Year's feast of this sort is not original with Mowinckel; see, for example, P. Volz, *Neujahrsfest Jahwes* (Tübingen: Mohr, 1912). For a more recent defense of Mowinckel's hypothesis with extensive use of Ugaritic texts, see J.C. de Moor, *New Year with Canaanites and Israelites* (Kampen: Kok, 1972); cf. the review of D. Marcus, *JAOS* 93 (1973), pp. 589-91. Some appeal was made in Mowinckel's argument to a comparison between the Israelite and Babylonian New Year's. Although this comparison has been criticized, it is not a necessary element of the theory. Moreover, the comparison has been defended with qualifications by K. van der Toorn, 'The Babylonian New Year Festival: New Insights from the Cuneiform Texts and their Bearing on Old Testament Study', in J.A. Emerton (ed.), *Congress Volume: Leuven 1989* (VTSup, 43; Leiden: Brill, 1991), pp. 331-44.

54. The association with the fall period might help to explain סתר רעם, 'the hiding-place of thunder', in Ps. 81.8.

55. For the relation between the two, Mowinckel, *The Psalms in Israel's Worship*, I, pp. 120-21.

the giving of divine teaching, the procession of the ark, purification and rededication of the Temple (reflected in the later feast of Yom Kippur).[56] Mowinckel described the ritual procession with the ark as a reflection of a drama re-enacting Yahweh's defeat over the cosmic enemy of Sea and Yahweh's resulting creation. Mowinckel saw this drama as descendant of the New Year's festival reflected in the Ugaritic Baal Cycle; here, similarly Baal conquers Sea, and as a result creation is renewed.

Mowinckel's powerful interconnection of themes and the theory's explanatory capacity to account for so many psalms found many supporters, such as J.H. Eaton and J. Gray.[57] However, the evidence for some aspects of Mowinckel's reconstruction is tenuous. His identification of the New Year's Festival and Sukkot requires further explanation in view of the two feasts' separation in biblical and later Jewish tradition. As a result of these difficulties, many scholars have denied the existence of a New Year's festival.[58] While Mowinckel may have extended his theory beyond the evidence, this is no demonstration of the feast's non-existence. Indeed, given the lack of a fall feast by the name of Sukkot outside of Israel, this feast may have been an inner-Israelite development evolving from an older fall festival associated with the turn of the year. An older festival was known in earliest Israel. In Judg. 21.19-20 the feast is not given a specific name; the passage refers to it as the annual feast of Yahweh and the later context indicates that it takes place at the time of wine-making, that is, after the harvest of the summer fruit, including grapes. It is also clear that Sukkot was known later to occur at the 'end of the year' (Exod. 23.16) or 'turn of the year' (Exod. 34.22). Sukkot would appear then to be the Israelite name given secondarily to this feast which occurs at the turn of the year. The name, 'New Year's Feast', is perhaps then to be

56. To Mowinckel's credit he distinguished between the ritual of the divine enthronement ('Yahweh's epiphany') and 'the complex of harvest and new year'. See Mowinckel, *The Psalms in Israel's Worship*, I, pp. 184-85.

57. J.H. Eaton, *Kingship and the Psalms* (Biblical Seminar, 3; Sheffield: JSOT Press, 1986), pp. 102-11, 227-28; J. Gray, *The Biblical Doctrine of the Reign of God* (Edinburgh: T. & T. Clark, 1979).

58. See de Vaux, *Ancient Israel*, II, pp. 502-506; H.J. Kraus, *Psalms 1–59: A Commentary* (trans. H.C. Oswald; Minneapolis: Augsburg, 1988), pp. 60-61; E. Kutsch, 'Sukkot', *EncJud* 15, pp. 497-98. See also B.A. Levine, *In the Presence of the Lord: A Study of Cult and Some Cultic Terms in Ancient Israel* (Leiden: Brill, 1974), pp. 39-41.

avoided, but the rejection of this detail of Mowinckel's theory hardly precludes the validity of some of his insights. Indeed, Zech. 14.16-19 points to Sukkot as a festival which celebrated divine kingship and the divine capacity to supply rain. Rain and the renewal of creation were the natural elements of the festival, and during the Davidic dynasty, divine kingship, directly or indirectly promoting human kingship, was the central cultural theme of the festival, only to be linked or perhaps displaced at some point in the post-exilic period by the theme of Israel's sojourn in the wilderness after the Sinai revelation. The promotion of divine kingship at the season of the Israelite storm-god's greatest meteorological beneficence would make sense.

In addition to the evidence from the Psalms, some circumstantial evidence would comport with a reconstruction of a royal Sukkot feast. First, the northern and southern dynasties seem to regard the autumn as the orientation point for royal cult. The Jerusalem temple was inaugurated in the fall (1 Kgs 8.2, 65), and Jeroboam I is said to institute the fall pilgrimage festival (1 Kgs 12.32-33).[59] The assemblage of symbols at both Jerusalem and Bethel was geared to the theme of enthronement (see the next section). An an aside, it is curious to note the fact that the inauguration of the Solomonic temple was celebrated for fourteen days (1 Kgs 8.65-66; cf. 2 Chron. 7.8-10), precisely the period which would cover both New Year's and Sukkot. If reflective of a historical tradition, perhaps it would point to a double-feast which included both New Year's and Sukkot, but this view is speculative. Second, despite the criticisms levelled against the interpretation of the Baal Cycle as a New Year's liturgical piece, it would appear that this cycle draws on the language and imagery of the fall period.[60] Finally, Jewish tradition associates the renewal of creation with the New Year's feast.

Given the prominence of rain at Sukkot, psalms that emphasize rain and the storm theophany might be located in the context of Sukkot. The time of year which would best fit the combination of no rain followed by a feast is the fall. The season when the rains are their most impressive and suggestive of a storm-theophany is the fall period

---

59. R.B. Coote, *Amos Among the Prophets: Composition and Theology* (Philadelphia: Fortress Press, 1981), p. 57. Cf. 2 Macc. 10.6-8; Josephus, *Ant.* 13, 14.5.

60. For discussion, see M.S. Smith, *The Ugaritic Baal Cycle.* I. *Introduction with Text, Translation and Commentary of the First Two Tablets (KTU 1.1–1.2)* (VTSup, 55; Leiden: Brill, 1994), pp. 68-69, 98-99.

when they arrive from the west. Candidates for Sukkot psalms include Psalms 29, 65, 68 and 85, although they are not reflections of a single liturgical complex, but vary widely in date and location.[61] Psalm 29 describes the appearance of Yahweh in the rains moving from the Mediterranean Sea across the Lebanon and anti-Lebanon mountain ranges and then into the Syrian desert. In the context of the eastward moving storm theophany, in Yahweh's Temple the divine glory (כבוד) is visible (Ps. 29.9c).[62] Psalm 65 is a prayer for rain. Verse 5 refers to the rich fare of the Jerusalem temple, and then vv. 6-14 ask Yahweh for rain which will bless the earth with growth. Ps. 68.10 makes specific reference to rain and theophany. Ps. 85.13-14 refers to the divine bounty of the land and then the procession of Yahweh. If the two verses are to be construed together, the psalm seems to refer to rain in conjunction with a theophany.

Psalms 29, 65, 68 and 85 seem to derive from different periods and locations. Psalms 29 and 68 are earlier than the other psalms, and the first, if originally Israelite, is northern in character and the second draws on southern traditions. Psalm 65 is clearly later and belongs to the Jerusalem cult. Psalm 85 is likewise later, but may derive from the northern kingdom. It is also difficult to know whether these psalms are to be located in a specific cultic setting. Here it might be helpful to note Psalm 63's distance from a particular cultic setting. While Psalm 63 may draw on the imagery of the fall rains and Sukkot, it is entirely metaphorical: v. 2 describes the psalmist as parched like a land without water and then v. 6 describes the psalmist as one sated on the rich fare of the Temple. It is possible that Psalm 65 draws on the imagery of the fall rains as a basis for praise without being located in a specific Sukkot setting. Psalms 29, 68 and 85 may not be metaphorical in the same manner, but it is important to be alert to the possibility that these three psalms refer to the different points in the fall period. Psalm 29

61. For the weather in Pss. 29 and 65, see M. Futato, 'A Meteorological Analysis of Psalms 104, 65, and 29' (PhD dissertation, The Catholic University of America, 1984).

62. I translate Ps. 29.9c: 'And in the temple, all of it, effulgence is seen'. I take כלו as the postpositive, a well-known construction in Hebrew, Aramaic and Ugaritic, but ignored by the commentators. I follow those who take אמר*, not 'to say', but 'to see, be visible', since כבוד, usually translated 'glory', is never met by a verbal response, 'Glory!' (as suggested by virtually all translations). Instead, כבוד is experienced as a visible phenomenon.

charts a fall storm, quite possibly at Sukkot. In contrast, Psalm 85 may be a lament for the delayed rain late in the season. The setting of Psalm 68 is very unclear. In sum, Psalms 29, 65, 68 and 85 have disparate positions in the Psalter and different geographical and temporal backgrounds. Therefore, they hardly appear connected to one another or to other psalms in a Sukkot liturgy.

In contrast, Psalms 93–100 may constitute some sort of Sukkot complex. The six psalms in question involve theophany and divine kingship. For example, Ps. 96.11 refers to the roaring sea, which would suggest a storm that bears the theophany of Yahweh mentioned in the previous verse.[63] The fields and trees of the forest therefore have good reason to 'shout for joy at the presence of Yahweh, for He is coming' in the storm in v. 12. Psalm 97 adds a theophany (vv. 2-5) not from the west, but from the east. The images of fire and ענן-cloud do not suggest a rainstorm, but the dry wind-storm coming from the eastern desert. Psalm 97 can indeed be read with the other psalms in Psalms 95–100, as the context of the fall, around the time of Sukkot, is the period when the east and west winds alternate until the west wind bringing the rains serves as the victorious sign of Yahweh's abundant care for Israel.

In view of the thematic congruence and juxtaposition of Psalms 93–100, I would be inclined to follow S. Mowinckel and A. Fitzgerald in viewing them, possibly in part or in whole, as a Sukkot complex. However, it is unclear whether these psalms were recited as part of a larger complex of the Sukkot liturgy or secondarily inspired by it. The second alternative may be all the evidence can presently afford (and therefore the first alternative is hardly disproven). As an analogy for the second possibility, some modern Christian hymnals juxtapose various Advent hymns, Christmas hymns and other such groupings despite the different historical backgrounds for the individual hymns within such groupings. The first alternative assumes that Psalms 93–100 are texts for liturgy, but the texts do not show specifically liturgical marks (e.g. refrains). Rather, a literary model fits the evidence better.[64] H.L.

63. I owe the following remarks on weather and Psalms 96–97 to Aloysius Fitzgerald.

64. So also M.Z. Brettler, *God is King: Understanding an Israelite Metaphor* (JSOTSup, 76; Sheffield: JSOT Press, 1989), pp. 150, 153, 158. According to Brettler, the idea of foreigners worshipping at Jerusalem is a matter of wishful thinking and the psalms with this theme and therefore the entire complex of Psalms 93–100

Ginsberg added a pertinent point in noting the literary dependence of Ps. 96.7-9 on Ps. 29.2-3.[65] This dependence would suggest scribal-liturgical activity of incorporating prior Sukkot psalmic materials into a single Sukkot group of Psalms 93–100 created for Jerusalem devotion (Pss. 97.8; 99.2) which may or may not have been used in liturgy (the evidence being insufficient to determine usage beyond reading).

In contrast to the psalms that combine theophany, kingship and the rain-storm, Psalm 81 and its theme of Sinai would have been appropriate at other times as well, and so perhaps it is not to be situated specifically at the time of Sukkot as Mowinckel proposed. A. Jepsen assigned Psalms 50 and 81 to Levitical tradition and not to a specific festival.[66] M. Weinfeld argues that these two psalms reflect covenant renewal within the context of the pilgrimage feast of Weeks (שבעת).[67] Given the disagreement over which feast these psalms should reflect, it is hard to know if covenant renewal and Sinai belong specifically to Sukkot. Also lacking in evidence is the ritual drama, such as the procession of the ark specifically for Sukkot or the ritual enthronement of Yahweh. It would be preferable to categorize the later theme under the rubric of 'the kingship of Yahweh'.[68]

are ideal expressions not based on real liturgy. Yet it is possible that such ideal expressions could be incorporated into liturgy possibly as the reflection of the practice of captives bringing gifts (Ps. 68.18, 29) or perhaps vassals submitting tribute to their overlord, the Judean king (see J.J.M. Roberts, 'The Religio-Political Setting of Psalm 47', *BASOR* 220 [1975], pp. 129-32). In any case, even in Brettler's literary model, setting remains a desideratum.

65. As observed in detail by H.L. Ginsberg, 'A Strand in the Cord of Hebrew Psalmody', *ErIsr* 9 (1969 = W.F. Albright volume), pp. 45-50.

66. Jepsen, 'Beiträge zur Auslegung', p. 303. Zimmerli likewise views the statement of divine self-revelation in the Exodus decalogue and these psalms in terms broader than the deuteronomic tradition (Zimmerli, *I am Yahweh*, pp. 23-28, 104). For further discussion, see Kraus, *Psalms 1–59*, pp. 490-91. J. Jeremias, followed by H.J. Kraus, categorizes Psalms 50 and 81 as 'Levitical sermons'. See Jeremias, *Kultprophetie und Gerichtsverkündigung in der späten Königszeit Israel* (WMANT, 35; Neukirchen–Vluyn: Neukirchener Verlag, 1970), pp. 125-27; Kraus, *Psalms 1– 59*, pp. 61, 490. See also R.J. Tournay, *Seeing and Hearing God with the Psalms: The Prophetic Liturgy of the Second Temple in Jerusalem* (trans. J.E. Crowley; JSOTSup, 118; Sheffield: JSOT Press, 1991), pp. 170-75.

67. See Weinfeld, 'The Uniqueness of the Decalogue', pp. 21-27. After Jepsen and others (mentioned in the preceding note), Weinfeld argues that both psalms quote the decalogue.

68. Following the thrust of Brettler's incisive comments. See Brettler, *God is*

The three feasts taken together recapitulated the central old, foundational events known in post-exilic liturgical memory. In celebrating the exodus from Egypt, Passover begins the chain of events. Shabuot continues by celebrating the divine gift of the Torah at Mount Sinai. Sukkot ends the series by recalling the years in the wilderness following the reception of the Torah. The pilgrimage feasts as well as Israel's others holidays, new moons and sabbaths were central celebrations for the priestly tradition. To anticipate the final chapter of this study, Israel's sacred places and times helped to shape the formation of the Pentateuch, in particular Exodus and Numbers.

3. *Jerusalem*

In pre-exilic Israel pilgrimages were made to regional and national shrines. Shiloh (Judg. 21.19-20; 1 Sam. 1) and Bethel (1 Sam. 10.3) are mentioned as regional shrines for pilgrims in the pre-monarchic period. During this period Israel undoubtedly had other shrines which served as pilgrimage sites. Based on his study of the Pentateuch, M. Noth deduced that pre-monarchic pilgrimage sites included Shechem and Bethel as well as the site of Sinai.[69] Bethel, Gilgal and Beersheba are likewise known as pilgrimage shrines in the time of Amos (5.4-6).[70] The national shrines built in Jerusalem by Solomon and in Dan and Bethel by Jeroboam I (1 Kgs 12.28-30) were the focus of national pilgrimages, with all of the political, social and economic ramifications that national centers entail. Of all the pilgrimage sites, it is Jerusalem that held the imagination of biblical writers and countless others since then: 'Look to Zion, the city of our sacred festivals' (Isa. 33.20a).

As the home of the Temple and the Davidic dynasty and the goal of pilgrimages, Jerusalem was the center of the Israelite world.[71] The city is called Yahweh's 'holy mountain', as it is Yahweh's home (Ps. 15.1b; cf. Pss. 24.3; 76.3). The symbol of Jerusalem as a mountain for

King, pp. 145-58. For criticism of the theory of ritual combat, see van der Toorn, 'The Babylonian New Year Festival', pp. 343-44.

69. Noth, *A History of Pentateuchal Traditions*, pp. 80-81, 83, 85, 138 (esp. n. 393), 199, 221.

70. Bethel is called 'a king's sanctuary' in Amos 7.13. For Bethel, see also Hos. 2.13, 4.15 and 10.5-6.

71. See Weinfeld, 'Zion and Jerusalem as Religious and Political Capital', pp. 75-115.

the divine dwelling reflects a common ancient Near Eastern idea: the deity dwells in his palace (reflected on the earthly level as the deity's temple) located on top of this mountain which links heaven and earth (Ezek. 38.12; 40.2).[72] The deity reigns from his temple-mountain where he exercises his royal rule, expresses his power in thunder, lightning and rain, defends his home against the enemies all around—both cosmic and terrestrial. Through victory in battle the deity renews the world. This mountain itself is imbued with the power and security, the beauty and holiness of the deity's abode, and on this mountain Yahweh's faithful may enjoy paradisial conditions.

As 'the holy dwelling-place of the Most High' (Ps. 46.5), the city also reflects God's own power. The city, for example, is the referent point for the sentiment that 'A Mighty Fortress is Our God', the opening line of Psalm 46, which inspired Luther's hymn by the same name. Jerusalem is a fortress whose patron-god repels the attack of all peoples (Pss. 2.1-6; 48.4-8; 76.3-4). Jerusalem came to be viewed as invulnerable to enemy attack (see Isa. 29.1-8; 31.1-6; 2 Kgs 18.13–20.19 = Isa. 36.1–39.18).[73] Ps. 50.2 speaks of God's appearance not from the temple, but from the city, and this sentiment is cast in aesthetic terms: 'From Zion, perfect in beauty, God shown forth'. The aesthetic dimension of the city is a theme also in Ps. 48.2-3 which describes 'the city of Our God' with a string of titles: 'His holy mountain, fair-crested, joy of all the earth, Mount Zion, summit of Zaphon, city of the great king'.

The aesthetic dimension is perhaps a reflection of the city's paradisial associations. Like the garden of paradise in Genesis 2, the city has 'a river whose streams gladden God's city' (Ps. 46.5a; cf. Isa. 33.21). The restored city of Jerusalem in Ezekiel 47 will include a river running from the temple flowing with miraculously curing waters (cf. Joel 4.18; Zech. 14.8). For all the richness of the paradisial associations of Jerusalem, the city inspired a deep affective response on the part of deity and humanity alike. Yahweh has an affection for this city unlike any other place (Ps. 87.2; NJPS):

72. See R.J. Clifford, *The Cosmic Mountain in Canaan and the Old Testament* (HSM, 4; Cambridge, MA: Harvard University Press, 1972), pp. 131-60; B. Ollenburger, *Zion the City of the Great King: A Theological Symbol of the Jerusalem Cult* (JSOTSup, 41; Sheffield: JSOT Press, 1987).

73. See J.H. Hayes, 'The Traditions of Zion's Inviolability', *JBL* 82 (1963), pp. 419-26; Clifford, *The Cosmic Mountain*, pp. 142-57.

Yahweh loves the gates of Zion,
His foundation on the holy mountains,
More than all the dwellings of Jacob.

Jerusalem inspired human concern and lament. Ps. 122.6 commends
pilgrims to the city: 'Pray for the welfare of Jerusalem'. A lament over
Jerusalem recalls: 'By the waters of Babylon, there we sat and wept,
as we thought of Zion' (Ps. 137.1).

Jerusalem and Yahweh are inextricably linked: the well-being of
Jerusalem is living proof of Yahweh's care for the city (Ps. 48.13-15):

Walk around Zion and circle it,
Count its towers.
Note its ramparts,
Pass through its citadels,
That you may recount to the next generation:
This is our God,
Our God forever and ever;
He is the one who shall guide us.[74]

The experience of Jerusalem was, however, prelude to the experience
in the temple.

To pass from holy city to holy temple, it was necessary to ensure
the holiness of visitors. Psalm 15 seems to reflect a ritual of passage to
the temple precincts. A religious leader asks, the pilgrim answers, and
the leader responds with an appropriate promise:

Question:
1 O Yahweh, who shall visit in Your tent,
Who shall dwell on Your holy mountain?

Answer:
2 The one who walks purely
and does what is right,
And speaks the truth in his heart;
3 The one who never went about with slander on his tongue,
Nor did evil to his neighbor,
Nor raised a reproach on his fellow;
4 In whose eyes the reprobate has been despicable,
But honors the reverers of Yahweh;
Who swore off doing evil,
And does not waver;

74. MT עַל מוּת in the final verse in this psalm is very problematic (see *BHS* for
the versions and various proposals).

5 Who never lent money at interest,
   Nor accepted a bribe against the innocent.

   Promise:
6 The person who does these things
   He will never be shaken.

The opening question presents Yahweh as the host who gives hospitality in his tent to those who visit there.[75] The tent also connotes the holy sanctuary of Yahweh, as in Ps. 27.5-6, and as clarified by the second question in v. 1. The place is the divine mountain, the place where the divine sanctuary is located. It is the point in the universe where heaven and earth meet, and where deity and human share each other's presence.

In vv. 2-5a, the qualifications for entry to the sanctuary are stated in positive and negative terms. The negative qualifications for entry to Yahweh's sanctuary are presented in the suffix verbal form, implying that these sorts of acts have never been done. In contrast, the positive qualifications are made with participles[76] and the prefix form of the verbs, suggesting that these qualities are always and continuously part of the admittant's character. Verses 2-3 seem parallel in content as the positive and negative realizations of one another[77]:

v. 2	v. 3
The one who walks purely	The one who never went about with slander on his tongue,
and does what is right,	Nor did evil to his neighbor,
And speaks the truth in his heart;	Nor raised a reproach on his fellow;

Verses 2a and 3a use a verb of travel to express the human condition. It may be said that v. 3a explains what 'to walk purely' in v. 2a means concretely. Similarly, vv. 2b and 3b both use a verb of 'doing' or 'making' to express right action. Verse 3b states a negative application compared with v. 2b. Finally, vv. 2c and 3c involve speech, the first

---

75. M.J. Dahood's nominal translation of the verb, 'who shall be a guest in your tent', also captures the theme of hospitality here. See Dahood, *Psalms I. 1–50* (AB, 16; Garden City, NJ: Doubleday, 1965), p. 83.

76. For this reason, the third word in v. 4a, נמאס (here translated, 'is despicable'), the *N*-stem participle should not be emended to the indicative suffix form (contra Dahood, *Psalms I*, p. 84).

77. For a detailed treatment, see P.D. Miller, 'Poetic Ambiguity and Balance in Psalm XV', *VT* 29 (1979), pp. 416-24.

expressing the notion of being truthful to the self and the second communicating the harm of verbal abuse.

Verse 4 is 'a swing or pivot verse',[78] both in terms of its formulation and its place in the psalm. The verse shows the only contrastive parallelism in the poem. It is also the only verse which mentions other persons in the arena of behavior: the reprobate and reverers of Yahweh. With vv. 4c and 5, the poem returns to the series of positive and negative statements about proper behavior. Verse 4c, if correctly interpreted, is a positive statement forswearing evil without wavering. Verse 5a-b returns to negative expressions of personal integrity. In the third and last part of the psalm, v. 5b promises that the one who does the things stated in vv. 1-5a 'shall never be shaken'. In what sense is this promise meant? For Ps. 15.5b the promise is Yahweh's general protection from the vicissitudes of life.

The poem shows three major parts of question, answer and promise. Within the answer there seems to be further symmetry, as vv. 2-3 and 4c-5a present positive and then negative statements. Inside these sections stands the middle element of v. 4a-b, contrasting the upright versus the reprobate. To summarize the structure thus far, this delineation of the psalm points to a general chiastic arrangement[79]:

A question (v. 1): two lines
   B positive-negative characterizations of behavior (vv. 2-3)
      C positive-negative contrast of persons (v. 4a-b)
   B' positive-negative characterizations of behavior (vv. 4c-5a)
A' promise (v. 5b)

The assumption of the psalm's structure is that the positive character applies to the reverers of Yahweh and the rejection of such a moral code of behavior and speech belongs to the reprobate. The psalm would appear to contrast not only two kinds of behavior, but also two types of persons associated with these behaviors. The contrast here echoes the way people are divided in Psalm 1 between the upright and the wicked.

78. Miller, 'Poetic Ambiguity', p. 423.

79. Here largely following the implications of Miller, 'Poetic Ambiguity', pp. 423-24. The bases for the further distinctions in the chiastic arrangement offered by M.L. Barré are thin. See Barré, 'Recovering the Literary Structure of Psalm XV', *VT* 34 (1984), pp. 207-11. For a more detailed analysis including sonant elements, see P. Auffret, 'Essai sur la structure littéraire du Psaume XV', *VT* 31 (1981), pp. 383-99.

The background of Psalm 15 has been related to Ps. 24.3-6 and Isa. 33.14-16, which provide further indication of a setting in Jerusalem. Psalm 15's three-fold structure—question, answer and promise—has been long recognized in Ps. 24.3-6 and Isa. 33.14-16[80]:

Psalm 24	*Isaiah 33.14-16*
	Narrative introduction:
	Sinners in Zion are frightened,
	The godless are seized with trembling:
Question:	
Who can ascend the mountain of Yahweh?	'Who of us can dwell with the devouring fire,
And who can go up to His holy place?	Who of us can dwell with the never-ending blaze?
Answer:	
The innocent of hands,	He who walks in righteousness,
And pure of heart	Speaks uprightly,
Who does not taken a false oath by My life,	Spurns profit from fradulent dealings,
And has sworn falsely.	Waves away a bribe instead of grasping it,
	Stops his ears against listening to infamy,
	Shuts his eyes against looking at evil.
Promise:	
He will receive blessing from Yahweh,	Such a one shall dwell in lofty security,
And justice from God, his Help.	With inaccessible cliffs for his stronghold,
Such is the circle of those who seek Him,	With his food supplied,
Of Jacob, who seek Your face.	And his drink assured.'

Psalm 24 incorporates the tripartite structure into a larger composition: vv. 1-2 declares the whole world to be Yahweh's creation in the past and Yahweh's possession in the present; and vv. 7-10 heralds the com-

---

80. See Kraus, *Psalms 1–59*, p. 227; the review also in H. Spieckermann, *Heilsgegenwart: Eine Theologie der Psalmen* (FRLANT, 148; Göttingen: Vandenhoeck & Ruprecht, 1989), pp. 201-203 n. 13; M. Weinfeld, 'Instructions for Temple Visitors in the Bible and Ancient Egypt', *Egyptological Studies* (ed. S. Israelit-Groll; Scripta Hierosolymitana, 28; Jerusalem: Magnes, 1982), pp. 224-50.

ing of the King of Glory witnessed by the city or Temple gates. The three pieces seem to fit together as parts of a theology of sanctuary: the Temple precinct is a microcosm for both the whole world made by Yahweh and the divine dwelling (vv. 1-2); the upright may be admitted to this sanctuary (vv. 3-6); the holy site awaits the return of its divine owner and ruler, the King of Glory (vv. 7-10).

Isa. 33.14-16 similarly reveals information pertinent to Psalm 15. Verse 14 provides a narrative introduction which associates the tripartite structure with 'sinners in Zion'. The sanctuary in question in both Psalms 15 and 24 is likely the Jerusalem Temple. The tripartite structure stands in Isa. 33.14-16 as a prophetic critique of sinners: the requirements listed in v. 15 are the criteria by which the devouring fire of Yahweh destroys sinners and refines the upright. The units on either side of Isa. 33.14-16 likewise mark a transition: Isa. 33.7-13 announces the coming of Yahweh's burning fire and Isa. 33.17-24 offers consolation with its claim of Zion's status as a stronghold. Isa. 33.14-24 assumes Zion as the place where God's people shall be preserved; the language of security and stronghhold marks both Isa. 33.16 and 20.

To return to Psalm 15, its most obvious distinguishing feature relative to Psalm 24 and Isa. 33.14-16 is its lack of context. The parallels with Psalm 24 and Isa. 33.14-16 would suggest that Psalm 15's setting is related to the Jerusalem Temple. It has been inferred from the psalm's content that it was a liturgical piece marking entrance into the sanctuary area.[81] M. Weinfeld notes similar Egyptian inscriptions on temples which contain ritual admonitions dealing with purity.[82] In sum, the three biblical texts forge an inextricable bond between moral commitments and the 'tent' and 'holy mountain' of Yahweh. The reverence for Yahweh manifest in concrete behavior and speech towards others is the condition prerequisite for, and appropriate to, association with Yahweh. In this sense, all life is liturgical life; speech and acts

81. So see Kraus, *Psalms 1–59*, p. 227. See also Spieckermann, *Heilsgegenwart*, pp. 201-203 n. 13 and Weinfeld, 'Instructions for Temple Visitors', pp. 230-31. One might also compare Deuteronomy 26 which describes the pilgrim's negative confession in handing over the tithe. The confession in this passage pertains to the agricultural goods transferred, while the confessions in Pss. 15, 24 and Isa. 33.14-16 pertain to the pilgrim's own 'pure' condition.

82. Weinfeld, 'Instructions for Temple Visitors', p. 239. As Weinfeld notes, there are some notable differences of content and setting which help to sharpen the insight into these biblical texts.

toward others form part of the reverence devoted to the One who lives in the tent on the holy mountain. Certain speech and behaviors not only mark association with the divine; it demarcates people as well. By these marks of behavior, people who revere Yahweh will find that they are never shaken.

Preparations for passage to the Temple informs the Exodus description of the requirements made of the people when they come into the divine presence in the cloud on Mount Sinai (Exod. 19.12-15; 20.15-18). The people are commanded to keep pure by washing their clothes and by refraining from sexual relations with a woman (Exod. 19.14-15). They are to remain at a distance from the mountain for three days. Only after the sound of the ram's horn on the third day may the people ascend the holy mountain. Then the people are ready to approach God's holy mountain (Exod. 19.16-17):

> On the third day, as morning dawned, there was thunder, and lightning, and a dense cloud upon the mountain, and a very loud blast of the horn; and all the people who were in the camp trembled. Moses led the people out of the camp toward God, and they took their places at the foot of the mountain.

Like the ancient Israelites in the wilderness who served as models for subsequent generations, pilgrims to Jerusalem would pass into the Temple precincts to take their places before the living God.

Chapter 2

THE TEMPLE AND ITS SYMBOLISM[1]

1. *The Courtyard*

According to 1 Kings 7, the outer courtyard at the Temple entrance contained an immense tank called 'the molten sea' (הים מוסק), ten 'lavers' or stands (מכנות), and two freestanding pillars (עמודים) flanking the temple porch entrance, which Hiram of Tyre had cast in bronze (1 Kgs 7.13-40). The lavers were positioned five to the right of the entrance and five to the left, and the tank was placed on the right, at the southeast corner (1 Kgs 7.39). Though not specified, it is presumed that 'the bronze altar' constructed during the reign of David or Solomon (1 Kgs 8.64; 9.25; 2 Kgs 16.14-15; 2 Chron. 6.13) also stood in the Temple outer court.[2]

Archaeological parallels have been cited for each of the courtyard objects. The columns named יכין and בעז (1 Kgs 7.15-22, 41-42) have been compared to flanking free-standing columns, column bases or מצבות from the Middle Bronze Age Shechem Migdal Temple, the Late Bronze Hazor Temple of Stratum I, and the Iron Age Tell Tainat Temple,[3] as well as the Melqart Temple of Tyre.[4] The two free-standing

---

1.   Dr Elizabeth M. Bloch-Smith's contributions to the first two sections of this chapter are based on two papers: '"Who is the King of Glory?" Solomon's Temple and its Symbolism', in M.D. Coogan, J.C. Exum and L.E. Stager (eds.), *Scripture and Other Artifacts: Essays on the Bible and Archaeology in Honor of Philip J. King* (Louisville, KY: Westminster/John Knox Press, 1994), pp. 18-31; and 'Solomon's Temple: The Politics of Ritual Space' (paper delivered at the national meeting of the American Schools of Oriental Research in November, 1995). With her permission I have made modifications and additions.

2.   T.A. Busink, *Der Tempel von Jerusalem von Salomo bis Herod.* I. *Der Tempel Salomos* (Leiden: Brill, 1970), pp. 321-24; S. Paul and W. Dever, *Biblical Archaeology* (Jerusalem: Keter Publishing House, 1973), p. 58; C.L. Meyers, 'Temple, Jerusalem', *ABD*, VI, p. 359.

3.   M. Ottosson, *Temples and Cult Places in Palestine* (Boreas, Uppsala Studies

pillars are generally agreed to attest to Yahweh's presence and power, although they have also been regarded as phalloi, stylish ornaments, fire-altars, imitations of Egyptian obelisks, and symbols for Yahweh.[5] Recent scholarship interprets the twin pillars as gateposts or mythological 'trees of life', symbolically announcing the indwelling of the god.[6]

The pillars, named 'He will establish' (יכין) and 'In strength' (בעז), were the words of a sentence-long dynastic oracle or prayer inscribed on them. In support of this interpretation, several Mesopotamian and biblical examples have been cited.[7] One Assyrian instance, apparently composed for the dedication of several wooden columns to a temple in the city of Kar Tukulti-Ninurta (dating to the second half of the thirteenth century), describes and provides measurements for the columns and their capitals erected upon orders from the king, and mentions royal dedicatory inscriptions. Following suit, יכין and בעז may be dedicatory names, meaning 'may He [i.e. Yahweh] establish in strength'. As for the implicit direct object of this blessing, evidence might suggest the temple or, perhaps more likely, the dynasty (and by implication, the people; cf. Ps. 29.11). For this second possibility, 1 Sam. 1.10 may be compared: 'May He [Yahweh] give strength to His king' (יתן עז למלכו). Indeed, prayer on behalf of the king or dynasty is standard in the repertoire in biblical psalms (Pss. 20, 72, 89; cf. Ps. 21.7; Jer. 22.18; 34.5) as well as other ancient Near Eastern literature.[8] In the following section on the Temple interior, it will be suggested that the

in Ancient Mediterranean and Near Eastern Civilizations, 12; Uppsala: Uppsala University Press, 1980); V. Fritz, 'Temple Archaeology: What Can Archaeology Tell us about Solomon's Temple?' *BARev* 13 (1987), p. 40.

4.   Busink, *Der Tempel von Jerusalem*, p. 318.

5.   See Busink, *Der Tempel von Jerusalem*, pp. 13-17 for a review of the literature.

6.   G.E. Wright, 'Solomon's Temple Resurrected', *BA* 4 (1941), p. 21; Paul and Dever, *Biblical Archaeology*, p. 257; Meyers, 'Jachin and Boaz', *ABD*, III, pp. 597-98; *idem*, 'Temple, Jerusalem', p. 360.

7.   V. Hurowitz, *I Have Built you an Exalted House: Temple Building in the Bible in Light of Mesopotamian and Northwest Semitic Writings* (JSOTSup, 115; ASOR Monograph Series, 5; Sheffield: JSOT Press, 1992), pp. 257-58 n. 2.

8.   The so-called 'Poem of the Righteous Sufferer' (*Ludlul bel nemeqi*) in tablet 2, ll. 27-28, 31-32, describes the speaker's piety in praying for the king, which reflects a general belief that prayer for the king is considered 'pleasing to the gods'. See B.R. Foster, *Before the Muses: An Anthology of Akkadian Literature* (2 vols.; Bethesda, MD: CDL Press, 1993), I, p. 314.

Phoenician pillars are an adaptation of an earlier Mesopotamian practice of erecting flowering trees or branches to symbolize an attribute and power of the deity resident in the temple. Seen from a distance, the ornate capitols atop the Jerusalem pillars may have given the columns a floral appearance. However, in Solomon's Temple the inscriptions would have made explicit the blessings that were once implicit in the pillar/post representation.

The lavers, wheeled carts decorated with reliefs of lions, oxen, cherubs, and palm trees (1 Kgs 7.27-38), have been reconstructed on the basis of similarly decorated bronze wheeled stands known from Ras Shamra, Megiddo, Enkomi, and Kition.[9] The presumed function of the so-called 'lavers' is based upon a Chronicles text explaining that the wheeled stands supported basins used for rinsing parts of the burnt offering (2 Chron. 4.6). Each of the ten lavers consisted of a square, wheeled stand or base (מכונה) supporting a basin (כיור). In relating the objectionable practices of Eli's sons at the shrine in Shiloh, the basin is mentioned in the context of boiling sacrificial meat (1 Sam. 2.12-16). The exaggerated size of the temple stands has been argued to have precluded their daily use for boiling sacrificial meat;[10] however, they may have served as functioning or mimetic 'hot carts' for Yahweh, in conjunction with the altar where the sacrificial meat was roasted for the deity. It is not coincidental that ten carts stood in the outer courtyard, five to each side of the Temple entrance, and ten lampstands stood in the main room of the temple (היכל), five to each side of the entrance of the holy of holies (דביר) (1 Kgs 7.49). Perhaps the ten carts represented ten constituent groups or tribes.[11]

Assyrian, Cypriot, and Syrian parallels are cited for the immense 'molten sea' which rested on the backs of twelve cast bronze oxen (1 Kgs 7.23-26). An Assyrian relief of Sargon II (dating to the last quarter of the eighth century) depicts two huge cauldrons resting upon bulls' forelegs at the entrance to the temple of Musasir. Two large stone bowls, approximately six feet in height and diameter, one of which had four handles on which bulls were carved in relief, were reported from

9. Busink, *Der Tempel von Jerusalem*, pp. 338-48, 350-52; Paul and Dever, *Biblical Archaeology*, p. 258.

10. For a review of the literature, see Busink, *Der Tempel von Jerusalem*, pp. 348-50.

11. Cf. the ten tribes that formed the pre-monarchic confederation recorded in the Song of Deborah in Judges 5?

the vicinity of Amatheus in Cyprus.[12] Additional bases rendered as oxen were uncovered in excavations from ninth-century Tell Halaf and eighth-century Tell Tainat.[13] By the time of the Chronicler, the 'molten sea' functioned in priestly ablutions (2 Chron. 4.6). However, the tank's great size in conjunction with the fact that no practical application is offered for the 'Sea' during the time of Solomon suits the supposition that the tank served a symbolic purpose. Either the 'cosmic waters' or 'waters of life' that emanated from below the Garden of Eden, or the 'great deep' of chaos, is most often cited as the underlying symbolism for the 'molten sea'.[14] Another possibility consonant with Jerusalem cultic theology is that the molten sea symbolized the conflict between Yahweh and the Sea, a conflict attested in West Semitic literature. According to the first major section of the Ugaritic Baal Cycle (*KTU* 1.2 IV), Baal fights Sea, known also as River.[15] The political function of the conflict story between the storm god and the cosmic sea has been long recognized, for example in an early eighteenth-century letter from Nur-Sin of Aleppo to king Zimri-Lim of Mari in which the god defeats Sea and then bestows the weapons upon the earthly king. Through Nur-Sin the storm god Adad proclaims, 'I set you on the throne of your father; I gave you the weapons with which I battled Sea'.[16] Just as Adad provided Zimri-Lim with the weapons to defeat Sea, so Yahweh empowered the Davidic king to subdue Sea and River, 'I will set his [the king's] hand upon the Sea, his right hand upon the rivers' (Ps. 89.26). The 'molten sea' may have symbolized Yahweh's cosmic victories and extension of divine powers to the king.

Each of the courtyard items was of unusually great size, and in the case of the tank and stands, significantly larger than the adduced ancient Near Eastern parallels. The pillars, called יכין and בעז, rose to a height of 23 cubits (c. 12.2 meters, henceforth m), consisting of a five-cubit-

---

12. Paul and Dever, *Biblical Archaeology*, p. 258.

13. Busink, *Der Tempel von Jerusalem*, p. 332.

14. C.L. Meyers, 'Sea, Molten', *ABD*, V, p. 1062.

15. F.M. Cross, *Canaanite Myth and Hebrew Epic: Essays in the History of the Religion of Israel* (Cambridge, MA: Harvard University Press, 1973), pp. 118-19; M.S. Smith, *The Early History of God: Yahweh and the Other Deities of Ancient Israel* (San Francisco: Harper & Row, 1991), p. 55.

16. J.M. Durand, 'Le mythologème du combat entre le dieu de l'orage et la mer en Mésopotamie', *MARI* 7 (1993), pp. 41-61; P. Bordreuil and D. Pardee, 'Le combat de *Ba'lu* avec *Yammu* d'après les textes ougaritiques', *MARI* 7 (1993), pp. 63-70.

high capital atop an 18-cubit-high stem. The immense tank, ten cubits in diameter (c. 5.3m), held nearly 38,000 liters. Including the height of the wheels and the band which supported the basin, each stand/ 'laver' measured 4 cubits square (c. 2.1m) and 7 cubits high (c. 3.7m). The basin supported by each of the ten stands had a capacity of 40 baths (c. 920 liters). Cosmic dimensions attributed to cities, temples, and deities convey spatial magnitude.[17] Deities' cosmic size conveys the magnitude of their power. The immense cherub throne in the Temple's 'Holy of Holies' or 'backroom' (דביר), 10 cubits high and 10 cubits wide (c. 5.3m square), attests to the Israelite vision of the deity as superhuman in size. The superhuman distances of divine travel in Ugaritic myths[18] and the meter-long footsteps carved into the portal and thresholds leading into the cult niche of the temple at 'Ain Dara[19] are further examples of late second to early first millennium Syrian conceptions of deities of superhuman size. Accordingly, the exaggerated size of the structures in the Solomonic Temple courtyard would suggest that they were not intended for human use, but belonged to the realm of the divine. The courtyard symbols perhaps conveyed Yahweh's triumphant enthronement. Upon defeating the chaotic forces of nature, as represented by 'the Molten Sea', the god of the Israelites accepted the sacrificial offerings of the ten constituent groups or tribes, and entered the Temple bestowing blessings on the king and the people, as recorded on the pillars flanking the Temple entrance.

2. *The Temple Proper*

The Palace–Temple complex or citadel was a common Near Eastern architectural feature. M. Ottosson noted that '*langhaus*-type [temples] always seem to share their courtyards with a "palace"'.[20] Syro-Palestinian examples have been excavated at Megiddo, Hazor, Beth Shan IX, and Shechem from the Bronze Age, and at Tell Qasile and

---

17. See M.S. Smith, 'Divine Form and Size in Ugaritic and Pre-Exilic Israelite Religion', *ZAW* 100 (1988), pp. 424-27; Hurowitz, *I Have Built you an Exalted House*, p. 337.

18. See M.S. Smith, 'Divine Travel as a Token of Divine Rank', *UF* 16 (1984), p. 397.

19. A. Abou-Assaf, *Der Tempel von 'Ain Dara* (Damaszener Forschungen, 3; Mainz: Philip von Zabern, 1990), pp. 15-16.

20. Ottoson, *Temples*, p. 51.

Beth Shan Lower V from the Iron Age.[21] Solomon's Temple was an imposing structure, bigger than its contemporaries in Syro-Palestine.[22] However, the national shrine was built in the shadow of the larger, adjacent palace, reflecting the more dominant structure in Solomon's architectural plan.[23] In comparing the Temple wall reliefs to Mesopotamian examples, a most striking feature is the absence of the deity and the king from the Solomonic depictions. An aniconic sensibility prevailed.[24] Even the 'cult niche' of the Holy of Holies (דביר) contained no representation of the deity, only a 'vacant throne' and the divine symbol of presence in the form of the ark.[25] Though it lacked explicit royal imagery, the Temple decoration conveyed divine endorsement of his kingship. Temple proximity to the royal palace and choice of courtyard symbols communicated to Temple worshippers Yahweh's enthronement and patronage of the human king. Solomon adopted a prevalent architectural plan which served to bolster his ideological position.

Several elements known from the Solomonic Temple were also incorporated into the contemporary 'Ain Dara level II temple (1000–900 BCE), located in northwest Syria not far from Tell Tainat. The temple was constructed according to the Phoenician tripartite plan, with two immense columns flanking the entrance. Monstrous lions and cherubs depicted with stylized palms guarded the entrances onto the temple platform and into the temple proper and the cella. The deity inhabiting the temple, probably the goddess Ishtar, was also of superhuman size. 'Divine' footprints, about one meter long, stand in the portico entrance, and then tread on the thresholds, first left and then right, leading into the cella. The single reported outer courtyard object was a large, but not immense, sacrificial basin found in the courtyard of the level III temple (a temple virtually identical to its predecessor),

21. Ottosson, *Temples*, p. 62.
22. Ottosson, *Temples*, p. 112.
23. See Busink, *Der Tempel von Jerusalem*, p. 161.
24. T.N.D. Mettinger, 'The Veto on Images and the Aniconic God in Ancient Israel', in H. Biezais (ed.), *Religious Symbols and their Functions* (Scripta Instituti Donnerians Aboensis, 10; Stockholm: Almqvist and Wiksell, 1979), p. 24. See also Mettinger, *No Graven Image? Israelite Aniconism in its Ancient Near Eastern Context* (ConBOT, 42; Stockholm: Almqvist & Wiksell, 1995), p. 16.
25. O. Keel, *Jahwe-Visionen und Siegelkunst: Eine neue Deutung der Majestätschilderungen in Jes 6, Ez 1 und Sach 4* (SBS, 84/85; Stuttgart: Katholisches Bibelwerk, 1977), pp. 37-45.

which measured approximately 1.6 by 3.5m.[26]

At least as early as the post-exilic period, the three-fold architectural structure of the Temple replicates in priestly conceptualization three levels of holiness corresponding to the differing degrees of holiness among the people, the priests in general and finally the high priest in particular.[27] According to post-biblical tradition, the people were permitted to enter the Temple as far as the outer court, the priests to the inner court and only the high priest could enter the holy of holies, and there only on Yom Kippur, the Day of Atonement (Leviticus 16), in order to make atonement on behalf of himself, his household and the rest of the people of Israel. While this particular delineation may not have been fully operative in Solomon's Temple, some distinction between the priesthood and laity may have been realized through architectural division. Holiness was thought to pervade the environs of the Temple, and degrees of holiness was probably reflected in the division of the Temple's major sections, culminating in the holiness of God within the Holy of Holies.[28]

Like the courtyard, the Temple proper incorporated symbolism associated with the Divine King. If the 'porch' (אולם) is reconstructed with a porticoed opening (1 Kgs 7.19, 21), worshippers may have dimly perceived the gilded carved wood reliefs of cherubs (כרבים), ornamental palms, and calyxes which adorned the doors leading into the central room in the Temple, the היכל. Identical gilded carvings adorned the shrine doors and interior walls as well. The exact configuration of the cherubs, palms and calyxes is uncertain. Ezekiel 41.18 describes wainscotted walls decorated with a pattern of 'cherubs and palm trees, with a palm between every two cherubs'. The lotus chain and guilloche border design of a wall painting at Kuntillat 'Ajrud may echo the decorative borders of the Temple carvings.[29] Cherubs with trees and blossoms

26. Abou-Assaf, *Der Tempel von 'Ain Dara*.

27. J. Milgrom, 'Israel's Sanctuary: The Priestly "Picture of Dorian Gray"', *RB* 83 (1976), pp. 390-99.

28. W. Houston has argued that the practice of כשרות (keeping kosher) developed in ancient Israel as part of the priestly sacrificial system of maintaining holiness in the temple. See Houston, *Purity and Monotheism: Clean and Unclean Animals in Biblical Law* (JSOTSup, 140; Sheffield: JSOT Press, 1993). In general, there is much merit to this approach to the origins of כשרות.

29. P. Beck, 'The Drawings from Horvat Teiman (Kuntillet 'Ajrud)', *TA* 9 (1982), pp. 56-58. For a discussion of the symbolism of the decoration including the floral border, see J. Strange, 'The Idea of Afterlife in Ancient Israel: Some Remarks

lined the temple walls and covered the doors. As represented by their bodily parts, cherubs combined the strength, ferocity, and regalness of a lion, with the flying capability of a bird, and the higher reasoning capabilities of a human. The resulting composite creature possessed superior intelligence and physical abilities. In the biblical texts, the brains and braun of a pair of cherubs were enlisted to guard the tree of life in the Garden of Eden (Gen. 3.24) and perhaps also sacred trees (1 Kgs 6.29-35; Ezek. 41.18-25). In addition, cherubs served as chariots to transport the deity (Ps. 18.11 = 2 Sam. 22.11; Pss. 80.2; 99.1), and as the divine throne (Exod. 25.18; 1 Kgs 6.23-27). The cherub's role at Shiloh may be inferred from the description of 'the Ark of the Covenant of Yahweh of Hosts Enthroned on the Cherubim' (1 Sam. 4.4; NJPS).

Egyptian sphinxes and Mesopotamian cherub (*kurību*) could be male or female, winged or non-winged.[30] By contrast, the biblical cherub was winged but of unspecified sex. This presentation is limited to the winged *kurību* and sphinx which are comparable to the biblical cherub. It is not possible to distinguish the *kurību* from the sphinx in Syrian art. (In conformity with general usage, the animal will be referred to here as a cherub except in cases of Egyptian sphinxes.) Individual and pairs of facing cherubs, almost always in a cultic context, are depicted on cylinder seals and metal stands through the second millennium. On a seal dated to the first half of the second millennium, the cherubs with raised paws face one another in the top register of the terminal. The primary scene is a revealing goddess standing before a god seated on his temple throne with the sun disc and crescent moon between them.[31] A contemporary, unprovenienced seal depicts cherubs flanking a stylized plant.[32] A third example comes from Middle Bronze IIB Hazor, roughly 1750–1550. On this seal, the facing cherubs raise their paws over a star-like depiction. Both a winged and a non-winged sun disc and crescent moon appear on the seal.[33]

---

on the Iconography in Solomon's Temple', *PEQ* 117 (1985), pp. 35-40. For a recent survey of the cherub, see T.N.D. Mettinger, 'Cherubim', *DDD*, pp. 362-67.

30. *CAD* K.559.

31. D. Collon, *First Impressions: Cylinder Seals in the Ancient Near East* (Chicago: University of Chicago Press, 1987), fig. 778.

32. Collon, *First Impressions*, fig. 453.

33. O. Keel and C. Uehlinger, *Göttinnen, Götter und Gottessymbole: Neue Erkenntnisse zur Religionsgeschichte Kanaans und Israels aufgrund bislang*

The seal impressions display primarily Syrian and Mesopotamian influence. The origin of the cherub and the locale from which it was introduced into Syrian art is still debated. A. Dessenne proposes an Egyptian origin, while noting that cherub existed in both the Egyptian and Mesopotamian repertoires by the end of the third millennium.[34] Northern Levantine cherubs are closer in style to Anatolian[35] and Mesopotamian examples which were depicted with clearly delineated wings. In contrast, Egyptian sphinxes often had such stylized wings that they were frequently unrecognizable. The motif of facing cherubs guarding a sacred tree developed in Late Bronze Age Mitanni and northern Syria, and from there spread throughout the Levant. A second motif was the cherub accompanying a nude goddess.[36] On a seal from Ugarit, cherubs guard a sacred/bouquet tree while a goat or another horned animal perhaps feeds above; there are circles in the sky and background.[37] Facing cherubs with raised paws guard a stylized tree on a seal from T. Atchana (ancient Alalakh) level II–I, dated roughly 1225–1175. Bulls support the winged sun disc with their horns, and the background circles are grouped into clusters referred to as 'rosettes'.[38] These rosettes are discussed below. In all these examples, cherubs do not feed from the trees; rather, they watch and protect it. Cherubs were also depicted on metal stands. The best metalwork illustration of cherubs flanking a stylized plant is a Cypriot rod

unerschlossener ikonographischer Quellen (Quaestiones Disputatae, 134; Freiburg: Herder, 1992), p. 49, fig. 35.

34. A. Dessenne, *Le Sphinx: Étude iconographique.* I. *Des origines à la fin du second millénnaire* (Bibliothèque des écoles françaises d'Athènes et de Rome, 186; Paris: Boccard, 1957), p. 175.

35. So J. Canby, 'The Walters Gallery Cappadocian Tablet and the Sphinx in Anatolia in the Second Millennium BCE', *JNES* 34 (1975), pp. 225-48.

36. Dessenne, *Le Sphinx*, pp. 66-74; B. Tessier, *Ancient Near Eastern Cylinder Seals from the Marcopoli Collection* (Berkeley: University of California Press; Beverly Hills, CA: Summa Publications, 1984), p. 96.

37. Kepinski, *L'arbre stylisé en Asie Occidentale au 2ᵉ millénaire avant J.-C.*, I–III (Bibliothèque de la délégation archéologique Française en Iraq, 1; Centre de recherche d'Archéologie Orientale, Université de Paris, 1.1; Editions recherche sur les civilisations, 7; Paris: Editions recherches sur les civilisations, 1982), #640.

38. D. Collon, *The Alalakh Cylinder Seals: A New Catalogue of the Actual Seals Excavated by Sir Leonard Woolley at Tell Atchana, and from Neighboring Sites on the Syrian–Turkish Border* (BAR International Series, 132; Oxford: British Archaeological Reports, 1982), fig. 105; *idem, First Impressions*, fig. 307.

tripod from the twelfth or early eleventh century. This tripod measures 0.34m in diameter and is adorned with nine cast plaques. On five
of the plaques, two winged male cherubs flank a stylized plant, perhaps a lily-bloom, and on the remaining four, two goats with unicorn-
like projections stand with a raised foreleg on either side of a highly
stylized 'sacred tree' evocative of the 'bouquet tree'.[39]

In all these second-millennium examples, cherubs are not associated
with any particular deity. They commonly appear in pairs, and are
often depicted in a protective stance flanking a stylized plant or tree.
What did the stylized plant or tree represent? The Hebrew word for
the trees carved into the Temple walls and doors is תמרות, which may
refer to stylized date palms. With its hanging clusters of fruit, the tree
symbolized fecundity and vitality. In ancient Near Eastern iconography animals (in addition to cherubs) feed from the branches or repose
to either side of the sacred tree, but they do not raise their paws or
forelegs in a protective stance. Painted examples of reposing and
feeding animals flanking a stylized tree abound on Late Bronze Age
pottery. The motif also appears on cylinder seals, including three Late
Bronze I (c. 1600–1400) examples. Goats flank a seven-branched tree
in the lower register, and a single cherub and a pole supports a winged
disc in the upper register of a seal from Alalakh IV.[40] A naked, winged
goddess stands directly above the seven-branched tree on a seal from
Akko Tomb B3.[41] Horned animals feeding from the sacred tree are in
turn flanked by a worshipper and a cherub on an example from
Megiddo; there is the seven-part rosette in the sky beside the worshipper.[42] The stylized tree protected by the cherub is similar in depiction to the trees which provided sustenance for the animal kingdom. It
may be concluded, therefore, that in different contexts the sacred tree
may have variously represented fecundity, or the sacred tree protected
by the cherub provisionally identified with the Tree of Life guarded
by the cherub. The motif continues into the Iron I period. A stamp seal
from Megiddo VIIa is carved with a schematic anthropomorphic tree
flanked by three-legged animals.[43]

39. H.W. Catling, *Cypriot Bronzework in the Mycenean World* (Oxford:
Clarendon Press, 1964), pl. 29 c, e.
40. Collon, *The Alalakh Cylinder Seals*, fig. 75.
41. Collon, *First Impressions*, fig. 264; Keel and Uehlinger, *Göttinnen*, fig. 63.
42. Keel and Uehlinger, *Göttinnen*, 63, fig. 52.
43. M. Shuval, 'A Catalogue of Early Iron Stamp Seals from Israel', in O. Keel,

Neither humans nor deities are depicted eating the fruit of the sacred tree. However, in the Late Bronze Age the 'Bouquet Tree' was often the focal point with one or more figures standing, kneeling, or sitting beside it, often touching it.[44] These examples derive from Late Bronze I Alalakh level V (c. 1550–1500),[45] Late Bronze I–II Gezer,[46] and Late Bronze II Alalakh II (c. 1250–1225).[47] D. Collon interprets the scene as beneficial minor deities protecting the tree of life and interceding for the owner of the seal.[48] If the tree is to be interpreted as the tree of life, then the seals may have depicted the divine beings who had exclusive rights to eat of its fruit (cf. Gen. 3.22). There is no iconographic indication either in specific details or in general context to suggest that the palm trees carved on the Temple walls and doors symbolized anything other than Yahweh's life-giving properties or the tree of life specifically. Unfortunately, the biblical description of the Temple decoration does not specify the arrangement of the cherubs and the trees. They may have been depicted either with cherubs flanking the trees as described by Ezekiel (Ezek. 41.18, 25) or in alternating position. Cherubs amid stylized palm trees and calyxes are the divine cherubs in a sacred garden, the Garden of Eden. Such a view comports with the common understanding of the Temple as the Garden of Eden, Yahweh's terrestrial abode.

A golden altar, the golden table for the bread of display and ten golden lampstands stood within this garden, before the throne of the deity. Ten lampstands (מנורות) stood five to either side of the entrance into the holy of holies. C.L. Meyers's reconstruction of the basic form of the stand allows for considerable speculation as to its appearance, function and interpretation.[49] The account in 1 Kings does not describe the stands; it merely provides the number and their placement. A single lampstand is described in the detailed instructions and description of

M. Shuval and C. Uehlinger (eds.), *Studien zu den Stempelsiegeln aus Palästina/ Israel. Band III: Die Frühe Eisenzeit, ein Workshop* (OBO, 100; Freiburg: Universitätsverlag; Göttingen: Vandenhoeck & Ruprecht, 1990), fig. 74.

44. Tessier, *Ancient Near Eastern Cylinder Seals*, p. 92.
45. Collon, *The Alalakh Cylinder Seals*, fig. 51.
46. Kepinski, *L'arbre stylisé*, #745.
47. Collon, *The Alalakh Cylinder Seals*, fig. 108.
48. Collon, *The Alalakh Cylinder Seals*, p. 12.
49. C. Meyers 'Lampstand', *ABD*, IV, pp. 141-43; *idem*, 'Was There a Seven-Branched Lampstand in Solomon's Temple?' *BARev* 5.5 (1979), pp. 46-57.

the Tent of Meeting (Exod. 25.31-36; 37.17-22). According to Meyers, the lampstand has יָרֵךְ וְקָנֶה, a hendiadys meaning 'central shaft', and כַּפְתֹּר וָפֶרַח, also a hendiadys meaning 'floral capital'. The resulting form is a cylindrical shaft, flaring at the base and perhaps also the top, decorated with a floral motif. Three non-functional branches, similarly embellished, extend from each side of the cylindrical shaft. Branches are not mentioned in the summary statement in 1 Kings, leading Meyers to suggest that the lampstands in the Solomonic Temple were branchless cylindrical shafts with floral embellishment. In the Tent of Meeting description in Exodus, seven lamps (נֵרוֹת) are described as discrete objects to be fashioned separately from the lampstand (Exod. 25.37; 37.23), and mounted either on top of the central shaft, follow- ing Meyers, or one lamp on top of each branch, following others. In support of her argument, Meyers notes that the seven lamps are referred to as a single lamp, or perhaps, collectively. This נֵר תָּמִיד or 'eternal light' was to burn continually, from evening to morning (Exod. 27.20; Lev. 24.2-3).

The lampstands may have symbolized the astral bodies, a view that can be traced back to Josephus and Philo.[50] Following this line of inter- pretation, the lampstands served as divine nightlights representing the heavenly hosts, perhaps the Pleiades. The sun, moon and the stars were identified in Mesopotamia as the seven great divinities.[51] In Israel per- haps the sun, moon and stars were similarly identified with the heav- enly hosts. The association of Yahweh with the stars was an old one in Israel. According to Judg. 5.20, stars constituted part of the heavenly host of the God of Israel. Stars came to Israel's aid:

> The stars fought from heaven,
> From their courses they fought against Sisera.

As part of his older identification with El,[52] Yahweh continued the

---

50. Josephus, *Ant.* 3.102-203, *War* 5.212-19; Philo, *Vit. Mos.* 2.76-108. So J. Blenkinsopp, *Sage, Priest, Prophet: Religious and Intellectual Leadership in Ancient Israel* (Louisville, KY: Westmnister/John Knox, 1995), pp. 113, 177 n. 66.

51. For the Mesopotamian evidence, see F. Rochberg-Halton, *ABD*, I, p. 506; I. Zatelli, 'Constellations', *DDD*, pp. 386-91, esp. p. 387. Note the listing together in Isa. 13.10.

52. S. Olyan, *Asherah and the Cult of Yahweh in Israel* (SBLMS, 34; Atlanta: Scholars Press, 1988), pp. 38-61; see also Smith, *The Early History of God*, p. 19. In Ugaritic literature, the moon-good is the gate-keeper in the house of El (*KTU* 1.114) and Dawn and Dusk seem to be children of El. The sun-goddess seems to

association with astral deities in the form of the 'host of heaven'. Zephaniah 1.5 and other passages associate the host of heaven with the cult of Yahweh.[53] One prophet, Micaiah ben Imlah, 'saw Yahweh seated on his throne with all the host of heaven standing to the right and to the left of him' (1 Kgs 22.19).[54] If Israelite tradition identified the heavenly host as astral divinities, it would explain a number of passages where the heavens and divine beings stand in parallelism (e.g. Job 38.7; LXX Deut. 32.43).[55] These passages reflect no polemic against the identification of astral bodies and the heavenly host led by Yahweh. In contrast, deuteronomistic literature criticizes astral deities within the cult of Yahweh under the rubric of the 'sun, moon and the stars'. It is possible that the criticism represented by deuteronomistic and other condemnations derived from the threat of the neo-Assyrian astral cult during the Iron II period,[56] but this would not diminish the indigenous character of the religious devotion paid to the sun, moon and stars.[57]

The Pleiades is a galactic cluster of over four hundred stars, with five to seven stars visible to the naked eye as part of the constellation Taurus. From as early as the Old Babylonian period, the symbol of seven dots is known as *sibittu*, literally, 'group of seven'. According to E.D. van Buren, the symbol evolved from the seven pellets or pebbles used in casting lots for divining the fate of individuals, to the rosette-star of Ishtar, and finally, with the growing Babylonian interest

---

hold a special relationship with El as his messenger. In South Arabian religion, Asherah (El's wife in Ugaritic literature) is associated with the moon. In Ugaritic religion it is evidence that Athtar is associated with the 'Venus star'. These diverse witnesses perhaps point to an old Levantine understanding of the pantheon in which El and his family were identified with various astral bodies. To be sure in a number of ways this system of identification was modified and complicated by the place of other deities at Ugarit, such as the storm-god, Baal, and his sister, Anat.

53. So J.G. Taylor, *Yahweh and the Sun: Biblical and Archaeological Evidence for Sun Worship in Ancient Israel* (JSOTSup, 111; Sheffield: JSOT Press, 1993), pp. 105-107, 200-206.

54. See Taylor, *Yahweh and the Sun*, pp. 105-107, 200-206; B.B. Schmidt, 'Moon', *DDD*, pp. 1098-113, esp. p. 1110.

55. See I. Zatelli, 'Astrology and the Worship of the Stars in the Bible', *ZAW* 103 (1990), pp. 92-93.

56. See H. Spieckermann, *Juda unter Assur in der Sargonidenzeit* (FRLANT, 129; Göttingen: Vandenhoeck & Ruprecht, 1982).

57. So Taylor, *Yahweh and the Sun*, pp. 177-78.

in astronomy, to the constellation of the Pleiades. Van Buren argues for the enduring association of the number seven with divining practices by citing a second century CE north Syrian example of seven inscribed stones used for casting lots.[58] Biblical כימה is identified as the constellation Pleiades on the basis of a Sumerian equivalent mul-mul, meaning 'stars', found in a lexical list from Ebla.[59] According to S. Gitin, the Pleiades are also depicted with a solar disk and the moon in a scene on a seventh-century silver medallion excavated from Tel Miqne, identified with ancient Ekron.[60] Biblical texts mention the Pleiades in conjunction with Orion (כסיל). Amos 5.8 praises the God of Israel, 'Who made the Pleiades and Orion, Who turns deep darkness into dawn, and darkens day into night'. In reproaching Job Yahweh implicitly extols his own abilities (38.31-33; NJPS):

> 'Can you tie cords to Pleiades, or undo the reins of Orion?
> Can you lead out Mazzaroth in its season, conduct the Bear with her sons?
> Do you know the laws of heaven or impose its authority on earth?'

With the god of Israel in command of the heavenly bodies, their presence in the Temple is plausible. Each lampstand with seven lights on top was lit only at night. Like the stars, the lights shone from dusk to dawn. The seven-spouted lamps form a rosette, like the iconographic representations of the star of Ishtar and the Pleiades on cylinder seals. According to this hypothesis, the ten lamps served the ten constituent tribes or the Solomonic alliance perhaps as omens of good or ill fortune, or to fight on behalf of the tribes, or to divine Yahweh's will, or as in the Old Babylonian period, to enforce the sanctity of oaths. If this astral interpretation of the Temple lampstands is correct, then astral representations installed in the Temple reflected Yahweh's rule within the cosmos just as the bronze sea in the courtyard outside the Temple reflected Yahweh's cosmic victory.

The lampstands were positioned before the Holy of Holies which

---

58. E.D. Van Buren, *Symbols of the Gods in Mesopotamian Art* (AnOr, 23; Rome: Pontifical Biblical Institute, 1945), pp. 74-82.

59. L. Zalcman, 'Pleiades', *DDD*, pp. 1240-42. Semitic cognates suggest a basic meaning of 'group' for BH כימה.

60. S. Gitin, 'Tel Miqne-Ekron in the 7th Century BCE: The Impact of Economic Innovation and Foreign Cultural Influences on a Neo-Assyrian Vassal City-State', in S. Gitin (ed.), *Recent Excavations in Israel. A View to the West: Reports on Kabri, Nami, Miqne-Ekron, Dor and Ashkelon* (Colloquia and Conference Papers, 1; Boston: Archaeological Institute of America, 1995), p. 71 fig. 4.14.

was filled with Yahweh's immense cherub throne. Zoomorphic thrones
for deities are depicted on cylinder seals as early as the third millennium. Ishtar sits on a lion throne,[61] and the sun-god stands on a throne of
fantastic animals.[62] Closer to Israel and nearly a thousand years later,
earthly kings sit on sphinx thrones. A Late Bronze II ivory panel from
Megiddo depicts a 'triumph scene' with bound captives presented to
the king seated on a sphinx throne. The winged sun-disc appears above
the horses of the captor's chariot. Megiddo also yielded a miniature
sphinx throne carved from ivory.[63] On both the Megiddo ivory panel
and the tenth-century Ahiram sarcophagus, earthly and not divine kings
sit on a cherub throne. However, the contemporary ceramic Ta'anach
cult stand likely depicts a divine cherub throne. In the second register
from the bottom, two cherubs face front flanking an empty space.
Given the cherubs' frontal pose and the absence of a sacred tree, the
cherubs likely appear in their function as a throne. Considering the
content of the other registers, the cherub throne was probably intended for a divine rather than a human ruler.

Perhaps the best general parallel for the joint use of date-palms,
stylized trees, cherubs, and a decorative border is found on the palace
mural at Mari. While the palace may date back to the reign of Yahdun-
Lim, the murals are probably to be attributed to Zimri-Lim, who
enlarged and rebuilt the palace in the early eighteenth cenury. Miraculously preserved, the mural was painted on a thin layer of mud plaster
just to the right of the entrance into the throne room (in Courtyard
106). Initially called 'L'Investiture du Roi', the central scene is now
thought to depict a royal ritual or ceremony, perhaps the annual induc-
tion of the statue of Ishtar into the palace.[64] A two-storied rectangular
structure fills the center of the mural. On the upper floor, the king
stands before a goddess, and below, two identical facing figures hold a

61. S. Schroer, 'Die Göttin auf den Stempelsiegeln aus Palästina/Israel', in
O. Keel, H. Keel-Lev and S. Schroer (eds.), *Studien zu den Stempelsiegeln aus
Palästina/Israel. II. Die Frühe Eisenzeit, ein Workshop* (OBO, 20; Freiburg:
Universitätsverlag; Göttingen: Vandenhoeck & Ruprecht, 1989), fig.49.

62. Keel, *Jahwe-Visionen*, p. 289; Schroer, 'Die Göttin', fig. 52.

63. R.D. Barnett, *Ancient Ivories in the Middle East* (Qedem, 14; Jerusalem:
Institute of Archaeology of the Hebrew University, 1982), p. 27; Keel and
Uehlinger, *Göttinnen*, p. 71.

64. A. Malamat, *Mari and the Early Israelite Experience* (The Schweich Lectures of the British Academy, 1984; Oxford: Oxford University Press, 1989), p. 23.

vase with flowing streams of water containing fish. Stylized trees and date-palms flank the structure, and an ornate decorative border frames the entire composition. Three tiers of animals stand alongside the stylized trees: at the bottom, a bull (possibly anthrocephalic) standing with forelegs on a mountain; above it is a griffin feeding from the tree; and on top, a winged sphinx or cherub wearing a feathered tiara. Human figures climb the date-palms to harvest the fruit, and mirror-image figures, with horned caps and arms raised as if in adoration, stand beyond the palm trees facing the central scene.[65]

According to M.T. Barrelet, the scene depicts a ceremony taking place in the cella and antecella of a temple. This view was based on the stylized trees flanking the temple which were interpreted as continuing the tradition of posts or emblems set up to frame the entrance to temples or animal stalls. Date-palms flanking the entrance to the Sin Temple at Khorsabad and depictions on cylinder seals from Tel Billa and Tel Agrab and on the stele of Gudea provide additional examples of this practice.[66] Such temple pillars or posts, which resemble flowering trees or branches, may have symbolized the divine attributes of longevity and fruitfulness, or virility and fertility, which could be bestowed upon supplicants or animals in the stalls (cf. Gen. 30.37-39). The Phoenician practice of erecting (inscribed) pillars flanking the temple entrance, known from the temples at Jerusalem, 'Ain Dara, or Tell Tainat, may have replaced the early palm or stylistic tree representations. The motif of composite creatures such as the cherub in association with palms or 'sacred trees' is also well-attested in the ancient Near Eastern minor arts, especially glyptic. On Mesopotamian cylinder sealings, a deity or divine emblem usually appears in the scene.[67]

---

65. A. Parrot, *Mission archéologique de Mari. II. Le palais: Peintures murales* (Institut Français d'Archéologie de Beyrouth; Bibliothèque archéologique et historique, 59; Paris: Geuthner, 1958), pp. 53-64.

66. M.T. Barrelet, 'Une peinture de la cour 106 du palais de Mari', *Studia Mariana* 4 (1950), pp. 9-15; see also Busink, *Der Tempel von Jerusalem*, pp. 318-21.

67. The competing cherub and calf representations of Yahweh in Israelite tradition may derive from the two different iconographic traditions depicting storm gods which are preserved on Syro-Mesopotamian cylinder seals. D. Collon (*The Alalakh Cylinder Seals*, p. 170) noted the change in animals attending the storm god beginning with second-millennium BCE representations. It was during the third-millennium Akkadian period that the winged composite creature was introduced as a chariot or throne for the god and goddess. In cylinder sealings of the period, the

The greatest number of representations of trees and composite winged creatures without deities originated in Mitanni, Syro-Palestine, and Cyprus.[68] As expected, the non-glyptic representations of winged sphinxes with 'sacred trees' derive from the same regions: a gold leaf relief from the Late Bronze–Early Iron Age Enkomi-Alasia Tomb 2, a Gezer cylinder seal, and the Samaria ivories.[69]

The extensive Israelite literature provides some information on the meaning of the associated elements for the Jerusalem cult. The Temple walls were depicted with palm trees and cherubs (1 Kgs 6.29, 32). Cherubs served as the divine chariot (1 Sam. 4.4; 2 Sam. 22 [Ps. 18].11).

---

storm god and goddess stand on the backs of winged lion-griffins (e.g. P. Amiet, *Art of the Ancient Near East* [trans. J. Shepley and C. Choquet; New York: Abrams, 1980], #769, appendix 5: 'Images of Gods and Goddesses'). First Dynasty Babylonian seals continue use of the motif (e.g. H. Frankfort, *Cylinder Seals: A Documentary Essay on the Art and Religion of the Ancient Near East* [London: Macmillan, 1939], pl. XXVIIi), and introduce a variant form, in which the storm god, standing in his chariot, cracks a whip over a winged monster spitting fire/lightning, on the back of which rides the nude storm goddess (e.g. Frankfort, *Cylinder Seals*, pl. XXIIa). Beginning in the second millennium, the storm god and goddess were also depicted with an attendant bull. First Dynasty of Babylon sealings show the storm god both with the winged-lion and with the bull/calf (Amiet, *Art of the Ancient Near East*, appendix 5). Second-millennium Syrian cylinder seals also depict the storm god with a bull/calf, on the back of which occasionally stands a nude goddess (e.g. E. Porada, *Mesopotamian Art in Cylinder Seals of the Pierpont Morgan Library* [New York: Pierpont Morgan Library, 1947], fig. 101; Amiet, *Art of the Ancient Near East*, appendix 5). On an Akkadian seal from c. 1500, the storm god brandishes a mace, and holds a flail and the leash of his bull (e.g. Collon, *First Impressions*, fig. 787). The Israelite (storm) god was eventually divorced from the nude goddess or consort present in both the winged creature and bull/calf iconographic traditions.

68. For example, Porada, *Mesopotamian Art*, p. 52, figs. 63, 107; M.L. Vollenweider, *Catalogue raisonné des sceaux cylindres et intailles* (vol. 1; Geneva: Musée d'art et d'histoire Genève, 1967), pl. 59.4, 5, 7; H. Frankfort, *The Pelican History of Art: The Art and Architecture of the Ancient Orient* (Harmondsworth: Penguin Books, 4th edn, 1970), pp. 135, 248, 260 fig. 296; Collon, *The Alalakh Cylinder Seals*, p. 12; figs. 271, 383; C.F.A. Schaeffer-Forrer, *Corpus des cylindres-sceaux de Ras-Shamra-Ugarit et d'Enkomi-Alasia*, I (Editions recherche sur les civilizations, 13; Paris: Association pour la Diffusion de la Pensée Française, 1983), R.S. 23.001, Chypre A12; B. Buchanan and P.R.S. Moorey, *Catalogue of Ancient Near Eastern Seals in the Ashmolean Museum*. III. *The Iron Age Stamp Seals* (Oxford: Clarendon Press, 1988), pl. IX.281.

69. Keel, *Jahwe-Visionen*, p. 18.

Like the Temple, the garden of Eden similarly was considered the original meeting-place of God and humans.[70] The Temple replicates paradise in other aspects as well, recalling the trees of paradise and the cherub who guards the Garden (Gen. 3.24). The Temple contained sources of water (Ps. 46), echoing the rivers that run in the Garden (Gen. 2.10-14). The elements embodied by both Eden and the Temple include divine presence, abundance of food and drink, the trees and cherubs, and the rivers.

While the story of the Garden of Eden evokes the tree of life in general terms, the Temple decoration specifies it as the תמרה, usually viewed as the date-palm. This term may simply refer to an ornamental tree or palmette, and not Phoenix dactylifera. Date-palms became a symbol for the righteous adherents of Yahwism who remained vital and virile even into old age (Ps. 52.8). As Ezek. 41.18 describes the iconographic configuration, the tree is the focus of attention, flanked by cherubs. In Mesopotamian sealings with this same configuration, a deity occasionally replaced the tree demonstrating that the tree represented either the god personified by a symbol for an attribute (the tree as a symbol of longevity and fruitfulness) or divine powers and blessings (virility/fertility). Therefore, according to the conventional meaning of the motif as employed in Mesopotamia, the tree symbolized divinity or divine powers. Solomon perhaps adopted the motif of tree with flanking cherubs on the strength of its representation of the cherub guarding the tree of life in the Garden of Eden.

The cherub transported Yahweh, formed his throne, and offered protection. In the innermost section of the Temple, supplicants were received by Yahweh 'enthroned upon the cherubs' (1 Sam. 4.4; see 2 Kgs 19.15 = Isa. 37.14-16; Ps. 99.1; 1 Kgs 6.23-28). The earliest representations of cherub thrones derived from the region of Syria-

---

70. M.S. Smith, *Psalms: The Divine Journey* (Mahwah, NJ: Paulist, 1987), pp. 40, 44-47. For further discussion, see G.W. Ahlstrom, *Aspects of Syncretism in Israelite Religion* (Horae Soederblomianae, 5; Lund: Gleerup, 1963), pp. 44-45 n. 1; J.D. Levenson, *Theology of the Program of Restoration of Ezekiel 40–48* (HSM, 10; Missoula, MT: Scholars Press, 1976), pp. 25-34; Strange, 'The Idea of After Life in Ancient Israel', pp. 35-40; H.N. Wallace, *The Eden Narrative* (HSM, 32; Chico, CA: Scholars Press, 1985), pp. 85-86; Smith, *The Early History of God*, p. 111 n. 98. For this theme in later literature, see G.A. Anderson, 'The Cosmic Mountain: Eden and its Early Interpreters in Syriac Christianity', in G.A. Robbins (ed.), *Genesis 1–3 in the History of Exegesis: Intrigue in the Garden* (Studies in Women and Religion, 27; Lewiston, NY: Edwin Mellen, 1988), pp. 187-224.

Palestine, including Byblos (Ahiram sarcophagus), Hamath, and Megiddo.[71] Later examples are known as well: a figurine from Ayia Irini in Cyprus, Egyptian depictions in the tomb of Panchesi and on an ostracon in the Gayer-Anderson collection in Stockholm, and Phoenician sealings of Melqart on a cherub throne.[72] A telling feature of Yahweh's cherub throne was its magnitude. As noted in the previous section, great size signified importance, sovereignty, and ultimately, divinity.[73] Many Ugaritic deities, when described travelling, cross superhuman distances. Ishtar's meter-long footsteps carved on the thresholds of the 'Ain Dara temple provide an indication of her projected size. As mentioned in connection with the courtyard objects, the enormous size symbolized the magnitude of the deity.

Israelite cultic texts may have served to articulate and transmit the symbolic meaning of the courtyard objects and their relationship to the Temple proper. The cultic repertoire, exemplified by 2 Samuel 22 (Ps. 18).8-16, Psalm 29, and early elements of Psalms 89 and 93,[74] recounted Yahweh's victories over the earth and its creatures, including the Sea, concluding with a description of the divine warrior-king enthroned in his temple for eternity. As the Temple represented the Garden of Eden, the 'molten sea' perhaps symbolized secondarily the primordial waters of Sea below issuing forth from Eden (Gen. 3.10), and the twin pillars modelled the trees (of life and knowledge) planted in the garden. This interpretation of the pillars and tank symbolizing Eden, while consistent with the interior decoration, needs to account for the stands and 'lavers' and the great size of all the courtyard objects. While the themes of Yahweh as creator and the Garden of Eden match the exterior and interior of the Jerusalem Temple complex, these areas more specifically express divine conflict and divine enthronement, further conveying divine patronage and empowering of the Jerusalemite king.

The outer courtyard symbols in conjunction with the Temple proper were constructed as a public display to convey Yahweh's triumphant enthronement and endorsement of the monarchy. After defeating the

71. So W.F. Albright, 'What Were the Cherubim?', *BA* 1 (1938), p. 2.
72. So Keel, *Jahwe-Visionen*, pp. 25, 29-30 n. 33, figs. 9, 15-17.
73. Keel, *Jahwe-Visionen*, p. 35.
74. Cross, *Canaanite Myth*, pp. 135, 152, 158-62. Cf. Kraus, *Psalms 1–59*, p. 258; *idem*, *Psalms 60–150: A Commentary* (trans. H.C. Oswald; Minneapolis: Augsburg, 1989), pp. 201-202, 232-3 for the difficulty in dating these psalms.

cosmic enemies, symbolized by the 'molten sea', Yahweh extended his powers to the monarch (Ps. 89.26), and designated Zion, the holy mountain won in battle, as the seat of eternal divine (and human) sovereignty (Exod. 15.1-18; 2 Sam. 22.8-16; Pss. 89, 93). Fed with offerings, Yahweh entered his Temple-palace and ascended his throne in the 'throne-room' of the terrestrial divine palace, namely the sanctuary of the Temple. Yahweh would bestow blessings on the king and the people, as recorded on the pillars flanking the Temple entrance. Solomon's choice of palmette and cherub motif to adorn the walls and doors conveyed to Temple visitors that the Temple proper recreated the Garden of Eden, Yahweh's terrestrial residence.[75]

3. *The Experience of God*

Within the Temple precincts pilgrims would experience the presence of God. 'Seeing God' is the pre-eminent expression for an audience with the divine King in the Temple (Pss. 17.15; 42.2; 63.2; 84.7; cf. 11.7; Job 33.26).[76] One psalmist who longs to make the pilgrimage

75. With the exception of 'Ain Dara, there are no roughly contemporary temples with preserved or detailed objects and decoration in relation to what can be identified as Solomon's innovations. Certain common Bronze Age cultic elements were not incorporated in the Temple. The first element is an anthropomorphic representation of the god. According to Shuval, Bronze Age anthropomorphic gods in sitting and smiting poses were replaced by Iron Age gods mounted on quadrupeds (Shuval, 'A Catalogue', p. 117). Neither the Bronze nor the new Iron Age tradition of anthropomorphic representation of the deity was adopted. The second element is the naked goddess, or consort. For nearly a thousand years, from the last quarter of the third millennium through the Middle Bronze Age, the storm god was accompanied by a nude female. A naked goddess poses on the Ta'anach cult stand, but no female graces Solomon's Temple. The third element is the winged sun-disc. This manifestation of the solar cult was a familiar symbol in Egypt and in the north, and appeared on the tenth-century Ta'anach cult stand. How can these omissions be explained? T.N.D. Mettinger argues for the aniconic tendency at work here ('The Veto on Images', pp. 15-29). Anthropomorphic god and goddess representations were considered unacceptable. The winged sun-disc would also have been objectionable since it functioned as an icon for the god. In contrast, the cherub, the sacred tree and the stars were not associated with a particular deity.

76. For the motif of 'seeing God', especially in connection with the notion of God as king, see J.H. Tigay, 'On Some Aspects of Prayer in the Bible', *American Jewish Studies Review* 1 (1976), p. 369; M.S. Smith, '"Seeing God in the Psalms": The Background to the Beatific Vision in the Hebrew Bible', *CBQ* 50 (1988),

laments: 'when shall I come and behold the face (פְּנִים) of God?'
(Ps. 42.3).[77] As noted at the outset of this chapter, Exod. 23.15 as well
as 34.20 (also vv. 23-24) allude to 'seeing' Yahweh as the cultic goal
of the three pilgrimage feasts. The traditional translations read: 'and
none shall appear before me empty-handed' (וְלֹא יֵרָאוּ פָנַי רֵיקָם). As
critics have long noted, the expression פָּנַי, literally 'my face' (with no
preposition), cannot be rendered 'before me' (with a preposition), and
the verb is to be repointed from an *N*-stem ('Niphal') to the *G*-stem
form ('Qal') יִרְאוּ, and translated 'and they shall not see my face empty-
handed' (i.e. they shall not come to the place where they see my face,
namely the temple, without proper offering). The verb is not to be
read as a 'Niphal' (*N*-stem form), as a preposition would be required
to govern פָּנַי.[78] Similarly, although the Hebrew Masoretic Text renders the forms of רָאָה* in Exod. 34.23, 24, 1 Sam. 1.22 and Ps. 42.3
as *N*-stem, it is more likely that *G*-stem ('Qal') forms originally governed the direct object 'the face of the Lord Yahweh/God' ([אֶת] פְּנֵי
(הָאָדוֹן) יהוה/אלהים)) in these passages (cf. נִרְאָה* אֶל in Lev. 9.4 etc.).

The various expressions for seeing the deity are not limited to the
divine 'face'. Ps. 27.4 mentions an aesthetic experience, namely 'to behold the beauty (נֹעַם) of Yahweh', a notion paralleled in Ps. 27.13, to
'see the goodness (טוּב) of Yahweh'. It is possible that these expressions mean to enjoy the beautiful and good place of Yahweh, that is,
the sanctuary,[79] but there are ancient Near Eastern parallels for the

pp. 171-83; *idem*, *The Early History of God*, pp. 115-20. These works cite parallels
from the realm of the human king. The religious usage is also known in ancient Near
Eastern texts outside of the Bible (for a late Egyptian example, see *ANET*, p. 32,
l. 18). On the motif of 'seeing God' in rabbinic literature, see D. Boyarin, 'The Eye
in the Torah: Oracular Desire in Midrashic Hermeneutic', *Critical Inquiry* 16 (1990),
pp. 532-50 (reference courtesy of Rabbi Arnold Wolf).

77. For the comparable Akkadian expression *amāru pānī*, 'to see the face of
(someone)', for personal visits, see *CAD* A, II, pp. 21-22; C.L. Seow, 'Face',
DDD, p. 609.

78. For discussion, see C.T. Fritsch, 'Greek Translations of Hebrew Verbs "To
See", with Deity as Subject or Object', *ErIsr* 16 (1982 = H.M. Orlinsky Volume),
pp. 51*-66*.

79. So for v. 4, J.C. Greenfield, 'The "Cluster" in Biblical Poetry', *MAARAV*
5–6 (1990) = E.M. Cook (ed.), *Sopher Mahir: Northwest Semitic Studies Presented
to Stanislav Segert* (Santa Monica, CA: Western Academic Press, 1990), p. 164.
Greenfield points to Ugaritic parallels. For an easily accessible Akkadian parallel, see
the prayer of Nabu in Foster, *Before the Muses*, II, p. 613.

experience of the deity's 'beauty'.[80] Psalm 17.15 refers similarly to witnessing the divine 'form' (תמונה), a notion which likewise enjoys ancient parallels (Num. 12.8; Job 4.16).[81] The priestly tradition does not include these expressions for the experience of the divine presence, preferring instead the less anthropomorphic notions of the divine כבוד, usually rendered 'glory', but better 'effulgence'[82] (Ezek. 1) or cloud of the divine presence (Exod. 24.15-18; 40.36-38; Num. 9.15-23; see below).

Although the texts use 'to see Yahweh' as a frozen expression for coming to the temple at the appointed times, the origins of the expression lie in a cultic experience of Yahweh as suggested by Ps. 42.3 and Exod. 24.10. Whether and the degree to which this notion of 'seeing God' was based on a solar theophany (as opposed to the storm theophany reflected in Sukkot psalms such as Psalm 29) is debatable.[83] Some psalms mentioning the visibility of God contain images of the sun. In Psalm 84 the pilgrimage (vv. 6-7) is followed by the statement that 'the God of gods is seen in Zion' (v. 8). The description of being in the courts of Yahweh (v. 11) is followed then by a description of Yahweh (v. 12): 'For Yahweh is a sun and shield'. Here the notion of divine visibility and the sun seems to be linked, if only metaphorically, but perhaps 'sun' here is only a traditional royal title, as known in the Amarna letters and Ugaritic correspondence.[84] A solar image underlies the prediction of Mal 3.20: 'and the righteous Sun will rise on you who fear my name, with healing in its wings'.[85] This passage may reflect an older belief lying behind psalms of vigil (such as Pss. 17, 27 and 63). These psalms do not reduce the experience of God's presence to a solar theophany, but the experience of the dawn after the night vigil may have helped to evoke the perception of the luminescent dimension of the divine presence.[86] So it would seem that the expression of 'seeing

80. See *ANET*, p. 34.
81. For discussion, see Smith, *The Ugaritic Baal Cycle*, pp. 350-52.
82. So J. Blenkinsopp, *The Pentateuch: An Introduction to the First Five Books of the Bible* (ABRL; New York: Doubleday, 1992), p. 219. See Cross, *Canaanite Myth*, p. 153 n. 30.
83. For a maximal position on this issue as well as a substantive treatment of the pertinent passages, see Taylor, *Yahweh and the Sun*, esp. pp. 237-39.
84. So Taylor, *Yahweh and the Sun*, pp. 219-20. For some examples of 'sun' as a royal title, see Smith, *The Early History of God*, p. 118.
85. See Morton Smith, 'Helios in Palestine', *ErIsr* 16 (1982), p. 205.
86. So Smith, ' "Seeing God in the Psalms" ', p. 181. See also Taylor, *Yahweh*

God' may have derived from an experience which may be labelled a solar theophany. The experience of God as Light at once conveys the proximity, the visibility of the Divine Presence as well as the wonder and unknown dimension of God. Later the visual experience became a more general expression for the experience of God in the Temple.

The visual experience of divine light informed a wide group of metaphors in the Psalter. The face of Yahweh provides light to worshippers as a sign of divine favor (Pss. 4.6; 34.5; 67.1; 80.3, 7, 19; 89.15; cf. Num. 6.24-26) or divine judgment (Ps. 90.8). The speaker in some psalms asks God to allow the divine face to shine upon them (Ps. 31.16).[87] In the case of these expressions, only the larger theophanic context would necessarily indicate whether an experience of the deity is actually requested rather than a more general sign of divine favor. In many biblical cases, only a more general indication is asked of the deity. Such usages are known as well outside Israel. In an Old Babylonian prayer, Apil-Adad asks his personal god: 'Let me see your face'. B.R. Foster explains: '"Let me see your face", that is, "show yourself capable of doing something"'.[88] In this Akkadian usage and perhaps the biblical examples as well, the request to see the divine face usually represents a cliché and not a request for an experience of the deity.

The visual experience of God belonged to a larger complex of experiencing the temple as paradise. Two psalmists describe the temple feasting and use it to evoke their experience of God. Ps. 36.7-9 proclaims:

> How precious is Your steadfast love, O God!
> People take refuge in the shadow of Your wings.
> They feast on the abundance of Your house,
> And You give them drink from the river of Your delights.

and the Sun, p. 239. As part of a group of idolatrous acts, Ezek. 8.16 (cf. *m. Sukk.* 5.4) describes priests in the temple bowing down to the sun, but this act of obeisance may be no more than worship of Yahweh mediated by the sun (so see Smith, *The Early History of God*, p. 116; Taylor, *Yahweh and the Sun*, pp. 147-58, 251-53) or the sun-chariot which was thought to carry Yahweh (so E. Lipiński, 'Shemesh', *DDD*, p. 1147).

87. For the 'hiding the (divine) face' as a sign of divine disfavor, see R.E. Friedman, 'The Biblical Expression *mastîr pānîm*', *HAR* 1 (1977), pp. 139-47; S.E. Balentine, *The Hiding of the Face of God in the Old Testament* (New York: Oxford University Press, 1983).

88. Foster, *Before the Muses*, I, p. 157. For similar expressions in Akkadian prayers, see Foster, *Before the Muses*, I, p. 301: 'Turn your face toward Esagila which you love'; p. 314: 'I called to my god, he did not show his face'.

> For with You is the fountain of life,
> In Your light we see light.

Here the emphasis in the visual experience is given to divine lumines-cence. These verses also epitomize the paradisial elements of the Temple experience, namely divine presence, abundant food and drink in the Temple. Indeed, in the phrase, 'your delights' (עֲדָנֶיךָ) reverberates the peaceful, abundant life in the Garden of Eden (עֵדֶן; Gen. 2.8, 15, etc.).

Similarly, Ps. 63.3-5 draws on the image of the Temple's luxuriance and abundance of feasting to describe the effect that 'seeing God' has on the psalmist:

> So I have looked upon You in the sanctuary,
> Beholding Your power and majesty.
> So I will bless You as long as I live;
> I will lift my hands and call on thy name.
> My soul is feasted as with marrow and fat,
> And my mouth praises You with joyful lips.

The visual experience of God dominates both passages, and it appears to represent the focal image for the pilgrimage experience of the Temple.

The prophet Isaiah sees God in Isaiah 6, which emphasizes the cultic trappings associated with this experience. The smoke of the sacrificial cult corresponded in Israel's experience to the cloud of the divine pres-ence filling the Temple in Isaiah's vision, also known from the descrip-tion of the Temple's inauguration (1 Kgs 8.10, 11).[89] In B.A. Levine's words: 'The cloud of incense... covered the *kappôret*, thus reproduc-ing the conditions of Yahweh's heavenly abode (1 Kings 8.12, 2 Sam. 22.12//Pss. 18.10, 97.2, Job 38.9)'.[90] The prophet's vision assumes an anthropomorphic presentation of Yahweh (Isa. 6.1). (In Ezekiel's vi-sion of 1.26, the prophet softens this anthropomorphism by describing the vision of Yahweh as 'the semblance of a human form' [NJPS].) At Mount Sinai the cloud concealing the divine presence covered this holy mountain (Exod. 24.15-18). This cloud of presence likewise would travel over the tabernacle as Israel moved from Mount Sinai to

---

89. See the important discussion of T.N.D. Mettinger, *The Dethronement of Sabaoth: Studies in the Shem and Kabod Theologies* (ConBOT, 18; Lund: Gleerup, 1982), esp. pp. 87-110.

90. B.A. Levine, *In the Presence of the Lord*, p. 72. See also Mettinger, *The Dethronement of Sabaoth*, p. 89.

the Promised land (Exod. 40.36-38; Num. 9.15-23). As T. Hiebert notes, 'The Priestly writer relates the divine cloud in which the deity appears above the cherubs to the cloud of incense produced by the priestly censer to cover these cherubs (Lev. 16.2, 12-13)'.[91]

Other features of liturgical practice also channeled and gave form to the experience of the divine.[92] The presence of God was announced by the blowing of the ram's horn (שׁופר). Descriptions of the divine presence on Mount Sinai are marked by lightning, thunder and the sounding of the horn (see Exod. 19.16, 19; 20.15), precisely the sort of theophanic experience of the Temple. There theophanies are likewise marked by the conjunction of storm imagery and the horn (Ps. 98.6; Zech. 9.14). Ps. 47.6 describes the cultic theophany: 'God ascends midst acclamation; the Lord, to the blasts of the horn' (NJPS). In Zech. 9.14 the role of blowing the horn is attributed to God manifest in the storm theophany (NJPS):

> And the Lord will manifest Himself to them,
> And his arrows shall flash like lightning;
> My Lord God shall sound the ram's horn
> And advance in a stormy tempest.

A hallmark of the pilgrimage feasts (Num. 10.10), the cultic sounding of the horn was perceived as announcing the divine presence. The blowing of the horn may be viewed also as giving form to the liturgical experience of the divine storm, especially the thunder.[93]

The Temple's cherub iconography likewise played a role in giving form to stormy descriptions of the divine. Psalm 18's mythic description of Yahweh flying on the cherub in order to rescue the king in the Temple is informed by the cherub iconography in the Temple. The language of the storm-theophany in this psalm indicates once again the

91. Hiebert, 'Theophany in the OT', *ABD*, VI, p. 510.
92. Cf. E. Sapir: 'the real world is to a large extent unconsciously built up on the language habits of the group. . . We see and hear and otherwise experience very largely as we do because the language habits of our community predispose certain choices of interpretation.' Quoted by M. Douglas, *Natural Symbols: Explorations in Cosmology* (New York: Vintage Books, 1973), p. 42. Or, in Douglas's words (p. 182), 'Here we come to Durkheim's insight that the shared experience of society structures the internal consciousness of the private person to match that of the collectivity.'
93. The liturgical context of all of these passages lives on in the Rosh Hashanah service (Shoferot verses).

procession that the stormy warrior-god made to the temple. As noted above, the entire layout of the Temple and its courtyard expressed the procession of the divine King into his palace following his victory over the cosmic enemies. The procession of God into the Temple area is described in Ps. 24.7-10:

> 7 Lift up, O Gates, your heads,
>   Lift up, O Eternal Gates,
>   That the King of Majesty may enter!
> 8 Who is this King of Majesty?
>   Yahweh, the Strong Warrior,
>   Yahweh, the Battle-Warrior.
> 9 Lift up, O Gates, your heads,
>   Lift up, O Eternal Gates,
>   That the King of Majesty may enter!
> 10 Who is this King of Majesty?
>   Yahweh of Armies—
>   He is the King of Majesty.

The warrior-king is recognized by the community, as he assumes his throne within the terrestrial palace, that is the sanctuary of the Temple. The theophanic experience in the Temple, storm-theophanies included, seems to have generally involved the procession of the warrior-king. The cultural traditions embodied in liturgical practice and Temple iconography lent expression and form to the experience of 'seeing God'. The Temple rituals and iconography and the people's liturgical experience of Yahweh reinforced one another.

To anticipate the discussion of liturgical life in Exodus (especially that in Chapter 9), this Temple complex of rituals, symbols and experiences informed the literary rendering of the divine presence in the book of Exodus, and here the classic priestly presentation of this experience in Exod. 19.18-22, 20.15 (NJPS) may be quoted:

> Now Mount Sinai was all in smoke, for the Lord had come down upon it in fire; the smoke rose like the smoke of a kiln, and the whole mountain trembled violently. The blare of the horn grew louder and louder. As Moses spoke, God answered him in thunder. The Lord came down upon Mount Sinai, on the top of the mountain, and the Lord called Moses to the top of the mountain and Moses went up. The Lord said to Moses, 'Go down, warn the people not to break through to the Lord to gaze, lest many of them perish. The priests also, who come near to the Lord, must stay pure, lest the Lord break out against them.'. . . All the people witnessed the thunder and lightning, the blare of the horn and the mountain smoking; and when the people saw it, they fell back and stood at a distance.

This passage contains basic priestly elements of the Temple experience: the delimitation of the holy place conceptualized as the holy mountain of Yahweh; the hierarchy of Moses, priests and people; the requirement of purity and holiness for all; the appearance of Yahweh in cloud which both signals and conceals the divine presence; and the dangerous character of holiness, not simply a human condition, but a divine one which threatens humans who participate out of keeping with their proper status. As G. von Rad commented: 'The recognition of a close relationship between the Sinai narrative and a cultic ceremony carries us a great step forward'.[94]

It should be recognized that this description points to one further essential feature of the pilgrimage experience, and that was divine teaching. In this passage from Exodus, it is the Ten Commandments that are the pre-eminent divine teaching to be received upon making pilgrimage to the holy mountain of God. Such teaching was likely part and parcel of pilgrimage feasts. Above it was noted in the discussion of Weeks that Psalms 50 and 81 reflect teaching in the context of the pilgrimage. Which pilgrimage feast was involved is unknown. Weeks and Booths are the two most common proposals. Yet it would seem that all three pilgrimage feasts would be appropriate occasions for the teaching of divine law. In either case, Isa. 2.3 (Mic. 4.2) reflects the association of divine teaching with making pilgrimage.[95] This verse begins with a future speech of non-Israelite pilgrims (cf. NJPS):

> And the many peoples shall go and say:
> 'Come, let us go up to the Mount of the Lord,
> To the House of the God of Jacob;
> That He may instruct us in His ways,
> And that we may walk in His paths'.
> For instruction shall come forth from Zion,
> The word of the Lord from Jerusalem.

As this passage suggests,[96] divine teaching belongs to the pilgrimage

---

94. Von Rad, *The Problem of the Hexateuch*, p. 21.
95. Von Rad, *The Problem of the Hexateuch*, p. 25.
96. On this passage, see Jensen, *The Use of Tôrâ*, pp. 84-95. Many would take issue with Jensen's emphasis on the 'wisdom sense of *tôrâ* in this passage' (p. 89). Jensen's claim is based on a questionable syllogism (implicitly recognized on p. 91): wisdom is often connected with kingship, Yahweh is the Divine King; therefore, torah here is influenced by wisdom. A more general view may be preferable: divine teaching derives from some cultic mediator, priestly or prophetic, which was expected

made to the presence of the Divine King. Indeed, divine teaching is presented here as a second level of pilgrimage. The first level is the literal journey to Jerusalem, while the second is the moral pilgrimage of walking in 'God's paths', here parallel to being instructed in the divine ways. This relationship between literal and moral journey underlies the dialogue between Yahweh and Moses in Exodus 33–34. To anticipate, Exodus 33–34 uses the notion of God's ways to link the journey of the Israelites with their moral and spiritual well-being.

Compared with Exodus 19–20, Exod. 24.1-11 was informed by an older presentation of this sanctuary experience.[97] An altar is erected at the foot of the mountain, sacrifices are offered on it and then an archaic description of 'seeing God' is described (Exod. 24.4-11). Moses and other Israelite leaders ascend Mount Sinai, eat the covenant meal and have the special experience of seeing God in his heavenly palace (Exod. 24.10; cf. Num. 12.8): 'there was under his feet as it were a pavement of sapphire stone, like the very heaven for clearness'. In the following verse seeing God is regarded as problematic, as it is elsewhere in Israelite literature (Gen. 16.13; Exod. 33.12-23; Deut. 4.12, 15; Judg. 6.22-23), but God does 'not lay his hand' on the Israelite leader, evidently the expected price for this visual experience. 'Seeing God' also lies at the heart of the dialogue between Yahweh and Moses in Exodus 33–34. These chapters draw on the liturgical Temple tradition in order to present a fuller reflection on the theological problem of how a holy deity can dwell in the midst of a sinning people.[98]

This traditional complex of liturgical experiences in the Temple made an impact on other literary descriptions of God's holy mountain. As noted above in the discussion of Genesis 2, the descriptions of paradise and Temple seem to influence one another.[99] The notion of

in the context of pilgrimage as mentioned in this passage. For this view, see the references provided by Jensen, *The Use of Tôrâ*, p. 89 n. 112. However, Jensen may be correct in that even this distinction might be overdrawn: instructional language might have belonged to the rhetorical repertoire of cultic teachers in the Jerusalem sanctuary, whether sages, prophets or priests (in other words, it may be impossible here to infer social location from language). Indeed, the fact that such putative wisdom usage appears in Isaiah according to Jensen militates in this direction.

97. On this passage, see below Chapter 10, section 2.
98. On this passage, see below Chapter 10, section 3.
99. Israelite descriptions of paradise incorporate three motifs known from Ugaritic tradition: the home of the heavenly council located on the top of a mountainous abode like Mount Olympus; the abode of the god, El situated at the meeting-point of divine

God's walking in the cool of the day in Eden in Genesis 2 echoes the notion of the divine footsteps uncovered in the 'Ain Dara temple mentioned above. Ezekiel 28 locates Eden on God's holy mountain, characterizing it as a divine garden with gold and every precious stone, protected by the cherub (vv. 13-14). Ezekiel 28 locates paradise on God's mountain (v. 16), just like the Temple in Jerusalem (Pss. 15.1, 24.3, 43.3 and 48.1-2). The 'stones of fire' in Ezek. 28.14 may allude obliquely to the tradition of the divine Temple or palace on the holy mountain of God. The idea of the divine palace on top of the holy mountain appears to lie behind the description of God's abode in Exod. 24.10. This description barely shows what was known of the heavenly Temple in ancient Israel. However, prior West Semitic tradition represented in the Baal Cycle (*KTU* 1.4 V-VII) and later Israelite literature of the Songs of the Sabbath Sacrifice suggest that the heavenly Temple or palace was known much more widely and in greater detail than the bare-bones allusions in Exodus 24 and Ezekiel 28 might suggest.[100]

In sum, the pilgrimage was like visiting paradise and temporarily recapturing the primordial peaceful and abundant relationship with God. It involved both holiness and pleasure, sacred and aesthetic space. It was an experience imbued with holiness, the beauty of the divine dwelling, and the very presence of God. The pilgrims' experience in the Temple was global in its effects. It saturated the psalmists' senses with all kinds of wonders: abundant food and incense, music and singing, gold and silver, palm trees, water and cherubs. This joyful experience led further to an experience of awe and holiness in the presence of God.

---

waters variously called 'rivers' or 'deeps'; and the temple–palace home of the storm god Baal atop his heavenly mountain. The first two may have been identified in Ugaritic tradition; they certainly were merged in biblical material as the home of God. And the third tradition, though separate in Ugaritic material, has likewise merged with the other two traditions in biblical tradition. For discussion, see H.N. Wallace, *The Eden Narrative*, pp. 60-172; Smith, *The Early History of God*, pp. 10, 33-34 n. 57; cf. p. 111 n. 98; *idem, The Ugaritic Baal Cycle*, pp. 225-34.

100. M.S. Smith, 'Biblical and Canaanite Notes to the Songs of the Sabbath Sacrifice from Qumran', *RevQ* 48 (1987), pp. 585-87. On Ezek. 28, see R.R. Wilson, 'The Death of the King of Tyre: The Editorial History of Ezekiel 28', in J.H. Marks and R.M. Good (eds.), *Love and Death in the Ancient Near East: Essays in Honor of Marvin H. Pope* (Guilford, CT: Four Quarters, 1987), pp. 213-14.

EXCURSUS: TEMPLE AND CREATION IN THE PRIESTLY ORDER
OF GENESIS 1

The priestly understanding of the Temple may be explored further in the first creation story in the Bible, Gen. 1.1–2.4a.[101] As a central expression of the priestly world-view, this text may be regarded as a charter text that informs other priestly passages in the Pentateuch. Genesis 1, for example, is deliberately echoed at the beginning and end of Exodus. To anticipate, this creation story combines two different visions of the cosmos: the first and older view that a cosmos as the stage where divine wills engage in conflict; and the second and largely priestly notion that the cosmos is a holy place analogous to a sanctuary.[102] This excursus first offers a cursory sample of ancient Near Eastern and biblical texts describing the cosmos as a stage of conflict and then describes the priestly background to the idea of the universe as a holy divine dwelling in Genesis 1.

1. *The Cosmos as a Stage of Conflict*

The ancient Near Eastern text perhaps cited most often as an example of the cosmos as a locale for conflict between divine wills is the Babylonian classic known from its first two words, Enuma Elish ('When on high. . . ').[103] In the cosmic world of this

101. The pre-priestly background of Gen. 1.1–2.4a is not the focus of attention here. For the theory that this text is 'based upon a poetic document probably of catechetical origin', see Cross, *Canaanite Myth*, p. 301, citing the Harvard dissertation of J.S. Kselman, 'The Poetic Background of Certain Priestly Traditions' (1971). The bibliography on the first creation story is immense. In addition to the commentaries and works cited below, see W.P. Brown, *Structure, Role, and Ideology in the Hebrew and Greek Texts of Genesis 1.1–2.3* (SBLDS, 132; Atlanta: Scholars Press, 1993); and S.L. Jaki, *Genesis 1 through the Ages* (London: Thomas More, 1992).

102. On creation, see most recently (and the works cited therein) R.J. Clifford, *Creation Accounts in the Ancient Near East and in the Bible* (CBQMS, 26; Washington: Catholic Biblical Association, 1994); and R.A. Simkins, *Creator and Creation: Nature in the Worldview of Ancient Israel* (Peabody, MA: Hendrickson, 1994). An excerpt based on C. Westermann's three-volume commentary on Genesis was published as *Creation* (trans. J.J. Scullion; Philadelphia: Fortress Press, 1974) and remains a helpful precis of pertinent information. For some further considerations of issues in this first section, see J.G. Janzen, 'On the Moral Nature of God's Power: Yahweh and the Sea in Job and Deutero-Isaiah', *CBQ* 56 (1994), pp. 458-78, esp. pp. 460-65.

103. See Foster, *Before the Muses*, I, pp. 351-402. The well-known older translation of E.A. Speiser is available in *ANET*, pp. 60-72, with additions rendered by A.K. Grayson in *ANET*, pp. 501-503. For an accessible discussion, see Clifford, *Creation Accounts*, pp. 82-93. This epic poem has been read against the political events of the late second millennium Babylon and the later neo-Assyrian and neo-Babylonian empires of the first millennium. For a recent discussion, see B.N. Porter, *Images, Power, and Politics: Figurative Aspects of Esarhaddon's Babylonian Policy* (Memoirs of the American Philosophical Society held at Philadelphia for Promoting Useful Knowledge, 208; Philadelphia: American Philosophical Society, 1993), pp. 115, 139-43; see also J. Oates, *Babylon* (London: Thames & Hudson, rev. edn, 1986), pp. 169-74. For further discussion of the theological milieu of the Babylonian version of Enuma Elish, see A. Livingstone, *Mystical*

text, deities face off in battle like the royalty who patronized the epic and their enemies; then in the wake of this divine conflict creation emerges. The cosmos of the epic corresponds to the human world in three ways: (1) the enemies of the divine king, Marduk, and their human counterparts can threaten the world; (2) both kings, divine and human, reign from Babylon at the center of the world; and (3) the temple of the god is the cosmic center linking both divine and human dominion.

A number of West Semitic texts likewise allude to the cosmic conflict between the storm god and his enemies. The use of the conflict story to reinforce human kingship appears in a variety of texts, hailing from the city of Mari on the Euphrates river all the way to Egypt. In a letter to Zimri-Lim of Mari, Nur-Sin of Aleppo quoting Adad (Baal) informs the king that 'I s[et] you on the thr[one of your father]; the weapons with which I battled against Sea I gave to you'.[104] In some of the Amarna letters, the pharaoh is compared with 'Baal in the heavens'.[105] A few Egyptian texts, such as the poetical stele of Tutmoses III,[106] dress the king in the storm imagery of Baal. Finally, the Baal Cycle, the longest religious text from the ancient city of Ugarit, does not make explicit the link between Baal and the Ugaritic king, but it may be sus- pected that the royal line whose patron god was Baal patronized the copying and transmission of the Baal Cycle precisely because this text embodied the royal ideals of the divine support of the Ugaritic dynasty.[107] Baal's enemies such as Sea and Death, as well as the better-known Leviathan, perhaps mirrored earthly powers sur- rounding Ugarit. In the case of the Mari letter the political expression of divine support does not simply construct a parallelism between the divine and human kings. Instead, it crosses the boundaries of this parallelism by making the king into a figure sharing the power of his patron storm god.[108] It is possible that the language was not merely a figurative ornament.[109] Rather, to use older metaphysical language, the human king was perhaps thought to 'participate in' the power of the divine king.[110]

The political use made of the conflict between storm god and cosmic enemies passed into Israelite tradition. Yahweh is not only generally similar to Baal as a storm god. Yahweh inherited the names of Baal's cosmic enemies such as Leviathan, Sea,

and *Mythological Explanatory Works of Assyrian and Babylonian Scholars* (Oxford: Clarendon Press, 1986).

104. See Durand, 'Le mythologème du combat', pp. 41-61; Bordreuil and Pardee, 'Le combat de *Ba'lu* avec *Yammu*', pp. 63-70; Smith, *The Ugaritic Baal Cycle*, pp. 108-10, 360.

105. For the evidence, see Smith, *The Early History of God*, p. 74.

106. E. Gaál, 'Tuthmosis III as Storm-God?' *Studia Aegyptiaca* 3 (1977), pp. 29-38. See also *ANET*, p. 249.

107. See Smith, *The Ugaritic Baal Cycle*, pp. 108-10, 360.

108. Cross, *Canaanite Myth*, p. 258 n. 177.

109. Cf. the self-comparison of Shalmaneser III with Hadad in *ANET*, p. 277; D. Damrosch, *The Narrative Covenant: Transformations of Genre in the Growth of Biblical Literature* (San Francisco: Harper & Row, 1987), pp. 55, 61, 70.

110. For further discussion, M.S. Smith, 'Mythology and Myth-Making in Ugaritic and Israelite Literatures', in G.J. Brooke, A.H.W. Curtis and J.F. Healey (eds.), *Ugarit and the Bible: Proceedings of the International Symposium on Ugarit and the Bible. Manchester, September 1992* (Ugaritisch-Biblische Literatur, 11; Münster: Ugarit-Verlag, 1994), pp. 309-21.

Death, and Tannin as well as the name of Baal's home on Mount Saphon, which is secondarily identified with Zion in Ps. 48.3. Given this evidence, it would appear that Yahweh's titles, 'Rider of the heavens' (Deut. 33.26; Ps. 104.3) and 'Rider of the Steppes' (Ps. 68.5), echo Baal's own title, 'Rider of the Clouds'.[111] The political use of this conflict language also passed into ancient Israel. The biblical parallel between Yahweh, the divine king, and the Davidic ruler, the human king, may be seen in Psalm 89. This psalm parallels the victorious power of Yahweh in vv. 5-18 with the divine help which Yahweh bestows upon the Davidic monarch in vv. 19-37. The parallelism between Yahweh and the king changes, however, in v. 26 and a different sort of notion appears: Yahweh promises to extend his power to the monarch in language associated in Ugaritic with the god, Baal: 'I will set his hand on Sea and his right hand on Rivers'.[112]

The monarchy was not only the only segment of Israelite society that used the creation-conflict to describe divine power. Non-royal texts also refer to the divine conflict between Yahweh and cosmic forces at the time of creation to illustrate Yahweh's ancient powers. Ps. 74.12-17 and Isa. 51.9-10a are often cited as two classic biblical examples.[113] This conflict is not only set in the primordial past, but it is set in the future as the definitive moment of Yahweh's salvation of Israel. Isa. 27.1 may be the most poignant instance of this theme: 'In that day the Lord with his hard and great and strong sword will punish Leviathan the fleeing serpent, and he will slay the dragon that is in the sea'. The apocalyptic visions of Daniel 7 and Revelation 13 present the beasts of the Sea whom Yahweh, the divine warrior, will ultimately sweep away. The political link between these beasts and world empires was no late invention, but echoed the mirroring of divine and human kings and the cosmic and human enemies known already in the second millennium. While this view of the cosmos is attested in all biblical periods, another view of the universe with at least equal influence in post-biblical tradition would emerge in Israel.

2. Genesis 1 and the Priestly Order of Creation

The first creation story in Gen. 1.1–2.4a points to a vision of a holy universe, which adds to the older model of the universe as a site of conflict. This priestly narrative

111. For further evidence of Yahweh's inheritance of other features associated specifically with Baal, see Smith, *The Early History of God*, pp. 50-55.

112. G.W. Ahlström, *Psalm 89: Eine Liturgie aus dem Ritual des leidenden Königs* (Lund: Gleerup, 1959), pp. 108-11; E. Lipiński, *Le poème royal du Psaume LXXXIX 1.5.20-38* (Cahiers de la Revue biblique, 6; Paris: Gabalda, 1967), p. 53; J.-B. Dumortier, 'Un rituel d'intronisation: Le Ps. LXXXIX 2-38', *VT* 22 (1972), p. 188 and n. 1; Cross, *Canaanite Myth*, p. 258 n. 177, pp. 261-62; P. Mosca, 'Ugarit and Daniel 7: A Missing Link', *Bib* 67 (1986), pp. 509, 512; *idem*, 'Once Again the Heavenly Witness of Ps 89.38', *JBL* 105 (1986), p. 33. Mosca ('Once Again', p. 33) points to other examples of 'mythico-religious terms' in Psalm 89: the king is the 'first-born' (v. 28) of 'my father' (v. 27), and serves as the 'Most High' (v. 28) with respect to earthly kings'. See also M. Weinfeld, 'Zion and Jerusalem as Religious and Political Capital', pp. 97-98.

113. Cross, *Canaanite Myth*, p. 137; Clifford, *Creation Accounts*, pp. 154-56, 168-72.

presents the cosmos as the divine holy place, even while it shows its debt to the old model of the cosmos as battlefield. Genesis 1 manifests the marks of the old royal model of the cosmos, but the story modifies this vision of the cosmos in three ways. First, as noted above, Enuma Elish and various biblical texts connect creation with divine conflict. Ps. 74.12-17 makes the divine conflict the basis for the establishment of the sun, moon and stars as well as the boundaries of the earth. In contrast, Genesis 1 shows only a hint of this old tradition. At the opening of Genesis 1, the audience expects the conflict, as the 'mighty wind', or possibly 'divine spirit' (רוח אלהים), hovers over the face of the cosmic waters. Rather than conflict, Genesis 1 has God speak or make, and creation happens. With but a word, without conflict, God effects the opening of creation. The silence of Genesis 1, in omitting the divine conflict, is so strong that the absence of this motif marks a paradigm shift in the presentation of creation.[114]

Secondly, the old language of human rule, associated with the royal model of creation as conflict, still appears in Genesis 1: humanity is to 'rule' (רדה*) over the terrestrial creation (v. 28) as a human governor on earth corresponding to the King of Kings in heaven.[115] Genesis 1 alters this royal motif in that the king on earth is not the Israelite king, but all humanity. Thirdly, the creation of the human person in Gen. 1.26, in the 'image' and 'likeness' of God, represents a major shift from the old royal model. The idea of 'the image' of the gods was, in ancient Near East, applied to the king.[116] It was the king who was the image of the deity. Gen. 1.26 changes this idea. For humanity, understood as the participant in the cosmic Sabbath (שבת), is to be the holy image of God on earth.

Parenthetically it is evident that Gen. 1.26 is actually two steps removed from the older royal theology of the image, when Gen. 1.26 is compared not only with royal theology, but with Ezek. 1.26 as well. Ezekiel 1.26 conveys the prophet's vision of the divine with the language of 'image' of the human person (דמות כמראה אדם, 'like the semblance of a human being'; NJPS).[117] In contrast, Gen. 1.26-28 presents a

---

114. For these points, see following a long line of continental scholarship, J.D. Levenson, *Creation and the Persistance of Evil: The Drama of Divine Omnipotence* (San Francisco: Harper & Row, 1988), pp. 53-127.

115. The royal model is especially pronounced in the study of B. Janowski, 'Herrschaft über die Terre: Gen. 1, 26-28 und die Semantik von רדה', in G. Braulik, W. Gross and S. McEvenue (eds.), *Biblische Theologie und gesellschaftlicher Wandel: Für Norbert Lohfink SJ* (Freiburg: Herder, 1993), pp. 183-98. See also P.A. Bird, 'Gen. 1.27b in the Context of the Priestly Account of Creation', *HTR* 74 (1981), pp. 138-44, esp. p. 140. The further issue is the degree to which the priestly account has moved away from a primarily royal background or model.

116. See the many interpreters cited by Kraus, *Psalms 1–59*, p. 183. Kraus rejects this view as missing the specifically priestly context of this passage, but this is to miss the borrowing and adaptation of the old royal language. For this usage of the divine image in Egyptian literature (which shows a long history of using this language for the king), see Merikare (*ANET*, p. 417; for further discussion, see Smith, 'Mythology and Myth-Making', pp. 321-22).

117. The use of *dmwt'* in lines 1 and 15 in the Old Aramaic Tell Fakheriyeh inscription, discovered in 1979, is striking, in view of J. Wellhausen's claim that this word was an Aramaic loan into Hebrew (*Prolegomena to the History of Ancient Israel* [Gloucester, MA: Peter Smith, 1973], p. 389). The Akkadian equivalent for the second instance of this word in the Aramaic portion is

vision of the human person in the likeness of the divine.[118] Ezekiel 1.26 describes Yahweh in anthropomorphic terms (albeit a considerably more limited one compared with prior prophetic texts), but Gen. 1.26-28 reverses the direction of the comparison in rendering the human person in divine terms. Perhaps drawing specifically on Isa. 6.1 or more generally on a tradition of prophetic visions, Ezek. 1.26 is a literary adaptation of the prophetic visionary experience in a Temple setting which casts the deity in human terms. In turn, Gen. 1.26-28 reflects theologically on humanity in divine terms. In sum, the view of humanity expressed in Gen. 1.26-28 stands at a considerable but discernible distance from the royal notion of the king as the image of the god.[119]

If these three features of Genesis 1 represent alterations to the royal model of creation involving divine conflict, then what is the new vision of reality? Often noted in Genesis 1 are the correspondences between the first and second sets of three days culminating in the seventh day.[120] This order is more than an orderly construction; it is a religious order and has a moral character. It is imbued by the word of God and seen as good. This universe intimates a priestly blueprint for human existence in three ways long recognized by scholars. The divine resting (שׁבת*) on the seventh day anticipates the priestly institution of the Sabbath in Exodus 20 and 31. Furthermore, Gen. 1.14 states that the lights in the firmament are to mark the times for feast-days, weeks and years, a central feature for maintaining priestly cult. Finally, the division of the universe into heavens, earth and seas, and the assignment of the animals to these spheres foreshadow another priestly prescription, namely the system of dietary requirements (later called כשׁרות, or the practice of 'keeping kosher').[121] These three themes point to the priestly service and holiness that are to characterize this new creation.

In Genesis 1, creation is no longer primarily a conflict; it is the result not of two wills in conflict, but of One Will expressing the word issuing in the good creation. This One Will places humanity in this creation. The life of this creation is to be holy, moral and good, and perhaps even priestly. Although it exceeds the evidence, it may be suggested that the cosmos in Genesis 1 was to be understood not simply as holy,

---

ṣalmu, cognate with BH צלם also used in Gen. 1.26-28 for 'image'. For the inscription, see A. Abou-Assaf, P. Bordreuil and A.R. Millard, *La statue de Tell Fekherye et son inscription bilingue assyro-araméenne* (Etudes Assyriologiques; Paris: Editions Recherche sur les civilisations, 1982), pp. 23, 28. The word is used to refer to the human depiction on the statue on which the inscription was discovered. In the *editio princeps* the word is accordingly translated 'statue'. For discussion especially of the Aramaic evidence, see D.M. Gropp and T.J. Lewis, 'Notes on Some Problems in the Aramaic Text of the Hadd-Yith'i Bilingual', *BASOR* 259 (1985), p. 47.

118. For a discussion of Ezek. 1.26 in the context of the prophetic visionary experience, see above Chapter 2, section 3.

119. For discussion, see Smith, *The Early History of God*, p. 102.

120. Cf. J.M. Sasson, 'Time... To Begin', in Fishbane and Tov with Fields, *'Sha'arei Talmon'*, p. 186.

121. So also independently Nelson, *Raising Up a Faithful Priest*, pp. 23, 36, 94; Blenkinsopp, *Sage, Priest, Prophet*, pp. 67, 101-104.

but as a holy place, such as a sanctuary.[122] The relation between Temple and creation was well known. As noted above in Chapter 2, the Temple in Jerusalem, decorated with the motifs of the cosmos and the Garden of Eden, mirrored the cosmos. Biblical descriptions of creation and temple-building have influenced one another and constitute, in J.D. Levenson's view, a 'homology'.[123] Ps. 78.69 expresses this view metaphorically: 'He built his sanctuary like the high heavens, like the earth which he has founded for ever'.[124] In Psalm 78 temple-building is rendered in terms of creation.[125] Ps. 150.1 likewise expresses this idea in poetic parallelism:

> Praise God in His sanctuary;
> Praise Him in the sky, His stronghold.[126]

In this case the divine sanctuary and the sky are poetic parallel terms which serve to explain one another: the heavens constitute the divine sanctuary. The sense of cosmos as sanctuary may lie behind Genesis 1 or may be evoked by it. Furthermore, the implicit evocation of כשרות in Genesis 1, if correct, may likewise suggest the notion of cosmos as Temple. W. Houston has argued that the practice of כשרות developed in ancient Israel in the priestly protection of Temple purity and holiness.[127] If this is right, Genesis 1's delineation of realms in the universe according to animals may evoke Temple practice and in turn a vision of the world as a kind of Temple. In any case, creation is built as a moral, good, ordered holy place, and humanity is placed in this holy site to imitate the rest, order and holiness of the Deity in whose image humanity is made.

Genesis 1 does not use conflict as the main element in its vision of the cosmos and the place of humanity in it. Instead, the priestly holiness of time and space overshadow the component of conflict.[128] This view made sense of a world in which

122. Without evidence this view is argued also by Blenkinsopp, *Sage, Priest, Prophet*, pp. 68, 104, 113. For the Temple background to Genesis 1, see M. Weinfeld, 'Sabbath, Temple and the Enthronement of the Lord—The Problem of the Sitz im Leben of Genesis 1.1–2.3', in A. Caquot and M. Delcor (eds.), *Mélanges bibliques et orientaux en l'honneur de M. Henri Cazelles* (AOAT, 212; Kevelaer: Butzon & Bercker; Neukirchen–Vluyn: Neukirchener Verlag, 1981), pp. 501-12; Levenson, *Creation and the Persistence of Evil*, pp. 78-87; B. Janowski, 'Tempel und Schöpfung: Schöpfungstheologische Aspekte der priesterschriftlichen Heiligtumskonzeption', *Jahrbuch für Biblische Theologie* 5 (1990), pp. 37-69.
123. Levenson, *Creation and the Persistence of Evil*, pp. 78-87.
124. For a reading of this verse based on parallels cited in the following note, see Hurowitz, *I Have Built you an Exalted House*, pp. 335-37.
125. This connection was made in the Syro-Mesopotamian world as well. See Gudea, Cylinder A, xxv, line 2: 'the house's stretching out. . . was like the heights of heaven awe-inspiring' (T. Jacobsen, *The Harps that once. . . Sumerian Poetry in Translation* [New Haven: Yale University Press, 1987], p. 419). For other examples, see Hurowitz, *I Have Built you an Exalted House*, pp. 335-37. See also the cosmic ramifications of Baal's palace in the Ugaritic Baal Cycle (for discussion, see Smith, *The Ugaritic Baal Cycle*, pp. 77-78).
126. The translation follows NJPS, apart from the capitalization of the first word and the lack of indentation in the second line.
127. Houston, *Purity and Monotheism*. See above Chapter 2, section 2.
128. For correlations between social groups and their cosmologies, see M. Douglas, *Natural Symbols*, esp. pp. 138-40, 169-71, 175-76, 195.

monarchy no longer protected Israel. This outlook would serve Israel well in exile and beyond when responsibility for community order passed from the Davidic dynasty to the priesthood of Aaron. Indeed, Genesis 1 has often been dated to the exilic or post-exilic period.[129] Genesis 1 reflects this change: to the royal model has been added a priestly model. The politics of creation have changed. There is still a king in this world, but it is the King of Kings, the One Will who rules heavens and earth alike, with no serious competition, and this King in Heaven is to be followed by humanity ruling on earth. There is no mirror, no single royal agent on earth, whose human foes mirror the cosmic foes of the divine king. Moreover, this king is, as importantly, the Holy One enthroned over the cosmos.[130] In sum, the vision of humanity in Genesis 1 anticipates the divine election of Israel as its prototypical servant of Sabbath, and in the foreshadowing of כשׁרות.

The priestly picture of the cosmos in Gen. 1.1–2.4a foreshadows the covenant on Mount Sinai. Holy time and space are only adumbrated in Genesis 1, but with the Sinai legislation the full picture of these dimensions of human life will become explicit. The maintenance of the sabbath and the other times as well as the sacred space of the Temple is a structure built into the fabric of the cosmos, according to the priestly picture in Genesis 1. With the Sinai covenant Israel will be able to participate in this holy order. At the center of this order lives the God who is at once signalled but concealed by the cloud on Mount Sinai. Yet the priestly redaction has connected this revelation with the opening creation of the cosmos. To anticipate the discussion in the next chapter, the priestly redaction of the beginning and end of Exodus evokes Genesis 1. As scholars have long noted, the priestly opening of Exodus 1, specifically in v. 7, describes how the Israelites had been fruitful and multiplied, an early echo of Gen. 1.28a, the divine command to be fruitful and multiply. Similarly, commentators beginning with Martin Buber and Franz Rosenzweig have observed that Exodus 39–40 consciously echoes the end of the priestly creation account (Exod. 39.43a//Gen. 1.31a; Exod. 39.32a//Gen. 2.1; Exod. 40.33b//Gen. 2.2a; and Exod. 39.43b//Gen. 2.3a).[131] Exodus 39–40 is thereby connected to the creation story of

---

129. See the instructive comments of P.A. Bird, ' "Male and Female he Created them": Gen. 1.27b in the Context of the Priestly Account of Creation', *HTR* 74 (1981), p. 143 n. 37, p. 152. The royal model informs the picture of Israel in Isa. 42.5-6, 55.3, as argued by many interpreters. See most recently Janzen, 'On the Moral Nature of God's Power', pp. 469-78. It may be noted further that according to Isaiah 40–55, the universe is not only the scene of divine conflict (51.9-10a), as noted above, but also a divine dwelling, specifically a tent (40.22; cf. 42.5). Cf. Isa. 66.1: ' "The heavens are My throne and the earth is My footstool. . . " '.

130. See Levenson, *Creation and the Persistence of Evil*, p. 88.

131. For discussion of Buber and Rosenzweig, see E. Blum, *Studien zur Komposition des Pentateuch* (BZAW, 189; Berlin: de Gruyter, 1990), pp. 306-307. See also J. Blenkinsopp, 'The Structure of P', *CBQ* 38 (1976), pp. 275-92; *idem*, *The Pentateuch*, pp. 62, 186, 218; P.J. Kearney, 'Creation and Liturgy: The P Redaction of Ex. 25–40', *ZAW* 89 (1977), p. 375; M. Fishbane, *Text and Texture: Close Readings of Selected Biblical Texts* (New York: Schocken Books, 1979), pp. 11-13; M. Weinfeld, 'Sabbath, Temple and the Enthronement of the Lord', pp. 501-12; Levenson, *Creation and the Persistence of Evil*, pp. 78-87; W.W. Hallo, *The Book of the People* (BJS, 225; Atlanta: Scholars Press, 1991), p. 60; B. Batto, *Slaying the Dragon in the Biblical Tradition* (Louisville, KY: Westminster/John Knox Press, 1992), p. 120.

Genesis: while the account of Genesis marks the creation of the world, the creation language of Exodus 39–40 heralds the new creation of Israel's cultic life with its deity. As Chapters 7 and 9 note, proposals have been made for further echoes of Genesis 1 in the priestly plague materials in the first half of Exodus and in the tabernacle sections of the second half of Exodus. According to the priestly perspective, with the book of Exodus Israel enters into the cosmic plan which Yahweh laid out at the beginning of the world.

Chapter 3

PRAYER: POSTURES, GESTURES AND SACRIFICE

The journey to Israel's deity, whether at Jerusalem or Sinai, issues in
Yahweh's communication with the community through Temple theophanies, matched by the community's expressions made to Yahweh in
the Temple liturgy. Drawing primarily from Exodus and the Psalms,
this chapter presents a brief sampling of non-verbal postures, gestures
and sacrifices offered in response to the presence of Yahweh in the
sanctuary. Prayer and praise (in conjunction with music), postures and
gestures, and offerings and sacrifices were interrelated ritual expressions aimed at God. Prayer is verbal expression addressed to God and
it is often paralleled by the non-verbal communication of bodily postures and gestures.[1] Postures express the basic disposition of the individual toward the deity, and gestures are combined with postures to
express more specific nuances. A third dimension related to these two
forms of communication to God is sacrifices, which constitute communication mediated by a non-personal offering. As H.J. Levine remarks,
'sacrifice can be seen as both a substitution for the self and a contribution of the self'.[2] Ps. 141.2 reflects the perception that prayer and
gestures were considered comparable and connected systems of communication with Yahweh: 'Take my prayer as an offering of incense, my
upraised hands as an evening sacrifice' (NJPS).[3] Prayer and music,

1.   The basic study of postures and gestures remains M.I. Gruber, *Aspects of
Nonverbal Communication in the Ancient Near East* (2 vols.; Studia Pohl, 12.2;
Rome: Pontifical Biblical Institute, 1980). The following remarks on postures and
gestures represent only a very partial summary of Gruber's findings, with some
modifications.
2.   Levine, *Sing unto God a New Song*, p. 50.
3.   Gruber, *Aspects of Nonverbal Communication*, pp. 30-31. For the juxtaposition of prayer and offering as related systems of communication, see Foster, *Before
the Muses*, I, p. 314: 'Prayer to me was the natural recourse, sacrifice my rule'; II,
p. 582: 'Accept of me my flour offering, receive my plea.'

posture and gestures and sacrifice appear in conjunction, and they jointly reflect the attitudes and wishes of the human participants in ritual. Like prayers and praise, postures, gestures and sacrifices are used in individual and communal contexts. The three forms of communication seem to reflect a division of labor (in the post-exilic period at least): the (Aaronid) priesthood ran the sacrifices, while the Levites led the people in music and prayer.[4] All three forms of communication assume and express in varying ways and degrees the position of the prayer before God as servants before a king: Yahweh is the Divine King, and when Israelites enter the Temple to pray, they enter the divine palace on earth in order to be received into the presence of this King.[5]

1. *Postures*

Different postures correspond to various types of psalms: dancing for hymns of praise and thanksgiving; standing, and later kneeling, for prayer including communal lamentation; sitting in the dust for individual lamentation; prostration as expression of homage. The first three bodily postures and activities seem to reflect varying degrees of joy or distress. The fourth posture of prostration perhaps reflects subservience as a statement of homage to the superior party.

Dancing to Express Joy
Praise and joy inspire the non-verbal communication of dance.[6] Dancing is the polar opposite of lament: 'You turned my lament into dancing' (Ps. 30.12). Hymns call for 'dance... timbrel and lyre' (Ps. 149.2). Thanksgiving and hymns offered in the Jerusalem Temple were occasions for music and dance (Pss. 87.7a; 149.3; 150.4; Isa. 38.19-20; Jer. 30.19). Victory in battle would inspire a response of dance and music (Judg. 11.34; 1 Sam. 18.6; see also 2 Sam. 6.5, 12).

---

4. For the Aaronids and Levites, see the excursus to Chapter 10. For this 'hierarchy' as represented by the houses of Aaron and Levi, and 'you who fear Yahweh', cf. Ps. 135.19-20.

5. On this point, see Tigay, 'On Some Aspects of Prayer', pp. 363-79. For this conceptual framework, see Brettler, *God is King*.

6. M.I. Gruber, 'Ten Dance-Derived Expressions in the Hebrew Bible', *Bib* 62 (1981), pp. 328-46. In addition to praise and joy, Mowinckel stressed cultic dance's power to induce ecstasy. See Mowinckel, *The Psalms in Israel's Worship*, I, pp. 10-11.

The victory over the Egyptians at the Sea was recalled as celebrated by Miriam and the Israelite women in dance, music and song (Exod. 15.20).

Standing and Kneeling to Pray
One standard position for prayer is standing. This position before a superior such as God denotes standing in attendance, as a courtier stands before the king, or a servant waits on a master.[7] As her comment to the priest Eli indicates, Hannah had been in a standing position when she prayed to God for a son (1 Sam. 1.26). Solomon prays to God before all Israel in a standing position (1 Kgs 8.22). Standing is the appropriate stance for waiting for a theophany (1 Kgs 19.11; cf. Exod. 34.5). When the people experience the theophany of Yahweh on Mount Sinai, they stand: 'All the people witnessed the thunder and lightning, the blare of the horn and the mountain smoking; and when the people saw it, they fell back and stood at a distance' (Exod. 20.15; NJPS). Standing would appear to be the communal stance in the temple as well. Communal lament would take place standing (Neh. 9.1-3).

Individuals may pray on their knees (Dan. 6.11; Ezra 9.5). 1 Kgs 8.54 combines kneeling with hands outspread. Kneeling is a recognition of an inferior party's deference before a superior party. This posture derived from the royal court, where all defer in this manner before the king (except for his own family).

Prostration to Express Homage
Bowing down, with nose to the ground, is a common act of recognition and submission of a lesser party before a superior, whether that superior is another human being (so Gen. 43.28; 1 Sam. 24.9, 28.14; 1 Kgs 1.16, 31), a deity (Gen. 24.26, 48) or a deity and human together (1 Chron. 29.20).[8] Being at the feet of another is a sign of subordination (Ps. 8.7). This posture is well-known from the royal court, where lesser parties would bow before the king (1 Sam. 24.9, 28.14). This etiquette was expressed also in the heavenly court, where according to the Ugaritic texts deities bow down before the god, El.[9] When Yahweh, the ultimate superior party, or an angel, appears in a theo-

---

7. P.A. Kruger, 'Nonverbal Communication and Symbolic Gestures in the Psalms', *BT* 45 (1994), p. 219.

8. Gruber, *Aspects of Nonverbal Communication*, pp. 97-128.

9. See Smith, 'Divine Travel', p. 397.

phany, prostration is an appropriate human response (Exod. 33.10, 34.8-9; Josh. 7.6; 1 Kgs 18.42; Ps. 29.1-2; Ezek. 1.28; Dan. 10.9-10; *1 En.* 24.24; Rev. 1.17).[10] When they learn of Yahweh's care for them through Moses and Aaron, the Israelites bow down low to the ground as an act of acknowledgment and homage (Exod. 4.31; cf. 12.27). Later Moses bows down as he makes his petition on behalf of Israel before Yahweh (Exod. 34.8).

2. *Gestures*

Removal of Footware
Removing one's footware before entering the place of a divine appearance is a non-verbal recognition of that place's holiness. Exod. 3.5 records the divine command to Moses on Sinai: 'Do not come closer. Remove the sandals from your feet; for the place on which you stand is holy ground' (see also Josh. 5.15).[11]

Hands to Express Invocation
Standing in prayer may be accompanied by outstretched or uplifted hands (Exod. 9.29, 33; 1 Kgs 8.22; Isa. 1.15). The non-verbal communication of hands lifted is the physical way to express prayer as suggested by Ps. 28.2:[12]

> Listen to my plea for mercy
> When I cry out to You,
> When I lift my hands
> Toward Your inner sanctuary.

Other psalms likewise know the gesture of outstretched hands to express prayer (Ps. 44.21).

In Pss. 63.5, 134.2 and Neh. 8.6 the gesture is used to bless God, an act of praise. Ps. 63.5 reads:

> I bless You all my life;
> I lift up my hands, invoking Your name.[13]

---

10. L. Hartmann and A.A. Di Lella, *The Book of Daniel* (AB, 23; Garden City, NY: Doubleday, 1978), p. 281.

11. For the relationship between these passages, see the discussion in J. van Seters, *The Life of Moses: The Yahwist as Historian in Exodus–Numbers* (Louisville, KY: Westminster/John Knox Press, 1994), pp. 37-38.

12. Gruber, *Aspects of Nonverbal Communication*, p. 34.

13. Gruber, *Aspects of Nonverbal Communication*, p. 34.

As the gesture is used for both prayer and praise,[14] it may be inferred that the purpose is not specific to either; rather, another basic purpose common to both underlies the gesture. It may be that the gesture in Ps. 63.5 is intended to draw God's attention. In other words, it corresponds to the verbal act of invoking God's name, an act which occurs in both prayer and praise. Job 11.13 seems to describe the non-verbal act of spreading the hands as the beginning point for addressing Yahweh: 'But if you direct your mind,/And spread forth your hands toward Him'.[15]

Washing Hands to Express Personal Innocence
Washing with water expresses externally an internal washing of the self. So Ps. 73.13 proclaims: 'I. . . washed my hands in innocence' (cf. Ps. 26.6). According to P.A. Kruger, this gesture was imported from legal usage (Deut. 21.6-7).[16]

Kissing to Express Loyalty
A kiss may serve as a gesture of loyalty of deities (1 Kgs 19.18; Hos. 3.2). Kisses to other humans are a mark of affectionate relations (Exod. 4.27; cf. Ps. 2.12).

Hiding the Face to Express Fear of Divine Presence
Before a theophany, worshippers may hide their faces in fear of its power (Exod. 3.6).

Before proceeding to sacrifices, it should be noted that music functioned to extend the expression of words, gestures and postures. Communal music was common for hymns and psalms of thanksgiving, while silence or quiet was expected of lamentation (1 Sam. 1.9-15). Accordingly, in Psalm 137, as the community laments its exile from Jerusalem, it sets aside its harps and cannot honor the request of its captors to sing one of the songs of Zion. Similarly, Job sits silently in lament over his affliction (Job 2.10), and his friends who had come to comfort him respond only in silence, 'for they saw how very great was his suffering' (Job 2.13; NJPS). In sum, laments, tears, sitting and silence are the polar opposites of hymns, laughter, dancing and music, which are often accompanied by sacrifices.

---

14. Kruger, 'Nonverbal Communication', p. 215.
15. Gruber, *Aspects of Nonverbal Communication*, p. 31.
16. Kruger, 'Nonverbal Communication', p. 220.

3. *Sacrifices*

The end of Exodus 20 (v. 21) provides a description of the communication between Yahweh and the Israelites[17]:

> Make for Me an altar of earth and sacrifice on it your burnt offerings
> (עולות) and your sacrifices of well-being (שלמים) with your sheep and
> oxen; at every cult-place where I cause my name to be called on I will
> come to you and I will bless you.

This passage requires the Israelite community to offer communication by means of presenting sacrifices and calling on the name of Yahweh, and in turn Yahweh promises presence and blessing. Sacrifices form part of the human-divine system of communication.[18] The main types of sacrifices can be noted for their own particular messages.

עולה

This sacrifice is the first one mentioned in the quotation above. It is usually understood as a 'burnt' offering or 'holocaust', as it is completely consumed by fire. On the semantic level, the word refers to something that 'goes up'. According to B.A. Levine, the sacrifice ascends to heaven as an 'attraction and invocation' in order to gain Yahweh's attention.[19] This understanding fits Exod. 20.21, and it is evident in 1 Kings 18 as well where Elijah and the prophets of Baal compete to gain the attention of their deity. This sort of sacrifice is ordained also for the pilgrimage festivals. As noted by Levine, this sacrifice precedes שלמים ('sacred gifts of greeting') in composite sacrifical rites.[20] Levine comments further:

> the deity had first to be attracted to the site and to indicate his readiness to
> descend and respond before humans could bring their petitions before
> him. . . The pleasing aroma of the burnt, altar offering rose heavenward,

17. B.A. Levine, '*Lpny YHWH*—Phenomenology of the Open-Air-Altar in Biblical Israel', *Biblical Archaeology Today 1990: Proceedings of the Second International Congress on Biblical Archaeology* (Jerusalem: Israel Exploration Society, 1992), p. 202.

18. For a helpful summary of Israelite sacrifice with some fine insights drawn from anthropological literature, see Nelson, *Raising Up a Faithful Priest*, pp. 55-82.

19. Levine, *In the Presence of the Lord*, pp. 22-27; *idem*, '*Lpny YHWH*', p. 201, citing Judg. 13.20 as an aetiology assuming this understanding.

20. Levine, '*Lpny YHWH*', p. 202.

taking over the vertical dimension [from incense offerings], while incense was moved indoors (or nearer the cult object representing the deity outdoors), and its function was horizontalized, so to speak. Incense now pleased the deity who had already arrived at the site![21]

Perhaps the עולה sacrifice then serves a function corresponding to verbal invocation of the deity: both are designed to attract the deity's attention. The response may be theophanic in character: 'A fire came forth from before Yahweh and consumed the burnt offering (עולה) and the fat parts on the altar. And all the people saw, and shouted, and fell on their faces' (Lev. 9.24; cf. NJPS).

מנחה

This sacrifice is usually known as the 'cereal offering', but outside the sacrificial context, מנחה may mean 'tribute' (see 2 Sam. 8.10; Ps. 72.10; Zeph. 3.10).[22] The sacrifice on this semantic level represents the submission of its offerer before the superior party, Yahweh. It 'connotes a gift to the deity in cultic terminology'.[23] It roughly corresponds then to prayer expressing the subordinate status of the speaker vis-à-vis the deity.

שלמים

This sacrifice, the so-called 'peace-offerings' (Lev. 3), accompanied great celebrations.[24] It was the central sacrifice in the inauguration of the Jerusalem Temple (1 Kgs 8.62-63). Levine deduces:

we see the *šᵉlāmîm* as originally a sacrifice related to royal and/or national celebrations of a distinctive character, and which only subsequently became incorporated into the regular cult.[25]

Underlying the entire history of the *šᵉlāmîm*, with its development in Israel, is the notion of sacrifice as an efficacious gift of greeting, offered 'in the presence of the Lord'.[26]

21. Levine, '*Lpny YHWH*', p. 202.
22. See Levine, *In the Presence of the Lord*, pp. 16-17; G.A. Anderson, *Sacrifices and Offerings in Ancient Israel: Studies in their Social and Political Importance* (HSM, 41; Atlanta: Scholars Press, 1987), pp. 27-34.
23. See Levine, *In the Presence of the Lord*, p. 16.
24. See Levine, *In the Presence of the Lord*, pp. 27-35.
25. See Levine, *In the Presence of the Lord*, p. 34. See also pp. 45-52.
26. Levine, *In the Presence of the Lord*, p. 52. See further Levine, '*Lpny YHWH*', p. 202.

Like praise, and more specifically thanksgiving and hymns, communal
שלמים-offerings express homage and greeting to the deity. (This function would fit Exod. 20.21 quoted above.) Individuals used this sort of
offering to repay vows, to make a thanksgiving offering or the נדבה,
the so-called 'volunteer' or 'generous' offering (Lev. 7.11-38; cf.
Prov. 7.14).[27]

חטאת

The purification-offering (literally, the 'sin-offering', in the sense of
removing it) is designed to rid persons of sin or places of contamina-
tion caused by human sin.[28] According to Numbers 28–29, the חטאת
was offered on every annual occasion in order to achieve the community's purified state. It was also used for specific, individual purposes,
for example, for purification of someone with a skin ailment (Lev.
14.1-32) or a woman after childbirth (Lev. 12.6-8).[29]

The sacrificial offerings were designed generally for celebrations (Joel
1.13). According to priestly instruction-literature, מנחה, עולה and
חטאת sacrifices were ordained for all three of the pilgrimage-feasts as
well as other annual events on the cultic calendar (Num. 28.16–29.29).
Jointly the three sacrifices may have represented a standard priestly
repertoire designed to invoke the attention of Yahweh (עולה), to express the subordinate status of the worshipper (מנחה), and to purify
the worshipper (חטאת). Leviticus 1–5 presents in order עולה (Lev. 1),
מנחה (Lev. 2), שלמים (Lev. 3), and חטאת (Lev. 4.1–5.13).[30] In terms
of the functions which each of these sacrifices signal by their name,
the order may be viewed as corresponding roughly to a typical order
of prayer: both begin with invocation, followed by statements of
homage and greeting to the deity (especially in the form of praise) and
request for forgiveness from sins in order to restore the relationship

---

27. Levine, *In the Presence of the Lord*, pp. 42-43.
28. See N. Kiuchi, *The Purification Offering in the Priestly Literature: Its Meaning and Function* (JSOTSup, 56; Sheffield: JSOT Press, 1987). For historical and
archaeological considerations regarding this sort of sacrifice, see Z. Zevit, 'Philology, Archaeology, and a *Terminus a Quo* for the P's *ḥaṭṭā't* Legislation', in Wright,
Freedman and Hurvitz (eds.), *Pomegranates and Golden Bells:*, pp. 29-38.
29. Levine, *In the Presence of the Lord*, pp. 111-12.
30. To which the אשם-offering (the so-called 'guilt'-offering) has been attached
(Lev. 5.14-16). For their relationship, see Levine, *In the Presence of the Lord*,
p. 109.

between the community and its deity.[31] Both verbal expressions of prayer and praise and the non-verbal expressions of postures, gestures and sacrifices were means to convey the community's intentions to repair and advance relations between Israelites and their Divine King. To cite Levine once more, 'sacrificial worship... occurs anew each time the deity is ritually invoked, or attracted. This is what is meant to say that a worshipper stood *lpny YHWH* in the presence of YHWH.'[32]

31. Cf. Blenkinsopp, *Sage, Priest, Prophet*, p. 97.
32. Levine, *'Lpny YHWH'*, p. 204.

Chapter 4

PILGRIMAGE AS PARADIGM FOR ISRAEL

The preceding chapters describe how, when and where pilgrimages
were made in ancient Israel, and they illustrate the impact of this historical practice on various passages in Exodus. Yet pilgrimage was not
only a religious practice. It also served as a literary paradigm for expressing future aspirations, present wishes and past identity. As noted
in Part 3 below, this use of pilgrimage as a literary pattern applies to
Exodus.

1. *Pilgrimage Future*

Three sorts of future pilgrimage are described in the prophetic books:
Israelite pilgrims journeying within Israel, Israelite pilgrims travelling
from outside Israel and the pilgrims of the nations travelling from
outside Israel. Jeremiah 31 describes the first two in tandem (NJPS):

I will build you firmly again,
O Maiden Israel!
Again you shall take up your timbrels
And go forth to the rhythm of the dancers.
Again you shall plant vineyards
On the hills of Samaria;
Men shall plant and live to enjoy them.
For the day is coming when watchmen
Shall proclaim of the heights of Ephraim:
Come, let us go up to Zion, to the Lord our God!

For thus said the Lord:
Cry out in joy for Jacob,
Shout out at the crossroads of the nations!
Sing aloud in praise, and say:
Save, O Lord, Your people,
The remnant of Israel.
I will bring them in from the northland,

Gather them from the ends of the earth. . .
They shall come with weeping
And with compassion will I guide them.
I will lead them to streams of water,
By a level road where they will not stumble,
For I am ever a Father to Israel,
Ephraim is My first-born.

The first part of this passage describes the restoration of the land, which in turn results in the restoration of the pilgrimage to Jerusalem. The second part predicts the divine restoration of exiled Israelites back to the land.[1] This progression resembles a pilgrimage, with Yahweh as the guide. Like the divine shepherd of Psalm 23 (discussed in the next section), Yahweh will lead the exiles to streams of water and the road will be made level to ease their travel. In sum, return from exile is construed as making pilgrimage.

In a well-known book, *The Exodus Pattern in the Bible*,[2] D. Daube explored the use of the Exodus as a pattern or paradigm elsewhere in the Bible. The connection of Exodus with return from exile appears in Mic. 7.15 and Zech. 10.8-12. Perhaps the most dramatic instance of the exodus theme with the return of the exiles from the nations appears in Isa. 43.16-21, as D. Daube, M. Fishbane and others have observed.[3] 'Second Isaiah'[4] is drawing, however, on the wider reservoir of pilgrimage imagery. Like Jeremiah 31, Isaiah 40 evokes the glorious

---

1. For the relations between these two parts of Jer. 31, see R.P. Carroll, *Jeremiah: A Commentary* (OTL; Philadelphia: Westminster, 1986), pp. 586-95.

2. D. Daube, *The Exodus Pattern in the Bible* (All Souls Studies, 2; London: Faber & Faber, 1963).

3. M. Fishbane, *Biblical Interpretation in Ancient Israel* (Oxford: Clarendon Press, 1986), pp. 363-64.

4. I place this well-known scholarly designation for Isa. 40–55 in quotation marks to indicate that this section, while representing a clear unit in Isaiah, has complex redactional relations with the rest of the book; the authors of this redactional activity did not regard 'Second Isaiah' as separate. See, for example, H.J. Hermisson, 'Einheit und Komplexität Deuterojesajas: Probleme der Redaktionsgeschichte von Jes. 40–55', in J. Vermeylen (ed.), *The Book of Isaiah. Le livre d'Isaïe: Les oracles et leur relectures: Unité et complexité de l'ouvrage* (BETL, 81; Leuven: Leuven University Press/Peeters, 1989), pp. 287-312; C.R. Seitz, *Zion's Final Destiny: The Development of the Book of Isaiah. A Reassessment of Isaiah 36–39* (Minneapolis: Fortress Press, 1991), pp. 196-208. As this issue specifically involves Isa. 40, see also C. Seitz, 'The Divine Council: Temporal Transition and New Prophecy in the Book of Isaiah', *JBL* 109 (1990), pp. 229-46.

restoration of the exiles. This chapter opens with the proclamation of the good news that a road is to be cleared in the wilderness (v. 3). On this road made level (as in the end of the section of Jer. 31 quoted above), the divine presence will progress with the exiles. Like the picture of Psalm 23, in Isa. 40.11, Yahweh will be the divine shepherd who will lead the sheep home. Just as 'Second Isaiah' begins with an evocation of the pilgrimage of the exiles back to the land, so this unit ends in this manner. Isaiah 55 contains three fundamental aspects of pilgrimage: journey, divine word and meal. Verses 1-5 contain a call to a meal. H.C. Spykerboer has argued that this invocation is precisely for a pilgrimage meal in Jerusalem, 'the new, restored city of abundance where God reigns as King'.[5] The second part of Isaiah 55, verses 6-11, present the divine word.[6] The third part of the chapter, namely vv. 12-13, places this conjunction of meal and law as the end-point of a pilgrimage. In sum, the return from exile frames 'Second Isaiah', and it does so in the language and imagery of the pilgrimage pattern.[7] To return to Daube's proposal, the exodus is the specific antecedent cited in Isaiah 43 to render the divine restoration of Israelites from among the nations, but Jeremiah 31 and the beginning and end of 'Second Isaiah' would suggest that fundamental to both exodus and return from exile is the pilgrimage paradigm. In both journeys God will be the Israelites' guide, leading them to the mountain where they will have rest from their enemies, plenty of food and drink to feast on, and repose in the divine presence. Underlying the exodus traditions is what I would call Israel's pilgrimage pattern, playing on Daube's expression, 'the Exodus pattern'. To anticipate a central point of this study, the book of Exodus reflects the pilgrimage patttern.

That the exodus was rendered in terms of pilgrimage is evident from Ps. 78.19-20. Describing the Israelites in the wilderness, the two verses recount (NJPS):

> They spoke against God, saying,
> 'Can God spread a feast in the wilderness?
> True, He struck rock and waters flowed,

---

5.   Spykerboer, 'Isaiah 55.1-5: The Climax of Deutero-Isaiah; An Invitation to Come to the New Jerusalem', in Vermeylen (ed.), *The Book of Isaiah*, p. 357.

6.   With the clusters of the Hebrew consonants שׁ and ב echoing the message of שׁוּב*, 'to return' (to Yahweh)?

7.   For proposed connections between Second Isaiah and Sukkot psalms, see the forthcoming studies of J.J. Ferrie, Jr. For the Sukkot psalms, see above Chapter 1.

    streams gushed forth;
    but can He provide bread?
    Can He supply His people with meat?'

Some scholars have argued that these verses' evocation of the exodus
served as the basis for the linkage of the divine images of shepherd
and host in Psalm 23.[8] However, to anticipate the next section, it would
appear that both Pss. 23.5 and 78.19-20 draw on pilgrimage ideas. In
the pilgrimage paradigm, Yahweh is both shepherd and host.[9] In sum,
the Bible shows many variations on the pilgrimage paradigm, which
served as the foundation for, and was in some texts transmuted into,
Daube's 'exodus pattern'.

The Israelites' return from exile was sometimes not rendered specifically in terms of the pilgrimage journey, but instead borrowed on the
imagery associated with pilgrimage harvests. Here the imagery is highly
evocative in using pilgrimage harvests to describe national restoration.
The national restoration predicted in Amos 9.11-15 evokes verbal associations with the feast of Booths (Sukkot). This resonance might be felt
first in v. 11's reference to the restoration of the Davidic dynasty:

    In that day I will set up again the fallen booth (סכה) of David. . .

The time of the Sukkot harvest of the grapes resonates then throughout
vv. 13-15:

    A time is coming—declares the Lord—
    When the plowman shall meet the reaper,
    And the treader of grapes
    Him who holds the [bag of] seed;
    When the mountains shall drip wine
    And all the hills shall wave [with grain].

---

8.   D.N. Freedman, 'The Twenty-Third Psalm', in L. Orlin (ed.), *Michigan
Studies in Honor of George G. Cameron* (Ann Arbor: University of Michigan Press,
1976), pp. 139-66; M.L. Barré and J.S. Kselman, 'New Exodus, Covenant, and
Restoration in Psalm 23', in C.L. Meyers and M. O'Connor (eds.), *The Word of the
Lord Shall Go Forth: Essays in Honor of David Noel Freedman in Celebration of
his Sixtieth Birthday* (ASOR Special Volume Series, I; Philadelphia: ASOR, 1983),
p. 97. For discussion and criticism, see Pardee, 'Structure and Meaning in Hebrew
Poetry: The Example of Psalm 23', in Cook (ed.), *Sopher Mahir*, pp. 276-67.
9.   As A. Cooper notes, this connection was made already in Exodus Rabba
25.7. See Cooper, 'Structure, Midrash and Meaning: The Case of Psalm 23', in
*Proceedings of the World Congress of Jewish Studies: Jerusalem, August 4–12,
1985. Division A. The Period of the Bible* (Jerusalem: World Union of Jewish
Studies, 1986), p. 109.

> I will restore My people Israel.
> They shall rebuild ruined cities and inhabit them;
> They shall plant vineyards and drink their wine;
> They shall till gardens and eat their fruits.
> And I will plant them upon their soil,
> Nevermore to be uprooted
> From the soil I have given them—said the Lord your God.

The future restoration, miraculous in the prosperous, abundant harvests, will be the time of Israel's restoration. The Israelites will replant and rebuild, and again here the crops emphasized are those of the late summer harvest. The final image of v. 15 nicely uses the imagery of planting vineyards and drinking wine to describe Israel's restoration. In sum, Amos 9.11-15 is laced with the imagery of the grape harvest associated with Sukkot.

Psalm 126.3-6 likewise draws on the pilgrimage harvest in evoking the joy anticipated in the return to Jerusalem (NJPS):

> Restore our fortunes, O Lord,
> like watercourses in the Negeb.
> Those who sow in tears
> shall reap with songs of joy.
> Though he goes along weeping,
> carrying the seed-bag,
> he shall come back with songs of joy,
> carrying his sheaves.

Here the agricultural cycle illustrates the cycle of national experience which, the speakers pray, will now be made complete: now the joy of harvest will inform the returns of the exiles. The paradigm running beneath the surface of this prayer is the pilgrimage at harvest time: now the Israelites will make the pilgrimage home to Jerusalem.

In addition to Israelites inside and outside of the land, a third group of persons called to make the pilgrimage in future expressions of restoration are the nations. According to Zech. 14.16 all the nations will make the pilgrimage to Jerusalem for the feast of Booths (Sukkot). This pilgrimage issues in the exaltation of Israel, which is to be recognized as Yahweh's chosen among the nations (see also Zeph. 3.8-13).[10] Isa. 25.6-8 describes the future restoration on God's holy mountain in paradisial terms—for both the peoples generally and for God's own

---

10. Whether or not this third type of future pilgrimage is related to an older practice of vassals paying homage to the Judean monarch is discussed in Chapter 2.

chosen people. This passage describes the final victory over Death and the great banquet to follow on God's holy mountain (NJPS):

> The Lord of Hosts will make on this mount
> For all the peoples
> A banquet of rich viands,
> A banquet of choice wines—
> Of rich viands seasoned with marrow,
> Of choice wines well refined.
> And He will destroy on this mount the shroud
> That is drawn over the faces of all the peoples
> And the covering that is spread
> Over all the nations:
> He will destroy death forever.
> My Lord God will wipe away tears from all faces
> And will put an end to the reproach of His people
> Over all the earth—
> For it is the Lord who has spoken.

The great banquet and defeat of death awaits both faithful Israelites and the other nations on the holy mountain. Sometimes as in this passage, the pilgrimage of the peoples to Jerusalem witnesses to the glory of Israel. Sometimes, however, the journey of the nations to attack Jerusalem issues in their condemnation, again employing the agricultural imagery of the harvest (Joel 3.9-13; Mic. 4.11-13).[11] In sum, the end of the future pilgrimage will know a restored, even miraculous Jerusalem. This city, God's holy mountain, will be the site of the pilgrimage banquet of banquets.

2. *Pilgrimage Present*

There is one very well-known psalm that uses the pilgrimage paradigm to describe the ideal life with a kind of depth otherwise unattested in biblical literature. This text is Psalm 23.[12]

---

11. For the use of the agricultural imagery in divine warfare, see R.M. Good, 'Metaphorical Gleanings from Ugarit', *JJS* 33 (1982 = Essays in Honor of Yigael Yadin), pp. 55-59; Smith, *The Early History of God*, pp. 63-64.

12. The bibliography is immense. I have consulted the following works (in addition to others cited below): Barré and Kselman, 'New Exodus, Covenant, and Restoration in Psalm 23', pp. 97-127; A. Cooper, 'Structure, Midrash and Meaning', pp. 107-14; O. Loretz, '*Marziḥu* im ugaritischen und biblischen Ahnenkult; Zu

Superscription
Type of Composition:
1. A song
   Putative Authorship:
   Of David.

Poem
Topic Sentence:

1. Yahweh is my shepherd,	I have no want.

God as Shepherd:

2. In green pastures	He lies me down,
3. Beside still waters	He leads me,
	He restores my soul.
He leads me in right paths,	For His name's sake.
4. Even though I walk	Through the darkest valley,
I fear no evil,	For You are with me,
Your rod and staff,	They comfort me.

God as Host:

5. You prepare a table before me,	Before my enemies.
You anoint my head with oil,	My cup overflows.
6. Surely goodness and mercy	
shall follow me,	All the days of my life,
And may I dwell	
in the house of Yahweh,	For the length of my days.

NOTES TO TRANSLATION

v. 3a: Held ('Hebrew *ma'gal*: A Study in Lexical Parallelism', *JANESCU* 6 [1974], p. 111) perhaps rightly regarded the line as 'a metrically defective hemistich.' Pardee's attempt to take v. 3 as a tricolon falters on two counts: the second line is disturbingly longer than the first (see Pardee, 'Structure and Meaning in Hebrew Poetry', pp. 275-80, esp. p. 250. The same problem afflicts Pardee's attempt to take

---

Ps. 23; 133; Am. 6. 1-7 und Jer. 16.5-8', in M. Dietrich and O. Loretz (eds.), *Meso-potamia–Ugaritica–Biblica: Festschrift für Kurt Bergerhof zur Vollendung seines 70. Lebensjahres am 7. Mai 1992* (AOAT, 232; Kevelaer: Butzon & Bercker; Neu-kirchen–Vluyn: Neukirchener Verlag, 1993), pp. 94-144; C. O'Connor, 'The Struc-ture of Psalm 23', *Louvain Studies* 10.3 (1984), pp. 206-30; D. Pardee, 'Structure and Meaning in Hebrew Poetry', pp. 275-80; M.S. Smith, *Psalms: The Divine Journey*, pp. 63-65; idem, 'Setting and Rhetoric in Psalm 23', *JSOT* 41 (1988) pp. 61-66; N.A. van Uchelen, 'Psalm xxiii. Some Regulative Linguistic Evidence', *OTS* 25 (1989), pp. 156-62.

v. 4b as a tricolon.) By way of content, v. 3a seems to follow the preceding line in v. 2c, and v. 3c seems to follow v. 3b.

v. 3b: The final clause means 'as befits His name' (so Held, 'Hebrew *ma'gal*', p. 111).

v. 4a: 'Valley of death' is perhaps a folk-etymology of this word which may originally have meant 'deep darkness' (see Lewis, *Cults*, pp. 11-12 n. 24). Could this folk-etymology have been ancient?

v. 4b: 'They comfort me' may seem unlikely for 'staff and rod', and as a result commentators have emended to the similar-looking verb נחה*, 'to lead', which suits the sense of the passage quite well. Word-play may be at work here, however, with נחה*, already used in v. 3b (cf. Kraus, *Psalms 1–59*, p. 304). This word-play of verbal roots extends also to נוח* in v. 2b.

v. 5a: See the discussion below in the following section.

v. 6b: MT וְשַׁבְתִּי is pointed as the converted suffix form of שׁוּב*, 'to return', but this root plus the preposition -בּ for -places is otherwise unknown, leading commentators to consider versional evidence, perhaps either the infinitive construct, *wešibtî* (< ישׁב*), 'my dwelling', based on LXX, or a converted perfect, *wᵉyāšabtî*, based on the Vulgate and other versions. The infinitive construct assumes a nominal sentence which departs from recognized poetic style, and the converted perfect *wᵉyāšabtî* adds a consonant to the text otherwise unknown, although it would be possible to reread the word as *yāsᵉbtî* by seeing the initial waw as yodh, a confusion well-known in the DSS. Kraus (*Psalms 1–59*, p. 304) tries to retain the MT by translating 'I will remain', but this translation is forced and semantically approximates ישׁב* more closely than שׁוּב*. M.L. Barré ('An Unrecognized Precative Particle in Phoenician and Hebrew', *Bib* 64 [1983], p. 416) has read the form as the 'precative perfect' of ישׁב*, but *šabtî* would not suit the proposed form as argued by Barré; rather *yašabtî* would be required. The attempt to posit ישׁב* is supported by grammar (noted above) and the comparable usage in Ps 27.4b, but an acceptable form of this verb cannot be achieved without emendation (see Pardee, 'Structure and Meaning in Hebrew Poetry', p. 241) or a hypothetical positing of *šabtî* as an otherwise unknown biform of this root. In either case, the reading of the form as a precative perfect is suggested on formal grounds. If the psalm is a song of trust, as is commonly claimed, then it should contain a request and this verb is the only candidate. It is important to observe that the poet perhaps plays on traditional themes as in v. 4b. I would see שׁוּב* here as a word-play on ישׁובב*, 'he restores', in v. 3a: Yahweh restores the speaker (v. 3a), as the speaker dwells in Yahweh's house (v. 6b).

The final phrase has no personal suffix, but perhaps the personal suffix in the preceding line ('all the days of my life') serves double-duty. 'Length of days' is an indeterminate amount of time stretching into the future. As a parallel with 'days of life', 'length of days' appears in royal blessings, such as Ps. 21.5 and the Karatepe inscription (KAI 26 A III 2-7) use the word-pair, *ḥyym*, 'life', and *'rk ymm*, 'length of days' (see Barré, 'An Unrecognised Precative Particle', p. 180). Parallels are noted also in Quintens, 'La vie du roi dans le Psaume 21', *Bib* 59 (1978), pp. 384-400. Cf. Tell Siran bottle inscription, ll. 6-8, for which see W.E. Aufrecht, *A Corpus of Ammonite Inscriptions* (Lewiston, NY: Edwin Mellen, 1989), pp. 202-11; cf.

K. Beyer, 'The Ammonite Tell Siran Bottle Inscription Reconsidered', in Z. Zevit,
S. Gitin and M. Sokoloff (eds.), חיים ליונה *Solving Riddles and Untying Knots:
Biblical, Epigraphic, and Semitic Studies in Honor of Jonas C. Greenfield* (Winona
Lake, IN: Eisenbrauns, 1995), pp. 389-91.

In expressing trust in Yahweh, this most beloved of psalms presents
two images for this deity which have been thought generally to correspond to the two sections in the psalm. The first major part, usually
taken as vv. 1-4, depicts Yahweh as shepherd, while the second section,
vv. 5-6, construes Yahweh as host.[13] While the two roles of shepherd
and host are almost universally recognized,[14] the relationship of the
two images to one another is a matter of debate. One common approach
to this problem is to see the shepherd and host images as royal in background, since both images are commonly applied to ancient Near
Eastern monarchs.[15] This reading is somewhat unsatisfying, however,
as it bears little on the relationship between the two sections, the movement of the psalm or the reference to the Temple in the final verse. A
different approach addressing these issues would follow the lead of
many later generations of readers,[16] for whom the psalm presents

13. A. Cooper divides the poem into two balanced units, vv. 2-4 and 5-6, with
v. 1 as the topic sentence governing the two parts: v. 1a refers to vv. 2-4 and v. 1b to
vv. 5-6. See Cooper, 'Structure, Midrash and Meaning', p. 111. I would, however,
take issue with his theory of the poem. Cooper's attempt to see in Psalm 23 'a poetic/
midrashic reflection on the life of Jacob' is likewise uncompelling on many grounds,
including the reference to the temple. Moreover, some of the counts of lines (p. 111)
belie the great differences in line-length. N.A. van Uchelen rightly notes the syntactical similarity between v. 1b and 4c as well as 2a and 4b (van Uchelen, 'Psalm xxiii.
Some Regulative Linguistic Evidence', pp. 156-62). He labels these two nominal
clauses as the topics of two sections, implying a division of the psalm into two sections, namely vv. 1-4b and 4c-6; I find the separation of v. 4c from the rest of the
verse unpersuasive.

14. For a dissenting voice, see M. Weiss, 'Psalm 23: The Psalmist on God's
Care', in Fishbane and Tov with Fields (eds.), *'Sha'arei Talmon': Studies in the
Bible, Qumran and the Ancient Near East*, pp. 31*-41*.

15. Barré and Kselman, 'New Exodus, Covenant, and Restoration in Psalm 23',
pp. 97-127; Pardee, 'Structure and Meaning in Hebrew Poetry', pp. 279-80; W.L.
Holladay, *The Psalms through Three Thousand Years*, p. 9. The reference to enemies is so common in the Psalms that it need not imply a specifically royal background.

16. See the inspiring survey of Holladay, *The Psalms through Three Thousand
Years*, esp. pp. 6-14 and 359-71.

pilgrimage as a paradigm for life.[17] Verses 2-4 present Yahweh as the shepherd who leads the psalmist on the pilgrimage-journey, while vv. 5-6 depict Yahweh as the host who cares for the psalmist at the conclusion of the pilgrimage in the Temple.

It is very difficult to pin down the historical backdrop of Psalm 23, and there is a good reason for this problem: the psalm lacks explicit historical and geographical references because it evokes the personal or internally oriented, spiritual experience of pilgrimage. Ps. 23.1-4 renders the pilgrimage-journey to the house of Yahweh, the Temple, and vv. 5-6 describe the psalmist's experience of God in the Temple. Comparing Psalm 23 with psalms that explicitly mention the pilgrimage suggests that Psalm 23 draws on the imagery of the pilgrimage in several ways. First, like Ps. 42.4, Psalm 23 names the Temple as the goal of the journey. Second, Psalm 23 refers to being led by God in vv. 2-3, and Ps. 43.3 implores God to send out the Divine Light and Truth to lead the pilgrim to Jerusalem. Third, like Ps. 42.5, Ps. 23.2 refers to the watering places that pilgims visit on their way to God. Finally, and most importantly, the spiritual states of the psalmists are mentioned in Ps. 23.3 and in the three-fold refrain of Pss. 42.5, 11 and 43.5. More specifically, both pilgrimage psalms and Psalm 23 reflect on how nature symbolizes the spiritual life of the psalmist. In Ps. 42.7-8, the waters of the springs remind the psalmist how threatening the waters of chaos are.

To an even greater degree than Psalms 42–43, Psalm 23 merges the psalmist's self-perceptions with the experience on the physical journey. The external experience includes pastures in v. 1 and waters in v. 2, the valley in v. 4, the table of God in v. 5 and the house of God in v. 6. All of these external phenomena are placed within the larger context of the psalmist's spiritual experience: the pastures and waters of vv. 1-2 belong to the psalmist's experience of divine guidance; the valley in v. 4 expresses divine protection against the worst threat even unto death; and the divine table and house in vv. 5-6 are sign and symbol of being enveloped in the divine presence. Because of this reframing of physical experience in terms of spiritual experience, Psalm 23 is, in many respects, a model pilgrimage-psalm. Other pilgrimage psalms balance the specific references to the historical or geographical world around them with allusion to the psalmists' personal perceptions, but

17. Smith, *Psalms: The Divine Journey*, pp. 64-65; *idem*, 'Setting and Rhetoric in Psalm 23', pp. 61-66.

Psalm 23 makes the personal perspective of the spiritual journey into the focal point. The pilgrimage is rendered precisely as a personal one in conjunction with the community of other pilgrims. Psalm 23 conveys the external world through a personal or spiritually oriented perspective and therefore conveys the world as it truly is, in the midst of an ongoing transformation by God.

Psalm 23 is a peaceful psalm for readers in part because it contains restful images. Readers transfer the sense of peace from the speaker's voice to their own as they pray, read and contemplate the words of the psalm. The peaceful, consoling character of the pilgrimage in Psalm 23 extends even to the psalm's structure. Each section of the poem correspond to different aspects of divine protection during the pilgrimage. The opening section, vv. 1-3, depicts God before the speaker, leading and protecting the psalmist. The middle of the poem, v. 4, describes God with the psalmist. The last two verses of the psalm, vv. 5-6, show the psalmist being followed by Divine Goodness and Mercy. Thus the structure of the poem, beginning, middle and end, corresponds to how the Divine Presence surrounds the speaker: before the psalmist in the initial section, with the psalmist in the central verse and after the psalmist in the final verses. This structure of protection is echoed through several wordplays: Yahweh restores (שוב*) the speaker in v. 3a who either dwells (ישב*) or returns (שוב*) in v. 6b to the presence of Yahweh in the Temple all the days of his life. The divine leadership (נחה*) in v. 3b is extended to function as a form of consolation (נחם*) in v. 4b and restfulness (נוח*) in v. 2b (which is combined with a further echo in 'He leads me', נחל*). Yahweh as 'shepherd' (רעי) in v. 1b offers protection against 'evil' (רע) in v. 4a and therefore the speaker does 'not fear' (אירא). The psalmist ends with an expression of hope meant to last an entire human lifetime, and that expression belongs to the speaker and audiences alike.

While fully steeped in the imagery of pilgrimage psalms, Psalm 23 also transcends the genre of pilgrimage psalms. The final verse gives the clue to this feature, for it notes that this pilgrimage is the pilgrimage not of a single feast. Rather, the pilgrimage is the pilgrimage of a person's entire life:[18] 'Surely goodness and mercy shall follow me, All the days of my life. And may I dwell in the house of the Lord for the length of my days.' Psalm 23 ends in such a way as to suggest that the

---

18. Alonso Schökel, *A Manual*, p. 198; Smith, *Psalms: The Divine Journey*, pp. 64-65; *idem*, 'Setting and Rhetoric in Psalm 23', pp. 61-66.

pilgrimage is not only a single or annual experience. The psalm expresses the view of the pilgrimage as a model for the psalmist's life. Pilgrimage becomes a vehicle for describing life as a whole in the presence of Yahweh.

3. *Pilgrimage Past*

Just as Israelite texts used pilgrimage to express their future return home and their exaltation over the nations as well as their present aspirations, so they also drew on the reservoir of pilgrimage motifs in order to describe the relations between their ancient forbears and their God. The book of Genesis occasionally uses the language of pilgrimage in the travels of the patriarchs. Both the Abraham cycle (Genesis 12–25) and the Jacob cycle (Genesis 26–36) are structured around journeys which are marked by stops at cult sites, many of which ancient Israelites knew later as pilgrimage destinations. The two cycles are parallel in the itineraries of these two patriarchs, both inside the land at sanctuary-sites (Beersheba, Shechem, Bethel, Mamre) and outside of it (Haran).[19] I would like to look at a few stories influenced by the pilgrimage paradigm. Genesis 22, known in Jewish tradition as the Akedah ('the binding' of Isaac),[20] might be characterized as an anti-pilgrimage. The stories in Genesis 28 and 32.23-33 do not involve pilgrimage in a strict sense, but in the context of Jacob's journey back to the land, these stops occur at momentous points of transition in and out of the

---

19. The cycles are further parallel in their family structures, except Jacob's is doubled that of Abraham: Jacob has two wives and two concubines, while Abraham has one of each (though, to be sure, on the point of his one wife and her twin children Isaac occupies a middle point). No separate Isaac cycle survived the later shaping of Genesis, unless one so regards the restricted 25.19–28.5, but even in these stories he appears largely either as Abraham's young son or as Jacob's old father. Rather, in the present form of the literature he is a connecting figure between his father and son. Unlike them, Isaac does not have a story that shows the change of his name and the 'naming' of his identity and destiny. For the older state of the Isaac cycle, see Noth, *A History of Pentateuchal Traditions*, p. 39 n. 146, pp. 102-15. For a sophisticated literary analysis, see G.A. Rendsburg, *The Redaction of Genesis* (Winona Lake, IN: Eisenbrauns, 1986), pp. 27-77. For a recent historical and source-critical analysis, see Z. Weisman, 'Societal Divergences in the Patriarchal Narratives', *Henoch* 17 (1995), pp. 11-27.

20. On this story, see most recently, Levenson, *The Death and Resurrection of the Beloved Son*, pp. 111-42.

land.[21] At a minimum it may be said that the Jacob sanctuary narratives contain a number of the features associated with pilgrimage.

In Genesis 22 Abraham is told to embark on a three-day journey in order to offer a burnt sacrifice on 'the mount of the Lord' (v. 14), Mount Moriah. This name may represent the paradigm pilgrimage site. Many commentators connect it with Jerusalem, as in 2 Chron. 3.1 (though the connection may be due to a post-exilic glossator).[22] As readers are aware, this is no pilgrimage of joyful expression, but one of Abraham's virtual silence, as he obeys the divine order to offer his own son. Fortunately, Abraham is repaid for his obedience; Isaac is spared. Even in the divine reward, the pilgrimage theme is first reversed in substituting Isaac for the animal, and then reversed back, now the animal serving in place of Isaac. In v. 13 Abraham is provided for miraculously,[23] with a ram as an offering instead of Isaac. This was just as Abraham himself had told his son in v. 8, but for readers this is ironic, since Abraham had not known that this would be the case. Finally, the aetiological explanation that 'on the mount of the Lord there is vision' (v. 14) is based not on the vision of God, the culmination of the pilgrimage experience discussed at the end of Chapter 2. Instead, it is the notion that 'the Lord sees', namely, the divine provisioning of the animal: as Abraham says in v. 8, 'God will see to the sheep for His burnt offering'.[24] In sum, Genesis 22 situates the test of

21. Because of these features, A. Alt, and his great student, M. Noth, posited ancient pilgrimage practices lying at the roots of narratives describing Jacob's visits at sanctuaries, in particular to Shechem and Bethel. See Noth, *A History of Pentateuchal Traditions*, pp. 80-81, 83, 85. For the cultic features to Gen. 28, see Levine, '*Lpny YHWH*', p. 203. For an argument for many of these cultic stories as reflections of contemporary ancestral devotion, see A. Cooper and B.R. Goldstein, 'The Cult of the Dead and the Theme of Entry into the Land', *BI* 1 (1993), pp. 285-303.

22. The connection apparently represents a late biblical identification. See Noth, *A History of Pentateuchal Traditions*, p. 114; and more recently, I. Kalimi, 'The Land of Moriah, Mount Moriah, and the Site of Solomon's Temple in Biblical Historiography', *HTR* 83 (1990), pp. 345-62; and Levenson, *The Death and Resurrection of the Beloved Son*, pp. 122, 174, 181.

23. The miracle involves timing, with אחר in v. 13 meaning 'at that moment', as proposed by M.H. Pope, 'The Timing of the Snagging of the Ram, Genesis 22.13', *BA* 49 (1986), pp. 114-17; reprinted in Pope, *Probative Pontificating in Ugaritic and Biblical Literature: Collected Essays* (ed. M.S. Smith; Ugaritisch-Biblische Literatur, 10; Münster: Ugarit-Verlag, 1994), pp. 305-10.

24. The connection is made by commentators and NJPS, p. 32 n. c.

Abraham within the contours of the pilgrimage journey, sacrifice and divine vision, yet at every turn the chapter reverses this experience.[25] Biblical pilgrimage here becomes an occasion for presenting not the joy of religious life, but its potentially terrifying side.

In Genesis 32 the journey of Jacob between Canaan and Aram is framed by pilgrimage themes. On his way to Aram, Jacob stops at Bethel, well-known to Israelite audiences as a sanctuary (Genesis 28). There the patriarch experiences a divine revelation through a dream. At the end of the story Jacob declares the stone as a symbol of God's abode (v. 22), and he promises to pay a tithe as a vow. An Israelite audience would have associated the tithe with the pilgrims' gift to the sanctuary. As evidenced by Hannah's vow at the sanctuary at Shiloh (discussed in Chapter 2), Jacob's personal vow, too, was an appropriate act in a sanctuary. On his return from Aram (Gen. 32.23-33), Jacob again experiences a divine revelation, one that defines his identity, and by implication the people known by his name: his new name of Israel identifies him as one who struggles with God[26] and with other people, is alone in the world, and is destined to return to the land.[27] Finally, Jacob realizes that he has experienced the special grace of seeing God and living (v. 31). While vv. 31-32 anchors this theme in an aetiological context to the place-name, Peniel/Penuel ('face of God'), these verses also evoke the classic pilgrimage experience of seeing God. In sum, while these stories incorporate other themes and concerns (e.g. the aetiological explanations in Gen. 22.14 and 32.33), for their Israelite

---

25. I would raise the question as to whether Jesus' journey to Jerusalem for the Passover is to be regarded likewise as an 'anti-pilgrimage'. The parallels between Jacob and Jesus as sacrifices of the first-born son have been beautifully laid out by Levenson, *The Birth and the Resurrection of the Beloved Son*, pp. 174-219, who shows further the Jewish background of some of the themes pertaining to Jesus as the first-born sacrificial victim. In particular, the transformation of Jacob into the martyr who atones for the sins of others and the connection of Passover to the Jacob story in Jewish tradition (Levenson, *The Birth and Resurrection of the Beloved Son*, pp. 182-83) provide helpful links between Jacob's and Jesus' journeys to Jerusalem as the intended sacrifice. The transformation of pilgrim into sacrificial offering becomes the model for early Christians who are to follow Jesus on the journey. On this point, see Lk. 9.31, 51; 23.26-32, 48-49, 55.

26. For this interpretation of Jacob's experience, see Hos. 12.4.

27. This summary of Israel's identity as revealed in this chapter was taught to me by Professor Michael D. Coogan.

audiences they also evoked the pilgrimage paradigm.[28] In the cases of both Genesis 22 and 32, their pilgrimage tales are stories of identity which reveal the relationship of Yahweh with Abraham (the obedient) and Jacob-Israel (the struggler). Long ago the patriarchs lived a pattern of religious life familiar to the Israelites, one which they, too, continued to live.[29]

Pilgrimage motifs appear in many psalms, prophetic speeches and Pentateuchal and historical narratives. From patriarchal past through apocalyptic future, what was the past pilgrimage pattern was not only prologue. The pilgrimage paradigm also provided hints of destiny which helped to shape present identity. Pilgrimage was a paradigm malleable to different situations and genres. The paradigm of pilgrimage also became the basis for one arrangement of one biblical book, and this book is Exodus.[30] The priestly arrangement of Exodus, described in Part II (Chap-ter 6), uses the pilgrimage pattern to describe the journey of Moses, first alone and then with the Israelites, to the holy mountain where they would receive their call and commission in the presence of Yahweh. Part II begins with an overview of the current state of scholarly studies on the book of Exodus.

28. That H. Gunkel assigned a whole stratum of patriarchal narratives to the pilgrimage traditions of various cult sites is indicative of the pilgrimage motifs embedded within these stories. See Gunkel, *Genesis übersetzt und erklärt* (HKAT; Göttingen: Vandenhoeck & Ruprecht, 1901), pp. 266-67; *idem, The Legends of Genesis: The Biblical Saga and History* (New York: Schocken Books, 1964), pp. 30-34. For discussion and criticisms, see R. Hendel, *The Epic of the Patriarch: The Jacob Cycle and the Narrative Traditions of Canaan and Israel* (HSM, 42; Atlanta: Scholars Press, 1987), pp. 6-13.

29. For a discussion of typology in the patriarchal narratives, see M.Z. Brettler, *The Creation of History in Ancient Israel* (New York: Routledge, 1995), pp. 48-61.

30. The book of Numbers might be regarded as a pilgrimage journey from the mountain to the sanctuary-land. Tentatively I would regard Numbers as a dialectic between the anti-pilgrimage of the older generation which departs Sinai and sins on the one hand, and on the other hand, the pilgrimage of the new generation born in the wilderness and prepared to reach the promised land. For a fuller description of Numbers in relation to Exodus, see Chapter 11 below. Another possibility for a book organized around the theme of pilgrimage is, according to R. Coote, the book of Amos (see Coote, *Amos among the Prophets*). Many passages in Third Isaiah are likewise informed by pilgrimage motifs. Pilgrimage in all its biblical permutations might serve as the basis for a larger biblical theology.

Part II

THE PRIESTLY ARRANGEMENT OF EXODUS

'And they saw the God of Israel.'
Exodus 24.11

Chapter 5

THE CURRENT STATE OF RESEARCH ON EXODUS

1. *Source Criticism*

Parts II and III of this study address the theology reflected in the priestly redaction of Exodus and Numbers. This proposed agenda raises some major methodological issues about the study of the Pentateuch as a whole. Given the emphasis on Exodus in this investigation, the following remarks on the current state of research will focus largely, though not exclusively, on this biblical book.[1] The long-reigning paradigm for examining the diachronic development of the Pentateuch is now undergoing serious criticism.[2] For over a century and a half the historical

---

1.　For the 'book of Exodus', I refer to the MT which in the main belongs to the same shorter text with LXX in contrast with the expansionist 4QpaleoExodus[m] and the Samaritan Pentateuch. For discussion, see P.W. Skehan, E. Ulrich and J.E. Sanderson, *Qumran Cave 4. IV. Palaeo-Hebrew and Greek Biblical Manuscripts* (DJD, 9; Oxford: Clarendon Press, 1992), pp. 53-130, esp. pp. 65-70. None of the preferred readings in the latter expansionist texts has any impact on the discussion of Exodus in this work. See further the Qumran Exodus manuscripts presented in E. Ulrich *et al.*, *Qumran Cave 4. VII. Genesis to Numbers* (DJD, 12; Oxford: Clarendon Press, 1994).

2.　For the continental discussion, see O. Eissfeldt, *The Old Testament: An Introduction* (trans. P.R. Ackroyd; New York: Harper & Row, 1965), pp. 158-241; H. Schmid, *Die Gestalt des Mose: Probleme alttestamentlicher Forschung unter Berücksichtigung der Pentateuchkrise* (Erträge der Forschung, 237; Darmstadt: Wissenschaftliche Buchgesellschaft, 1986); W.H. Schmidt, *Exodus, Sinai und Mose* (Erträge der Forschung, 191; Darmstadt: Wissenschaftliche Buchgesellschaft, 1983); the essays in A. de Pury (ed.), *Le Pentateuque en question*; E. Blum, *Studien zur Komposition des Pentateuch*; A. Schart, *Mose und Israel im Konflikt: Eine redaktionsgeschichtliche Studie zu den Wüstenerzählung* (OBO, 98; Freiburg: Universitätsverlag; Göttingen: Vandenhoeck & Ruprecht, 1990), pp. 23-36; P. Haudebert (ed.), *Le Pentateuque: Débats et recherches: Quatorzième congrès de l'ACFEB, Angers (1991)* (LD, 151; Paris: Cerf, 1992). See also specifically for Exodus, B.S. Childs, *The Book of Exodus* (OTL; Philadelphia: Westminster Press, 1974). For the debate

study of the Pentateuch has been dominated by source-criticism that divides the text into the Yahwist/Jahwist source (J), the Elohist source (E) and the Priestly source (P). The synthesis achieved in the works of M. Noth represents a high point in source-criticism.[3] In Noth's words:

> The most probable solution of the literary riddle of the Pentateuch has proved to be the hypothesis that the present Pentateuch is the result of a working together of different, originally independent 'written sources', each of which, in a separate literary work, had fixed the material of the Pentateuchal tradition in writing.[4]

Although source-criticism has stood as an assumption of Pentateuchal study, it should be noted that the character and dating of the sources have been heavily controverted over the twentieth century.[5] In general, however, J has been considered a southern narrative source dating to the United monarchy.[6] E has been viewed as a northern narrative

in Britain, see the summaries in S.R. Driver, *An Introduction to the Literature of the Old Testament* (Gloucester, MA: Peter Smith, 1972), pp. 22-42; C.R. North, 'Pentateuchal Criticism', in H.H. Rowley (ed.), *The Old Testament and Modern Study: A Generation of Discovery and Research* (Oxford Paperbacks; Oxford: Clarendon Press, 1961), pp. 48-83; J. Barton, *Reading the Old Testament: Method in Biblical Study* (Philadelphia: Westminster Press, 1984), pp. 20-29; E.W. Nicholson, *God and His People: Covenant and Theology in the Old Testament* (Oxford: Clarendon Press, 1986). For discussion in the United States since 1980, see D.A. Knight, 'The Pentateuch', in D.A. Knight and G.M. Tucker (eds.), *The Hebrew Bible and its Modern Interpreters* (Philadelphia: Fortress Press; Decatur, GA: Scholars Press, 1985), pp. 263-96; J.H. Tigay, 'Introduction', in J.H. Tigay (ed.), *Empirical Models for Biblical Criticism* (Philadelphia: University of Pennsylvania Press, 1985), pp. 1-19; T. Dozeman, *God on the Mountain: A Study of Redaction, Theology and Canon in Exodus 19–24* (SBLMS, 37; Atlanta: Scholars Press, 1989), pp. 1-12; Blenkinsopp, *The Pentateuch*, pp. 1-30; A.F. Campbell and M.A. O'Brien, *Sources for the Pentateuch: Texts, Introductions, Annotations* (Minneapolis: Fortress Press, 1993), pp. 1-19. For further discussion, see below. (I am grateful to Professor Gordon Davies for bringing the works of Schmid and Schmidt to my attention.)

3. See Noth, *A History of Pentateuchal Traditions*. For a recent presentation of Noth's Pentateuchal sources, see Campbell and O'Brien, *Sources for the Pentateuch*. For the book of Exodus, see M. Noth, *Exodus: A Commentary* (trans. J.S. Bowden; OTL; Philadelphia: Westminster Press, 1962).

4. Noth, *Exodus*, pp. 12-13.

5. See North, 'Pentateuchal Criticism', pp. 48-83.

6. For a defense of a date of ca. 950, see K. Berge, *Die Zeit des Jahwisten: Ein Beitrag zur Datierung jahwistischer Vätertexte* (BZAW, 186; Berlin: de Gruyter, 1990).

source[7] or a collection of editorial additions[8] produced during the divided monarchy.[9] (For the book of Exodus, E is regarded even in the source-criticism of A.W. Jenks as a supplement to J except in the Sinai narrative material.[10]) This approach sometimes reconstructs a redactor of JE in addition to a priestly source and redactor, and deuteronomistic additions.[11] The oral background of pre-JE material, while difficult to pin down, has played a major role in discussions of source criticism of Exodus.[12]

The revolution within Pentateuchal studies over the last twenty years makes it impossible to assume the JEP source model at the outset, although such studies have appeared in the United States over the last fifteen years, mainly from students of F.M. Cross.[13] Assaults on the

7. See A.W. Jenks, *The Elohist and North Israelite Traditions* (SBLMS, 22; Missoula, MT: Scholars Press, 1977); *idem*, 'Elohist', *ABD*, II, pp. 478-82; R.E. Friedman, 'Torah (Pentateuch)', *ABD*, VI, pp. 609-14.

8. So S. Mowinckel, 'Der Ursprung der Bil'amsage', *ZAW* 48 (1930), pp. 233-71; P. Volz and W. Rudolph, *Der Elohist als erzähler ein Irrweg der Pentateuchkritik?* (BZAW, 63; Giessen: Töpelmann, 1933); W. Rudolph, *Der 'Elohist' von Exodus bis Josua* (BZAW, 68; Giessen: Töpelmann, 1938). For criticisms of this view, see Noth, *A History of Pentateuchal Traditions*, pp. 21-22; Jenks, *The Elohist and North Israelite Traditions*, pp. 9-12. For more recent views along these lines, see F.V. Winnett, 'Re-Examining the Foundations', *JBL* 84 (1965), pp. 1-19; J. van Seters, *Abraham in History and Tradition* (Yale Near Eastern Researches; New Haven: Yale University Press, 1975). For further discussion, see R.R. Wilson, 'The Hardening of Pharaoh's Heart', *CBQ* 41 (1979), p. 23 n. 18; *The Book of J* (translated from the Hebrew by David Rosenberg; interpreted by Harold Bloom; New York: Grove Weidenfeld, 1990), p. 22.

9. For a study in this vein, see R.E. Friedman, *Who Wrote the Bible?* (New York: Summit Books, 1987).

10. See Jenks, *The Elohist and North Israelite Traditions*, p. 42.

11. See below.

12. See Noth, *A History of Pentateuchal Traditions*, pp. 38-41, 52-53, 77, 229-34. Childs (*The Book of Exodus, ad loc*) frequently discusses the oral tradition prior to and often shared by J and E.

13. For example, Clifford, 'Exodus', *NJBC*, I, pp. 44-60; R.B. Coote and D.R. Ord, *The Bible's First History* (Philadelphia: Fortress Press, 1989); R.B. Coote, *The Elohist: In Defense of Revolution* (Minneapolis: Fortress Press, 1991); Friedman, *Who Wrote the Bible?*; B. Halpern, *The Emergence of Israel in Canaan* (SBLMS, 29; Chico, CA: Scholars Press, 1983), pp. 37-40, 42-43, 116-17, 156-63 (etc.); Hendel, *The Epic of the Patriarch*; S.D. McBride, 'Biblical Literature in its Historical Context: The Old Testament', in J.L. Mays (ed.), *Harper's Bible Commentary* (San Francisco: Harper & Row, 1988), pp. 14-26; P.K. McCarter, 'Exodus', in

source-critical paradigm have come from three directions, specifically modifications of source theories, newer redactional theories and synchronic approaches. The first of the attacks on traditional source-criticism, namely the attempts to redate or relocate sources,[14] continues an old debate. In more recent years, J. van Seters,[15] H. Schmid[16] and J. Blenkinsopp[17] have proposed an exilic dating for J. All of these scholars draw J into the orbit of deuteronomic tradition,[18] but van Seters goes further. Based largely on thematic criteria, van Seters sees J as dependent on Deuteronomy, the Deuteronomistic History as well as prophetic and wisdom traditions.[19] Van Seters allows for great literary diversity in J (otherwise unseen in the other great works of D and P).[20] This diversity is used to account for almost all material attributed in traditional source-criticism to E or D, including differences in the use of divine names, place-names, phraseology and themes. Van Seters is highly criticial of others for invoking hypothetical oral traditions, alternate sources (such as E) or generally redactional

Mays (ed.), *Harper's Bible Commentary*; W.H. Propp, *Water in the Wilderness: A Biblical Motif and its Mythological Background* (HSM, 40; Atlanta: Scholars Press, 1987); Wallace, *The Eden Narrative*; Levenson, *The Death and Resurrection of the Beloved Son*.

14. For a recent discussion of the *status questionis* of source criticism, see R.W.L. Moberly, *The Old Testament of the Old Testament*, pp. 176-91.

15. J. van Seters's two decades of research on the Yahwist is conveniently collected in his two books, *Prologue to History: The Yahwist as Historian in Genesis* (Louisville, KY: Westminster/John Knox Press, 1992), and *The Life of Moses*. See also van Seters, '"Comparing Scripture with Scripture": Some Observations on the Sinai Pericope of Exodus 19–24', in G.M. Tucker, D.L. Petersen and R.R. Wilson (eds.), *Canon, Theology and Old Testament Interpretation* (Philadelphia: Fortress Press, 1988), pp. 111-30.

16. H. Schmid, *Der sogenannte Jahwist: Beobachtungen und Fragen zur Pentateuchforschung* (Zürich: Theologischer Verlag, 1976).

17. Blenkinsopp, *The Pentateuch*, p. 93. For the provisional argument that J assumes P in Genesis 1–11, see Blenkinsopp, *The Pentateuch*, pp. 78, 80-81.

18. R.N. Whybray regards the Pentateuch ultimately as the product of a single author who intended it to serve as the preface to the Deuteronomistic History. See Whybray, *The Making of the Pentateuch: A Methodological Study* (JSOTSup, 53; Sheffield: JSOT Press, 1987); *idem*, *Introduction to the Pentateuch* (Grand Rapids: Eerdmans, 1995).

19. For all of these materials in J, see van Seters, *The Life of Moses*, pp. 63, 460, 465.

20. 'Diversity' is van Seters's term. See van Seters, *The Life of Moses*, p. 177.

materials (apart from P), but the literary model that van Seters employs assumes literary relationships which are equally hypothetical and overlook major differences in theme or language between his putative J and passages outside the Pentateuch.[21] Van Seters is to be credited for some forceful criticisms of the traditional model of source-criticism and helpful comparisons between Pentateuchal and extra-Pentateuchal texts, but his methodology is often unpersuasive. Other views of J have been raised. In some of these discussions of dating sources, the possibility of several Js or of a rolling J corpus has been proposed, following an old suggestion of J. Wellhausen.[22] G.A. Rendsburg raises old suspicions against the assumption that E and D are northern in provenience.[23] He asserts rather that there are no distinctive northern linguistic features in E and D.[24] The date of much P material has been raised several centuries from the exile or post-exilic period to the divided monarchy.[25]

One of the most important criteria for source-criticism, namely the

21. See van Seters, *The Life of Moses*, pp. 16-19, 211-12. For the method, see the comments on pp. 177, 193, 202, 214. Many of the complaints levelled by van Seters against other scholars could be applied to van Seters's own claims if his word, 'literary', were to be substituted for 'oral' (see p. 214, under (1) and (2) and also the second sentence in the second full paragraph).

22. E.W. Nicholson, 'The Pentateuch in Recent Research: A Time for Caution', in J.A. Emerton (ed.), *Congress Volume: Leuven 1989* (VTSup, 43; Leiden: Brill, 1991), p. 21.

23. So Mowinckel, 'Der Ursprung', regarding E.

24. G. Rendsburg, *Linguistic Evidence for the Northern Origin of Selected Psalms* (SBLMS, 43; Atlanta: Scholars Press, 1990), p. 12 n. 50, p. 81 n. 54.

25. See A. Hurvitz, *A Linguistic Study of the Relationship between the Priestly Source and the Book of Ezekiel* (Cahiers de la Revue biblique, 20; Paris: Gabalda, 1982); *idem*, 'The Evidence of Language in Dating the Priestly Code', *RB* 81 (1974), pp. 24-56; *idem*, 'The Language of the Priestly Source and its Historical Setting: The Case for an Early Date', *Proceedings of the Eighth World Congress of Jewish Studies 1981* (Jerusalem: World Union of Jewish Studies, 1983), V, pp. 83-94; *idem*, 'Dating the Priestly Source in Light of the Historical Study of Biblical Hebrew a Century after Wellhausen', *ZAW* 100 supplement (1988), pp. 88-99; G. Rendsburg, 'Late Biblical Hebrew and the Date of "P"', *JANESCU* 12 (1980), pp. 65-80; Z. Zevit, 'Converging Lines of Evidence Bearing on the Date of P', *ZAW* 92 (1982), pp. 481-511; Milgrom, *Leviticus 1–16*, pp. 3-6. For an opposite view from a linguistic perspective, see B.A. Levine, 'Late Language in the Priestly Source: Some Literary and Historical Observations', *Proceedings of the Eighth World Congress of Jewish Studies 1981* (Jerusalem: World Union of Jewish Studies, 1983), V, pp. 69-82.

distribution of divine names, has been criticized of late. According to the standard source-critical view, J uses *yhwh* after Gen. 4.26, E uses אלהים generally, and P uses אלהים until Exod. 6.3 after which the tetragrammaton is employed. R.E. Friedman qualifies this point by noting that J's use of the divine name is maintained in narration, not dialogue.[26] R.W.L. Moberly denies the value of the divine names as a criterion for distinguishing material.[27] Moberly further rejects the standard source-critical view of Gen. 4.26b ('And at that time people began to call on the name of Yahweh'). Most scholars had seen the Yahwist's version of the revelation on the divine name as parallel to the E and P versions in Exodus 3 and 6 respectively.[28] According to Moberly, however, the Yahwist shares with the other Pentateuchal sources the view that revelation of the divine name took place first to Moses: 'all the pentateuchal writers share a common tradition that the divine name was first revealed by God to Moses, and yet all feel free to use the divine name where they consider appropriate in the patriarchal stories'.[29] This includes Gen. 4.26b and the other uses of the tetragrammaton in J prior to Moses. Moberly perhaps correctly criticizes the historical difficulties with the traditional view of Gen. 4.26b, but his solution for this verse is less persuasive. It is not clear why J could not have resorted to the more generic term for 'God' (אלהים) as in E and P, if that is what the J narrative wished to express. More to the point for this study, Moberly notes that the tetragrammaton appears in material generally assigned to E and P (Gen. 20.18; 22.11, 14 [E]; 17.1; 21.1b [P]), but he also recognizes that source-critics may justly account for these departures.[30] Furthermore, the exceptions noted by Moberly are relatively rare and do not disprove the criterion of divine names for sources.[31]

26. Friedman, 'Scholar, Heal Thyself; Or How Everybody Got to be an Expert on the Bible', *The Iowa Review* 21.3 (1991), p. 37; *idem*, 'Torah', p. 610a.

27. Moberly, *The Old Testament of the Old Testament*, pp. 43-45; see also pp. 176-91.

28. Moberly, *The Old Testament of the Old Testament*, pp. 36-78.

29. Moberly, *The Old Testament of the Old Testament*, p. 36.

30. Moberly, *The Old Testament of the Old Testament*, p. 43. It may be noted further that the compound title יהוה אלהים is attested in Gen. 2.4b-5, material attributed usually in source-critical treatments to J. It is quite possible that the second title was a priestly glossing on the first, the J divine name.

31. For a defense of the traditional criterion of divine names, see Friedman, 'Torah', p. 610a. Moberly's position seems contradictory: he is sharply critical of

The study of the Pentateuch may not decrease but increase the number of sources,[32] in keeping with the process of accumulation and redaction of documents known from Mesopotamian sources[33] and arguably attested in the Ugaritic Baal Cycle, based on internal evidence.[34] Accordingly, that J and E were transmitters as well as possibly redactors and authors would comport with models available from other ancient Near Eastern cycles of texts. Given this supposition, three alternatives might be envisioned: either J and E were independent strata subsequently redacted by a further party, or J was redacted into E, or vice-versa. The first hypothesis, the classic form of the documentary hypothesis,[35] has long suffered from the assumption that the redactor omitted duplicated material, a problem since in fact in many places the text retains duplicates so often.[36] This approach is further problematic since ancient Near Eastern literary cycles tend to retain material and modify it rather than omit it.

The second approach, based on the premise that J was redacted into E,[37] suits the general weight of material assigned to the two. As E lacks much material,[38] it appears as if it may serve to supplement the themes and narrative of J. The plague material assigned to E is a good example.[39] However, in some cases it would be difficult to read E as the redactor of J. Genesis 22, a text classically assigned to E, shows an

---

source-criticism, but he uses it to sketch his position of the theology of the Pentateuch.

32. As supposed by some of the older critics. For examples, see North, 'Pentateuchal Criticism', pp. 54-55.

33. See J.H. Tigay, 'The Evolution of the Pentateuchal Narratives in the Light of the Evolution of the *Gilgamesh Epic*', in J.H. Tigay (ed.), *Empirical Models for Biblical Research* (Philadelphia: University of Pennsylvania Press, 1985), pp. 21-52.

34. See Smith, *The Ugaritic Baal Cycle*, pp. 29-36, 58, 96-114.

35. For a major alternative, see Cooper and Goldstein, 'Exodus and *Maṣṣôt* in History and Tradition', pp. 15-37, esp. p. 25. Cooper and Goldstein see the redactor of J and E (themselves not 'throrough-composed' written sources as such), as a northerner who was the principal author of the Exodus and Sinai materials in that they see 'no alteration of R^JE's basic chronology or story line by subsequent redactors' (p. 25). For Exodus Cooper and Goldstein attribute very little to a Judean background. In terms of the general disposition of materials in Exodus, this position shares much in common with the third position outlined below.

36. See Campbell and O'Brien, *Sources for the Pentateuch*, p. 161.

37. See above n. 8.

38. See Campbell and O'Brien, *Sources for the Pentateuch*, pp. 166-190.

39. See Wilson, 'The Hardening of Pharaoh's Heart', p. 23 n. 18.

apparent intrusion of a Yahwistic marker into a putative E narrative (vv. 11, 15-18). Such instances would require some other interpretation.

The third approach, that E was redacted into J, may begin on the assumption that the material designated E was primarily a cycle of stories dealing with Abraham, Isaac, Jacob and Joseph in Genesis and Moses and the people in Exodus.[40] The patriarchal stories anticipate the themes and motifs of the Moses narratives concluding in the covenant on the mountain. The travels of Abraham to Egypt and to the holy mountain foreshadow Moses and the people in Egypt and Horeb (Sinai). If correct, it might be argued that this cycle was brought south in the aftermath of the north's demise in 722. The larger literary creation that source critics label as 'J' subsequently incorporated the E cycle into the larger southern cycle of material. One advantage of seeing J either as the text into which E was redacted or as the redactor of E as well as a source of narratives may be found in intrusions of apparently Yahwistic redactional touches in narratives assigned to E. The classic example of Gen. 22.11 has just been noted (see also Gen. 28.21; Exod. 3.15). Another advantage of this approach is the placement of the bulk of E material at the end of J blocks, at least in the patriarchal narratives. Campbell and O'Brien note that 'the overall impression is of addition of variant aspects of Israel's tradition at nodal points in the Yahwist narrative, with some extensive variants expressed in the Jacob-Esau cycle and the Joseph story'.[41] In most respects this approach is the most persuasive of the source critical approaches, but it suffers from the relative meagerness of material involved in a putative E cycle. Finally, there is a problem with the concept of 'J' as well. It is unclear that 'J' is a single piece, given the differing literary character of the Joseph cycle compared with the narratives detailing the lives of the other patriarchs. Different levels of materials or cycles may underlie the material traditionally identified as 'J',[42] but a convincing

---

40. The evidence for E in Num. 20–23 is unclear and it may have belonged to a group of journey stories on the way to the mountain. See Campbell and O'Brien, *Sources for the Pentateuch*, pp. 190-93. For this approach to E, see recently Weisman, 'Societal Divergences', pp. 11-27.

41. See Campbell and O'Brien, *Sources for the Pentateuch*, p. 162.

42. This approach would be able to deal with apparent anachronisms in the J material such as the mention of Pithom (so van Seters, *The Life of Moses*, p. 24).

detailed reconstruction of such a development seems beyond our grasp.

None of the three basic hypotheses for J and E and their juxtaposition and interpenetration is fully satisfactory. Either a considerably more complex set of relations must be envisioned for the different sets of materials assigned to J and E, or the present scholarly capacity to understand this material along source critical lines may be doubted. At this point it would seem that the capacity to penetrate this 'JE' material along source critical lines stands in serious jeopardy. The assignment of older material remains a problematic enterprise for both older source critics and newer redaction critics. Indeed, it may be time to prescind from over-confident judgments, especially about non-priestly material. Here Moberly's admonishment about Pentateuchal criticism is well-placed: 'But there are times when it may perhaps be best to say "We just don't know"'.[43]

2. *Redactional Theories*

As a result of many questions, source-criticism has been challenged more severely by newer models of redaction criticism. In the final passage of his work, *The Problem of the Process of Transmission in the Pentateuch*, R. Rendtorff criticizes modifications of source-theory:

> It would be following a false trail methodologically, I think, if 'new' or 'late' sources were now to replace the 'old' pentateuchal sources, or if one wanted to try to repeat the global interpretation of the 'Yahwist' or other 'sources' with another dating and on the background of other time-conditioned circumstances. That would be to pour new wine into old skins. The problem of the process of tradition in the Pentateuch lies deeper. One must tackle it, as von Rad demanded in one of his last statements: 'we urgently need a comprehensive new analysis of the narrative material of the Pentateuch'.[44]

The new analysis that Rendtorff proposes is form-critical: analysis of units should proceed from their oldest stage to their arrangement in the present form of the five books without the *a priori* presupposition of source-criticism.[45] For Rendtorff, form-critical work on the Penta-

---

This particular problem has been explained away by some, however (see T.F. Wei, 'Pithom', *ABD*, V, pp. 376-77).

43. R.W.L. Moberly, *At the Mountain of God: Story and Theology in Exodus 32–34* (JSOTSup, 22; Sheffield: JSOT Press, 1983), p. 43.

44. Rendtorff, *The Problem*, pp. 205-206.

45. For some programmatic statements, see Rendtorff, *The Problem*, pp. 172,

teuch has been obstructed by the documentary hypothesis since this hypothesis was always assumed rather than demonstrated to represent part of the tradition's development. In Rendtorff's view this assumption is unwarranted.

Rendtorff, followed by others,[46] identifies old traditional material within large blocks of material that underwent priestly and deuteronomistic redactions. Echoing M. Noth's proposal for the major themes of the Pentateuch,[47] Rendtorff and his followers call for analysis within blocks of materials such as the primeval history, patriarchal narratives, the Joseph cycle, the Sinai traditions, etc. with the results across blocks to be analyzed after examination of each block is complete. Compared with traditional source-criticism, this approach involvesa major shift in the diachronic model applied to the text. Sources with opposing characteristics such as divine names no longer function as the major determinants of the paradigm. Rather, the Pentateuchal tradition seems to represent several blocks of material, each one a rolling corpus, with successive redactions and varying interpretations of the material; these blocks achieve connectedness through redactional 'cross-references'.[48] This approach seems to obviate the great difficulty in splitting material between sources in passages where such an approach produced only atomistic units of unlikely construction.[49] Furthermore, this approach does not assume relatively uniform strata across wide blocks of material, but allows for greater variety across blocks. For Rendtorff, the older materials within different blocks of material are to be treated on their own terms. A difficulty with this approach, albeit not a major one, is that while these blocks of material may be relatively easily distinguished within Genesis (i.e. the primeval history, the patriarchal narratives, the Joseph cycle), the same cannot be said for all the narrative materials in Exodus. The narrative materials in

---

175, 188-89. Rendtorff has returned to these themes in his article, 'The Paradigm is Changing: Hopes—and Fears', *BI, Sample Issue* (1992), pp. 6-12.

46. Dozeman, *God on the Mountain*; Blum, *Studien*; and B. Renaud, *La théophanie du Sinaï, Exod. 19–24: Exégèse et théologie* (CahRB, 30; Paris: Gabalda, 1991). See H. Gese, *Alttestamentliche Studien* (Tübingen: Mohr–Siebeck, 1991), who also works with deuteronomistic and priestly redactions.

47. Noth, *A History of Pentateuchal Traditions*, pp. 46-62.

48. Rendtorff, *The Problem*, pp. 46, 183.

49. So, for example, Moberly (*The Old Testament of the Old Testament*, pp. 47-48) on source-critical treatments of Exod. 3.

Exodus reflect tradition-histories that blur distinctions between purportedly separate blocks of material. Delineation of the Sinai tradition
in relation to chs. 16–18, 'Israel's stay in the desert',[50] is by no means
obvious as Rendtorff himself acknowledges in passing.[51]

In general, it is also interesting to observe how contrasting features
play out differently in the analyses of source and redaction critics.
The older block of material for source-critics generally showed some
contrasts since J and E both represented narrative sources with their
own characteristic marks. For newer source critics who date J late,
contrasts are a matter of chronological development within sources.[52]
For newer redaction critics contrasts do not inhere in the older core
of material. Instead, such contrast implies that the material either is
deuteronomistic or belongs to independent tradition. In a redactional
model, less contrast might be expected, since redaction occasions more
extensive rewriting.[53] Perhaps apart from Blum's study of Genesis[54]
and the ongoing studies of Cooper and Goldstein on Exodus,[55] the
newer redactional studies have less displaced the theory of sources as
much as challenged the specificity with which they have been presented and the bases for the assignment of some texts to them. Despite their
major differences, both older and newer source-criticism and the

---

50. Rendtorff, *The Problem*, pp. 38-39.

51. Rendtorff, *The Problem*, p. 187.

52. The sometimes linear argumentation developed by van Seters has come in for
criticism. Rendtorff (*The Problem*, pp. 204-205) especially criticizes the argumentation for drawing conclusions from the absence of evidence in pre-exilic literature.

53. J.H. Tigay writes:

> To the extent that the Temple Scroll is analogous to Pentateuchal narratives... I
> would argue that the analogy applies basically to those pericopes in the Torah which
> critics have found difficult to analyze thoroughly, and it would support the assumption
> that the difficulty is sometimes due to extensive rewriting by the redactor...

See J.H. Tigay, 'Conflation as a Redactional Technique', in *idem* (ed.), *Empirical
Models for Biblical Criticism*, p. 84 n. 71. Tigay's italics. See also his important cautionary remarks in 'The Stylistic Criterion of Source Criticism', *Empirical Models
for Biblical Criticism*, pp. 172-73.

54. Blum, *Die Komposition der Vätergeschichte* (WMANT, 57; Neukirchen–
Vluyn: Neukirchener Verlag, 1984). See also T.L. Thompson, *The Origin Tradition
of Ancient Israel. I. The Literary Formation of Genesis and Exodus 1–23* (JSOTSup,
55; Sheffield: JSOT Press, 1988).

55. See Cooper and Goldstein, 'Exodus and *Maṣṣôt* in History and Tradition',
esp. p. 25.

newer redactional work on the Pentateuch represented by Rendtorff, Blum and Dozeman overlap in positing older material, and deuteronomistic and priestly redactions.

3. *The Older Material in the Book of Exodus*

Both older and newer source-criticism and the newer redactional work on the Pentateuch assume an older stock of narrative material received by the priestly redaction. For the older source critical approach this would be the JE material. In contrast, the newer approach does not flesh out an idea of the older inherited material. Blum refers little to the material prior to the deuteronomistic and priestly redactions, and Dozeman likewise offers a limited description of the background of such prior material.

Some texts in Exodus that may been assigned to 'JE' have parallels in the Deuteronomistic History[56]:

(1)   the naming of Gershom in Exodus 18 (cf. Judg. 17.7);
(2)   the curing of the waters at Marah in Exod. 15.22-27 (cf. 2 Kgs 2.19-22);[57]
(3)   the story of the Golden Calf in Exodus 32 (cf. 1 Kgs 12.28);[58]

---

56. For the larger context for these issues, see E.L. Greenstein, 'The Formation of the Biblical Narrative Corpus', *AJS Review* 15 (1990), pp. 151-78, esp. pp. 171-72. Following older commentators, Greenstein especially notes a set of similarities between J stories in Genesis and the David stories. See also J.D. Pleins, 'Murderous Fathers, Manipulative Mothers, and Rivalrous Siblings: Rethinking the Architecture of Genesis-Kings', in A.B. Beck *et al.* (eds.), *Fortunate the Eyes That See: Essays in Honor of David Noel Freedman in Celebration of his Seventieth Birthday* (Grand Rapids: Eerdmans, 1995), pp. 121-36.

57. Y. Zakovitch, *'And You Shall Tell Your Son...' The Concept of the Exodus in the Bible* (Jerusalem: Magnes, 1991), pp. 75-76. Zakovitch also compares 2 Kgs 3. See also van Seters, *The Life of Moses*, pp. 176-77

58. Much of Exod. 32 has been attributed traditionally to E, but there are many tensions in the narrative, noted by H.L. Ginsberg (*The Israelite Heritage of Judaism* [New York: The Jewish Theological Seminary of America, 1982], pp. 84-91) and harmonized by H.C. Brichto (*Toward A Grammar of Biblical Poetics: Tales of the Prophets* [New York: Oxford University Press, 1992], pp. 91-101). For the origins of this story, see Cross, *Canaanite Myth*, pp. 73-75, 198-200; Jenks, *The Elohist and North Israelite Traditions*, p. 104. The pro-Levitical and anti-Aaronid polemic of this chapter is evident. Ginsberg's analysis of the tensions in the chapter is penetrating, but his historical reconstruction overlooks the parallel of Exod. 32.4 with 1 Kgs 12.28 noted by Cross. M. White emends Cross's analysis by attributing

(4) contacts between the figures of Moses and Elijah;[59]
(5) contacts between the figures of Moses and Joshua.[60]

E.L. Greenstein offers helpful reflections on such correspondences. He would not attribute such similarities to different redactions of a single tradition or to two variations of an orally transmitted story. Rather, Greenstein comments:

> I would imagine a different history to these and many of the other story pairs we have identified in the Torah—and Genesis in particular—and the so-called Deuteronomistic History. I cannot say where all of the narratives came from—no one could. We possess so little historical documentation. But I do suspect that there arose in ancient Israel various stories concerning the early kings, David of Judah and Jeroboam of Israel in particular. Elements of their stories served as the material of later narrators and writers. Some of these elements became recombined into new sequences; others became transformed through substitutions in details and other modifications.[61]
>
> I would place the source of the primary legends as we now find them in the early monarchy. The reasons that I do not view the patriarchal and

Exod. 32.4 to a Deuteronomistic editor rather than to E (*pace* Cross) because 1 Kgs 12.28 is taken as deriving from the Deuteronomistic history (White, 'The Elohistic Depiction of Aaron: A Study in the Levite-Zadokite Controversy', in J.A. Emerton (ed.), *Studies in the Pentateuch* [VTSup, 41; Leiden: Brill, 1990], pp. 151-57). Brichto's theological attempt at harmonizing Aaron's responsibilitiy in this chapter with his high status elsewhere in Exodus reflects the fundamental inadequacy of a purely diachronic reading (*Toward A Grammar*, p. 98). It remains to mention the intriguing suggestion of C.F.A. Schaeffer ('Nouveaux témoignages du culte de El et de Baal à Ras Shamra et ailleurs en Syrie Palestine', *Syria* 43 [1960], p. 16) followed by N. Wyatt ('Of Calves and Kings: The Canaanite Dimension in the Religion of Israel', *SJOT* 6 [1992], pp. 78-83) that El and not Yahweh was the god of Jeroboam I. Wyatt reads אל, 'El', for אלה in Exod. 32.4 and 8. See further Greenstein, 'The Formation', pp. 175-76; and Zakovitch, *'And You Shall Tell Your Son.. . '*, pp. 87-97.

59. For more recent comparisons, see Cross, *Canaanite Myth*, pp. 191-94; G. Savran, '1 and 2 Kings', in R. Alter and F. Kermode (eds.), *The Literary Guide to the Bible* (Cambridge, MA: The Belknapp Press of Harvard University Press, 1987), pp. 162-63; Zakovitch, *'And You Shall Tell Your Son.. . '*, pp. 70-72.

60. Zakovitch, *'And You Shall Tell Your Son.. . '*, pp. 60-67; H.C. Schmitt, 'Das sogenannte vorprophetie Berufungsschema: Zur "geistigen Heimat" des Berufungsformulars von Exod. 3,9-12; Jdc 6,11-24 und I Sam 9,1-10,16', *ZAW* 104 (1992), pp. 202-16.

61. Greenstein, 'The Formation', p. 175.

other Pentateuchal narratives as primary are largely traditio-historical. . . Sometime during the centuries from David until the Babylonian exile, the narrative corpus was formed. . . I imagine the Josianic era as a suitable period for the composition of most of the narratives as we have them. Because of the complexity of the corpus I could not with confidence develop a more precise and intricate reconstruction of the overall literary history. A flexible combination of models would seem to be in order.[62]

This approach is also consistent with the most proximate ancient Near Eastern parallels to Pentateuchal stories. The parallels between Exodus and the Deuteronomistic History reached a formative point of collection, and this literary activity holds implications for the dating of such material in the Pentateuch.

Some examples might suggest the Neo-Assyrian or Iron II period as the formative period for the Pentateuch. One text that may point to the Neo-Assyrian period as the formative period for Exodus 2 is the so-called 'Birth Legend of Sargon', identified as Sargon II. As W.W. Hallo notes,[63] there is no indication that this text predates the late eighth century. To take another Pentateuchal example outside of the book of Exodus, the Joseph story in Genesis 37–50 is often compared with other narratives of Jewish heroes living in foreign lands such as Daniel, Esther, Susanna.[64] While these stories are post-exilic, the same type of story is known of the figure of Ahiqar who has been identified as a figure in the Neo-Assyrian court. One *ummanu*, or learned man and official, belonging to the court of Esarhaddon, had the Akkadian name Aba-enlil-dari, but was known to the Ahlamu (Arameans) as ^{l}a-ḫu-'u-qa-a-ri. [65] Perhaps the Israelite theme of the wise figure in the foreign court developed initially during the Neo-Assyrian period,[66] and this may represent the temporal background of the Joseph cycle.[67] Such a

62. Greenstein, 'The Formation', pp. 177-78. Cf. Wellhausen, *Prolegomena*, p. 327. This is a reprinted edition of the 1883 original, itself a revision of Wellhausen's first volume of his two-volume *History of Israel* of 1878.

63. Hallo, *The Book of the People*, p. 48.

64. For a discussion of research, see L.M. Wills, *The Jew in the Court of the Foreign King: Ancient Jewish Court Legends* (HDR, 26; Minneapolis: Fortress Press, 1990), pp. 1-12.

65. For a summary as well as further supporting evidence, see J.C. Vanderkam, 'Ahikar/Ahiqar', *ABD*, I, p. 114.

66. See Wills, *The Jew in the Court*, pp. 39-55.

67. Another argument for the monarchic background of the Joseph stories is given by K.D. Schunck ('Benjamin', *ABD*, I, p. 671): 'Since Ephraim, together with

reconstruction would fit a period after the fall of the northern kingdom when life in a foreign land became an issue in Israel.

To these kinds of observations, lexical items might be added in order to identify the period of the formation of Pentateuchal stories. The famous comparison between אברך in Gen. 41.43 and *hbrk* in line 1 of the Karatepe inscription may be cited in this regard. The words, both meaning 'steward' or the like,[68] would appear to represent a loan from Akkadian *abarakku* during the Neo-Assyrian period, although it is to be noted that the word is attested already at Ebla.[69] In short, different kinds of evidence, namely parallel stories and wordings in the Deuteronomistic history and elsewhere in the Bible, extra-biblical parallels, and a single (but somewhat valuable) lexical item, fit the period from the eighth century onwards as the formative period of the narrative material in Exodus. The parallels between some of the stories in Exodus and the Deuteronomistic History may also suggest an older northern background.[70] These may have been transmitted and further modified in southern circles, a development which may explain why 'E' narrative lacks characteristically northern linguistic items.[71] The possibility of northern material predating a deuteronomistic redaction of Exodus cannot be excluded in some cases, especially as the specific characteristics of deuteronomistic language, images or theology are absent from these texts. Whether one wishes to call this material E or pre-deuteronomic material may matter little in the long run.[72] It is impor-

the tribe of Manasseh, was subsumed under the rubric "house of Joseph" during the monarchy, it is also clear why Benjamin usually appears alongside Joseph in the tribal lists (Gen. 35.24; 46.19, 21; 1 Chr. 2.2) and why the fictive tribal ancestor is Joseph's only full brother who receives special treatment: thus Benjamin plays a special role in the Joseph novella (Gen. 42.4, 36; 43.14-16, 29, 34; 44.12; 45.12, 14, 22)'. See further G.A. Rendsburg, *The Redaction of Genesis* (Winona Lake, IN: Eisenbrauns, 1986), esp. p. 119.

68. Delitzsch and Sayce, cited in BDB, p. 8; Rosenthal, *ANET*, p. 653 n. 1.

69. See W.W. Hallo, 'The First Purim', *BA* 46 (1983), pp. 20, 25; *idem, The Book of the People*, pp. 39-41. For a more technical discussion, M. Krebernik, '*hbrk b'l* in den phön. Karatepe-Inschriften und '*à-ba-ra-gú* in Ebla', *WO* 15 (1984), pp. 89-92.

70. See Greenstein, 'The Formation', p. 177 n. 102. For further indicators of northern provenience, see Friedman, 'Torah', p. 613.

71. For this issue, see above.

72. W.H. Propp (personal communication) informs me that his forthcoming commentary on Exodus assigns more material to the E source than do previous

tant, nonetheless, to bear in mind the conflicting views over the identification, date and relations among the materials assigned to J and E.

For this study, it is not of primary importance to resolve the identity and nature of the material traditionally assigned to J and E (and for that matter D) because this study's selective discussion of non-priestly material is designed to understand better the larger interpretative moves underlying the priestly redaction of the book. Furthermore, the weight of the study falls on the side of the synchronic arrangement, and diachronic considerations are subordinated to this end. At times the following discussion refers to some material as J and E, first because these sigla provide a common frame of understanding, and secondly, because newer criticism has yet to substitute a convincing framework.

4. *The Priestly 'Source' and Priestly Redaction in Exodus*

Older and newer approaches to the Pentateuch show many areas of agreement about priestly material in Exodus. Apart from some literary approaches to Exodus, scholars agree that the book shows a significant amount of priestly material as well as a marked priestly redaction. Some narratives, the genealogies,[73] a number of the itinerary notices,[74]

---

commentators. Cf. the remarks of Friedman ('Torah', p. 619b): 'while J is heavily focused upon the patriarchs and the patriarchal covenant, E is essentially focused on the age of Moses, the Exodus, and Sinai, and it does not even have a patriarchal covenant'.

73. See Noth, *A History of Pentateuchal Traditions*, pp. 10, 235; Cross, *Canaanite Myth*, pp. 301-305; S. Tengström, *Die Toledotformel und die literarische Struktur der priestlichen Erweiterungsschicht im Pentateuch* (ConBOT, 17; Lund: Gleerup, 1971).

74. Noth, *A History of the Pentateuchal Traditions*, p. 14; Cross, *Canaanite Myth*, pp. 308-17; G.I. Davies, 'The Wilderness Itineraries and the Composition of the Pentateuch', *VT* 23 (1983), pp. 1-13. If Davies is correct in seeing Num. 33 as the basis for the non-priestly itinerary notices, their priestly redaction in both this chapter and the priestly itineraries within Exodus and Numbers might be taken to indicate that priestly redactional activity remains responsible for their placement within these books. In this case, Cross correctly assigns this activity to late priestly redaction. Discussion below of the itineraries assumes this view. For the historical background to the literary notices, see the further studies by Davies: 'The Wilderness Itineraries: A Comparative Study', *TynBul* 25 (1974), pp. 46-81; *The Way of the Wilderness: A Geographical Study of the Wilderness Itineraries in the Old Testament* (SOTSMS, 5; Cambridge: Cambridge University Press, 1979); 'The Wilderness Itineraries and Recent Archaeological Research', in J.A. Emerton (ed.), *Studies*

the legal (or instructional) literature of Exodus 25–31 and its narrative execution in 35–40, as well as numerous glosses have been generally regarded as priestly. Despite the consensus on these points, Pentateuchal scholarship has varied over some issues involving the priestly material. Older source-critical reconstructions exemplified by the work of M. Noth and G. von Rad[75] argue for a priestly narrative stratum, a *Priesterschrift*, independent of older material ('JE' in traditional source-critical terms), but other commentators deny this notion.[76]

Noth's view has retained support in recent years. In favor of an independent priestly narrative in Exodus, K. Koch argues that the priestly call of Moses in Exodus 6 was not likely written as a planned addition to the call in Exodus 3.[77] Friedman states similarly: 'The parallels of persons, events, and order between P and JE are so close as to indicate that J and E were edited together and then were known to and followed by the person(s) who composed P'.[78] In his treatment of the priestly narrative in Numbers 20, A. Schart posits a priestly narrative that is literarily independent. For Schart this narrative deliberately echoes the older version of the story in Exod. 17.1-7, which he assumes the priestly writer's audience knows.[79]

in the Pentateuch (VTSup, 41; Leiden: Brill, 1990), pp. 161-75.

75. Noth, *A History of Pentateuchal Traditions*, pp. 8-19; G. von Rad, *Die Priesterschrift im Hexateuch* (BWANT, 4; Berlin/Stuttgart, n.p., 1934). For explicit statements of P's dependence on JE, see Noth, *A History of Pentateuchal Traditions*, p. 234; idem, *Exodus*, p. 16. For the book of Exodus, see Noth, *Exodus*. For a recent presentation of Noth's P source in Exodus, see Campbell and O'Brien, *Sources for the Pentateuch*, pp. 35-61. See also L. Schmidt, *Studien zur Priesterschrift* (BZAW, 214; Berlin: de Gruyter, 1993); cf. the criticisms of M. Moore, Review of *Studien zur Priesterschrift*, by L. Schmidt, *CBQ* 56 (1994), pp. 778-90. The older work of S.E. McEvenue, *The Narrative Style of the Priestly Writer* (AnBib, 50; Rome: Pontifical Biblical Instutute, 1971), depends on K. Elliger's modifications of Noth's view of P (McEvenue's work is also confined to Genesis).

76. For a valuable recent survey of these questions, see M. Vervenne, 'The "P" Tradition in the Pentateuch: Document and/or Redaction? The "Sea Narrative" (Exod. 13,17–14,31) as a Test Case', in C. Brekelmans and J. Lust (eds.), *Pentateuchal and Deuteronomistic Studies: Papers Read at the XIIIth IOSOT Congress, Leuven, 1989* (BETL, 94; Leuven: Leuven University Press/Peeters, 1990), pp. 67-76. The following consideration of the issues is restricted to the book of Exodus.

77. K. Koch, 'P—Kein Redaktor! Erinnerung an zwei Eckdaten der Quellenscheidung', *VT* 37 (1987), pp. 446-67.

78. Friedman, 'Torah', p. 616a.

79. Schart, *Mose und Israel im Konflikt*, pp. 97-121.

Scholars working out of widely varying frameworks have opposed this position.[80] It is not clear from a cursory glance at the blocks of priestly narrative that the priestly narrative was more than a supplement to the older material. Exodus shows no sizable narrative block of priestly material until ch. 6. One may suspect that the priestly call in 6.2-8 represents a composition incorporating three themes derived from other material. First, the initial instance of the priestly statement (and its variations), 'they shall know that I am Yahweh', appears in the commission (Exod. 6.7; 7.5).[81] In the old material this formulation expresses the terms of conflict between Pharaoh and Yahweh in the plague narrative (e.g. 7.17; 8.18; 9.14, 16, 29; 14.31), but the priestly material extended this statement to other parts of the book (14.18; 16.6, 12; 18.11; 25.22; 29.43; 31.18).[82] Secondly, the priestly call and commission identify the plagues as 'great deeds', שׁפטים גדלים (6.6; 7.4), a priestly usage applied to divine deeds against foreign nations (12.12; cf. Ezek. 5.10, 15; 8.22, 26; 11.9; 14.21; 25.1; 30.14, 19; 39.41). Thirdly, the priestly material extends the theme of the hardening of Pharaoh's heart from the plague narrative to this section.[83] Other themes have correspondences in other material. The theme of the patriarchs and the use of the root ראה* in Exod. 6.3 may have been modelled on 3.2, 4, 6. Similarly, the divine recognition of Israelite affliction and promise of the land in 6.5-8 follows 3.7-9. There is no reason why either a separate priestly 'source' or redactor could not have composed this call. In sum, the best text-case for an independent *Priesterschrift* in Exodus remains open to question.

The argument for the *Priesterschrift* suffers in other sections of

80. Commentators denying this view include M. Löhr, P. Volz and F.M. Cross who operate with traditional source-critical assumptions; J. van Seters, who radically alters source-criticism; and R. Rendtorff and E. Blum who employ redactional models. See Löhr, *Der Priesterkodex in der Genesis* (BZAW, 38; 1924); Volz, in his work with Rudolph, *Der Elohist als Erzähler*, pp. 135-42; Cross, *Canaanite Myth*, pp. 301-21; van Seters, *The Life of Moses*, pp. 108-12, 122-23; Rendtorff, *The Problem*, p. 170; *idem*, 'The Paradigm is Changing', p. 10; Blum, *Studien*, pp. 221, 229-30.

81. For the priestly background of the expression, 'I am Yahweh', see Zimmerli, *I am Yahweh*, pp. 1-28, esp. pp. 2-13.

82. See Z. Zevit, 'The Priestly Redaction and the Interpretation of the Plague Narrative in Exodus', *JQR* 66 (1976), pp. 194-205. Cf. the deuteronomistic-sounding formulation in 10.2.

83. Wilson, 'The Hardening of Pharaoh's Heart', pp. 23-35.

priestly narrative in Exodus. The independent priestly plague narrative is confined to the two plagues of 7.19-22[84] and 9.8-12.[85] The priestly material in Exodus 14 encounters a similar question. The traditional source critic, R.E. Friedman,[86] regards the priestly material in the following terms: 'The Song of the Sea appears to have been a source that the J author used in constructing his source, and J and the Song of the Sea were in turn sources for the P author'. A more redactionally oriented scholar, M. Vervenne, likewise views the priestly material in Exodus 14 as the result of redactional compositional activity: 'the Priestly redaction has *worked over* an existing narrative into a new composition'.[87] The priestly narrative material in Exod. 15.22–18.40 is confined largely to Exodus 16.[88] Noth considered 24.15b–28.43 as a continuation of the *Priesterschrift*, with chs. 29–31 representing secondary additions.[89] The narrative material in Exodus 35–40 was also considered secondary by Noth.[90] It is questionable whether the instructions in 25–31 originated as part of a priestly narrative. C. Cohen has instead identified this legal material as 'priestly instructional literature',[91] based on comparisons with Mesopotamian and Ugaritic instruc-

84. So Noth, *Exodus*, p. 79. See Campbell and O'Brien, *Sources for the Pentateuch*, p. 38.

85. So Noth, *Exodus*, p. 70: 7.19, 20aα, 21b, 22. See Campbell and O'Brien, *Sources for the Pentateuch*, p. 38.

86. Friedman, 'Torah', p. 620b.

87. Vervenne, 'The "P" Tradition in the Pentateuch', p. 87. Vervenne's italics. From 13.17 through ch. 14, Vervenne takes the following as priestly: Exod. 13.20; 14.1-4, 8aβ, 9b, 10a, 11-12, 15-18, 21-23, 26-27, 28aβ, 29, 31. This largely follows Noth (*Exodus*, p. 105): 14.1-4, 8, 9aβb, 10aβb, 15-18, 21aαb, 22, 26, 27aα, 28-29. See Campbell and O'Brien, *Sources for the Pentateuch*, pp. 40-41.

88. Noth (*Exodus*, pp. 128, 131, 138) assigns to P 15.22a, 27; 16.1-35a (with v. 8 taken as secondary); 17.1abα (see Campbell and O'Brien, *Sources for the Pentateuch*, pp. 41-43). According to Childs (*The Book of Exodus*, pp. 266, 275) the priestly material in this section consists of 15.22aα, 27; 16.1-3, 6-13a, 32-35aα, b;17.1abα. For a detailed discussion, see Schart, *Mose und Israel im Konflikt*, pp. 122-48.

89. Noth, *Exodus*, pp. 229, 234, 239. See Campbell and O'Brien, *Sources for the Pentateuch*, p. 49 n. 57.

90. Noth, *Exodus*, p. 274.

91. C. Cohen, 'The Genre of Priestly Instructions in the Torah and the Isolation of a New Torah Source—PI', (unpublished paper, cited with permission). For some preliminary considerations involving this genre of priestly literature, see Cohen, 'Was the P Document Secret?' *JANESCU* 1.2 (1969), pp. 39-44. See further below.

tional literature. The genre of priestly instruction in Exodus 25–31 would militate against an assignment to a narrative source. The priestly narrative based on this instructional literature comprises the bulk of Exodus 35–40.

If there were an independent priestly narrative level in the Pentateuch, then one might expect further examples of, and continuity between, independent priestly narrative, especially involving events of priestly concern.[92] Accordingly, A.F. Campbell and M.A. O'Brien ask:

> For those who see P as an independent document, it is possible to argue that the P account of the Sinai covenant was suppressed in favor of the more colorful JE account. . . In this case, it is strange that a redactional process using P as a base narrative should have sacrificed the entire P version of so critical a passage, again given P's extensive coverage of the Sinai traditions.'[93]

If a separate *Priesterschrift* existed, it might have been expected that the real hero of the priestly (specifically Aaronid) tradition, namely Aaron, might be represented in priestly narrative in a less mechanistic manner, but no stories render Aaron in anything approximating the level of characterization of Moses. Aaron remains something of a 'stick-figure'. The hypothetical question of why priestly narrative is lacking where it might be expected undermines the theory of an independent *Priesterschrift*.[94]

Following these considerations, it may be argued that at least some priestly narrative which knows the earlier material ('JE') may be regarded as essentially supplemental in character. A helpful starting-point for discussing the range and character of priestly redaction is Cohen's discussion of glosses in chs. 25–31. Based on parallel instructional literature in Mesopotamia and Ugarit, Cohen argues that first-person speech does not belong to the priestly instructional genre and therefore provides an indication of the redactional hand in Exodus 25–31 and 35–40. Priestly additions to the instructional literature are evident from the criteria established by Cohen, especially first-person

---

92. 'Wilderness journey' seems preferable to 'wilderness wandering' in order to avoid the implication that the text connotes Israelites lost in the desert. Such a characterization would inadvertently privilege Pharaoh's statement in 14.3.

93. Campbell and O'Brien, *Sources for the Pentateuch*, p. 43 n. 55.

94. The issue may remain open pending further work. See Vervenne, 'The "P" Tradition in the Pentateuch', p. 88.

divine speech. Accordingly, priestly redactional additions in Exodus 25–31 include 25.2, 8-9, 21-22, 30, 40; 26.30; 27.8b; 28.3-4, 41; 29.1, 35, 42-46; 30.31; and 31.[95] Two of these passages, Exod. 25.1-7 and ch. 31, represent extensive redactional compositions. The same argument might be argued for Exodus 6. This story may have been composed with Exodus 3–4 in mind and used narrative conventions well known to the priestly tradition.[96] In sum, the fragmentary character of the priestly narrative material in Exodus would suggest that in addition to the final priestly redactional touches added to Exodus, the priestly tradition created and transmitted stories modelled on existing narratives, but not strung into a continuous narrative source as a pre-existing *Priesterschrift*.

Given the potentially long development of 'priestly instructional literature', it may be preferable to speak of a priestly tradition that produced instructional literature, narrative and other redactional material over several centuries. This approach leaves open the number of priestly redactions, since it cannot be assumed at the outset that all priestly glosses and redactional activity derived from a single hand. It is possible that the priestly redaction of Exodus involved multiple hands or redactional levels. M. Noth pointed to several priestly sections which he considered secondary to the *Priesterschrift*.[97] As a result, one might posit a priestly tradition of redactional activity evidenced by Exodus. By the same token, the literary arrangement of the priestly redaction, proposed in the following chapter, may imply a single general priestly organizing of the book which developed over a period of time. This major priestly redaction combined older arrangements of material and may have received additional glossing. In Cross's words, 'The Priestly work, JEP, was essentially the Tetrateuch in its penultimate form. Later changes, including the rearrangement which created a Pentateuch, were relatively minor.'[98] In sum, the

95. I. Knohl regards such divine first-person speech as Holiness as opposed to priestly. See Knohl, *The Sanctuary of Silence*, p 64. For discussion of Knohl's work, see below.

96. See Rendtorff, *The Problem*, p. 192.

97. The most covenient way to read these secondary texts is to examine the passages italicized in Campbell and O'Brien, *Sources for the Pentateuch*, pp. 35-61.

98. Cross, *Canaanite Myth*, p. 325. The addition of Deuteronomy was not literarily minor in the sense that it served to balance the book of Genesis. On this point, see below, Chapter 12. Cross (*Canaanite Myth*, p. 315, esp. n. 77) generally distin-

priestly tradition, understood in this sense, was responsible for the literary arrangement presented in the next chapter.[99]

This discussion of priestly material holds some ramifications for the date of the priestly materials. The view that P is a pre-exilic source has been championed by numerous critics, including Y. Kaufman, M. Haran, J. Milgrom, M. Weinfeld, R.E. Friedman, Z. Zevit and G.A. Rendsburg.[100] This view has found less acceptance among continental scholars, as well as some Americans such as H.L. Ginsberg[101] who generally place the priestly material in the post-exilic period. Milgrom and Friedman both appeal to A. Hurvitz's linguistic arguments for the linguistic priority of P to Ezekiel,[102] which imply that much of P may date from the second half of the monarchy.[103] Furthermore, it is argued that the priestly material uses the pre-exilic meanings of many terms that undergo semantic changes in the post-exilic period.[104] Similarly, demonstration of priestly archaizing, which would point to a post-exilic date, would benefit from clear examples of anachronism in the priestly document, but such instances are lacking.[105]

guishes between the priestly tradent and the redactor of the Pentateuch, but the basis for this distinction is not made clear.

99. It may be preferable to speak of a tradition or series of priestly redactions (perhaps some involving little more than glosses) which maintained the general priestly arrangement achieved by the major priestly redaction (or what Cross calls 'JEP').

100. Kaufman, *The Religion of Israel: From its Beginnings to the Babylonian Exile* (trans. and abridged by M. Greenberg; New York: Schocken Books, 1972), pp. 153-211; M. Haran, *Temples and Temple Service in Ancient Israel: An Inquiry into Biblical Cult Phenomena and the Historical Setting of the Priestly School* (Oxford: Clarendon Press, 1978; repr.: Winona Lake, IN: Eisenbrauns, 1985), pp. 1-12, 140-48; *idem*, 'The Character of the Priestly Source', *Proceedings of the Eighth World Congress of Jewish Studies: Jerusalem, August 16–21, 1981* (Jerusalem: World Union of Jewish Studies, 1983), pp. 131-38; Weinfeld, 'Literary Creativity', in A. Malamat and I. Eph'al (eds.), *World History of the Jewish People. First Series: Ancient Times. IV.2. The Age of the Monarchies: Culture and Society* (Jerusalem: Masada, 1979), pp. 28-33; Milgrom, *Leviticus 1–16*, pp. 3-6; *idem*, 'Priestly ("P") Source', *ABD*, V, pp. 454-62, esp. pp. 458-59; Friedman, 'Torah'; Zevit, 'Converging Lines of Evidence', pp. 481-511; Rendsburg, 'Late Biblical Hebrew', pp. 65-80.

101. Ginsberg, *The Israelian Heritage*.

102. See above n. 25.

103. Milgrom, *Leviticus 1–16*, pp. 3-6.

104. Milgrom, 'Priestly ("P") Source', p. 459.

105. Milgrom, 'Priestly ("P") Source', p. 459.

Thematic arguments are sometimes invoked as well for a pre-exilic date.[106]

There are some methodological flaws to this general line of argumentation, even if one were able to posit a priestly narrative stratum (and as indicated above, this view remains unproven at least for the book of Exodus). First, the date of the texts cited from Ezekiel are highly debated. Many of them may be post-exilic.[107] Secondly, while the linguistic approach taken by Hurvitz and followed by others is appealing, it remains debatable as to whether or not it constitutes a sufficient basis to posit a general date for both priestly instructional literature and priestly narrative. Methodologically, only those sections of the Pentateuch that manifest the linguistic criteria established by Hurvitz could be clearly dated prior to Ezekiel, and it is evident that Hurvitz's analysis covers only priestly instructional literature and not priestly narrative and other redactional additions.[108] Even if Hurvitz's argument pertaining to the date of these materials could be accepted and extended to the instructional literature as a whole, the date of the priestly narrative and redactional material in the Pentateuch would remain open. Indeed, the nearly lone dissent of B.A. Levine on the linguistic criteria remains a helpful reminder as to the difficulties involved in the linguistic argument.[109] The linguistic and thematic criteria involve

---

106. For a list, see Friedman, 'Torah', pp. 616b-17a; see also pp. 614a-15a. Friedman's list of allegedly pre-exilic passages showing dependence on texts in Exodus includes only ch. 6 which he takes as the source for Ezek. 20. For a thematic comparison of Ezekiel and P which comes to the same conclusion as to P's relative priority, see Haran, 'The Law-Code of Ezekiel XL–XLVIII and its Relation to the Priestly School', *HUCA* 50 (1979), pp. 45-71.

107. For a chronological study of Ezekiel based on linguistic evidence (in the vein of A. Hurvitz's approach), see M.F. Rooker, *Biblical Hebrew in Transition: The Language of the Book of Ezekiel* (JSOTSup, 90; Sheffield: JSOT Press, 1990).

108. Hurvitz, 'The Language of the Priestly Source', p. 87:

> A further investigation included an analysis of nine characteristic terms and expressions which represent a highly variegated cross-section of the Priestly vocabulary. These words are used in connection with genealogical lists. . . sacrificial regulations. . . religious offerings and services. . . technical descriptions of cultic objects, structures, and activities. . . cloth used for sacred purposes; and designations of Temple.

109. B.A. Levine, 'Late Language in the Priestly Source', pp. 69-82. I am not prepared to follow Levine in arguing that some terminology of the instructional literature originally reflected the exilic or post-exilic period (although it could have been used or interpreted secondarily in this manner) even though some of the instructional literature could postdate the monarchy.

a limited selection of passages, and as a result, the dating of the rest of the priestly material requires further investigation.[110]

Thirdly, the arguments about archaizing and priestly use of terms in their pre-exilic meanings are not compelling, as one advocate of these criteria, J. Milgrom, admits: 'the possibility must be granted that the priestly redaction may have succeeded in concealing its true (late) period'.[111] The pre-exilic meanings of terms in the priestly material may have continued after the exile usage; a specialized priestly usage of such terms is not unrealistic. The same point applies to those thematic criteria which have been invoked to sustain a pre-exilic date.[112] Because of the various sorts of material grouped under the rubric of P, E.A. Speiser and B.A. Levine argue that the priestly material developed over a long period of time.[113] Levine concludes:

> P, as we have it, is the product of extended literary activity. On this basis, some of P may be later than the period of the First Return, and other literary components—earlier. Some parts of P may date to the exilic period, when there was considerable editorial activity on materials originating from the period of the First Temple. Finally, there may be some material in P that dates from the pre-exilic period, and which was committed to writing at that time.[114]

Given the evidence, Levine's view as expressed here appears most

110. Blenkinsopp, *The Pentateuch*, p. 238.

111. Milgrom, 'Priestly ("P") Source', p. 459.

112. A credible post-exilic setting for the priestly institutions described in Exodus has been presented *in nuce* by B.A. Levine (*The JPS Torah Commentary. Leviticus,* אֶרְקְיָּו: *The Traditional Hebrew Text with the New JPS Translation* [Philadelphia: The Jewish Publication Society, 1989], pp. xxxi-xxxix, 218-21).

113. E.A. Speiser, 'Leviticus and the Critics', in M. Haran (ed.), *Yehezkel Kaufman Jubilee Volume* (Jerusalem: Magnes, 1960), pp. 29-45; Levine, 'Late Language in the Priestly Source', p. 70; *idem, The JPS Torah Commentary. Leviticus,* pp. xxix-xxx. It is instructional to compare the conclusions about the range of priestly material by Wellhausen, *Prolegomena*, p. 376 n. 1, p. 385. Despite his exceedingly disparaging remarks about priestly material and Judaism (e.g. *Prolegomena*, p. 341 n. 1, pp. 342, 348, 412), and his acceptance of P's lateness (*Prolegomena*, p. 3), Wellhausen nonetheless recognized the variety of priestly materials, not all of which were late. For further discussion of Wellhausen's autobiographical reflections on his aversion to 'the Law', see L.H. Silberman, 'Wellhausen and Judaism', in D. Knight (ed.), *Julius Wellhausen and his* Prolegomena to the History of Israel (Semeia, 25; Chico, CA: Scholars Press, 1983), pp. 75-82. On the social location of the priestly material in the Aaronid tradition, see the excursus to this chapter.

114. Levine, 'Late Language in the Priestly Source', p. 70.

reasonable. In sum, the priestly genealogies and instructional literature may be regarded generally as pre-exilic. The priestly glosses (including glosses to narrative, such as 1.13-14 and 2.23-25,[115] and legal sections such as 26.30) and priestly narratives (including narrative based on the instructional literature) as well as the literary arrangement of priestly redaction of Exodus as a whole, would suit either an exilic or post-exilic setting. The priestly itinerary notices as well as the incorporation of the non-priestly itinerary notices probably belong to the priestly structuring of narrative material and would therefore comport better with a later stage of development.

The nature of the discussion regarding the priestly redaction of Exodus has been affected recently by the important study of I. Knohl.[116] According to Knohl, the Holiness Code (Lev. 17–26) is later than P. Furthermore, based on similarities between the Holiness Code and many redactional additions to the Pentateuch, he argues that the priestly school responsible for the Holiness Code (H) redacted P. Based on his analysis of P and H, Knohl reconstructs two schools, the Priestly School and the Holiness School. Both are priestly in thought and expression, although some verbal and theological differences distinguish them. With respect to the book of Exodus, Knohl views H as the final, major redactor responsible for 4.21b; 6.2–7.6; 9.35; 10.1-2, 20-23, 27; 11.9-10; 12.1-20, 43-49; 16 (especially vv. 12, 23, 32); 20.11; 24.12-18; 25.1-9; 27.20-21; 28.3-5; 29.38-46; 30.10; 31.1-17, 18; 32.15; 34.29-35; and 35–40.[117] Many of these passages constitute precisely the material that the next chapter identifies as seminal to the literary arrangement of the priestly redaction of Exodus. This study and Knohl's often agree as to the later redactional material of Exodus. This agreement includes some of the passages, such as Exodus 6.2–7.7 and 31.18, which are crucial for discerning the literary arrangement of the priestly

---

115. Childs, *The Book of Exodus*, pp. 7, 28.

116. Knohl, *The Sanctuary of Silence*. Knohl is not alone in reversing the traditional scholarly chronology of H and P. See also Milgrom, *Leviticus 1–16*, pp. 13-42. Cooper and Goldstein ('Exodus and *Maṣṣôt* in History and Tradition', p. 25 n. 35) regard H as a redaction post-dating P; they call H a 'midrash' on P. Compare the opposite view of Cross (*Canaanite Myth*, p. 297 n. 18, p. 319) that P reworked H in Lev. 26.

117. See Knohl, *The Sanctuary of Silence*, esp. pp. 15-7, 19-20, 21, 47, 52, 61-68, 104-105.

redaction proposed in this work.[118] As a result of Knohl's work, the priestly redaction of Exodus might be defined further as largely an H redaction. Viewed in these terms, the purpose of this study is to attempt to build on Knohl's contribution by inquiring into the literary arrangement which the holiness redaction, in combination with earlier priestly structuring materials (such as the priestly itineraries), achieved with the book of Exodus.

While Knohl's study of the linguistic items distinguishing P and H appears well-grounded, a number of questions surrounding the reconstruction of the H redaction may be raised. The extent of H is debated. Questions may be raised, for example, regarding H in some narrative sections. The argument for H in Exodus 6–11 is tenuous at times, as it is built on a syllogistic logic: (1) an H formula ('I am the Lord. . . ') is found in Exod. 6.2-8, and this passage is therefore H; (2) 7.1-6 stands in chiastic relationship with 6.2-8, and is therefore H; and (3) 11.9-10 forms an *inclusio* with 7.1-6, and is therefore H.[119] In some instances the basis for attributing a passage to H is primarily linguistic, and in many of these cases Knohl appears on firmer ground. Yet as in the cases of 7.1-6 and 11.9-10, the argument rests on stylistic criteria of chiasm and *inclusio*. The argument is quite plausible, but generally not as well founded.[120]

118. Knohl, *The Sanctuary of Silence*, pp. 61, 67, 145.
119. Knohl, *The Sanctuary of Silence*, pp. 61-62.
120. The only other major disagreement with Knohl's book bearing on this study involves his view of the Sabbath in P as opposed to H. According to Knohl (*The Sanctuary of Silence*, pp. 18, 61-62), P does not forbid human work on the Sabbath despite its view of God as resting on the seventh day in Gen. 1.1-2.4a. Many scholars have argued that divine rest appears to be paradigmatic for human rest on Sabbath. Accordingly, the notion of human rest seems to be implicit in Gen. 1.1–2.4a which all scholars, including Knohl, attribute to P (see below Chapter 6). If, as Knohl would argue, the point of this passage is not that God's rest is paradigmatic for humans (and anticipatory for Israel), then the full theological thrust of this crescendo of the priestly creation requires an alternative explanation. Furthermore, the apparently priestly redaction of Exod. 20.8-11 would seem to highlight the connection between divine and human rest. It is therefore hardly surprising that Knohl assigns v. 11 to HS (*The Sanctuary of Silence*, pp. 67, 104, 102 n. 144), but the connection between the Sabbath and desisting from work is made already in v. 10 which would suggest that the requirement of rest predates HS. It would appear that the Sabbath is just as important to P as it is to H. What is different is H's attempt to give the Sabbath greater currency and application to the people, as Knohl demonstrates so well with so many other features of H theology. The ideology which

Furthermore, there is some disagreement over the setting of H. Knohl would date it to some point from the time of Hezekiah to the Persian period, while Milgrom would allow a range from Hezekiah down to the exilic period. The evidence for these dates is minimal. The historical reconstruction for H is not fully evident and consistently presented. Knohl presents H as the successor school to the priestly school effected by the prophetic critique of priestly ritual.[121] The evidence for such a historical succession (as opposed to overlap) is unavailable. It is not even clear that the linguistic evidence insightfully proposed by Knohl translates into the sociological delineation which he constructs between the holiness and priestly 'schools'.[122] Knohl generally refers to them as schools, but at one point he implies a rather different sociological model: 'HS [Holiness School] reflects a profound ideological change occurring within PT [Priestly Theology] circles'.[123] From this formulation it might be inferred that not two schools are involved, but only one, with competing views and some chronological overlap. Such a view would also suit Knohl's own demonstration of the massive debt that H owes to P. Therefore, it might be argued that the material designated as H by Knohl may prove to represent a later priestly redactional level which held the sort of theological views that Knohl attributes to H (this is the force of the argument in Part III of this study). In sum, Knohl's two priestly schools are hypothetical reconstructions which would benefit from evidence beyond the insightfully examined linguistic items and theological views.[124]

Despite these relatively minor quibbles, Knohl's work is to be heralded not simply for the importance of his bold hypothesis for understanding the redaction of the Pentateuch, but also for the methodical analysis which undergirds the study. However one regards H, the final

Knohl assigns to HS with respect to the Sabbath seems to be found also in Isa. 58.13 (is the putative position of HS on the Sabbath influenced by Levitical circles, by way of reaction to them?).

121. Knohl, *The Sanctuary of Silence*, p. 220.

122. Similarly, R.E. Friedman argues that the reconstruction of 'the Deuteronomistic School', especially in the work of M. Weinfeld, rests more on presumption than evidence. See Friedman, 'The Deuteronomistic School', in Beck *et al.* (eds.), *Fortunate the Eyes That See*, p. 80.

123. Knohl, *The Sanctuary of Silence*, p. 200.

124. It is scarcely necessary to raise other potential criticisms, as they do not affect this study. Furthermore, they hardly detract from the weight of the contribution that the book makes to Pentateuchal research.

literary arrangement represents a cumulative product of priestly tradition, since both the holiness and priestly schools are priestly in character and social location. Knohl regards H as priestly,[125] and Milgrom has emphasized the overall proximity between the two.[126] Milgrom has raised questions about the relationship between the two within specific passages. For these reasons, the redaction of Exodus outlined and discussed in the following chapters of this work is to be regarded generally as priestly.

In closing, it should be noted that the basic goal of this study, to determine the literary arrangement of the priestly redaction in Exodus, remains generally unaffected by the three major areas of controversy surrounding P discussed so far: (1) the existence of a priestly narrative stratum (which, following Cross and others, I do not accept); (2) an older independent collection of priestly instructional materials (including H) separate from the priestly narrative and redactional material (which I accept); and (3) the nature, date and extent of H (which stands in need of greater study).

5. *The Question of Deuteronomistic Redaction in Exodus*

Both source and redactional approaches recognize deuteronomistic material in the book of Exodus. In the older approach some of this material was viewed as including a series of additions that highlighted specific themes as well as other material reflecting a redactional stratum. The newer redactional views vary in their views of deuteronomistic material in Exodus. Rendtorff's view of a relatively minimalist deuteronomistic redaction following a priestly redaction echoes older source-critical arguments.[127] For the book of Exodus this view con-

---

125. Knohl, *The Sanctuary of Silence*, p. 200.

126. Milgrom, *Leviticus 1–16*, p. 42.

127. Rendtorff, *The Problem*, pp. 99-100:

> One usually calls the layering of reworking of which we are speaking here 'deuteronomistic' or more recently 'early deuteronomic' or 'protodeuteronomic'. In any case, it is a matter of a reworking which in its ideas and language is closely related to Deuteronomy. It has been shown that this reworking has left the texts at hand essentially unchanged and has inserted interpretive additions at definite places. It presupposes therefore the present text more or less in the form in which it lies before us.

Cf. L. Perlitt, *Bundestheologie im Alten Testament* (WMANT, 36; Neukirchen–Vluyn: Neukirchener Verlag, 1969), pp. 156-238; Blum, *Studien*; *idem*, 'Israël à la

forms essentially to Noth's reconstruction which involved relatively little material that could be classified as deuteronomistic: Exod. 12.24-27, 13.1-16, 15.25b-26, 16.4, 28, and 32.9-14.[128] Blum, Dozeman and Johnstone differ from Rendtorff in two ways. Dozeman and Johnstone posit a *major* deuteronomistic redaction and Blum a *major* deuteronomistic composition. All three authors place this work *prior* to the priestly redaction.[129]

Much of the deuteronomistic material especially in chs. 12–13 appears to constitute a supplemental 'agglomeration of ritual materials of quite varied character and provenance'.[130] In contrast, the briefer items in Exod. 15.25b-26, 16.4, 28 may be redactional touches. In a quite different vein, it has been argued that Exodus 19–24 shows the order and elements of a larger deuteronomistic redaction. The basis for this view might be traced to the work of G. von Rad.[131] Once von Rad observed the massive patterning akin to both Exodus 19–24 and the book of Deuteronomy, it was logical to assign the formation of these chapters to a deuteronomistic redactor. Von Rad viewed the similarity

montagne de Dieu', pp. 271-95 (and 'Débat sur la contribution de E. Blum', pp. 297-300). For linguistic evidence for deuteronomistic language in Exodus, see also F. Postma, E. Talstra and M. Vervenne, *Exodus: Materials in Automatic Text Processing*. I. *Morphological, Syntactical and Literary Case Studies* (Instrumental Biblica, 1.1; Amsterdam: Turnhout; Brepols: Vu Boekhandel, 1983), pp. 98-108. See also on Exod. 20.22, M. Weinfeld, *Deuteronomy and the Deuteronomic School* (Oxford: Oxford University Press, 1972), pp. 206-207 n. 4; and Mettinger, *The Dethronement of Sabaoth*, p. 48 n. 37; Exod. 34.11-16, noted by many commentators (see Ginsberg, *The Israelian Heritage of Judaism*, pp. 62-66, and below); Exod. 34.25b, so Mettinger, *The Dethronement of Sabaoth*, p. 72 n. 28a.

128. For a summary, see Campbell and O'Brien, *Sources for the Pentateuch*, pp. 198-99, esp. nn. 28, 29, 31-33, 38. See further M. Fuss, *Die deuteronomische Pentateuchredaktion in Exodus 1–17* (BZAW, 126; Berlin: de Gruyter, 1972).

129. Blum, *Studien*, p. 222; Dozeman, *God on the Mountain*, pp. 9, 11-12, 37-86; W. Johnstone, *Exodus* (OTG; Sheffield: JSOT Press, 1990), pp. 75, 84-85; *idem*, 'Reactivating the Chronicles Analogy in Pentateuchal Studies, with Special Reference to the Sinai Pericope in Exodus', *ZAW* 99 (1987), pp. 16-37; and 'The Decalogue and the Redaction of the Sinai Pericope in Exodus', *ZAW* 100 (1988), pp. 361-85. For the claim for deuteronomistic redaction of Exod. 32 (as in Johnstone's first article), see C.T. Begg, 'The Destruction of the Calf (Exod. 32,20/Deut. 9,21)', in N. Lohfink (ed.), *Das Deuteronomium: Entstehung, Gestalt und Botschaft* (BETL, 68; Leuven: Leuven University Press/Peeters, 1985), p. 250.

130. M. Greenberg, 'Exodus', *EncJud*, VI, p. 1054.

131. Von Rad, *The Problem of the Hexateuch*, pp. 26-40.

between Exodus 19–24 and Deuteronomy through the lens of source-criticism, and attributed the shape of chs. 19–24 to the cult of Shechem as recorded in the Deuteronomistic history. In contrast, the newer paradigm of Rendtorff, Blum and Dozeman took the evidence of the Deuteronomistic history as support for a deuteronomistic redactor of Exodus 19 and 24. While Exodus 19–24 does lend itself to the view of a deuteronomistic redaction, this approach is not without substantial questions and difficulties.

First, some scholars have criticized the lack of clear deuteronomistic language and themes in passages newly assigned to the deuteronomistic redaction of Exodus.[132] Secondly, the distribution of this redaction within Exodus is uneven. Even if a maximal view of this redaction were taken to include the narrative sections of chs. 19–24,[133] the character of the redaction remains debatable. Parenthetically, this point would suggest different tradition-histories in various blocks of material in Exodus. Thirdly, the reassignment of E material to a deuteronomistic redaction constitutes a difficulty in some cases. In the attempts to describe a deuteronomistic redaction, much material newly assigned to this redaction was attributed previously to E. The result of this shift was to erase some of the doublets from the older core of material in redactional treatments. Given the common background posited for E and D,[134] this reassignment was understandable. If the two cannot be distinguished on the basis of language, then one criterion remaining for positing a deuteronomistic redaction rather than an Elohist source is a matter of editorial style. Such an issue would be complicated by the redactional view of E, proposed by P. Volz and W. Rudolph in the 1930s.

The arguments for a deuteronomistic redaction versus an Elohistic source may not be so divergent as their proponents imagine. Both have been attributed to a common Levitical tradition-stream. Whether E is redactional material or a parallel source, it may be possible to

132. Moberly, *At the Mountain of God*, p. 184; J.D. Levenson, *Sinai and Zion: An Entry into the Jewish Bible* (San Francisco: Harper & Row, 1985), p. 25.

133. See Blum, *Studien*, pp. 9-43, esp. pp. 30-37; J. Blenkinsopp, Review of *Studien zur Komposition des Pentateuch*, by E. Blum, *CBQ* 54 (1992), p. 312.

134. This background is considered to be northern Levitical by Wilson, *Prophecy and Society in Ancient Israel* (Philadelphia: Fortress Press, 1980), pp. 146-66; Friedman, *Who Wrote the Bible?*, pp. 120-29, 189-90, 196. For the similarities between E and D, see also Jenks, *The Elohist and North Israelite Traditions*, p. 48.

equate it with some of the materials identified as the deuteronomistic
redaction by Blum and Dozeman. Under either reconstruction, this
material was received by the priestly redaction. In this case identifying whether or not a specific phrase or sentence belongs to an Elohist
source or a deuteronomistic redaction (or possibly a third origin) may
be moot. Other materials assigned to the deuteronomistic redaction
may represent a different level of the tradition. T.H. Vriezen observes
verbal parallels between Exod. 1.6 and 8 and Judg. 2.8 and 10 and suggests that the two texts share a common literary pattern.[135] Rendtorff
and Blum take this parallel as evidence of deuteronomistic editorial
reworking.[136] Assuming the validity of their argument,[137] this redactional connection would date presumably to a point when the Deuteronomistic History was undergoing its larger redaction, and this might
appear to date from a time later than the priestly redaction of Exodus
19. Pinpointing the relative dating of large collections of material
such as the Pentateuch and the Deuteronomistic History is very difficult, but it would seem logical that such collections were redacted and
related to one another at a stage after the priestly redaction of an individual section within a book. If this is correct, it would imply two
levels of tradition within Exodus that might be identified in some sense
as deuteronomistic. This approach appears in the work of Blum.
A. Schart likewise posits for Exod. 15.22–18.27 a deuteronomistic redaction to JE ('Dje') and a deuteronomistic redaction to P ('Dp').[138]
The criteria used for this redaction are debatable at times, and the differing views of the deuteronomistic and priestly redactions perhaps
highlight the problem.

In comparison with the priestly redaction, the hypothesis of a
major deuteronomistic redaction is difficult and remains a question.
Rendtorff's arguments for this redaction are modest at best, and Blum
as well as Dozeman seem to have accepted the thematic and terminological arguments broached by Perlitt, though perhaps without a sufficient winnowing of the claims involved. It is especially curious that
many passages that Rendtorff takes as deuteronomistic reworking or

135. T.H. Vriezen, 'Exodusstudien Exodus 1', *VT* 17 (1967), pp. 334-53, esp.
p. 339.
136. Rendtorff, *The Problem*, p. 198; Blum, *Studien*, p. 102.
137. Vriezen views the parallel in rather different terms. For him, the two texts
draw on a common literary pattern.
138. Schart, *Mose und Israel im Konflikt*, pp. 245-47, 252-53.

cross-references are remarkably devoid of characteristically deutero-nomistic language. Similar problems affect Blum's claims. He acknowl-edges that his 'D-composition' ('K^D') lacks the linguistic features otherwise associated with deuteronomistic works in contrast to the one clearly deuteronomistic Exod. 32.9-14.[139] How else is one to identify a biblical work or section of one as deuteronomistic? As argued below in Chapter 9, the linguistic items attributed variously to a deuterono-mistic stratum, editorial work or composition are better understood as priestly reworkings of deuteronomistic themes and expressions. On this view it may be preferable to view Exodus 19–34 (and I would say, Exodus 19–40) as 'K^P' or some sort of priestly 'composition', which used older materials including the distinctly deuteronomistic Exod. 32.9-14. For example, as noted above, the deuteronomistic motif of the tablets becomes a priestly redactional motif for framing 19–31 and 32–40. If this point were to be carried to its logical conclusion, it might suggest that late priestly redactional activity may have been re-sponsible for some or all of the deuteronomistic materials in Exodus. All of these issues will be revisited in further detail in Chapter 10 of this study, but suffice it to say that deuteronomistic supplements seem more plausible than deuteronomistic strata or redactional schemas. In sum, the clearer deuteronomistic items reflect relatively minor supple-ments rather than a substantive redaction.

In retrospect, newer source-critical and redactional studies share two major methodological changes in contrast with older source-critical studies. A relative priority has been given more recently to thematic criteria over linguistic ones in texts other than priestly material. This priority is evident in J. van Seters's redating of J and in Blum's attempts to identify the deuteronomistic redaction. It is perhaps ironic that both scholars rely on the same theme of the land for their highly divergent views.[140] This emphasis on thematic criteria may represent a reaction against the limits imposed by the use of older lists of lin-guistic features to identify sources or redactions. Heavy reliance on

139. See especially Blum, 'Israël à la montagne de Dieu', p. 288. Blum's reconstruction involves an inherent chronological contradiction: he attributes 'K^D' to the inheriters of the classic deuteronomistic school, but he regards the passages in Deut. 5 and 9 as 'prolongement' of Exod. 19 and 24 .

140. J. van Seters, 'The So-Called Deuteronomistic Redaction of the Pentateuch', in J.A. Emerton (ed.), *Congress Volume: Leuven 1989* (VTSup, 43; Leiden: Brill, 1991), pp. 58-77; Blum, *Studien*, p. 103.

thematic criteria may prove equally inadequate, however, in the long run. Finally, most critics of either approach depart from older critics in their decided shift against reading Pentateuchal literature against the purported historical background of the sources or redactions. There seems to be less appeal made to a purported *Sitz im Leben* of either sources or redactors, in part because knowledge of both seems increasingly problematic to venture despite some recent attempts to do so.[141]

6. *Literary Readings and Exodus*

The field of biblical studies is moving away from the tendency to equate the interpretation of literature with its purported historical background. This change seems to reflect two larger hermeneutical issues. One is literary, the other theological. The climate in historical-critical study has been sufficiently affected by literary study to consider issues of literary character. Furthermore, theologically informed readings have reacted against purely historicist models of interpretation and the limits they place on theological appropriations of the biblical text. Theologically oriented inquiry now questions whether the study of the Bible is to be reduced to the historical background of texts.

As a result of these changes, diachronic approaches to the Pentateuch have been supplemented in recent years by synchronic study. Critics have taken refuge in this approach not only because they find too many overly speculative and unsupported hypotheses in diachronic analyses. These critics also deny that diachronic concerns should eclipse synchronic analysis. For the book of Exodus, synchronic work includes the studies of R.W.L. Moberly and H.C. Brichto on Exodus 32–34.[142] Moberly's goal is an essentially synchronic reading that attempts to do justice to the theology of the text. Synchronic analysis is certainly valid. The accurate assessment of a work on the synchronic level remains a valuable enterprise even for historians who wish to understand their written sources. Synchronic studies by biblicists and literary critics alike have produced valuable results for biblical studies. From the perspective of either literary criticism or historical-critical studies, synchronic analysis is limited, however, if it is severed from diachronic considerations.

141. See Friedman, *Who Wrote the Bible?*
142. Moberly, *At the Mountain of God*; H.C. Brichto, *Toward a Grammar*, pp. 88-121. See also Moberly, *The Old Testament of the Old Testament*, pp. 176-91.

The relationship between diachronic and synchronic study has long been a tension in literary studies and there have been a wide variety of viewpoints on the place of historical background in understanding a literary work.[143] The spectrum of views ranges from construing the literary work in terms of its author's biography to denying any relevance of historical background. Indeed, this is one major battlefield of literary debate. New Criticism denied, or at the least greatly subordinated, historical considerations. In the last three decades, a flood of new diachronic considerations have reacted against New Criticism's construal of the relationship between diachronic and synchronic reading.[144] Ideological and cultural aspects of texts and their authors have become a major diachronic dimension of reading literature since the 1960s. T. Eagleton concludes his survey of literary criticism by remarking: 'It is not a question of debating whether 'literature' should be related to 'history' or not: it is a question of different readings of history itself'.[145] The conceptualization of history has changed dramatically over the last decade. Rather than the subject of objective or even scientific inquiry, history has become recognized as a category of discourse, subject to a variety of ideological manipulations. Indeed, as M. Roth observes, many historians 'use and comment upon historical discourse knowing that History has been undone'.[146] The relationship of literature to 'history' and to historical settings has become again a central question in literary criticism, but on entirely different terms.[147] As S. Fish warns, interpretation is not simply the result of investigation; rather 'interpretation is the source of texts, facts, authors and intentions'.[148]

In this environment of questioning the processes and underpinnings of interpretation, literary criticism has returned to diachronic factors in reading texts. No literary critic could envision understanding Dante

143. See the survey of views in T. Eagleton, *Literary Theory: An Introduction* (Minneapolis: University of Minnesota Press, 1983).

144. See C. Porter, 'History and Literature: "After the New Historicism"', *New Literary History* 21.2 (1990), pp. 253-54.

145. Eagleton, *Literary Theory*, p. 209.

146. M.S. Roth, 'Introduction', *New Literary History* 21.2 (1990), p. 242.

147. For different views in the debate, see *New Literary History* 21.2 (1990), which contains several articles devoted to this topic.

148. S. Fish, *Is There a Text in this Class? The Authority of Interpretive Communities* (Cambridge, MA: Harvard University Press, 1980), p. 16.

and Milton without recognizing their debt to the Christian tradition. Yet this is exactly what some literary critics such as R. Alter[149] presently practice in the area of biblical studies. To be sure, Alter pays lip service to the achievement of diachronic study of the Bible, but it remains unintegrated into his work.[150] This oddity contradicts the practice of literary criticism of other literatures and does not excuse the literary-critical enterprise from investigating a biblical work in part through its historical background. It might be argued that some literary critics who approach the Bible ignore diachronic dimensions of the texts because this sort of biblical work is not part of their training or field. One might follow R.E. Friedman in putting H. Bloom's *The Book of J* in this category.[151] Bloom's previous work such as *The Anxiety of Influence*[152] revolves around understanding authors in relation to one another, but *The Book of J* shows no understanding of J relative to its antecedent material.[153] P. Trible's view that Bloom's 'Book of J' should be called 'The Book of B' might suggest the figure against whom Bloom is reading J is Bloom himself.[154] In any event, Bloom gives the impression that J sprang full-blown onto the literary stage, despite his uncritical assumption of the validity of source-criticism and despite his appreciation of diachronic factors in his other work.

Whether on historical-critical or literary grounds, synchronic readings need diachronic considerations of the literary conventions and historical background of the age. It represents the interests of both literary and historical inquiry to understand either how a work came to achieve its form or how it responds to or incorporates prior tradition. Just as a work cannot be reduced entirely to historical considerations, so too it cannot be stripped of its historical importance and setting. There are

149. R. Alter, *The Art of Biblical Narrative* (New York: Basic Books, 1981).

150. Alter, *The Art of Biblical Narrative*, pp. 11-12.

151. See R.E. Friedman's review of *The Book of J*, in his article, 'Scholar, Heal Thyself', pp. 33-47. The standard criticisms of Bloom's interpretative shortcomings are treated in Friedman's article as well as in the other articles in *The Iowa Review* 21.3 (1991).

152. H. Bloom, *The Anxiety of Influence: A Theory of Poetry* (London: Oxford University Press, 1975).

153. So J.A. Holstein, 'How Not to Read the Hebrew Bible', *The Iowa Review* 21.3 (1991), p. 50. For the literary antecedents to the J material of Gen. 2–3, see Wallace, *The Eden Narrative*.

154. P. Trible, 'The Bible on Bloom', *The Iowa Review* 21.3 (1991), p. 30.

other considerations involving assumptions underlying synchronic study of texts. Moberly is inclined to assume synchronic unity unless otherwise indicated, but this assumption appears as unwarranted as the over-confident presuppositions made in diachronic analysis of Pentateuchal books.[155] If diachronic analysis relies on the differences between materials in order to establish different sources or redactions, synchronic analysis appears to rely more on similarities within the text to sense the order in the apparent mélange of materials, but the perception of similarities runs the risk of subjective judgments no less than the perception of differences by source critics. Indeed, the criteria for an intelligible synchronic arrangement of Exodus are not always self-evident. And the examination of a literary work's synchronic arrangement may elude firm criteria in part because each work is *sui generis*.

155. Moberly, *At the Mountain of God*, p. 39.

Chapter 6

THE LITERARY ARRANGEMENT
OF THE PRIESTLY REDACTION OF EXODUS

1. *Introduction*

Over the last century scholarly discussion of Exodus has revolved
largely around the character and date of sources, their relation to one
another and their tradition-histories.[1] Generally overlooked in this
discussion is the nature of the final product achieved by the priestly or
deuteronomic redactions. The purpose of this chapter is to address one
of these issues, specifically the literary arrangement produced by the
priestly redaction of Exodus. Diachronic analysis has been joined rarely
to a discussion of the synchronic arrangement of the book. To be sure,
this approach has been ventured for specific sections of Exodus,[2] but
the agenda proposed here has not been executed for the biblical book
as a whole.

This agenda raises some methodological issues, however. The long-
reigning paradigm for examining the diachronic development of Exodus has come under serious attack. For over a century and a half the
historical study of Exodus has been pursued by examining the Yahwist
source (J), the Elohist source (E) and the Priestly source (P) as well as
deuteronomic (D or dtr) additions, although these sources have been

---

1. For the scholarly discussion, see Chapter 5, section 1. For further discussion,
see below.

2. For example in G.F. Davies's recent analysis of Exod. 1–2 (see Davies,
Israel in Egypt: A Reading of Exodus 1–2 [JSOTSup, 135; Sheffield: JSOT Press,
1992]; and in R.W.L. Moberly's study of Exod. 32–34 (Moberly, *At the Mountain
of God*). B.S. Childs has called attention to what he perceives to be the 'canonical
influence' of the relationship of the various parts of Exodus. See Childs, *Introduction to the Old Testament as Sacred Scripture* (Philadelphia: Fortress Press, 1979),
p. 173. Whatever this influence may have been, it plays no explicit role in the analysis to follow.

vigorously debated during this period.[3] As discussed in the previous chapter, assaults on this paradigm have come from three general directions: modifications of source theories, redactionally oriented theories, and synchronic approaches. This chapter is premised on the general consensus reached on the priestly material discussed in the previous chapter (especially in section 4). Scholars largely agree that the book shows a significant amount of priestly material as well as a marked priestly redaction. To summarize, priestly narrative has been read as either a continuous narrative stratum or editorial composition supplements. In either case, the basic goal of this study, to determine the literary arrangement of the priestly redaction, remains relatively unaffected by the status of the issue of existence of a priestly narrative stratum. Moreover, a priestly redaction of the book has been generally upheld. Exodus shows a number of priestly glosses and compositions, and many scholars now maintain a major priestly redaction of the book.[4]

To date, diachronic discussions have generated relatively few attempts to describe the literary character of the book. Three recent synchronic suggestions may be noted. First, B. Jacob bases his arrangement largely on mathematical considerations.[5] According to Jacob's figures, the two halves, the first focusing on Egypt and the second on Sinai, tally to 494 and 716 verses. Each half contains three sections: Exod. 1.1–7.13, 7.14–11.10 and chs. 12–18 belong to the first while chs. 19–24, 25–34 and 35–40 belong to second. Apart from the gross difference in the two halves, this mathematical schema overlooks the break between Moses at Midian in ch. 2 and on the mountain in ch. 3. The division of the book into two major parts has been recognized by a number of scholars,[6] and it is adopted and modified below.

Secondly, J.P. Fokkelman offers the following structure (omitting the subheadings within these sections):[7] Exposition 1.1–6.27; Confrontation

3. See North, 'Pentateuchal Criticism', pp. 48-83.
4. I. Knohl has identified much of this redaction as the work of the 'Holiness School'. See Knohl, *The Sanctuary of Silence*, pp. 60-68, 104-105.
5. B. Jacob, *The Second Book of the Bible: Exodus* (trans. W. Jacob with Y. Elman; Hoboken, NJ: Ktav, 1992), pp. xxxv, 1083-87.
6. M. Greenberg divides the book into Exod. 1–19 and 20–40. See Greenberg, *Understanding Exodus* (New York: Behrman, 1969), p. 3. See also P.K. McCarter, 'Exodus', p. 129; Friedman, 'Torah', p. 605b.
7. J.P. Fokkelman, 'Exodus', in R. Alter and F. Kermode (eds.), *The Literary*

182   *The Pilgrimage Pattern in Exodus*

6.28–15.18; Introduction: Making for Sinai 15.22–18.27; Revelation on Sinai and Covenant I 19–31; Revelation on Sinai and Covenant II 32–40. The last two sections of this proposal are defensible on both synchronic and diachronic grounds. As argued below, the priestly re-daction of the book likewise made this division and thematically linked these two sections with parts in the first half of the book. The rest of Fokkelman's delineation appears somewhat arbitrary by comparison.

Finally, R.J. Clifford suggests the following schema (without his subheadings):

(I) The Hebrews Freed from Pharaoh in Egypt (1.1–15.21)
    (A) Danger (1.1–2.22)
    (B) God Commissions Moses: First Narrative (2.23–6.1)
    (C) God Commissions Moses: Second Narrative (6.2–7.7)
    (D) The Ten Plagues (7.8–13.16)
    (E) The Destruction of the Egyptian Armies and the Thanksgiving of Miriam (13.17–15.21)
    (F) The Journey to Sinai and Canaan after the Egyptians Have Been Destroyed (15.22–18.27)

(II) Israel at Sinai (19.1–40.38)
    (A) Solemn Concluding of the Covenant (19.1–24.18)
    (B) Divine Command to Build and Maintain the Dwelling (chs. 25–31)
    (C) Apostasy and Renewal of the Covenant (chs. 32–34)
    (D) Building of the Dwelling and the Descent of the Glory (chs. 35–40)

Clifford reiterates the notion of two major halves in Exodus. Based on the priestly itinerary notices as fundamental indicators of the 'P' arrangement of the book, he suggests two 'interlocking' halves, 1.1–15.21 and 12.37–40.38.[8] Clifford's delineation of two commissions reflects a long-standing consensus. To anticipate an argument made below, the pairs of commissions recognized by Clifford and the double-covenant scheme of chs. 19–40 observed by Fokkelman mirror one another structurally and thematically within the larger arrangement of the book. Of the three proposals only Clifford's relates the synchronic arrangement to a diachronic framework, specifically the priestly redaction of the book. Clifford correctly views the basic arrangement as the result of a priestly redaction, as the next section indicates.

Guide to the Bible (Cambridge, MA: The Belknap Press of Harvard University Press, 1987), pp. 57-58.

  8. Clifford, 'Exodus', *NJBC*, I, pp. 44-45. Clifford's analysis of 12.37–40.38 is based largely on Cross, *Canaanite Myth*, pp. 293-325, esp. pp. 310-14.

Before proceeding to the description of this arrangement, it is important to raise a few questions about some of Clifford's suggestions. The proposal for 'interlocking halves' reflects a fundamental problem of how Exod. 13.17–15.21 fits into the larger arrangement, and it will be argued that, for the priestly redaction, 'the Song at the Sea', 15.1-21, serves as the pivoting center of the book. It may be noted that not all of the itinerary notices function in Clifford's schema as points of major division. More specifically, while the notice in 19.1-2a represents a major marker in Clifford's schema, the notices in 12.37, 13.20 and 15.27 do not. Itinerary notices as such do not represent the markers for the major sections in the priestly redaction, and indeed 19.1-2a differs from the other three notices. In sum, the three proposals make important contributions toward understanding the arrangement of Exodus, and Clifford's proposal pursues this agenda in the context of diachronic considerations. In this respect, J. Blenkinsopp's comment on Exodus 24 applies as well to the priestly redaction of the book: 'We do not have to choose between synchronicity and diachronicity'.[9]

2. *Methodological Steps for Delineating the Priestly Redaction*

Step One

The first step in delineating the priestly arrangement of the book involves the question as to whether the book of Exodus may be treated as a unit within the priestly redaction of the Pentateuch. This issue may be addressed by asking to what degree chs. 1 and 40 demarcate beginning and end points for the priestly redaction. Exod. 1.1-7 and 40.36-38 constitute the prologue and epilogue to the book.[10] Chapter 1 was a beginning point inherited and expanded by the priestly redaction. While the priestly addition in 1.1-7 is designed to connect the book of Exodus back to the Joseph narrative in Genesis,[11] there is a thematic break between the books. The priestly material notes the deaths of the old generation of Jacob-Israel's clan (1.6)[12] and marks the appearance of the people, בני ישראל (1.7) who have been fruitful (פרה*) and have multiplied (רבה*). This expansion echoes the priestly injunction in

9. Blenkinsopp, *The Pentateuch*, p. 191.

10. So M. Greenberg, *Understanding Exodus*, pp. 2-3; N. Sarna, 'Exodus, Book of', *ABD*, II, p. 690b.

11. Childs, *The Book of Exodus*, pp. 1-2; Fokkelman, 'Exodus', p. 58.

12. See Blenkinsopp, *The Pentateuch*, p. 134.

Gen. 1.28 'to be fruitful and multiply'. Exod. 1.7 also says that the Israelites 'swarmed' or 'teemed' (שׁרץ*), a verb which echoes Gen. 1.20-21. In addition, the material inherited by P tells how a new Egyptian king ignorant of the Israelites has replaced the old monarch who knew and benefitted Joseph and his family. As a result, ch. 1 would appear to mark a new narrative stage.

The case for Exodus 40 as a particular break-point in the priestly redaction is more difficult to make. It is well-known that while Genesis and Deuteronomy are self-contained units by comparison, the same cannot be claimed for Exodus, Leviticus and Numbers. It is also clear that the priestly redaction runs through these three books. Moreover, it is sometimes argued that Exodus 25–31 and 35–40 cannot be separated from Leviticus 8–9, as Leviticus 8 provides the fulfillment of the command in Exodus 29.[13] Finally, the apparent literary structure proposed for Exodus through Numbers creates problems for seeing Exodus 40 as a break-point. Scholars have noted the chiastic arrangement of features in Exodus through Numbers, with the Sinai material of Exodus 19 through Numbers 10 standing as the middle and obviously major element.[14] Extending this chiastic arrangement, it may be argued that Exodus 25–31 + 35–40 corresponds to Numbers 1–10 in that both sections deal with the divine sanctuary. Exodus 25–31 + 35–40 which provides the first priestly legislation after arriving at Sinai deals with the construction of the divine sanctuary while Numbers 1–10 addresses the arrangements for travel with the divine sanctuary, the final legislation before departing from Sinai.[15]

As a result of these observations, any claim for Exodus 40 as a break-point must be situated within a larger discussion of Exodus, Leviticus and Numbers. By the same token, it is necessary to point out that the larger chiastic arrangement of these books does not exclude additional literary structures. Structural evidence for the book of Numbers as a separate work has been noted,[16] and the same may be done

13. See Hurowitz, *I Have Built you an Exalted House*, pp. 111-12; Milgrom, *Leviticus 1–16*, p. 61.

14. See J. Milgrom, *The JPS Torah Commentary*. במדבר *Numbers* (Philadelphia: The Jewish Publication Society, 1990), pp. xvii-xviii. Echoing observations of J. Wellhausen, A. Schart has proposed a 'Ringstruktur' surrounding the Sinai legislation. See Schart, *Mose und Israel im Konflikt*, p. 52.

15. For a discussion of these points, see Chapter 11.

16. See D. Olson, *The Death of the Old and the Birth of the New: The Frame-*

for the book of Exodus. Closer examination of the legal corpus suggests that within the larger priestly redaction of Exodus through Numbers, Exodus 40 does constitute a break-point or at least a caesura in the narrative. If Leviticus 1–7 represents an addition placed between the tabernacle material in Exodus and Leviticus 8–9, as noted above, then it must be observed that this addition alters the shape of the material preceding and following it.[17] This change creates a new beginning for the book of Leviticus and thereby a new ending for the book of Exodus. Furthermore, internal and external considerations suggest that the priestly redaction signals a narrative caesura or break-point at the end of ch. 40. Internally, the legal material in Exod. 40.33a ends a long section pertaining to the tabernacle, and a priestly narrative in 40.33b-38 divides the tabernacle material from the sacrificial materials beginning in Leviticus 1. With the work on the tabernacle finished (40.33b), the divine cloud covers the 'tent of meeting' (אהל מועד) and the divine 'glory' or 'effulgence'[18] (כבוד) fills the tabernacle (משכן) in Exod. 40.34. Moses' relationship to Yahweh is thereby changed: he no longer enters the tent of meeting to communicate with Yahweh, and a new stage in the divine-human communication is reached (40.35). The entry of the deity into the tabernacle marks the climax of a set pattern in temple and palace building.[19] Switching from the simple past forms of the previous verses, the final verses of the book (40.36-38) use durative past prefix verbal forms in describing how the movements of the wilderness journeys were signalled by the divine 'cloud'. According to J. Milgrom,[20] this is intrusive material which together with Num. 9.15-23 forms a bracket around the intervening material. In sum,

---

work of the Book of Numbers and the Pentateuch (BJS, 71; Chico, CA: Scholars Press, 1985); *idem*, 'Numbers', *Harper's Bible Commentary* (ed. J.L. Mays; San Francisco: Harper & Row, 1988), pp. 182-83.

17. So Greenberg, *Understanding Exodus*, p. 3. For a synchronic explanation of this apparent displacement, see Milgrom, *Leviticus 1–16*, p. 494. Note the opposite approach of B. Levine who regards 'Exod. 29,1-37 as a response to Leviticus 8, and Exod. 29,38-46 as a probable response to Num. 28,1-8 in requiring two *tamîd* sacrifices' (Levine, Review of *Leviticus 1–16*, by J. Milgrom, *Bib* 74 [1994], p 283).

18. So Blenkinsopp, *The Pentateuch*, p. 219. See Cross, *Canaanite Myth*, p. 153 n. 30.

19. See the important studies of A.V. Hurowitz, 'The Priestly Account of Building the Tabernacle', *JAOS* 105 (1985), pp. 21-30; *idem*, *I Have Built you an Exalted House*, p. 267-68.

20. Milgrom, *Leviticus 1–16*, p. 61.

internal indicators suggest that Exod. 40.36-38 signals a break-point
between the books of Exodus and Leviticus.

Externally, contacts between the priestly creation account in Gen.
1.1–2.3 and Exodus 39–40 indicate that the end of Exodus marks a
break in the Sinai legislation. Commentators beginning with Martin
Buber and Franz Rosenzweig have observed that Exodus 39–40 consciously echoes the end of the priestly creation account (Exod. 39.43a//
Gen. 1.31a; Exod. 39.32a//Gen. 2.1; Exod. 40.33b//Gen. 2.2a; and
Exod. 39.43b//Gen. 2.3a).[21] Exodus 39–40 is thereby connected to the
creation story of Genesis: while the account of Genesis marks the creation of the world, the creation language of Exodus 39–40 heralds the
new creation of Israel's cultic life with its deity. For the priestly tradition Sinai would represent the site of the definitive covenant and model
for later cultic remembrances. The conclusion formula of Exod. 39.32/
40.33 echoing Gen. 2.1-2[22] signals for the priestly tradition a definitive
covenantal moment in the religious history of Israel. In sum, the specifically priestly elements in the first and final chapters in Exodus signal new beginnings at either end of the book, the first beginning of the
Israelites in Egypt and the second beginning of their life with Yahweh
tabernacling in their midst.

Step Two

The second step in arguing for the literary arrangement of the priestly
redaction is to demonstrate the extent of the priestly redaction throughout the book.[23] While the priestly redaction of Exodus is regarded generally as major in character, the basic facts for this view deserve mention. The priestly shaping of 6.2 through ch. 12 is evident from the
priestly call narrative of 6.2–7.7 (incorporating the genealogy of Moses
and Aaron) and the priestly redaction of the plague narrative.[24] The
next pieces of evidence are the itinerary notices, which in Exodus structure material from the departure from Egypt to the arrival at Sinai.

21. For discussion of Buber and Rosenzweig, see Blum, *Studien*, pp. 306-307.
See also Blenkinsopp, 'The Structure of P', pp. 275-92; *idem, The Pentateuch*, pp.
62, 186, 218; Kearney, 'Creation and Liturgy', p. 375; Fishbane, *Text and Texture*,
pp. 11-13; M. Weinfeld, 'Sabbath, Temple and the Enthronement of the Lord', pp.
501-12; Levenson, *Creation and the Persistence of Evil*, pp. 78-87; Hallo, *The Book
of the People*, p. 60; Batto, *Slaying the Dragon*, p. 120.
22. Blenkinsopp, *The Pentateuch*, pp. 217-18.
23. Cf. Friedman, 'Torah', pp. 617b-618a.
24. Zevit, 'The Priestly Redaction', pp. 194-205.

More specifically, the itinerary notices in 12.37a, 13.20, 15.22a, 15.27, 16.1, 17.1 and 19.1-2a, provide the order and arrangement for the intervening material.[25] It has been long argued that the itinerary notices in Exodus and Numbers are to be attributed to P.[26] Even if not all of the itinerary notices are priestly,[27] several which demarcate major sections (i.e. 13.17, 15.22; 19.1-2a) are priestly. The third piece of evidence for the priestly redaction of the book involves Exodus 19–40. The arrangement by the priestly redaction is indicated by the priestly reuse of the deuteronomic motif of the tablets. It is possible that the motif of the tablets in this verse was originally deuteronomic.[28] However, in Exodus the motif is patently priestly. Exod. 31.18 as well as 32.15 and 34.29 use the priestly expression, 'tablets of the Pact' (לוחת העדות),[29] as opposed to the deuteronomic 'the tablets of the Covenant' (לוחת הברית), attested in Deut. 9.9, 11, 15.[30] The priestly redaction has adopted the motif of the tablets for its own redactional purposes in 31.18 which, as its free-standing character suggests, closes the section:[31] 'And He [God] gave to Moses, after He had finished speaking with him on Mount Sinai, the two tablets of the pact (לוחת העדות), tablets of stone written by the finger of God'. Thus far the priestly redaction covers chs. 6 through 40. Finally, from the priestly glosses in chs. 1–2, it would appear that the priestly redaction inherited and incorporated the structure of Exod. 1.1–6.1 into its larger redactional plan in 6.2 through the end of ch. 40.

---

25. Cross, *Canaanite Myth*, pp. 310-12.

26. See Cross, *Canaanite Myth*, pp. 311-12, 314; Davies, 'The Wilderness Itineraries and the Composition of the Pentateuch', pp. 1-13.

27. Noth attributes 12.37a and 13.20 to J. van Seters's arguments about the two notices in Exod. 19.1-2 are hardly compelling: both could be priestly. As a result, claims for J as author of the itinerary notices are controvertible. See van Seters, *The Life of Moses*, p. 156.

28. So Noth, *Exodus*, p. 247.

29. More specifically for Knohl, the label of the 'Holiness School'. See Knohl, *The Sanctuary of Silence*, p. 67 n. 21, p. 108.

30. As discussed below in greater detail in Chapter 9, section 2. See M. Weinfeld, *Deuteronomy 1–11* (AB, 5; New York: Doubleday, 1991), p. 36. On the priestly background of the term עדות, see Noth, *Exodus*, p. 247; Cross, *Canaanite Myth*, pp. 300, 312-14; Kearney, 'Creation and Liturgy', p. 382; C.L. Seow, 'Ark of the Covenant', *ABD*, I, p. 387. See BDB, p. 531.

31. Cf. Cross, *Canaanite Myth*, p. 314. For the argument that 'the tablets of the pact' (לוחת העדות) is a priestly expression, see especially Chapter 9, section 2.

Step Three

The third step in identifying the priestly arrangement of material within Exodus is to identify the major divisions of sections that the priestly redaction used and/or created:

1. 1–2.[32] The end of ch. 2 and the beginning of ch. 3 is the first of the two non-priestly divisions that the priestly redaction inherited. Fokkelman argues that 2.23-25 provides a transition to the following section.[33] That these chapters are self-contained[34] is suggested by a thematic frame: the section begins with the genealogical list of ancestors' names and ends with Moses' naming of his son. Stylistically the brief narrative segments in these chapters contrast with the long scene in 3.1–4.17.

2. 3.1–6.1.[35] The first call narrative marks a new point in the narrative[36] and constitutes the second of two non-priestly divisions that the priestly redaction inherited.

3. 6.2–14.31.[37] The priestly call passage separates 6.2f. from the preceding section.[38] Exod. 13.16 marks the end of the plague narrative, and Exod. 13.17 could therefore mark the beginning of the scene at the Sea which includes 14.1–15.21. However, Exod. 14.29 points to the priestly redaction for the end of ch. 14, perhaps demarcating the poem as a separate unit.[39]

---

32. Priestly material: 1.1-7, 13-14 and 2.23abβ-25. See Noth, *Exodus*, pp. 20, 22, 33; Campbell and O'Brien, *Sources for the Pentateuch*, pp. 35-36. See also Greenberg, *Understanding Exodus*, p. 18; Childs, *The Book of Exodus*, pp. 7, 28.

33. Fokkelman, 'Exodus', p. 58.

34. For the following points, see Davies, *Israel in Egypt*, p. 20.

35. Zero priestly material. See Noth, *Exodus*, pp. 38-56; Childs, *The Book of Exodus*, pp. 51-53; Campbell and O'Brien, *Sources for the Pentateuch*, pp. 132-36, esp. p. 131 n. 92.

36. See Childs, *The Book of Exodus*, p. 51.

37. Priestly material: 6.2–7.7; 7.8-13, 19-20a, 21b-22; 8.1-3 (RSV 5-7), 11b (RSV 15b), 12-15 (RSV 16-19); 9.8-12, 35; 11.9-10; 12.1-20, 28, 40-51. So Noth, *Exodus*, pp. 58, 70, 92; Campbell and O'Brien, *Sources for the Pentateuch*, pp. 36-40; Childs, *The Book of Exodus*, pp. 111, 131, 184. Noth adds 9.22, 23aα and 10.12, 13aα, 20-22. Childs assigns only 9.35b to P.

38. For Knohl, 6.2-8, 9-13, 26-30 and 7.1-6 are Holiness School compositions; the insertion of the priestly genealogy in 6.14-25 was the work of the Holiness School redaction as well. See Knohl, *The Sanctuary of Silence*, p. 61.

39. Interestingly, 4QExod^c moves directly from Exod. 13.16 to 15.1. For the

Accordingly, the defeat of the Egyptian army at the sea in ch. 14 is the culmination of the plague stories for the priestly redaction.[40]

4.   15.1-21.[41] Exod. 15.19 shows enough similarity to Exod. 14.29, customarily assigned to P, that a priestly redactional setting for the poem appears indicated; both verses relate how 'the Israelites went on dry land in the midst of the water'. So B.S. Childs comments on Exod. 15.19: 'The close parallel to the Priestly source—the last colon has been taken *verbatim* from 14.29—would point rather to the work of the final Priestly editor'.[42]

5.   15.22–18.27.[43] The priestly itinerary notices of 15.22 and 19.1-2a[44] delimit this unit for the priestly redaction. The priestly itinerary notice in 19.1-2a separates the pre-priestly material in 15.22–18.27 from the material after 19.2.

6.   19–31[45] and 32–40.[46] To create these units, the priestly

text, see Ulrich *et al.*, *Qumran Cave 4*, pp. 127-28.

40. See Zevit, 'The Priestly Redaction', pp. 194-205. See further van Seters, *The Life of Moses*, p. 77 n. 2.

41. Priestly material: 14.1-4, 8aβ, 9b, 10a, 15-18, 21-23, 26-27, 28aβ, 29; 15.19. For the P material in Exod. 14, see Noth (*Exodus*, p. 105): 14.1-4, 8, 9abβ, 10abβ, 15-18, 21aαb, 22-23, 26, 27aα, 28-29 (see Campbell and O'Brien, *Sources for the Pentateuch*, pp. 40-41). Excluding minor variations, Childs (*The Book of Exodus*, p. 220) also assigns to 13.20 to P, while Vervenne ('The "P" Tradition', p. 85) adds to P 13.20, 14.11-12, 31. For 15.19 as P, see Childs, *The Book of Exodus*, p. 248.

42. Childs, *The Book of Exodus*, p. 248. Childs's italics.

43. Priestly material: 15.22a, 27;16.1-35a; 17.1a. Noth (*Exodus*, pp. 128, 131, 138) assigns to P 15.22a, 27; 16.1-35a (with v. 8 taken as secondary), and 17.1abα (see Campbell and O'Brien, *Sources for the Pentateuch*, pp. 41-43). According to Childs (*The Book of Exodus*, pp. 266, 275) the priestly material in this section consists of 15.22aα, 27; 16.1-3, 6-13a, 32-35aα, b; 17.1abα. This rather sizable difference has no bearing on the following remarks. For a different reading of the unit's delineation, see E. Zenger, 'Tradition and Interpretation in Exodus XV 1-21', in J.A. Emerton, *Congress Volume: Vienna 1980* (VTSup, 32; Leiden: Brill, 1981), pp. 460-83.

44. See Cross, *Canaanite Myth*, p. 84 n. 15.

45. Priestly material: 19.1-2a; 19.5bβ-6a, 11b, 12aβ-13, 15b, 16aα, 18 (?); 19.20-25; 24.1-2, 6, 8-11 (?); 24.15b-18a; 25.1–31.18. So for Exod. 19 and 24, Dozeman, *God on the Mountain*, pp. 106-36. Noth, *Exodus*, pp. 155, 200 (Campbell and O'Brien, *Sources for the Pentateuch*, pp. 43-52) assigns to P 19.1-2a,

redaction used the motif of the two sets of tablets especially in 31.18, as noted above.

Of these markers Knohl argues that the Holiness School's redaction contributed both the second call narrative of 6.2–7.7 and 31.18.[47] The two are central pieces providing the framework for the two halves of the book. The other markers, specifically, the itinerary notices, were inherited and used by this redaction to provide the rest of the structure in Exodus.

3. *The Literary Arrangement of the Priestly Redaction*

These markers produced a delineation of sections which shows an overall arrangement. Proceeding from these presuppositions, the priestly redactional arrangement of Exodus may be outlined in the following manner:

I. Egypt
    A. Chapters 1–2: Moses' movement from Egypt to Midian
    B. Two calls and two confrontations
        i. 3.1–6.1: Moses' first call and confrontation with Pharaoh
        i′. 6.2–14.31: Moses' second call and Yahweh's confrontation with Pharaoh

                The conflict between the powers of Egypt and Sinai
                15.1-21: Victory at the sea

II. Sinai
    A′. 15.22–18.27: Israel's movement from Egypt to Midian
    B′. Two covenants and two sets of tablets
        i. Chapters 19–31: Israel's first covenant with Yahweh; the first tablets
        i′. Chapters 32–40: Israel's second covenant with Yahweh; the second tablets

In the most general terms the book may be regarded as containing two larger parts divided geographically. As J.D. Levenson has suggested,[48] Egypt, the land of the power of Pharaoh, is the overall setting for the

24.15b-18, and chs. 25–31 (with 29.1–31.17 as secondary expansions of the priestly document). Noth regards 19.3-8 as E, 10-15 as J, 16-20 as JE, and 21-25 as secondary.

    46. Priestly material: 35–40. Noth, *Exodus*, pp. 274-75 (Campbell and O'Brien, *Sources for the Pentateuch*, pp. 53-61) with several secondary elements.

    47. Knohl, *The Sanctuary of Silence*, pp. 61, 67 n. 21, 108.

    48. Levenson, *The Hebrew Bible*, pp. 127-59.

first half of Exodus, while Sinai, the realm of Yahweh's power, dominates the second half of the book. Moreover, in the two halves of the book the lives of Moses and the Israelites are parallel in general terms: both flee Egypt and both come to the divine mountain and receive the divine word. The conflict in the middle of the book resolves the struggle between these two domains. With Yahweh's victory at the Sea, the power of the One of Sinai is made fully manifest. While this schema generally holds, it should be noted as well that Sinai plays a role already in the first part in Moses' initial commission which anticipates the role the mountain will play in the second half of the book. Even in the first half Sinai looms as the ultimate goal (Exod. 3.12). Finally, this schema highlights the central, pivotal place of Exod. 15.1-21 within the priestly redaction of the book. The poem might be viewed as the ending to section B (6.2–14.31), but it serves a larger function as a fulcrum-point in Exodus. The poem in its redactional context looks back at the events leading up to the victory at the sea (vv. 1-12) and anticipates the events at the mountain following the victory (vv. 13-18).

This chapter and those that follow focus on arguments concerning the literary arrangement created by the priestly redaction. The following chapters illustrate how the priestly redaction arranged Exodus as a double journey to, and sojourning at, the holy place of Sinai. In this way, pilgrimage constitutes the basic pattern of the book.

Chapter 7

THE PRIESTLY ARRANGEMENT OF EXODUS 1.1–14.31:
SECTIONS A, B I AND B I'

1. *Section A: Moses' Movement From Egypt to Midian (Chapters 1–2)*

This section provides the initial setting of the book.[1] It presents the
shared origins of Moses and Israel in Egypt and anticipates their shared
destiny on the mountain of God. Section A ends by bringing Moses to
the land of Midian, the area of the divine mountain, just as section A'
(Israel's movement from Egypt to Midian) brings Moses and the people
to Mount Sinai.[2] The priestly addition in 1.1-5 connects Exodus to the
end of Genesis.[3] The priestly additions in 1.13-14 and 2.23-25 emphasize the oppressiveness of the Egyptians and thereby begin building
toward the divine punishment administered in section B i' ('Moses' second call and Yahweh's confrontation with Pharaoh').[4]

2. *Section B i: Moses' First Call and Confrontation with Pharaoh
(Chapters 3.1–6.1)*

This section begins with the first call of Moses in Midian (3.1–4.17), the
travel and arrival to Egypt (4.18-31), and the failed confrontation between Moses and Pharaoh (5.1-23).[5] Given the lack of priestly material

1. The most recent work on this section by Davies (*Israel in Egypt*) defends this
division and remarks on the relationship between sections A and A'.
2. So Clifford, 'Exodus', p. 44.
3. For another priestly list with the introductory formula אלה שמות*, see Num.
13.4. Num. 13.16 closes the list with a resumptive use of the same formula.
4. I.M. Kikawada ('Literary Conventions of the Primeval History', *Annual of
the Japanese Biblical Institute* 1 [1975], p. 13-18) argues that the structure and development of Gen. 1–11 is duplicated in the original redaction of Exod. 1–2. This view
is cited and accepted in Zevit, 'The Priestly Redaction', p. 202 n. 32.
5. This division follows the general consensus. For another proposal, see
P. Weimar, *Die Berufung des Mose: Literaturwissenschaftliche Analyse von Exodus*

in this section, the purpose of the following remarks is to mention
material pertinent to priestly material elsewhere in the book, especially in the following section. In Exod. 3.1-4 Moses is tending his
flock on Mount Horeb when he turns aside to see the burning bush,
called הסנה, which is 'not consumed' (איננו אכל).[6] The first of many
cultic motifs in Exodus, this site is couched in terms associated with a
sanctuary. Like the divine speech addressed to Joshua at Jericho in
Josh. 5.15, the divine speaker in Exod. 3.5 informs Moses: 'Remove
your sandals from your feet, for the ground on which you are standing is holy ground'.[7] This presentation of the site anticipates the emphasis placed on holiness when the Israelites arrive at the mountain in
ch. 19. Moses enters holy ground where he experiences the divine
presence and commission (3.1-6; cf. 19.9, 12-25; 20.18-21), with a
similar goal that the people might believe (4.31; cf. 19.9). The only
theophanies of Exodus begin in chs. 3 and 19, and these chapters stand
at the beginning of sections B and B'. Moses speaks alone with God in
chs. 3–4 and 20[8] and the elders play a role in the narratives only in
chs. 3 and 24.[9]

Moses is charged with a mission in Exod. 3.10 to go to Egypt and
the ensuing dialogue between Moses and the deity involves a sign anticipating the people's encounter with God at Sinai. Attention in this passage is usually given to the sign in vv. 13-15 (assigned to E in tradition
source-criticism), namely the divine name, interpreted as אהיה אשר
אהיה, literally 'I will be/am who/what I will be/am'. Numerous commentators agree that this name is an interpretation or elaboration of

---

2,23–5,5 (OBO, 32; Freiburg: Universitätsverlag; Göttingen: Vandenhoeck &
Ruprecht, 1980), pp. 19-25.

6.   The verbal form is unlikely to be a D-stem passive ('pual') perfect as in the
MT pointing, given that this root has an active G-stem but no active D-stem and given
that אין* usually governs a participle. Recourse to the G-stem passive participle *qatūl
is also unlikely given the absence of waw in the consonantal writing; only if it were
argued that the form is *defectiva* could this form be posited. The form is explained
better as an old alternative G-stem passive participle. Other examples of this second
type of G-stem passive participle include היולד in Judg. 13.8 and לקח in 2 Kgs 2.10
(see M.H. Pope, *Song of Songs* [AB, 7; Garden City, NY: Doubleday, 1977], pp.
599-600). It might be argued that this secondary passive participle was formed
secondarily from the G-stem perfect form.

7.   See above Chapter 2, section 2.

8.   Moberly, *The Old Testament of the Old Testament*, p. 15.

9.   Moberly, *The Old Testament of the Old Testament*, p. 16.

the tetragrammaton.[10] Levenson translates the sentence, 'I will be where I will be',[11] based on the older West Semitic background of the article אֲשֶׁר as a locative particle,[12] but this background is at best only vestigial in Hebrew; it is unlikely that the meaning 'where' in this sort of clause was used in the period of the monarchy or later. The context suggests a different interpretation of the name. The passage perhaps offers a clue as to how the sentence-name was understood in this particular context. Exod. 3.12 (traditionally assigned to E) precedes the actual revelation of the name by Yahweh's promise to Moses that 'I will be with you' (אֶהְיֶה עִמָּךְ). The pressing theological issue often voiced in Israelite literature is whether or not Yahweh will be or can be present on behalf of Israel. Perhaps this theological understanding informs the interpretation of the divine name in this context as expressed by Yahweh's message to Moses in 3.12.[13] In the perspective of this interpretational context, the sentence might mean (perhaps not

---

10. So Cross, *Canaanite Myth*, p. 67 n. 81; F.I. Andersen and D.N. Freedman, *Hosea* (AB, 24; Garden City, NY: Doubleday, 1980), p. 199. Cross and Freedman interpret the name as a *C*-stem verb constituting a sentence name with an implied object. In contrast, L. Koehler ('Vom hebräischen Lexikon', *OTS* 8 [1950], pp. 17-18) argues that the initial yodh represents a nominal prefix and translates the name 'Leben, Sein, Wirklichkeit, ser Seiende'. Hos. 1.9c might be cited in support of the view that אֶהְיֶה in Exod. 3.14 is a variant form of the tetragrammaton: לֹא אֶהְיֶה לָכֶם וְאָנֹכִי. This is glossed by NJPS: 'and I will not be your [God]'. The bracketed addition is intended to smooth out the perceived omission of אֱלֹהֶיךָ or the like (so *BHS*). However, if אֶהְיֶה in Hos. 1.9 is a form of the divine name, then there is no such difficulty (so Cross, *Canaanite Myth*, p. 67 n. 81; Andersen and Freedman, *Hosea*, p. 4, pp. 197, 198-99). Moreover, if it is the divine name, then Hos. 1.9c more closely approximates 1.9b (כִּי אַתֶּם לֹא עַמִּי) in syntax (so Andersen and Freedman, *Hosea*, p. 199). Given that the possible affinities between Hosea and the material attributed to the so-called E source or redaction, such an understanding of אֶהְיֶה would be plausible.

11. Levenson, *Sinai and Zion*, p. 22.

12. See BDB, p. 82, #4b. This use of אֲשֶׁר reflects its original West Semitic background as a noun meaning 'place' used to mark relative clauses of place; this usage was apparently extended to BH relative clauses in general. See D. Pardee, 'A Further Note on *PRU* V, No. 60', *UF* 13 (1981), pp. 152, 156; Smith, *The Early History of God*, p. 109 n. 65. See also M.H. Gottstein, 'Afterthought and the Syntax of Relative Clauses in Biblical Hebrew', *JBL* 68 (1949), pp. 42-47.

13. For related views, see Greenberg, *Understanding Exodus*, pp. 81-83; A. Caquot, 'Les énigmes d'un hémistique biblique', *Dieu et l'Etre* (Paris: Etudes augustiniennes, 1978), pp. 17-26.

so felicitously from a grammatical view): 'I will be with whomever I will be'. In this context, that person is Moses. The accompanying sign in v. 12 will be Moses' return to 'this mountain' (ההר הזה). The pun between הסנה and Sinai was probably not lost on later readers.[14] In any case, the revelation of the divine name appears also in the call in Exod. 6.2, suggesting an important parallel between this section and the next. The divine name plays a comparable role in both Exod. 20.2, 6 and in 34.6.

Chapter 4 introduces two elements which are greatly expanded in the following section. The sign of Exod. 4.1-9 (J) consists of unusual acts which Moses will perform before the Egyptians. These signs, the whitening of Moses' hands and the turning of Nile water into blood, anticipate the events of the next section. Chapter 4 also introduces Aaron's place in the narrative. In v. 20 Moses has returned to Egypt, but in v. 27 Aaron meets Moses on the mountain of God. However this narrative tension is to be resolved, it reinforces the importance of the mountain, not only for Moses, but also for Aaron, and anticipates the later arrival of the Israelites to the mountain as well as the significance of Aaron and his sons.

Chapter 5 closes the section in presenting the initial mission of Moses and Aaron to Pharaoh. This section does not contain the wonders or signs mentioned previously or those rendered in the following section. The conflict between the opposing parties remains at the level of Moses and Aaron versus Pharaoh, but in the following section, this dynamic is altered radically.

3. Section B i': Moses' Second Call and Yahweh's Confrontation with Pharaoh (Chapters 6.2–14.31)

a. Call and Commission (6.2–7.7)
The call and commission in this section is placed within the context of Moses' discouragement over his first attempt to persuade Pharaoh. Here the second call and commission serves as the divine answer to Pharaoh's refusal and added burden placed on the Israelites. The section begins with the priestly call and commission of Moses, which includes Aaron in the divine plan (v. 13). The genealogy that follows (vv. 14-27) explains the identity of Moses and Aaron. The narrative

14. See Wellhausen, *Prolegomena*, p. 339 n. 1; Greenberg, *Understanding Exodus*, p. 69.

resumes[15] the commission with 6.28–7.5, which Moses and Aaron perform (7.6). The section closes with information about the ages of Moses and Aaron when they spoke to Pharaoh.

The basic priestly commission begins and ends with the basic statement 'I am Yahweh' (6.2b, 8b). Exod. 6.3a identifies the name by which Yahweh appeared (but was not known) to the patriarchs as אֵל שַׁדַּי, usually translated 'God Almighty' (on the basis of the Greek version): 'but by my name YHWH I did not make myself known' (וּשְׁמִי יהוה לֹא נוֹדַעְתִּי).[16] Exod. 6.3 uses the word 'name' (שֵׁם) with the pronominal suffix, suggesting that the grammatical apposition between the deity and the name in Exod. 6.3 expresses a relationship of identity.[17] For the priestly tradition (or, more specifically, the Holiness School[18]), the statement, 'I am Yahweh', represents the foundational basis for Yahweh's relationship with Israel. In the words of W. Zimmerli, 'the phrase, "I am Yahweh" carries all the weight and becomes the denominator upon which all else rests... everything Yahweh has to announce to his people appears as an amplification of the fundamental statement, "I am Yahweh"'.[19] The statement of divine self-revelation is prefaced by the theme of knowledge in Exod. 6.7: 'they shall know that I am Yahweh'. This 'recognition formulation'[20] represents a deeper expres-

15. Friedman ('Torah', p. 617) cites this text as an instance of epanalepsis or resumptive repetition.

16. NJPS has essentially the same translation also reading the *N*-stem form as reflexive. W.R. Garr ('The Grammar and Interpretation of Exodus 6.3', *JBL* 111 [1992], p. 385) renders: 'But, I, my name Yahweh, was not known to them'. The paranomasia with נוֹעַדְתִּי in the priestly glosses in Exod. 25.22 and 29.43 and its possible theological significance are discussed below.

17. A proximate grammatical and thematic (but generally unnoted) analogue appears in Kothar's words in *KTU* 1.2 IV 11b-12 and 19 addressed to Baal's weapons. Like וּשְׁמִי in Exod. 6.3b, 'your name' (*šmk*) stands in initial position. Furthermore, the name is stressed by the addition of the pronominal element standing in apposition. In *KTU* 1.2 IV it is the independent pronoun that heightens the direct address to the weapon, while in Exod. 6.3b the pronominal element is constitutive of the verbal form. It may argued that the grammatical apposition between each name and the pronominal element communicates not only emphasis, but it also expresses an identity between them. In contrast, the presumed wielder of the weapons in *KTU* 1.2 IV, Baal, remains in the background. See Smith, *The Ugaritic Baal Cycle*, p. 342.

18. Knohl, *The Sanctuary of Silence*, p. 16.

19. Zimmerli, *I am Yahweh*, p. 9.

20. So Zimmerli, *I am Yahweh*, p. 109.

sion of revelation in the priestly material.[21] In the old material this formulation expresses the terms of conflict between Pharaoh and Yahweh in the plague narrative (e.g. 7.17; 8.18; 9.14, 16, 29; 14.31),[22] but the priestly material turned this statement into a monotheistic declaration by extending it to other parties in the book (14.18; 16.6, 12; 18.11; 25.22; 29.43; 31.18).[23] This use of the 'recognition formula' may be compared with similar formulations in Ezekiel (also priestly), applied to wicked counsellors in Judah (Ezek. 11.10), 'all the trees of

21. According to Y. Muffs, the revelation of the new name is to say 'God is not called Deus any more, He is called Zeus!' See Muffs, *Love and Joy: Law, Language and Religion in Ancient Israel* (New York: Jewish Theological Seminary, 1992), p. 50. In Exod. 6.2 the deity was identified previously not generically as 'God' (אלהים), but as אל שדי, a more specific label (more precisely, a title).

22. W. Brueggemann offers the interesting hypothesis that in 'the final form of the text' (p. 33) Yahweh's dealings with Pharaoh assumes the notion that Yahweh is the overlord of a recalcitrant vassal. See Brueggemann, 'Pharaoh as Vassal: A Study of a Political Metaphor', *CBQ* 57 (1995), pp. 27-51. This view assumes that the knowledge of Yahweh is of the same sort found in treaty documents. Exod. 3–15 lacks explicit treaty terminology (Brueggemann appeals for support to the multiple uses of the verb, 'to know' [ידע*], known from treaties, but it also appears in cultic contexts as noted here.) If treaty language as well as the larger royal paradigm are to be seen in the Exodus story, they are submerged in the cultic sensibility of the knowledge of God as discussed by Zimmerli. As Brueggemann observes, the rounds of the exchanges between Pharaoh and Moses are marked by references to sacrifices and pilgrimage which the people should make and by the former's pleas to the latter to pray on his behalf.

23. See Zevit, 'The Priestly Redaction', pp. 194-205. Cf. the deuteronomistic-sounding formulation in 10.2. For other examples of the priestly use of this formula, see Ezek. 5.13; 6.7, 10, 13, 14; 7.4, 9, 27; 11.10, 12; 12.15, 16, 20; 13.14, 21, 23; 14.8. This may serve as one of the central bases for Zakovitch's claim ('And You Shall Tell Your Son. . . ', p. 133) that the story of the Exodus 'was created in order to encourage the Israelites to accept the revolution of monotheism and to believe that they make up an exceptional creation completely different from the nations surrounding them'. While the Exodus story probably did originate as a foundational story for Israelite origins, it functioned later to reinforce nationalist identity both externally in terms of Israelite identity vis-à-vis the nations and internally through the special relationship between Yahweh and Israel (in royal thought mediated through the monarchy). A monotheistic perspective is consonant with deuteronomistic and priestly material in Exodus, but the monotheism of these traditions is proceeded by the monolatrous expressions of the special relationship between Yahweh and Israel (which allows for deities in foreign lands) witnessed in the older ('JE') material.

the field' (17.24), 'all the inhabitants of Egypt' (29.6) and 'the nations' (36.23, 36; 37.28; 39.7, 23).[24]

The expression of the knowledge of Yahweh undergirds the divine recollection of the covenant with the patriarchs, and it will lead to the divine conquest of Egypt, the liberation of the Israelites from slavery, and finally the granting of the land (Exod. 6.4-9). This section identifies the plagues as שְׁפָטִים גְדֹלִים, 'great deeds' (6.6) which will provide a basis for Egypt's and Israel's knowledge of Yahweh.[25] The priestly material also adds the theme of the hardening of Pharaoh's heart from the plague narrative to this section in order to show further Yahweh's control over the Israelites' destiny.

The next block of material (Exod. 6.9–7.7) provides the setting for Aaron's introduction into the commission (6.9-13), inserts the genealogy of Moses and Aaron (6.14-25), resumes the narrative (6.27-30), and finally represents the commission as a joint mission of Moses and Aaron (7.1-7). The genealogy gives a precedence to Aaron which the priestly additions to the plague stories also reflect in three details, as S.R. Driver notes:

1.   The formula 'say to Aaron' (7.19; 8.5, 16; 7.9; 9.8).
2.   Pharaoh's not listening to 'them', i.e. Moses and Aaron (7.22; 8.15b, 19; 9.12; cf. 7.13).
3.   Aaron's role as spokesman before Pharaoh (in contrast to Moses' speaking alone in 4.10-16).[26]

The force of the genealogy and the surrounding material is to transform the initial commission (6.2-8) into a team commissioning of Moses and Aaron (7.1-7). The repetitions in the commissions in 6.2-8 and 7.1-7 comport with this view:

1.   וִידַעְתֶּם/וְיָדְעוּ כִּי אֲנִי יהוה, 'and you/they shall know I am Yahweh' (Exod. 6.7; 7.5).
2.   שְׁפָטִים גְדֹלִים, 'great deeds' (Exod. 6.6; 7.4).
3.   'to raise' (נָשָׂאתִי)//'to give' (בְּנֻתְתִּי/וְנָתַתִּי) the divine 'hand' (יָד) (Exod. 6.8; 7.4, 5).

24.   Zimmerli, *I am Yahweh*, p. 109. Zimmerli adds Ezek. 21.4 where 'to see' (רָאה*) rather than 'to know' (יָדַע*) is used for the recognition of 'all flesh' that 'I am Yahweh'.

25.   See J.L. Ska, 'Quelques remarques sur P^g et la dernière rédaction du Pentateuque', in de Pury (ed.), *La Pentateuque en question*, p. 103.

26.   Driver, *An Introduction*, p. 24.

4. the divine claim that 'I will bring out. . . from under the burdens of
    Egypt/the land of Egypt', מצרים/מארץ סבלות מצרים מתחת . . . והוצאתי
    מצרים (6.6; 7.4).[27]

Exod. 6.3-8 uses these expressions to communicate Yahweh's relationship with, and action on behalf of, Israel. Exod. 7.1-7 employs these
motifs, however, to stress Yahweh's opposition to, and action against,
Egypt. Other expressions also convey this contrast. Yahweh 'heard'
(שמע*) the Israelites (6.5), but Pharaoh 'will not hear' (שמע*) Yahweh
(7.4), a theme continued in the priestly plague material (7.13; 8.11b,
15; 9.12; 11.9). All of these expressions may be taken to indicate the
shift in divine role in the next set of encounters with Pharaoh: it is not
Moses and Aaron who will encounter him, but Yahweh.

b. *The Priestly Plagues (7.8-13, 19-20a, 21b-22; 8.1-3, 11b, 12-15;
9.8-12, 35; 11.9-10).*
The priestly plagues proceed in four stages: (1) Yahweh gives Moses
instructions necessary to produce the plagues; (2) instructions follow
and the plague begins; (3) the Egyptian magicians attempt to duplicate
the plague, and either fail or succeed; and (4) whatever the result of
(3), the heart of Pharaoh is hardened.[28] As noted above, most of the
priestly themes in this section appear in the priestly commission.
Z. Zevit argues that the plagues have been rendered by the priestly
redaction as a reversal of creation.[29] For the priestly redaction, the
first three plagues—blood, frogs and lice—correspond to the three
parts of creation—water, land and heavens. These three plagues then
represent 'the reversal. . . of divine blessing to mankind in Gen. 1.28'.[30]
The plagues of flies, pestilence and boils destroy all the animals (cf.
Gen. 1.21, 25), while the hail and locust destroy all the remaining vegetation (cf. Gen. 1.12). With the ninth plague, the earth reverts to

27. Ska also notes some verbal contacts in 7.1-5 with chs. 4–5. See Ska,
'Quelques Remarques', pp. 121-23.
28. Wilson, 'The Hardening of Pharaoh's Heart', p. 34.
29. Zevit, 'The Priestly Redaction', pp. 193-211; see also Batto, *Slaying the
Dragon*, pp. 113, 114. In accordance with the discussion above in Chapter 5,
section 3, I am inclined to follow the view of J. van Seters, who identifies the author
of priestly narrative with the priestly redactor in the priestly plague materials. See van
Seters, 'A Contest of Magicians? The Plague Stories in P', in Wright, Freedman and
Hurvitz (eds.), *Pomegranates and Golden Bells*, pp. 569-80. Yet such a view is
hardly necessary.
30. Zevit, 'The Priestly Redaction', p. 205.

darkness, a reversal of the establishment of the distinction between light and darkness in Gen. 1.4. For Zevit, the tenth and final plague and the destruction of the Egyptians at the Sea represent a reversal of the creation of humanity (Gen. 1.28) localized in Egypt.[31] Zevit's view is compatible with R.R. Wilson's interpretation of the priestly use of the motif of the hardening of Pharaoh's heart in the plague narrative. The priestly development of the hardening motif as holy war and P's use of this motif in ch. 14 (vv. 4, 8, 17) contributes toward a reinterpretation of the plagues as a holy war which culminates in the victory at the sea.[32] The priestly creation leads to the creation of all humanity, while the priestly rendering of the plagues leads to the destruction of all Egyptians, culminating in the divine victory over the Egyptians at the sea.

In support of his argument, Zevit cites verbal items within the priestly redaction that echo the priestly creation story, for instance, the term 'collection' (מקוה), used with respect to water in both Gen. 1.10 and Exod. 7.19. That the priestly redaction connected the JE use of 'swarm, teem' (שרץ*) in Exod. 7.28 and its appearance in Gen. 1.20 may be inferred from the priestly use of this root in 1.7.[33] For Zevit, the ambiguity of the word, מצרים ('Egypt, Egyptians') as the land of Egypt, Pharaoh or all Egyptians in ch. 14 contributes to the priestly redaction's perspective that the plagues killed all Egyptians who did not drown at the sea. In this respect the plagues then figure together with the victory at the sea as the crowning act of the Egyptians' return to a state of complete chaos. Zevit views the extension of the plagues to cover all Egypt as a reversal of creation for all Egypt. Zevit comments: 'P''s [The priestly redactor's] image of Egypt at the conclusion of his plague-exodus is of a land with no people, no animals, no vegetation (cf. Gen. 1.1-2; 2.4-5)'.[34] Zevit concludes his discussion by suggesting

---

31. In a similar vein, T. Fretheim ('The Plagues as Ecological Signs of Historical Disaster', *JBL* 110 [1991], pp. 385-96) notes the sign-value of the plagues in that they anticipate Egypt's ultimate fate. For example, Aaron's staff turns into תנין which swallows (בלע*) those of Pharaoh's magicians just as the sea swallows (בלע*) Egypt in 15.12.

32. Wilson, 'The Hardening of Pharaoh's Heart', p. 34.

33. Zevit argues for a number of less tangible connections: the use of היה* (Exod. 7.19) instead of the J use of הפך* (7.15) echoes the creation style; the roots היה* and יצא* in Exod. 8.12, 14 also appear in Gen. 1.24; and ערוב links to עוף in Gen. 1.20 insofar as both are flying creatures.

34. Zevit, 'The Priestly Redaction', p. 210.

that priestly redaction's expansion to ten plagues reflects the ten divine utterances by which the world was created and ordered in Genesis 1.[35] Given the reverberations of language from the priestly creation account which were noted above, it is quite possible that the language of the creation account in Genesis informed the priestly interpretation of the plague story, especially since the priestly creation account exercised influence on other parts of Exodus. To anticipate, the influence of the priestly creation account on the priestly interpretation of the plague narratives suggests a reversion to the state of chaos for the Egyptians while the creation language used in the priestly redaction in the corresponding section B′ i′ suggest a new creation of the relationship between Yahweh and Israel through the tabernacle and its accompanying cultic mechanisms.

E.L. Greenstein has underscored three reasons given for the plagues: divine retribution against the Egyptians for their treatment of Israel; Yahweh's claim on all first-born males, including the Egyptians', executed by the tenth and final plague; and an aetiological reason to create an underpinning for the celebration of Passover.[36] All three contribute to the larger notion that it is the knowledge of God that the plagues achieve for both the Egyptians and the Israelites.[37] More importantly, the cultic theme of Yahweh's claim over all the first-born marks the culmination of a larger, liturgical sensibility evident in Exodus 1–15. Yahweh's initial demand that Israel be released so that it can make the three-day pilgrimage and worship (Exod. 5.3[38]) is now complete in the final plague's demonstration of Yahweh's claim on both the first-born of Egypt and on Israel, which Israel acknowledges in the cultic celebration of Passover.

35. Zevit, 'The Priestly Redaction', p. 211.

36. E.L. Greenstein, 'The First-Born Plague and the Reading Process', in Wright, Freedman and Hurvitz (eds.), *Pomegranates and Golden Bells*, pp. 555-68, esp. pp. 566-67.

37. So see Knohl, *The Sanctuary of Silence*, p. 138.

38. For the characterization of Exod. 5.3 as pilgrimage, see Noth, *A History of Pentateuchal Traditions*, p. 71 n. 1. Based on קרא*, 'to invite to a meal', C. Rabin argues that the idiom קרא על* in this verse and in 3.18 (which reads קרה*) refers to a divine invitation to a religious banquet. Rabin renders: '(the God of the Hebrews) has asked us to hold a banquet for Him.' See Rabin, 'Etymological Miscellanea', *Scripta Hierosolymitana* 8 (1961), p. 399.

c. *Relations between the Two Calls of Moses and Confrontations with Pharaoh (Sections B i and i')*

A parallel relationship between Exod. 3.1–6.1 and 6.2–13.16 is suggested by the two call narratives. Following older commentators such as A. Alt,[39] B.S. Childs notes the 'striking similarity in the form of the two narratives which includes commission, objection, divine response, and sign, which would confirm its parallel role'.[40] Yet Childs stresses that while the two calls were originally parallel, they now stand in sequential order, as the different locations of the two encounters between Moses and Yahweh/Elohim indicate.[41] Section B i', Moses' second call, in its present setting serves as the priestly filter on material in B i, Moses' first call. This effect is achieved less through material alteration than by the priestly redaction's juxtaposition of the priestly material in section B i' to non-priestly material in section B i. In his study of narrative in the Pentateuch and the Deuteronomistic History, D. Damrosch notes how redactional juxtaposition of materials produced rereadings in biblical texts:

> Certainly it is not necessary to return to the old view, no longer widely held among historians, that the later 'redactors' did little to shape their material, but it is reasonable to agree that the later composers of the text did not have complete freedom in their appropriation of the older material. Sometimes the later authors do indeed find ways to build an additive complexity through the assembling and creation of complementary parallels, but at other times it seems clear that the later author really wishes to *suppress* the earlier source, or at least to co-opt it and impose on it a structure and emphasis that guide the reader toward a new perspective in preference to the old.[42]

39. A. Alt, *Essays on Old Testament History and Religion*, pp. 14-15. See also J.F. Wimmer, 'Tradition Reinterpreted in Ex. 6.2-7.7', *Augustianum* 7 (1967), pp. 405-18.

40. Childs, *The Book of Exodus*, p. 111. See also Driver, *An Introduction*, pp. 23, 24. Whether Exod. 6.2-8 is form-critically part of a call narrative has been debated. See Ska, 'Quelques Remarques', pp. 98-107. The differences noted by Ska and other scholars would contribute in my mind to the view that this passage assumes the call narrative of Exod. 3–4. Ska also notes the affinities of Exod. 6.2-8 with the vocabulary and theme of divine authority and power in Exod. 5.1–6.1.

41. Childs, *The Book of Exodus*, p. 111. So also Moberly, *The Old Testament of the Old Testament*, pp. 34-35.

42. Damrosch, *The Narrative Covenant*, p. 304 (Damrosch's italics).

Sections B i and B i′ form one such 'complementary parallel' in that section B i is read through the lense of section B i′.

This point may be explicated by noting some of the differences between the two sections. First, the second call changes the picture of Moses. B. Scolnic remarks: 'Moses, in chapter 6, is placed within a genealogy, in the context of his people, which gives a very different impression than the story in Exodus 2–3 of an Egyptian noble who has been disloyal'.[43] Scolnic also stresses the function of the genealogy in presenting Moses 'as a member of his people, inside a community and its social institutions' in his second mission unlike the first mission where Moses 'is very much alone in terms of both Egyptians and Israelites'. The genealogy's attention appears, at least equally, on Aaron, with the purpose of showing his originally joint role in the Exodus. Nor is Aaron's role in the second commission one of subordination, in contrast with the rendering in the older material in Exod. 4.16.

Secondly, the character of the two missions in sections B i and i′ differ. Unlike the first call and mission, the second time the mission directly involves the plagues.[44] The initial call and mission involved JE material; this time the P redaction presents a further version of the mission to which it adds the JE and P traditions of the plagues.[45] The priestly redaction postpones J's version of the success of Moses before Pharaoh in order to place the wonders of the JE version together with

43. Scolnic, 'Strangers in the PaRDeS: Conservative Judaism and the Torah', *Study Guide to the Discovery* (ed. E.S. Schoenberg; New York: Jewish Theological Seminary, n.d.), p. 8.

44. See Moberly, *The Old Testament of the Old Testament*, p. 35.

45. See Zevit, 'The Priestly Redaction', pp. 193-211. The biblical plagues compare with Egyptian stories or descriptions of adverse natural conditions. For the image of the river turned to blood in Egyptian literature, see the 'Admonitions of Ipuwer' in M. Lichtheim, *Ancient Egyptian Literature. I. The Old and Middle Kingdoms* (Berkeley: University of California Press, 1973), p. 147. The competitions between foreign and Egyptian magicians set in the court of Pharaoh sometimes involve 'plagues'. See for example 'Setne Khamwas and Si-Osire' (also called 'Setna II') in M. Lichtheim, *Ancient Egyptian Literature. III. The Late Period* (Berkeley: University of California Press, 1980), pp. 138-51. This example includes foreign magic aimed at causing darkness throughout the land for three days and three nights. For further discussion, see Sarna, 'Exodus, Book of', *ABD*, II, p. 698; J.K. Hoffmeier, 'Egypt, Plagues In', *ABD*, II, p. 377. For an Egyptian parallel to the victory at the sea, see B. Couroyer, 'L'Exode et la bataille de Qadesh', *RB* 97 (1990), pp. 321-58.

those in the priestly version, following the P version of the call and commission beginning of 6.1.

Thirdly, the character of the deity differs in the two sections. J. Wellhausen noted the theophany of the initial call and the absence of any theophany from the second call.[46] The mission to Pharaoh in section B i is not miraculous or wondrous. In contrast, the mission to Pharaoh in section B i′ is full of wonders.[47] While divine power or presence is absent from Moses' first encounter with Pharaoh in section B i, in section B i′ divine power charges the entire sequence of interactions.[48] Both the plagues and the language of holy war change the encounter from a conflict between Moses and Pharaoh as found in section B i to a conflict between Yahweh and Pharaoh, paralleled by the contests of Moses and Aaron on the one hand, and Pharaoh's magicians on the other. Yahweh and Pharaoh's obstinate opposition to the Israelite deity replace the picture of two mortals competing in the sight of Pharaoh with a confrontation of cosmic importance.

46. Wellhausen, *Prolegomena*, p. 339 n. 1. See also B. Scolnic, 'Theme and Context in Biblical Lists' (PhD dissertation, The Jewish Theological Seminary of America, 1987), p. 287.

47. B. Scolnic considers the P version of the call in section B i′ less dramatic than that of JE in section B i. In Scolnic's words ('Strangers', p. 8), the P version

> emphasizes the idea that God speaks to Moses not in the Loneliness of the desert, but in the midst of the Jewish community, a community in exile. The Voice of God can be heard in exile, the P version states, and thus must have been a message of great comfort and inspiration to the exiles in Babylonia.

48. See Fretheim, 'The Plagues', pp. 385-96.

Chapter 8

THE POETICS OF EXODUS 15 AND ITS POSITION
IN THE PRIESTLY REDACTION

1. *Introduction*

Over the last century scholarly discussion of the poem of Exodus 15
has focused on two issues: the poem's tradition-history, especially in
relation to Exodus 14,[1] and its date, in particular within the corpus of
'ancient Yahwistic poetry'.[2] The second issue has been especially dominant in the United States, and if only as a reaction, in Europe as well.[3]
Scholarly work has generally neglected the question of the poem's relation to the rest of Exodus, although some commentators have raised
the question of late.[4] The second issue has been posed by reference to
other poems contained in narrative. Genesis 49 and Deuteronomy 32
and 33 occur toward the end of biblical books. The Song of Deborah
in Judges 5 and the poems of Numbers 22–24 are dependent on the

1. See F.M. Cross and D.N. Freedman, 'The Song of Miriam', *JNES* 14
(1955), pp. 237-50; G.W. Coats, 'The Traditio-Historical Character of the Reed Sea
Motif', *VT* 17 (1967), pp. 253-65; B.S. Childs, 'A Traditio-Historical Study of the
Reed Sea Tradition', *VT* 20 (1970), pp. 406-18; P.C. Craigie, 'Psalm XXIX in the
Hebrew Poetic Tradition', *VT* 22 (1972), pp. 143-51; Cross, *Canaanite Myth*, pp.
131-42, 310; Halpern, *The Emergence of Israel in Canaan*, pp. 32-43.
2. Cross and Freedman, 'The Song of Miriam', pp. 237-50; D.N. Freedman,
'Archaic Forms in Early Hebrew Poetry', *ZAW* 72 (1960), p. 105; D.A. Robertson,
Linguistic Dating in Dating Early Hebrew Poetry (Missoula, MT: Scholars Press,
1972), pp. 28-31; Cross, *Canaanite Myth*, pp. 121-31; D.N. Freedman, *Pottery, Poetry and Prophecy* (Winona Lake, IN: Eisenbrauns, 1980), pp. 187-227; C. Kloos,
*Yhwh's Combat's with the Sea: A Canaanite Tradition in the Religion of Ancient
Israel* (Amsterdam: van Oorschot; Leiden: Brill, 1986), pp. 127-214.
3. See R. Tournay, 'Chronologie des Psaumes', *RB* 65 (1958) pp. 340, 357;
Brenner, *The Song of the Sea*, pp. 11-15.
4. J.W. Watts, *Psalm and Story: Inset Hymns in Hebrew Narrative* (JSOTSup,
139; Sheffield: JSOT Press, 1992), pp. 41-62.

place of the character in the narrative to whom they are attached. Deborah's place in the book of Judges is dependent on the tribe to which she belongs in the book's south to north framework. Balaam's poems in the book of Numbers hinge on his place in the geographical itinerary in Transjordan. It is arguable that the position of the poem in Exodus 15 follows a principle governing the place of the poem in Judges 5. Like Judges 5, the poem in Exodus 15 is a victory hymn attached to the narrative of the victory.[5]

_ This approach is correct only for vv. 1-12, since vv. 13-18 have little bearing on the victory described in the preceding narrative.[6] These verses have been explained as anticipating events after the Egyptians' defeat. Scholars have noted that 'You [God] led' (נחית) in v. 13 refers to the period of the journey following the victory at the Sea,[7] but the text in their minds varies from Numbers[8] to passages in Deuteronomy, Joshua and Judges.[9] This approach regards vv. 13-17 as anticipatory in character. The task of understanding the poem in the priestly redactional context might be advanced by studying its textual relations to its immediate setting within the book of Exodus.[10]

The main purpose of this chapter is to add to this point by noting the relationship between the poem and both preceding and following material. This chapter first considers aspects of the 'present' form of the poem which have gone largely unnoted in recent scholarly discussion. More specifically, the following discussion will address the poetics of the poem, especially its verbal word-play between its two main sections. Then the poem's place in the book of Exodus is addressed. This issue will be construed largely in terms of the literary arrangement of

---

5. Childs, *The Book of Exodus*, p. 248; N. Sarna, *Exodus: The Traditional Hebrew Text with the New JPS Translation* (Philadelphia: The Jewish Publication Society, 1991), p. 75; A.J. Hauser, 'Two Songs of Victory: A Comparison of Exodus 15 and Judges 5', in E.R. Follis (ed.), *Directions in Biblical Hebrew Poetry* (JSOTSup, 40; Sheffield: JSOT Press, 1987), pp. 265-84; Watts, *Psalm and Story*, pp. 41-62. Watts suggests that 'psalm's placement here had the whole preceding account in view [13.17–14.31], and not just one or two of the sources'.

6. So Watts, *Psalm and Story*, pp. 41-62.

7. Cross, *Canaanite Myth*, p. 141; Childs, *The Book of Exodus*, p. 244.

8. R. Alter, *The Art of Biblical Poetry* (New York: Basic Books, 1985), p. 54.

9. Watts, *Psalm and Story*, pp. 41-62.

10. Childs makes essentially this point: 'Regardless of its prehistory, the fundamental issue is to determine the effect of joining the poem to the preceding narrative' (Childs, *The Book of Exodus*, p. 248).

the priestly redaction. To anticipate, the victory at the sea stands at a fulcrum point in the book for the priestly redaction of the book of Exodus. The two halves of the poem in Exodus 15 recapitulate the events of the book in the priestly redaction: vv. 1-12 refer generally to the events leading up to and including the victory at the Sea rendered in the first half of the book, while vv. 13-18 anticipate the events following the victory at the sea, as described in the second half of the book. While certainly not the only plausible approach, this reading has the merit of considering the two issues in tandem. Indeed, text and context constitute dual aspects of the poem. The effect is to see how the poem in its present context looks both backward to the preceding victory from slavery in Egypt and forward to the journey to Mount Sinai. As a result, the poem functions as the fulcrum-point of the book of Exodus.

2. *The Poetics between the Two Major Parts of the Song*

How the poem functions in the book is related to its structure. As a result, it is necessary to look first at the poem. Included first is a line-by-line translation of the poem, given for the sake of convenience in the smallest units possible; it is accompanied by the Hebrew text so that readers can better appreciate the discussion of the poetry which follows.

Text	*Translation*	*Words/syllables*[11] *per line*
Part One[12] (verses 1-12)[13]		
1b אשירה ליהוה	I sing to Yahweh[14]	2/6
כי גאה גאה	For He was highly exalted.	3/5

11. The purpose of the counts here is to give readers an idea of line-lengths. Both words and syllables are counted to serve as a check against each other. Sometimes words are numerous but short, or few but long which might give a skewed impression of length or brevity. Despite the inherent difficulties of counting syllables, all MT syllables are counted, even in items known to date later than the biblical period (such as the 'furtive' patah and the second vowel of segholate nouns) or features that are disputed in Masoretic grammar, but conventionally accepted (such as the existence of the 'vocal' shwa; for the argument against this phenomenon, see T. Muraoka, 'Much Ado About Nothing? A Sore Point or Two of Hebrew Grammarians', *JEOL* 32 [1991–92], pp. 131-40). The reason for this procedure is to avoid an arbitrary approach which runs the risk of proving what one wishes to demonstrate (*metri causa sui causa*). The convention for counting two syllables for the tetragrammaton is followed.

12. The division of the poem into two basic parts, vv. 1-12 and 13-18, is found

סוס ורכבו	Horse and his rider	2/5
רמה בים	He cast into the sea.	2/4
2 עזי וזמרת יה	My strength and protection[15] is Yah,	3/6
ויהי לי לישועה	He became my salvation.[16]	3/6
זה אלי ואנוהו	This one is my god, and I will glorify Him,	3/7
אלהי אבי וארממנהו	The god of my father, and I will exalt Him.	3/11
3 יהוה איש מלחמה	Yahweh is a man of war,	3/6
יהוה שמו	Yahweh is His name.	2/4
4 מרכבת פרעה וחילו	The chariots of Pharaoh and his army	3/8
ירה בים	He threw into the sea.	2/4
ומבחר שלשיו	And his choice charioteers	2/6
טבעו בים סוף	Were sunk in the Sea of Sup.	3/6
5 תהמת יכסימו	Deeps covered them,	2/7

in Cross, *Canaanite Myth*, pp. 127-31; Childs, *The Book of Exodus*, p. 252; McCarter, 'Exodus,' p. 146; Clifford, 'Exodus,' p. 50; M. Howell, 'A Song of Salvation; Exodus 15, 1b-18' (Doctoral dissertation, Faculty of Theology, Katholieke Universiteit Leuven, 1986), pp. 219-21. S.R. Driver (*The Book of Exodus* [CB; Cambridge: Cambridge University Press, 1911], pp. 129-40; reference courtesy of M. Howell) also divides between vv. 12 and 13. For a survey of late nineteenth- and twentieth-century views, see Howell, 'A Song of Salvation,' pp. 160-212.

13. Driver's proposal for the division of the poem addresses form and content (*The Book of Exodus*, pp. 129-40; summarized in Howell, 'A Song of Salvation', p. 168): Introduction: v. 1b; Part I: vv. 2-5; Part II: vv. 6-10; Part III: vv. 11-18, divided further into vv. 11-12 and 13-18. Kloos (*Yhwh's Combats with the Sea*, p. 138) suggests that vv. 1-12 alternate praise of Yhwh with the description of the defeat of the enemy.

14. The translation is literal. The lengths of lines given in the transcription and translation largely follow Cross, *Canaanite Myth*, pp. 127-31. For philological notes, see Cross, *Canaanite Myth*, pp. 127-31 (notes); and Kloos, *Yhwh's Combats with the Sea*, pp. 128-30.

15. See S.B. Parker, 'Exodus XV 2,' *VT* 20 (1970), pp. 358-59. For a recent discussion of זמרת, see M.L. Barré, '"My Strength and My Song" in Exodus 15.2', *CBQ* 54 (1992), pp. 623-37. Based on Akkadian texts referring to the personal god as 'protector' and 'vigor', Barré takes עזי וזמרת as 'protective deity', but these nouns may be abstracts used for a concrete description, like the parallel term ישועה* in Exod. 15.2.

16. This line could be more woodenly translated: 'He became for me salvation'. The noun of abstraction is used instead of an agent noun, 'saviour' (such as מושיע as in Isa. 43.11; 45.15, 21; 63.8; Hos. 13.4) and the dative of advantage with the personal suffix is employed instead of the suffix directly attached to the agent noun (see משעי in 2 Sam. 22.3). Finally 'to become' in English often expresses a change in state. Here it seems to indicate the divine posture toward the speaker. The line might be rendered more idiomatically: 'He acted as my saviour'.

Hebrew	English	Ratio
ירדו במצולת	They descended into the depths	2/6
כמו אבן	Like a stone.	2/4
6 ימינך יהוה	Your right hand, O Yahweh,	2/6
נאדרי בכח	Is mighty[17] with strength.	2/6
ימינך יהוה	Your right hand, O Yahweh,	2/6
תרעץ אויב	Shattered the enemy.	2/4
7 וברב גאונך	And in Your great majesty	2/7
תהרס קמיך	You smashed Your enemies.	2/6
תשלח חרנך	You sent Your fury,	2/7
יאכלמו כקש	It consumed them like stubble.	2/6
8 וברוח אפיך	And by the blast of Your nostrils	2/7
נערמו מים	The waters were piled.	2/5
נצבו כמו נד נזלים	The swells stood like a heap.[18]	3(4)/9
קפאו תהמת	The Deeps foamed[19]	2/5
בלב ים	In the heart of the sea.	2/3
9 אמר אויב	The enemy had said.	2/4
ארדף אשיג	'I will pursue, I will overtake,	2/4
אחלק שלל	I will divide spoil.	2/5
תמלאמו נפשי	My appetite will be filled with them,	2/5
אריק חרבי	I will unsheathe my sword,	2/4
תורישמו ידי	My hand will disinherit them.'	2/6

17. For the form of נאדרי, see W.L. Moran, 'The Hebrew Language in its Northwest Semitic Background', in G.E. Wright (ed.), *The Bible and the Ancient Near East: Essays in Honor of William Foxwell Albright* (Garden City, NY: Doubleday, 1965), p. 67; B.K. Waltke and M.P. O'Connor, *An Introduction to Biblical Hebrew Syntax* (Winona Lake, IN: Eisenbrauns, 1990), pp. 127-28.

18. The word נד is usually related to Arabic *nadd*, 'high hill; earth-heap, sand-heap' (E.W. Lane, *An Arabic–English Lexicon* [London: Williams & Norgate, 1963–93; repr. Beirut: Librairie du Liban, 1968], p. 2778); for example, see BDB, p. 623. The context would suggest the sense of 'heap' (cf. Cross, *Canaanite Myth*, p. 128 n. 58). The picture seems to be one of higher and higher waves. Cross rightly questions the notion that this verse bears any relation to priestly notion of a wall of water in ch. 14 (cf. NJPS to Exod. 15.8: 'The floods stood straight like a wall').

19. See Cross, *Canaanite Myth*, pp. 128-29 n. 59. Kloos (*Yhwh's Combat with the Sea*, pp. 136-37) questions Cross's etymology, but the three attestations constitute a poor base of data to use to exclude the meaning suggested by Cross. While 'to churn' is quite possible (so Cross), the meaning 'to foam' may be preferable, since it suits disturbed waters and has the benefit of a contextual parallel with *qp* in Ahiqar noted by Cross. Like NJPS (see previous note), Kloos takes the metaphors in v. 8b and 8c in a literal sense. However, the comparative particle in v. 8c suggests a simile and by parallelism with v. 8b a metaphor in that line as well. Kloos also criticizes the picture yielded by Cross's translation. The picture may be an evocative one which does not spell out the details of the defeat.

10	נשפת ברוחך	You blew with Your wind,	2/7
	כסמו ים	Sea covered them.	2/4
	צללו כעופרת	They sunk like lead	2/7
	במים אדירים[20]	In the mighty waters.	2/6
11	מי כמכה	Who is like You	2/4
	באלם יהוה	Among the gods, O Yahweh?	2/5
	מי כמכה	Who is like You,	2/4
	נאדר בקדש	Mighty among the holy?	2/5
	נורא תהלת	Awesome of praises,	2/5
	עשה פלא	Wonder-worker.	2/4
12	נטית ימינך	You extended Your right hand,	2/7
	תבלעמו ארץ	The Underworld swallowed them.	2/6

Part Two (verses 13-18)

13	נחית בחסדך	You led by Your faithfulness	2/7
	עם זו גאלת	The people whom You had redeemed.	3/5
	נהלת בעזך	You guided by Your strength	2/7
	אל נוה קדשך	To Your holy habitation.	2/6
14	שמעו עמים ירגזון	Peoples heard, they trembled,	3/8
	חיל אחז	Writhing seized	2/3
	ישבי פלשת	The inhabitants of Philistia.	2/6
15	אז נבהלו	Then they were frightened,	2/4
	אלופי אדום	The chiefs of Edom.	2/5
	אילי מואב	The leaders of Moab,	2/4
	יאחזמו רעד	Panic gripped them.	2/6
	נמגו כל	Entirely melted were	2/4
	ישבי כנען	The inhabitants[21] of Canaan.	2/6
16	תפל עליהם	Upon them fell	2/5
	אימתה ופחד	Terror and fear.	2/6
	בגדל זרועך	By Your strong arm	2/6
	ידמו כאבן	They were dumb like a stone.	2/6
	עד יעבר	While cross did	2/4
	עמך יהוה	Your people, O Yahweh,	2/5

20. See J.L. Mays, 'Some Cosmic Connotations of *Mayim Rabbîm*,' *JBL* 74 (1955), p. 17. The possibility that Ugaritic *gšm 'adr*, 'mighty rain' (*KTU* 2.38.14) bears on this expression has been raised by P. Bordreuil ('Recherches ougaritiques', *Sem* 40 [1991], pp. 29-30) who also suggests that the Ugaritic expression may mean the *gšm* of (the month of) Adar. Whatever the value of the second proposal, with regard to the first it is to be noted that the Ugaritic phrase refers to rain water from above while the BH expression often denotes the cosmic waters below.

21. Or possibly, 'the enthroned', and therefore 'rulers', in accordance with the parallelism with 'the leaders of Moab'. So Cross, *Canaanite Myth*, p. 130.

עד יעבר	While cross did	2/4
עם זו קנית	The people whom You had established.[22]	3/5
17 תבאמו ותטעמו	You brought them and planted them	2/9
בהר נחלתך	On the mount of Your inheritance,	2/7
מכון לשבתך	The establishment for Your dwelling	2/6
פעלת יהוה	You made, O Yahweh,	2/5
מקדש אדני	The sanctuary, O Lord,[23]	2/6
כוננו ידיך	Your hands made.	2/6
18 יהוה ימלך	May Yahweh reign	2/4
לעלם ועד	Forever and ever.	2/5

The division of the Song is a very difficult issue. N. Sarna argues for 13 as the end of a unit and proposes four strophes: vv. 1-10, 11-13, 14-16 and 17-18.[24] A division at the end of v. 12 is proposed by D.N. Freedman.[25] The verbs, 'You extended' (נטית) and 'You led' (נחית), in vv. 12-13 provide syntactical, morphological and sonant connections which might appear to militate in favor of taking the two verses together as the beginning of the second half. This criterion is hardly definitive, however. Freedman's further suggestion that v. 12 serves as a connecting link between the two strophes may mitigate this point. Furthermore, v. 11 appears to represent a 'refrain' (in Freedman's terminology), perhaps implying the end of the unit. However, the 'refrain' v. 16 obviously does not close the unit. As a further possibility, the poem may be divided generally into two parts consisting of vv. 1-12 and 13-18.[26] These sections mirror one another in theme and poetics. The content of v. 12 belongs with the preceding verses, as the Egyptians in the first half of the poem correspond to the enemies named in the second half.[27] The brevity of v. 12 matches that of v. 18, which

22. Unless the context were to suggest otherwise, a past verb in a relative clause dependent on a main verb in the past issues may be rendered in English as a pluperfect.

23. On אדני, see J. Goldin, *The Song at the Sea: Being a Commentary on a Commentary in Two Parts* (New Haven: Yale University Press, 1971), p. 45 n. 48; Cross, *Canaanite Myth*, p. 131 n. 70; cf. Waltke and O'Connor, *An Introduction to Biblical Hebrew Syntax*, p. 124.

24. Sarna, *Exodus*, p. 76.

25. Freedman, *Pottery, Poetry and Prophecy*, pp. 180, 185, 209.

26. Childs, *The Book of Exodus*, p. 252; Freedman, *Pottery, Poetry, and Prophecy*, p. 211; Alter, *The Art of Biblical Poetry*, p. 54.

27. Childs, *The Book of Exodus*, p. 252; Freedman, *Pottery, Poetry, and Prophecy*, p. 211; Alter, *The Art of Biblical Poetry*, p. 54.

closes the second half of the poem. The parallelism of sound (or 'sonant parallelism'[28]) between these two verses is notable: *yᵉmînᵉkâ*, 'Your right hand' (v. 12) and *yimlōk̲*, 'May He reign' (v. 18); *tib̲lā'ēmô*, '[the Underworld] swallowed them' (v. 12) and *lᵉʿōlā̲m*, 'forever' (v. 18). In sum, the demarcation between vv. 12 and 13 remains the most defensible. Two features might suggest a further division of vv. 1-12, specifically between vv. 1-6 and 7-12.[29] The motif of 'Your right hand' (*yᵉmînᵉkā*) in vv. 6 and 12 might suggest units of vv. 1-6 and 7-12. The hymnic character of vv. 6 and 11 noted by Muilenberg and Childs might be taken as further support for these units.[30] As a result, three parts to the poem may be suggested: vv. 1-6, 7-12, and 13-18.[31]

However, many important poetic and thematic features, especially sonant pairs, decidedly link vv. 1-12 and 13-18. A. Berlin proposes three criteria for identifying sonant pairs: (1) the words are pairs, namely words in close proximity; (2) at least two sets of consonants must be involved; and (3) the 'same or similar consonant' refers to an identical phoneme, an allophone, or two phonemes which are articulated similarly.[32] Exodus 15 shows sonant pairs not only within close proximity,

28. See below.

29. Alter (*The Art of Biblical Poetry*, pp. 50-54) argues for three strophes consisting of vv. 1-6, 8-11 and 12-18. In a letter dated 17 July 1993, W.H. Propp favors three units of vv. 1-7, 8-12, 13-18. I would be prepared to accept a division of this sort, but this particular issue does not affect the essential approach here.

30. J. Muilenberg, 'A Liturgy on the Triumphs of Yahweh,' *Studia Biblica et Semitica: Theodoro Christiano Vriezen* (Wageningen: Veenman & Zonen, 1966), pp. 233-51; Childs, *The Book of Exodus*, p. 252. See also Freedman, *Pottery, Poetry and Prophecy*, pp. 178-79. Muilenberg and Freedman view vv. 6, 11 and 16cd as refrains. For older views along these lines, see M. Howell, 'A Song of Salvation', pp. 194, 197, 237 n. 51.

31. Many commmentators propose additional delineations of smaller strophes. For a survey of late nineteenth- and twentieth-century views, see Howell, 'A Song of Salvation', pp. 160-212. Cross (*Canaanite Myth*, p. 126 n. 45) posits strophes where a change in meter occurs. Howell ('A Song of Salvation', pp. 219-66) proposes strophes at vv. 1b, 2-3, 4-5, 6-7, 8-10, 11, 12, 13, 14-16, 17, 18. The irregularity of length in these units does not recommend this division. For another proposal, see Zenger, 'Tradition and Interpretation', pp. 454-60.

32. A. Berlin, *The Dynamics of Biblical Parallelism* (Bloomington: Indiana University Press, 1985), pp. 104-105. This approach is not intended to privilege these correspondences at the expense of others within lines or within other units smaller within the major sections of the poem. For a helpful discussion, see E.L. Greenstein, 'Aspects of Biblical Poetry', *Jewish Book Annual* 44 (1986-87), pp. 39-42, esp. p. 40.

but also across verses. Identifying the pairs that meet Berlin's second
and third criteria may advance the understanding of Exodus 15's
poetry. The following sonant correspondences between vv. 1-12 and
13-18 meet the second and third of Berlin's criteria (to reinforce the
visibility of these correspondences, English transliterations are used
here):

Verses 1-12	*Verses 13-18*
'ozzî, 'My strength' (v. 2)	*bᵉ'ozzᵉkâ*, 'by Your strength' (v. 13)
wᵉ'anwēhû, 'and I will glorify Him' (v. 2)	*nᵉwēh*, 'habitation' (v. 13)
wᵉḥêlô, 'and his army' (v. 4)	*ḥîl*, 'writhing' (v. 14)
kᵉmô-'āben, 'like a stone' (v. 5)	*kā'āben*, 'like a stone' (v. 16)
tir'aṣ, '[Your right hand] shattered' (v. 6)	*rā'ad*, '[panic] gripped' (v. 15)
bā'ēlīm, 'among the gods' (v. 11)	*'êlê*, 'the leaders' (v. 15)
baqqōdeš, 'in holiness' (v. 11)	*miqqᵉdāš*, 'the sanctuary' (v. 17)
'ōśēh pele', 'wonder-worker' (v. 11)	*yōšᵉbê pᵉlāšet*, 'the inhabitants of Philistia' (v. 14)
nāṭîtâ...tiblā'ēmô,' You extended ... swallowed them' (v. 12)	*tᵉbi'ēmô wᵉtiṭṭā'ēmô*, 'You brought them and planted them' (v. 17)

Other possible sonant parallels, such as *gā'ô gā'â*, 'He was highly exalted' (v. 1) with *gā'āltā*, 'You had redeemed' (v. 13), *milḥāmâ*, 'war'
(v. 3) with *yimlōk*, 'He [Yahweh] reign' (v. 18), and *bayyām...bēyam*
(v. 4) with *'am* (vv. 13, 16), are distant at best, but such general
sonant correspondences add to the density of other features linking the
two parts.

Some of the parallels listed above reinforce divine victoriousness
in the two sections of the poem: *'ozzî* (v. 2)/*bᵉ'ozzᵉkâ* (v. 13); *wᵉḥêlô*
(v. 4)/*ḥîl* (v. 14); *kᵉmô-'āben* (v. 5)/*kā'āben* (v. 16); *bā'ēlīm* (v. 11)/
'êlê (v. 15); *'ōśēh pele'* (v. 11)/*yōšᵉbê pᵉlāšet* (v. 14). Other correspondences stress that the central act of the second part, though a result of
the divine victory, does not involve warfare as such, but the divine
establishment of a people: *wᵉ'anwēhû* (v. 2)/*nᵉwēh* (v. 13); *baqqōdeš*
(v. 11)/*miqqᵉdāš* (v. 17); *nāṭîtâ... tiblā'ēmô* (v. 12)/*tᵉbi'ēmô wetiṭṭā'ēmô*
(v. 17). The group of words for the divine arm shows both associations. While 'Your right hand', *yᵉmînᵉkā* (vv. 6, 12) and 'Your arm',
zᵉrô'ᵃkā (v. 16) refer to divine victoriousness, 'Your hands', *yādêkā*
(v. 17) pertains to the creation of the divine sanctuary. The same contrast underlies the use of personal referents employed in verbs and
pronominal suffixes: these forms focus on Yahweh's victory in the

first section, but in the second section they redirect the audience's attention to the creation of the people in the sanctuary-land.[33]

One detail in the first part of the poem perhaps plays on the theme of temple-building in the second part. Following Targum Onkelos and the great Jewish medieval commentator, Rashi, NJPS translates אנוהו in v. 2 as 'I will enshrine him', making an explicit connection with נוה in v. 13,[34] although the word refers to habitation.[35] Onkelos understands this word in the sense that 'I will build for him a temple' (לה מקדשא ואבני),[36] and in suppport of this view Rashi cites Isa. 33.20 and 65.10.[37] This view would suggest that אנוהו, at least in terms of word-play, anticipates the theme of the sanctuary in the second half of the poem. Like אנוהו, its parallel verb in v. 2, 'and I will exalt Him' (וארממנהו), might evoke not only its literal meaning of exaltation of the deity, but also the construction of a sanctuary, as the verbal root רום*, 'to raise', shows this sense of 'erect, construct' in the *D*-stem ('Piel') in Ps. 78.69 and Ezra 9.9 as well as the Ugaritic Baal Cycle (*KTU* 1.2 III 7 [partially reconstructed]; 1.4 V 52, 54).[38] In sum, the poem in Exodus 15 presents a double-image of divine victoriousness in both Egypt and in the Transjordan. Furthermore, the first part may be viewed as anticipating the theme of the sanctuary-building in the second part.

3. *The Poem in the Context of the Book*

The division of the poem may relate more widely to the book as a whole. This question may be pursued from the point of the priestly redaction of both the poem and the book of Exodus. While the introduction in 15.1 shows no indication of a specific redactional hand, the

33. Cross, *Canaanite Myth*, pp. 125-26, 142.

34. See I. Drazin, *Targum Onkelos to Exodus: An English Translation of the Text with Analysis and Commentary (Based on the A. Sperber and A. Berliner Editions)* (n.p.: Ktav/Center for Judaic Studies University of Denver/Society for Targumic Studies, 1990), p. 152 n. 12; Sarna, *Exodus*, p. 77.

35. Freedman (*Pottery, Poetry, and Prophecy*, p. 137 n. 18) cites Jer. 31.23 for the parallelism between נוה and הר.

36. Drazin, *Targum Onkelos*, pp. 152-53.

37. See M. Rosenbaum and A.M. Silbermann, *Pentateuch with Targum Onkelos, Haphtaroth and Rashi's Commentary: Exodus* (Jerusalem: The Silbermann Family, 1930), p. 75b.

38. Y. Avishur, 'RWM (RMM)—BNY in Ugaritic and the Bible', *Leš* 45 (1981), pp. 270-79.

verse immediately following the poem is more indicative. A comparison of Exod. 15.19 with Exod. 14.29, customarily assigned to P, indicates a priestly redactional context.[39] Moreover, parts of Exodus 14 including the priestly stratum show literary dependence on the poem in Exodus 15.[40] The priestly redaction either accepted the poem in its present position or placed it there.[41]

The second question is how the priestly redaction interpreted the mountain in v. 17. It is usually contended that the original referent of 'the mountain of Your inheritance' (הר נחלתך), was probably a sanctuary in the land (see the excursus). Indeed, there is no doubt that the language of the mountain partakes of the traditional language for the divine home that was attached to Jerusalem. Chapter 1 (section 1, specifically in the discussion of Jerusalem) charts the religious associations of Jerusalem as the mountainous abode of Yahweh. As found in Exodus 15, this holy mountain is the sanctuary-home of the deity's own making. To this mountain the deity leads the covenant-people in order that they may dwell together.

However, it is not clear that the priestly redaction identified the mountain in Exod. 15.17 as a divine mountain in the land. According to B. Halpern, Sinai constitutes the referent of the mountain in the priestly reading of Exod. 15.16-17:

39. So Childs, *The Book of Exodus*, p. 248.

40. Halpern, *The Emergence of Israel*, p. 38 nn. 66, 42-43. See also Vervenne, 'The "P" Tradition in the Pentateuch', pp. 67-90.

41. According to Halpern (*The Emergence of Israel*, pp. 38-39), the J material shows literary dependence on the poem (but not vice-versa; see Cross, *Canaanite Myth*, pp. 133-34) and the P material appears to combine details of Exod. 15 and J's notion that the sea was dried up. For Childs (*The Book of Exodus*, p. 245), tradition-historical grounds suggest a different relationship between the poetic and J versions. Since the crossing of the sea stands within the exodus-conquest traditions in the poetic version but in the prose context with the wilderness traditions, the poetic version represents an account parallel to J which would suggest an older tradition predating both accounts. In either reconstruction, P could draw on both the poem and J. For further discussion, see Blum, *Studien*, pp. 256-62. This involves a complicated debate which cannot be addressed satisfactorily in this context, much less solved. Such a resolution is, however, irrelevant for a synchronic consideration of the priestly redaction, except in the case of Brenner's exceptionally late dating of Exod. 15 and van Seters's position that the poem postdates both J and P (see Brenner, *The Song of the Sea*, pp. 11-15; van Seters, *Life of Moses*, p. 147). Both scholars ignore the relative density of older features.

Exodus 15 starts with two statements of the defeat of Egypt (vv. 1, 2-5); it then repeats the tidings (vv. 6-8); it then repeats the tidings again (vv. 9-10); and it repeats the tidings once more still (vv. 11-12). Only at this point, after five rehearsals of the victory over Egypt, does the poet proceeed to the migration (v. 13) and Israel's entry in Canaan (vv. 14-16). It is more than possible that in some circles, as in modern traditional circles, vv. 13-17 were seen not as an account of the conquest, but as a sixth recital of the victory at sea, and as one culminating in the arrival of Israel at Sinai! [42]

For the priestly redaction, the end-point of the journey, 'the mountain of Your inheritance'[43] in v. 17, may have been Sinai. The identification of Sinai as the mountain likely predated the priestly redaction of Exodus. For Exod. 3.12, usually assigned to E in traditional source-criticism, the goal of the journey is the mountain of God located in the wilderness:[44] 'And when you have freed the people from Egypt, you shall worship God at this mountain'. That the priestly redaction could have understood Sinai as the referent of 15.17 was therefore not exceptional.

There are two reasons for supposing that the priestly redaction read Sinai as the referent of the mountain in Exod. 15.17. The first reason is structural. The mountain may not have played such a central role in the pre-priestly strata of Exodus, but with the older mountain traditions of Exodus 3 and 32–34 now set at Sinai and the priestly insertion of Exod. 19.1–Num. 10.10, Sinai dominates not only the second half of the book, but also the book as a whole. The second and related reason is theological. In the priestly theology of the Pentateuch Sinai occupies an absolutely central place. With the priestly insertion of Exod. 19.1–Num. 10.10,[45] Sinai becomes the Mount Everest of priestly theology which looms larger than the cultic sites in the land such as Jerusalem. On this issue M. Noth comments:

> For the P narrative is not oriented toward an impending occupation of the land; rather, its real goal was reached with the presentation of the regulations established at Sinai, regulations which became valid immediately rather than being put off until a later occupation.[46]

42. Halpern, *The Emergence of Israel*, pp. 38-39 (Halpern's italics).
43. For the piling-up of epithets for the sanctuary, see *KTU* 1.3 III 29-31, IV 19-20 and Ps. 48.2-3.
44. McCarter, 'Exodus', p. 130.
45. Blenkinsopp, *The Pentateuch*, pp. 137-38, 162-63, 191, 194.
46. Noth, *A History of Pentateuchal Traditions*, p. 9.

Sinai not only anticipates the land. For the priestly theology Sinai defines how life inside and outside of the land is to be led. According to the priestly gloss in Exod. 29.46 (see also Lev. 22.32-33; Num. 15.41), Yahweh freed the Israelites from the slavery of Egypt in order 'to dwell among them'. This purpose is made possible only through the sacral order established at Sinai. The priestly tradition does not emphasize the land as the goal of the Exodus (cf. the deuteronomic statement in Deut. 6.23). Indeed, within the priestly theology the promises of progeny and land play important roles (Gen. 1.1–2.4a; 17; cf. Exod. 1), but Sinai is regarded not only as proleptic for the land; it also defines it. For the priestly tradition Sinai would represent the site of the definitive covenant and model for later liturgical remembrances in the land.

If this reading were to be placed into the historical context of the post-exilic period, Zion, perhaps the original referent of the poem, would have been understood as Sinai experienced cultically. Zion was the actual earthly location, but there Sinai's covenant and theophany was liturgically realized. Or, in J.D. Levenson's words,

> God's continuing availability is at Zion, not Sinai, but the canonical division of the Pentateuch from the rest of the Bible.. .insures that the heir will be eternally subordinate to the testator, Zion to Sinai, David to Moses. By limiting the concept of Torah proper to the Pentateuch, the canonical process speaks more directly to an Israel on the move, its promises of land and rest as yet unrealized, than to the Israel of the Zionistic traditions. . . The presence is the presence of Zion, but the voice is the voice of Sinai.[47]

For the priestly redactor of Exodus, this mountain was to function as the cultically pure site of Israel's God and its priesthood, echoing the original place of theophany and covenant.[48] In sum, Exod. 15.17 may have referred originally to a sanctuary in the land (as discussed in the excursus to this chapter). However, it was applied secondarily to Sinai by virtue of the new interpretation of the poem in accordance with the priestly redaction of Exodus 19–40.

47. Levenson, *Sinai and Zion*, p. 188.

48. Here note the comment of Lohfink: 'In its literal meaning, the song of Moses already was composed in such a way that later saving acts of Yahweh could be introduced and read into its account of history' (*The Inerrancy of Scripture*, p. 84). In view of the interpretation that I am offering about the the reading of the mountain in v. 17 as Sinai, I would add 'earlier' saving acts as well.

If this approach to Exod. 15.13-17 is correct, then three further
details in the poem may have been interpreted accordingly. First, the
priestly redaction may have understood 'it [your people] crossed'
(יעבר) in Exod. 15.16 as the crossing through the wilderness to the
mountain of Sinai. The verb 'to cross' (עבר*) is used of traversing
land in Deut. 2.18 (see also Num. 20.17, 21.22; Deut. 2.4, 27, 30).[49]
This view of יעבר in Exod. 15.16 would seem to follow from the
apparent reference to the wilderness journey as suggested by the verbs
in Exod. 15.13. Secondly, the reaction of the peoples in Exod. 15.14-
16 may have been read secondarily as the fearful response at a great
distance.[50] The foreign peoples' reaction would represent a miraculous
fear that the Israelite god's reputation could inspire in these peoples at
such a remove.[51] Other passages likewise indicate that the reputation
of the Israelite victories precede them (Exod. 18.1; Josh. 2.9-10, 5.1;
cf. Deut. 2.25; Josh. 9.1; Isa. 7.2). The theme of fear inspired at a
great distance could have been interpreted in accordance with Sinai as
the referent of the mountain. Finally, 'sanctuary' (מקדש) of Exod.
15.17 might be viewed as playing on the tabernacle of Exodus 25–31,
35–40 called מקדש in Exod. 25.8. In sum, the victory at the sea stands
at a fulcrum point in the book for the priestly redaction of the book of
Exodus. The two halves of the poem in Exodus 15 recapitulate the preceding and following events of the book. The chapter draws together
Israel's past and future in one poetic moment that has been paradigmatic for centuries.

---

49. I wish to thank Professor Michael Fishbane who brought this usage to my
attention. It is interesting to note that P. Haupt took יעבר in v. 16 as a misplaced
gloss from v. 8 which he believed originally referred to the crossing of the Reed Sea
(see Haupt, 'Moses' Song of Triumph', *AJSL* 20 [1904], p. 162 (reference courtesy
of M. Howell). Cf. Halpern, *The Emergence of Israel*, pp. 38-39.

50. For the physical reaction of the nations, see N.M. Waldman, 'A Comparative
Note on Exodus 15.14-16,' *JQR* 66 (1978), pp. 189-92.

51. Cf. Alter, *The Art of Biblical Poetry*, p. 54.

EXCURSUS: THE UNITY AND DATE OF THE POEM

The preceding argument about the text and context of the poem entails some further scholarly issues, specifically its unity, original date and setting.

1. *The Poem's Unity*

The unity of the poem has been challenged on grounds of meter, grammar, content and genre, by a number of scholars who regard vv. 13-17 or 18 as secondary.[52] Under this view the composer of these verses skillfully drew on the sounds and senses of words in the older composition of vv. 1-12. The main support for this view is form-critical: a song[53] celebrating the victory at the sea issuing in divine kingship has been augmented with the general schema of Pentateuchal events. In short, the first part of the poem relates to the defeat of the Egyptians at the Sea while the second part of the poem concerns the divine guidance of the people to the divinely established sanctuary.

As a logical premise, different content in different parts of an ancient Near Eastern text serves as a poor criterion for establishing a composite text. Numerous ancient Near Eastern hymns addressed to deities involve different sorts of content,[54] but this fact is not an argument for the composite character of these texts. The much-vaunted comparison with the Baal Cycle likewise suffers as an indicator of a composite text in the poem of Exodus 15. According to J. Jeremias, the apparent Ugaritic antecedent of the Baal Cycle (*KTU* 1.1-1.6) suggests that vv. 1-12 is to be separated from the rest of the poem, in keeping with the sequence of Baal's victory over Sea and divine kingship in *KTU* 1.2 IV.[55] For Jeremias, this Ugaritic conflict story while compa-

---

52. J.D.W. Watts, 'The Song of the Sea—Ex. XV', *VT* 7 (1957), pp. 371-80; G.W. Coats, 'The Song of the Sea', *CBQ* 31 (1969), pp. 1-17; S.I.L. Norin, *Er spaltete das Meer: Die Auszugsüberlieferung in Psalmen und Kult des Alten Testament* (ConBOT, 9; Lund: Gleerup, 1977), pp. 77-107; E. Zenger, 'Tradition und Interpretation', pp. 452-82; and Spieckermann, *Heilsgegenwart*, pp. 96-115.

53. While other form-critical assessments have been proposed, the category song follows from the first word of the poem. Song of victory seems the best label to cover the contents.

54. For some easily accessible examples, see the Sumerian Hymn to Enlil and Inanna and the Nanshe Hymn (Jacobsen, *The Harps*, pp. 101-42); the Akkadian Gula Hymn of Bullutsa-Rabi (Foster, *Before the Muses*, II, pp. 491-99) and the Shamash Hymn (Foster, *Before the Muses*, II, pp. 536-44); and the Egyptian Great Hymn to Khnum (M. Lichtheim, *Ancient Egyptian Literature*, III, pp. 111-15).

55. J. Jeremias, *Das Königtum Gottes in den Psalmen: Israels Begegnung mit dem kanaanäischen Mythos in den Jahwe-König-Psalmen* (FRLANT, 141; Göttingen: Vandenhoeck und Ruprecht, 1987), pp. 93-106; and followed by T. Dozeman, 'The Tradition-Historical Development of the Song of the Sea', paper presented to the Old Testament Theology group at the national meeting of the Catholic Biblical Association, August, 1993. I wish to thank Professor Dozeman for his gracious consent to cite his essay. While I take issue with his arguments and conclusion, I am especially appreciative of Professor Dozeman's kindness in allowing me to cite this piece. Moroever, my own arguments have benefited from reflecting on his essay. Several criticisms noted below arose from the session at the Catholic Biblical Association national meeting devoted to

rable in some ways with vv. 1-12 shows no parallels with vv. 13-17. However, the comparison is somewhat misleading, for in the Baal Cycle, the victory over Sea in *KTU* 1.2 IV is not complete until the establishment of Baal's house at his holy abode, Mount Sapan, in *KTU* 1.4 V–VII; so, too, in Exodus 15, the victory of vv. 1-12 is only complete with the establishment of the house of v. 17 at the holy abode mentioned also in v. 13.[56] In both cases, the victory cannot be separated easily from the house-building.[57] These parallels with the Baal Cycle may be used to argue for the unity of the poem in Exodus 15.[58]

The more basic problem with this methodology lies in using extra-Israelite literature as a norm for evaluating Israelite literature. After all, Exodus 15 like other early poems such as Judges 5 shows some specifically Israelite themes unknown in Ugaritic literature. To know whether a division is to be understood between vv. 12 and 13, it is necessary to understand whether in Israelite literature such linkage is made between putatively disparate themes as the victory at the Sea and the guidance to the sanctuary-land. In fact, many examples of such linkage occur in Israelite literature, even in a single verse such as Ps. 114.3. The multiplication of different reasons upon which to praise the deity occurs not only in biblical literature, but also in hymns in the ancient Near East. The argument from different themes to different compositions is not compelling.

The basis for seeing the poem as a composite does not lie in the meter, as the poem shows a basic pattern of shorter lines with some longer lines which are not confined to either vv. 1-12 or 13-17 (18); these occur certainly in vv. 5, 8 and 14. Nor may the grounds for a composite text be found in different time-frames in the poem.[59] The time-frame is narrative past (or perhaps historical present) throughout the poem even in vv. 13-17: the suffix verbs in vv. 13 and 14 refer to the past, and the construction of עָז ('then') + the suffix form נִבְהֲלוּ ('they were frightened') in v. 15 signals the continuation of the sequence in the past (i.e. the next action took place), this time involving the reaction of the nations which is continued in v. 16. A

Professor Dozeman's essay; these are noted as personal communications from various members of the Old Testament Theology group.

56. Batto (*Slaying the Dragon*, p. 113) claims that the poem exhibits 'the same basic structure' as the Ugaritic Baal Cycle, although only in *KTU* 1.2 and 1.4 (and nothing of 1.3 or 1.5–1.6) and Enuma Elish (see S. Rummel, 'Narrative Structures in the Ugaritic Texts and Hebrew Bible', in S. Rummel (ed.), *Ras Shamra Parallels III: The Texts from Ugarit and the Hebrew Bible* [AnOr, 51; Rome: Pontifical Biblical Institute, 1981], pp. 234-77). See further, Cross, *Canaanite Myth*, pp. 131-32; Kloos, *Yhwh's Combat with the Sea*, pp. 141-42, 152, 153-57; Levenson, *The Hebrew Bible*, p. 141.

57. On this point, see especially Rummel, 'Narrative Structures', pp. 236-60.

58. It might be argued that the Baal Cycle parallels the whole of the poem more deeply than the critics sometimes allege. After his defeat of Sea, Baal's house is built, and Baal engages in a victory tour capturing 'sixty-six cities' and 'seventy-seven towns' of terrestrial enemies (*KTU* 1.4 VII 7-10) and then a theophanic expression of power which frightens his enemies (1.4 VII, pp. 29-37). Exod. 15.13-17 might be viewed as combining the victory-tour with the ongoing expression of power following the defeat of Sea. These events compare only generally with Exod. 15.13-16, but such comparisons are as precise as the points of comparison offered by Jeremias and Dozeman.

59. Contra Brenner, *The Song of the Sea*, pp. 36-39.

switch to a future time-frame does not appear indicated even in v. 16b which uses the expression 'until it did cross. . . ' (עד יעבר). Here the nations show their fearful response during the time-frame continuously through the time when the people crossed over.[60] The construction of עד plus prefix form to express a past time-frame is not exceptional (Josh. 10.13, Ps. 73.17, 2 Chron. 29.34).[61] Many of the prefix verbs in vv. 13-17 may be of the grammatical form, archaic *yaqtul* preterites, as Cross argues.[62] In any case, attempts to see a break between vv. 12 and 13 on the basis of different time-frames appear misguided.

Despite the many difficulties with seeing the poem as composite, T. Dozeman takes the theory further in regarding vv. 13-17 as specifically deuteronomic.[63] As support, Dozeman argues that the so-called archaic grammatical features of the poem are lacking in vv. 13-17, and that these verses contain some well-known examples of deuteronomic language. On the first point Dozeman misconstrues the evidence. D.A. Robertson points to several archaic features in these verses.[64] According to Robertson, Exodus contains a high clustering of old forms and syntactical features without any forms standard to the later classical Hebrew. As evidence for his second point, Dozeman points specifically to the verbs of divine guidance; the theme of the fear of the nations; the root עבר* in Josh. 2.10, 4.23 and 5.1; and the use of the word יבשה for dry land. The theory suffers in a number of respects. First, Dozeman's attempt to sever v. 17 from the pre-deuteronomistic version of the poem seems forced. On the one hand, as Dozeman notes, it contains many of the characteristics of the older themes shared by the Baal Cycle and other texts celebrating divine kingship. On the other hand, this verse assumes the content of v. 16 or something akin to it. Secondly, Dozeman acknowledges that vv. 13 and 17 contain the themes of temple-building which often accompany the divine battle and assumption of kingship, for example in the Baal Cycle and Enuma Elish.[65] Yet Dozeman separates these themes in Exodus 15, preferring to understand the putatively original poem of vv. 1-12, 18 as exploring the themes of divine conflict and kingship, while vv. 13-17 dwell on the the divine temple-building. This separation appears forced, resulting in a thematically misplaced division of the poem. Thirdly, if vv. 1-12, 18 were separated from vv. 13-17, the party on whose behalf Yahweh fights would be missing from the original poem, which seems unlikely.[66] Finally, Dozeman takes specific words as deuterono-

---

60. For this sense of עד, see Judg. 19.26 (discussed in *GBH* 113m).

61. See *BDB* 725; Cross, *Canaanite Myth*, p. 130 n. 67. Cf. 1 Sam. 1.22 (*GBH*, p. 112i).

62. See A.F. Rainey, 'The Hebrew Prefix Conjugation in the Light of Amarnah Canaanite', *Hebrew Studies* 27 (1986), pp. 4-19, esp. pp. 4, 10-12; J. Huehnergard, 'The Early Hebrew Prefix Conjugations', *Hebrew Studies* 29 (1988), pp. 19-23, esp. pp. 21-3; Waltke and O'Connor, *An Introduction*, pp. 514-17 (with further references). The verb ירגזון ('they trembled') in v. 14 is not the archaic preterite *yaqtul* form (since no preterite *yaqtul* forms have the ending, -*ûn*).

63. Dozeman, 'The Tradition-Historical Development'.

64. Robertson, *Linguistic Evidence*, pp. 28-31, 61, 64, 67, 70, 72, 109, 135, 138, 147, 149-50, 153-54, 155, 156.

65. Dozeman presupposes that the divine battle with the Sea akin to that of the Baal Cycle is presented in the poem, but for reasons noted above, the parallel may be of a more general character.

66. J.J. Collins (personal communication).

mic. It is true that עבר* is used frequently for the crossing of the Jordan River in deuteronomic works, and it is also true that יבשה is attested with frequency in deuteronomic passages. Indeed, this noun appears with עבר* in two deuteronomic passages (Josh. 4.22, Neh. 9.11). Yet non-deuteronomic passages use עבר* for crossing either land or water (it might be asked what other verb would be used).[67] In the case of יבשה, the noun is attested only fourteen times. Many of them are not deuteronomic, which is arguably not a terribly indicative distribution. In short, nothing in vv. 13-17 is specifically deuteronomic. Furthermore, Dozeman assumes that because parallel language and themes are found in deuteronomic literature, this corpus is the indicator of the provenience of the verses involved. In sum, there are no compelling grounds for regarding the poem in Exodus 15 as a composite text.

2. The Poem's Original Date and Setting

The date of the poem is difficult to establish. It has been dated from the pre-monarchic period through the Hellenistic era.[68] While Cross and Freedman and others view the poem as pre-monarchic, others date it to the early monarchy[69] or the late monarchy.[70] There are two primary approaches to the issue of dating. One is based on history of traditions. This approach largely places the poem within the Zion tradition. The Zion tradition, however, lacks otherwise any theology of the Exodus until Second Isaiah and later literature (Isa. 11.15-16;[71] cf. Jer 23.7-8[72]). The Zion tradition may have derived this theology secondarily from another cultic tradition. Moreover, appeal to 'the establishment for Your dwelling' (מכון לשבתך) in v. 17 as a specifically Jerusalemite expression is hardly compelling, as the notion of the divine place of enthronement appears already in Ugaritic literature. The general problem with this approach of dating by tradition-history is that determining the tradition depends on the other attested written materials defining the tradition; but if these other materials which serve as the basis of comparison are substantially later, or if the available materials are unrepresentative for ancient Israel, then the history of traditions approach is insufficient to adjudicate the issue.

The second means of dating by appealing to archaic grammatical features is not a superior criterion, since the standards for dating poetry prior to the eighth-century prophets are poorly attested. The relative chronology offered for poems based on

---

67. B. Batto (personal communication).

68. See Brenner, *The Song of the Sea*, pp. 11-15.

69. J. Day, *God's Conflict with the Dragon and the Sea: Echoes of a Canaanite Myth in the Old Testament* (Cambridge: Cambridge University Press, 1985), p. 99.

70. Spieckermann, *Heilsgegenwart*, p. 113; Jeremias, *Königtum Gottes*, p. 103; Mettinger, *The Dethronement of Sabaoth*, pp. 26-27.

71. This passage has been connected with a late redaction level of the book as it refers to a post-exilic diaspora. So among some recent commentators, see W.H. Irwin in J. Jensen and W.H. Irwin, 'Isaiah 1–39', *NJBC* 1.238; O.H. Steck, 'Tritijesaja im Jesajabuch', in Vermeylen (ed.), *The Book of Isaiah*, pp. 382-84.

72. See S.E. Loewenstamm, *The Evolution of the Exodus Tradition* (trans. B.J. Schwartz; Jerusalem: Magnes, 1992), pp. 42-43.

archaic grammatical features rests on the assumption that a density of features provides a reliable standard for dating. While this argument is sensible to a degree especially for poems exhibiting an especially high or low degree of archaic features, it otherwise provides neither an absolute nor even a precise relative chronology. The problem is all the more complicated by the fact the prophetic corpus has been heavily redacted and does not provide an absolute standard for eighth-century and later poetry.[73] Given the insufficient sample for establishing a chronology for pre-prophetic poetry, it is impossible on the basis of grammar to precisely date poems such as the one in Exodus 15. The language of the poem seems archaic,[74] but archaic in this context is relative only to the prophetic corpus. When the antiquity of a poem's grammar and content is evident (e.g. the bulk of Judg. 5 and possibly the sayings of Gen. 49), then a pre-monarchic date may be sustained. In contrast, the content of Exodus 15 is amenable to either an early monarchic or pre-monarchic date. (Given the character of the language, it is difficult to hold a late date or even a date after the eighth-century prophets.[75]) Despite the problems, the grammar of the poem appears to predate the eighth century. After this point, suggestions for dates are less well-grounded. A tenth- or ninth-century date is reasonable, but there is no evidence disproving an eleventh-century date.[76]

The original setting of the poem is related to the question of the original referent of the mountain mentioned in v. 17. As with many features in this poem, this issue is a matter of dispute. The reaction of the Philistines, the Edomites, the Moabites and the Canaanites (v. 15) does not suggest Sinai as the final destination of Yahweh's guidance, although this view has been advocated.[77] Instead, it has been long argued

73. Kloos, *Yhwh's Combat with the Sea*, p. 130.

74. See the list in Kloos, *Yhwh's Combat with the Sea*, pp. 131-32; and Robertson, *Linguistic Evidence*, pp. 28-31, 61, 64, 67, 70, 72, 109, 135, 138, 147, 149-50, 153-54, 155, 156.

75. Robertson, *Linguistic Evidence*, pp. 28-31, 61, 64, 67, 70, 72, 109, 135, 138, 147, 149-50, 153-54, 155, 156; Cross, *Canaanite Myth*, pp. 121-31; Freedman, *Pottery, Poetry and Prophecy*, pp. 187-227; Kloos, *Yhwh's Combat with the Sea*, p. 130. See also E.Y. Kutscher, *A History of the Hebrew Language* (ed. R. Kutscher; Jerusalem: Magnes; Leiden: Brill, 1982), pp. 79-80.

76. If the original referent of Exod. 15.16-17 was Shiloh, then the poem could date to any point in the Iron I period from the eleventh century through the tenth century (see I. Finkelstein, *The Archaeology of the Israelite Settlement* [Jerusalem: Israel Exploration Society, 1988], pp. 220-34; *idem*, 'Seilun, Khirbet', *ABD*, V, pp. 1069-72; B. Halpern, 'Shiloh', *ABD*, V, p. 1214). Dr Elizabeth M. Bloch-Smith reminds me that the archaeological evidence for a temple at the site, the concern reflected in Exod. 15, is circumstantial at best. Indeed, Finkelstein describes the evidence in precisely this way (*Archaeology*, p. 233; see also pp. 216-18, 219).

77. So J.P. Hyatt, *Exodus* (NCB; London: Oliphants, 1971), pp. 166-67 (reference courtesy of M. Howell); Freedman, *Pottery, Poetry, and Prophecy*, pp. 136, 141; Andersen and Freedman, *Hosea*, p. 524; Levenson, *Sinai and Zion*, p. 136. This view was anticipated by Ibn Ezra (noted by Sarna, *Exodus*, p. 248 n. 55). Freedman (*Pottery, Poetry, and Prophecy*, p. 136 n. 14) notes that in an unpublished manuscript Albright suggested either Sinai or a site in Canaan as possibilities. Howell ('A Song of Deliverance,' p. 154) criticizes Freedman's identification of the mountain with Sinai on two grounds: (1) Freedman's identification appears prejudiced by his view that the poem is very early; (2) his argument that the poem does not mention conquest and therefore does not refer to a site in the land is irrelevant.

that a cultic site such as Gilgal,[78] Shiloh,[79] Jerusalem,[80] the hill-country of early Israel,[81] or the land of Judah as a whole,[82] is the original referent of the mountain mentioned in Exod. 15.17.[83] Correspondingly, v. 16 apparently referred originally to crossing the Jordan into the land, as Targum Onkelos, Rashi and other commentators have long noted.[84] As von Rad and Noth emphasized,[85] Sinai is conspicuous for its absence from almost all[86] other accounts of the exodus. The land is the end-point of the journey in Exod. 3.8, 17; 34.11-12;[87] Deut. 26.5-11;[88] Josh. 24.7-8; as well as later poetic texts such as Pss. 105.37-45; 114; and Isa. 51.9-11.[89]

---

78.   See Cross, *Canaanite Myth*, p. 142; Batto, *Slaying the Dragon*, p. 109. Cross, followed by Batto, suggests Gilgal based largely on the combination of exodus and conquest motifs in Exod. 15 and Josh. 3–5. Cf. the comments of Noth (*A History of Pentateuchal Traditions*, p. 52 n. 170): 'This rejects von Rad's thesis. . . that the claim upon the land in the tradition of the occupation was formulated specifically at the sanctuary of Gilgal near Jericho. This thesis rests solely on what seems to me the untenable literary-critical presupposition that the old materials of the Book of Joshua, with their Benjaminite narratives adhering to Gilgal, constitute the continuation and conclusion of the narrative of the old Pentateuchal tradition.'

79.   For this possibility, see BDB p. 874; Goldin, *The Song at the Sea*, pp. 34-58; Halpern, *The Emergence of Israel*, p. 35.

80.   See Childs, *The Book of Exodus*, p. 252; Spieckermann, *Heilsgegenwart*, p. 113; Jeremias, *Königtum Gottes*, p. 103; Mettinger, *The Dethronement of Sabaoth*, p. 27; cf. pp. 75, 109; Batto, *Slaying the Dragon*, pp. 216-17 n. 11. This view is found also in Targum Onkelos (Drazin, *Targum Onkelos*, pp. 158-59 at v. 17) and in traditional commentaries noted by Sarna, *Exodus*, p. 248 n. 57. Cf. the view of Freedman (*Pottery, Poetry, and Prophecy*, p. 195) that the final form of the poem is to be attributed to the Jerusalem cult under the united monarchy. See below for his two interpretations of the mountain in v. 17. In a similar vein, Mettinger and Batto see this verse as a patent reference to Zion, which indicates a date from the tenth century on. The lack of an explicit reference to Zion might seem unusual for royal theology, but the same argument might be levelled against identifications with the other sites.

81.   For this proposal, see Halpern, *The Emergence of Israel*, p. 35; *idem*, 'Jerusalem and the Lineages', p. 68.

82.   Freedman, *Pottery, Poetry, and Prophecy*, p. 214; Clifford, 'Exodus', p. 50. See traditional commentaries noted by Sarna, *Exodus*, p. 248 n. 56.

83.   Though inclining toward a specific site, Kloos (*Yhwh's Combats with the Sea*, pp. 134-35, 150) reckons with the possibility that the site is purely mythological, and prescinds from any identification.

84.   Drazin, *Targum Onkelos*, pp. 158-59 at v. 16. See also the discussion of Kloos, *Yhwh's Combat with the Sea*, pp. 135-36.

85.   See von Rad, *The Problem of the Hexateuch*, pp. 1-78, esp. pp. 8-13.

86.   See below.

87.   McCarter, 'Exodus', p. 130.

88.   For a recent assessment of this passage, see D.R. Daniels, 'The Creed of Deuteronomy XXVI Revisited', in J.A. Emerton (ed.), *Studies in the Pentateuch* (VTSup, 41; Leiden: Brill, 1990), pp. 231-42. Despite attempts since von Rad's early dating of this passage to see it as deuteronomic and late, Daniels views the passage as Proto-Deuteronomy (dated to about 700), but dates its pre-Deuteronomic form to the pre-monarchic period given the later Israelite-Aramean hostilities.

89.   One may note the linkage of the conquest with the crossing of both the Reed Sea and the Jordan imputed to Josh. 3–5 (which would fit into Cross's argument for Gilgal as the sanctuary named in Exod. 15.17, as noted above). Ps. 106 contributes little to this question. While Horeb appears in Ps. 106.19, it plays no role in the giving of the law or coming to the mountain of God.

As the many proposals for the original referent of v. 17 indicate, there is no con-
clusive evidence to prove any one of them. Of the proposed sites for the original
referent of v. 17, Shiloh perhaps holds some circumstantial evidence. Like the poem
of Exodus 15, Psalm 78 reviews the ancient traditions of Israel including the event of
the Exodus, the wilderness journey and the arrival to the holy mountain, held in
Psalm 78 to be Shiloh.[90] Psalm 78 then explains that due to the people's disobe-
dience, Yahweh 'forsook the tabernacle of Shiloh' (v. 60) and selected Zion-Jeru-
salem and the Davidic dynasty in its place (vv. 68-72).

Exodus 15 and Psalm 78 describe the victory at the sea and the establishment of
the people in some of the same terms.[91] First, Exod. 15.8 and Ps. 78.13 both use
the term 'hill' (נֵד) for the piling up of the waters.[92] Secondly, Exod. 15.16-17 and
Ps. 78.54 also share 'the same verb in a closely parallel context'[93] and other words
(as marked by the Hebrew words in parentheses):

Ps. 78.54. He brought them (וַיְבִיאֵם) to His holy realm (קֹדֶשׁ),
            The mountain (הַר) which His right hand acquired (קָנְתָה).

Exod. 15.16. While Your people crossed, O Yahweh,
              While the people whom You had acquired (קָנִיתָ) crossed.
        17   You brought (תְּבִיאֵמוֹ) and planted them
              On the mount (הַר) of Your inheritance. . .
              The sanctuary (מִקְּדָשׁ), O Lord,

Thirdly, Ps. 78.60 also speaks of a 'sanctuary' (מִשְׁכָּן) in Shiloh, which resembles
the language used in Exod. 15.17.[94] Exod. 15.17 and Ps. 78.54 share a theology of
the divine mountain as the residence of Yahweh's people, in contrast with the usual
Jerusalemite theology that the mountain is the deity's own residence. From these
parallels, it seems possible that Exod. 15.17 contains a Shilohite tradition for the
divine mountain. J. Goldin saw Exodus 15 as an old poem fashioned as a Shilohite
polemic against the southern royal theology, specifically against the rival Solomonic

This text may minimize motifs pertinent to the land as the psalm recites negative acts of Israel's
consorting with other nations' deities in order to justify its exile among the nations.
    90. So B. Duhm, *Die Psalmen* (KHAT, 14; Tübingen: Mohr–Siebeck, 1899), pp. 204-205; C.
and E. Briggs, *A Critical and Exegetical Commentary on the Book of Psalms* (ICC; Edinburgh: T.
& T. Clark, 1907), II, p. 189; A.F. Kirkpatrick, *The Book of Psalms* (Cambridge: Cambridge
University Press, 1957), p. 475; M. Dahood, *Psalms II. 51–100* (AB, 17; Garden City, NY:
Doubleday, 1968), p. 245; Kraus, *Psalms 60–150*, p. 129; A.A. Anderson, *The Book of Psalms*. II.
Psalms 73–150 (NCB Commentary; Grand Rapids: Eerdmans; London: Marshall, Morgan & Scott,
1972), p. 573; C. Stuhlmueller, 'Psalms', *Harper's Bible Commentary* (ed. J.L. Mays; San
Francisco: Harper & Row, 1988), p. 470. The referent is sometimes questioned. Some commenta-
tors take Mount Sinai and not the land or a site in it as the referent of v. 54 (W.O.E. Oesterly, *The
Psalms* [London: SPCK, 1962], p. 362; Sarna, *Exodus*, p. 80).
    91. See Goldin, *The Song at the Sea*, pp. 51-55; and Halpern, *The Emergence of Israel*, p. 34.
    92. See Cross, *Canaanite Myth*, pp. 134-35; Halpern, *The Emergence of Israel*, p. 34.
    93. So Freedman, *Pottery, Poetry, and Prophecy*, p. 214.
    94. So Goldin, *The Song at the Sea*, p. 51 n. 84. The proximity of language between Exod.
15.11 and Ps. 89.6-9 is not telling. See the interesting notice comparing Jerusalem and Shiloh also
in Jer. 26.6.

temple of Jerusalem.[95] The poem of Exodus 15 may be the forerunner to the theology of Psalm 78, which was applied to Jerusalem by the cult supported by the southern monarchy. The psalm implies that Zion assumed the mantle of tradition which Shiloh held previously. This inherited tradition may have included the theology of Exodus, the wilderness journey and the establishment of the people on God's holy place.

---

95. So Goldin, *The Song at the Sea*, pp. 51-55. According to Goldin, the army of Pharaoh in Exod. 15 would signal a polemic against Solomonic relations with Egypt.

Chapter 9

THE PRIESTLY ARRANGEMENT OF EXODUS 15.22–40.38:
SECTIONS A′, B′ I AND B′ I′

1. *Section A′: Israel's Movement from Egypt to Midian
(Chapters 15.22–18.27)*

This section is structured by the priestly itinerary notices (15.22a, 27; 16.1; 17.1a). These notices provide a progression of Israel from the waters of the sea to the mountain of Sinai.[1] This movement echoes the movement of Moses to the land of Midian in section A, as noted above. Moses and Israel share common origins in Egypt and both are drawn to their destiny at Sinai.[2] The priestly arrangement has affected some details in the five narratives in this section: (1) Exod. 15.22-27: the water at Marah and the springs at Elim; (2) Exodus 16: manna and the quail; (3) Exod. 17.1-7: water in the wilderness of Sin; (4) Exod. 17.8-16: the battle against Amalek; and (5) Exodus 18: the meeting of Moses and Jethro.

Two pieces of evidence might suggest that the narrative parallelism between the beginning of the book and the middle of the book was probably not original with the priestly redaction. First, in using the word 'reed' (סוף) in Exod. 2.3, 5, the older narrative material punned on 'the Sea of Suph' (ים סוף, often translated 'the Sea of Reeds') in the

1.   P's addition of the 'wilderness of Sin' מדבר סין (Exod. 16.1; 17.1; cf. Num. 33.11, 12) further connect the movement in this section to Sinai. The two place names may be related (so Wyatt, 'Of Calves and Kings', p. 77), as -y is found as an ending on place-names. See M.E.J. Richardson, 'Ugaritic Place-Names with Final -y', *JSS* 23 (1978), pp. 298-315.

2.   Cf. Sarna, *Exodus*, p. xii. D.O. Setel ('Exodus', in C.A. Newsom and S.H. Ringe (eds.), *The Women's Bible Commentary* [London: SPCK; Louisville, KY: Westminster/John Knox Press, 1992], p. 28) also notes: 'Moses' initial hesitation at the responsibilities of leadership (4.10) is later echoed in the people's resistance to the demands of freedom (in 16.23)'.

old poem in Exod. 15.4, 22.[3] For the older material both Moses and Israel were viewed as moving from the threatening waters to the mountain. In Moses' case these waters are the waters of the Nile while for the Israelites they are the waters of the Reed Sea. Similarly, the cry of the Israelites is a motif in the old material in both 1.23 and 14.10b. Secondly, ch. 18, which scholars agree preserves ancient material,[4] shows a connection with ch. 2[5] through the aetiology given to

3.   See Sarna, 'Exodus, Book of', *ABD*, II, p. 695. According to W.H. Propp (personal communication), Isa. 63.11-12 also links the episodes of the waters for Moses and Israel. If so, the connection stands on the level of paranomasia.

4.   Childs, *The Book of Exodus*, p. 323. Cross (*Canaanite Myth*, p. 201) associates the traditions surrounding Jethro in these chapters with southern levitical sanctuaries, based largely on Moses and his putative Levitical lineage. Wilson (*Prophecy and Society in Ancient Israel*, p. 152) also regards the E tradition of 18.13-27 as Levitical. Cf. the cautionary remarks of Childs, *The Book of Exodus*, pp. 322-24; L.E. Axelsson, *The Lord Rose up from Seir: Studies in the History and Traditions of the Negev and Southern Judah* (ConBOT, 25; Stockholm: Almqvist & Wiksell, 1987), p. 61. Since Eduard Meyer, many commentators have based on these traditions a theory locating the origins of the cult of Yahweh among the Midianites and/or Kenites. For the so-called older proponents and critics of these hypotheses, see H.H. Rowley, 'Moses and the Decalogue', *BJRL* 34 (1951 = repr. Manchester: The Librarian, the John Rylands Library, Manchester University, 1951), pp. 97-98; G. von Rad, *Old Testament Theology*. I. *The Theology of Israel's Historical Traditions* (trans. D.M.G. Stalker; New York: Harper & Brothers, 1962), pp. 8-10. For more recent, judicious endorsements of these theories, see Cross, 'Reuben, First-Born of Jacob', *ZAW* 100 (1988), pp. 57-63; K. van der Toorn, 'Ritual Resistance and Self-Assertion: The Rechabites in Early Israelite Religion', in J. Platvoet and K. van der Toorn (eds.), *Pluralism and Identity: Studies in Ritual Behavior* (Leiden: Brill, 1995), pp. 244-48. While these theories have merit, it is important to point out that the extant witnesses to the old Yahweh traditions from the south do not include the tradition of the Exodus. In turn Wyatt ('Of Calves and Kings', pp. 83-88) regards El and not Yahweh as the god of the Exodus taking support from passages such as Num. 24.8. How to explain the linkage between two traditions remains a major desideratum of biblical research.

5.   As Chapter 11 discusses in greater detail, this is not to deny the correspondence between Exod. 18 and Num. 10.29-32 surrounding the Sinai legislation as a whole. On the two names for Moses' father-in-law, see W.F. Albright, 'Jethro, Habab and Reuel in Early Hebrew Tradition', *CBQ* 25 (1963), pp. 1-11; Cross, *Canaanite Myth*, p. 200 n. 26; R. de Vaux, 'Sur l'origine kénite ou midianite du Yahvisme', *ErIsr* 9 (1969 = W.F. Albright Festschrift), pp. 28-30. Albright takes a largely text-critical approach to the different names, while de Vaux attributes them to the variety of traditions; the latter approach is preferable to Childs (*The Book of Exodus*, p. 332).

the name of Gershom. The older referent may have been the itinerant status of at least some Levitical priests as suggested by Judg. 17.7 which mentions that a 'youth' or 'servant' (נער) had come from Judah: 'and he was a Levite and he was sojourning there' (והוא לוי והוא גר שם; cf. Deut. 18.6).[6] The older material applied this aetiology in Moses' words regarding Gershom in both 2.22 and 18.3. In contrast, the putative quotation attached to the birth of Moses' second son, Eliezer, in 18 has no antecedent and refers to the exodus in general. It might be suggested further that taken together the quotations attached to the two sons recapitulate events up to ch. 18. The name of the first son focuses on the identity of Moses and that of the second on the identity of Israel. In the present context the kinship of the two sons may symbolize the interconnected character of the origins and destinies of Moses and the people whom he serves.[7] In any case, it would appear from

6.   For discussion especially of נער as sons other than the first-born who had to find occupations apart from working the family land, see Stager, 'The Archaeology of the Family', p. 26. This status may suggest the (secondary?) derivation of לוי from לוה*, 'to attach' (to a sanctuary [?]). It is evident that the tradition of the exodus was transmitted through various Levitical sanctuaries including Dan which is reflected by Judg. 17–18 (Cross, *Canaanite Myth*, pp. 197-99). McCarter ('Exodus', p. 134) has noted that the Levitical priesthood manifests a number of names that are Egyptian in origin (e.g. Moses, Phinehas, Hopni and Merari) which 'does suggest that a portion of the tribe of Levi may have lived in Egypt at some time'. Aaron has been interpreted as an Egyptian name. Furthermore, one of the Egyptian-derived names, Phinehas, is both a Levitical name (1 Sam. 1.3, 2.12-36) and an Aaronid one (Exod. 6.25; 1 Chron. 6.4, 20) which might appear to suggest that the Aaronids originally represented one line of the Levites (see below). The Levitical background of Aaron's line predated P, as it is attested in J (Exod. 4.14; cf. Josh. 21.4, 10). In addition to the Egyptian proper names, the historical kernel to the Exodus traditions lies in the observation that the tradition of slavery is more likely to be historical than not, since 'a people would be more likely to invent a story of being descended from gods or kings than from slaves' (Friedman, 'Torah', p. 620b). For a recent historical reading of the Exodus tradition as well as additional but less persuasive 'evidence', see R. Albertz, *A History of Israelite Religion in the Old Testament Period*. I. *From the Beginnings to the End of the Monarchy* (trans. J. Bowden; OTL; Louisville, KY: Westminster/John Knox Press, 1994), pp. 40-66; K. Kitchen, 'Exodus, The', *ABD*, II, pp. 704-707; Sarna, 'Exodus, Book of', *ABD*, II, p. 697.

7.   These sections share some minor elements as well. Section A describes the threat to Moses' life from Pharaoh's decree of death against 'Hebrew' newborn males (1.22), whereas section A′ describes the threat of death posed to Moses' life from the Israelites (17.4). The symbolism of water coincides in the two stories as well.

these features that the priestly redaction formalized the narrative parallelism between chs. 1–2 (sections A) and 15.22–18.27 (section A′).

The priestly arrangement produced a number of alterations. First, the priestly arrangement of material may explain why the older tradition in ch. 18[8] originally placed at 'the mountain of God' (v. 5) has been displaced in the priestly redaction[9] to a point in the wilderness prior to reaching Sinai in ch. 19. It has been long noted that the Jethro story in ch. 18 appears out of place, perhaps displaced from a point after the legislation such as Num. 10.29-32 which contains another Jethro story. Secondly, the priestly redaction affected the understanding of Horeb in Exod. 17.1-7. W.H. Propp comments:

> 'The ṣûr [rock] in Horeb' in Exod. 17.6 must denote this mountain or at least part of it (cf. Exod. 33.21-22 [J?]). Admittedly, scholars have generally assumed, influenced by Exod. 19.1 (P), that the Sinai-Horeb pericope begins in Exodus 19, but under this assumption both the reference to Horeb here [17.6] and the mention of the Mountain of God in 18.5 (cf. v. 12) are incomprehensible.[10]

For many scholars including Propp, Exod. 17.1-7 and 18.5 belonged to old Sinai–Horeb material prior to P, which was responsible for repositioning this material as part of the journey to the mountain. Following a long line of continental scholarship, Blenkinsopp attributes this material to an original Kadesh tradition which has been displaced in its present context by the insertion of Sinai material of Exod. 19.1– Num. 10.10.[11]

Thirdly, the selection and general tone in the first three stories in Exod. 15.22–17.7 may be due in part to the purposes of the priestly redaction. These stories draw on an old complex of wilderness stories attested also in Numbers 11 and 20 (cf. 21.4-9) as well as Ezekiel 20, Nehemiah 9, and Pss. 78.15-31, 105.40-41 and 106.13-15.[12] Two

---

8. According to Childs (*The Book of Exodus*, p. 321), most commentators assign ch. 18 to E, but detect some J influence in vv. 1-12 as well as secondary expansion in vv. 2-4 and 15-16.

9. Cf. the similar displacement at 4.20 versus 4.27.

10. Propp, *Water in the Wilderness*, p. 60.

11. Blenkinsopp, *The Pentateuch*, pp. 137-38, 162-63, 191, 194.

12. Y. Zakovitch has also compared Elisha's curing the waters of Jericho in 2 Kgs 2.19-22 which suggests the legendary background of this type of story; see Zakovitch, *'And You Shall Tell Your Son. . . '*, pp. 75-76. Zakovitch also compares 2 Kgs 3. The origins of the wilderness journey-stories (as opposed to the miracles

patterns in the wilderness stories have been discerned.[13] However one understands these patterns and their overlap,[14] they differ in the way the people are presented. In the first pattern, found in Exod. 15.22-27; 17; and Num. 20.1-13 (see also Ps. 105), the people make legitimate requests to Yahweh the successful provider; in the second pattern, attested in Num. 11.1-3, 17.6-15 and 21.4-10 (see also Ezek. 20, Neh. 9 and Pss. 78 and 106), the people complain illegitimately. Commenting on Exod. 17.1-7, Propp observes: 'We find little that fits the poetic references... Here we have no apostasy, no fertility, no strife among the Levites, no priestly ordination, no punishment.'[15]

While these different patterns predate the redaction of Exodus, it is evident that the more negative accounts appear in the book of Numbers while Exodus contains no purely negative examples. Childs argues that unlike J, the priestly material did not 'follow the scheme of assigning stories of Pattern I to the period before the Golden Calf'.[16] Nonetheless, the general tone of Exod. 15.22–17.7, including the priestly story in ch. 16, is positive relative to the comparable narratives in Numbers. The relatively positive tone in Exod. 15.22–17.7 results from a long and complicated tradition-history, as Childs shows. The question is why the priestly redaction left the positive tone relatively intact (the single priestly story in this section, namely ch. 16, is likewise generally positive). It may be suggested that the priestly redaction may have interpreted the Exodus passages as the people's pilgrimage to the mountain. (M. Noth argued that an actual ancient practice of pilgrimage underlies Exod. 18.1-12.[17] Such a connection may be represented in later tradition by the links between the Elijah's journey to the divine mountain in 1 Kgs 19.8 and Moses' visit to Sinai in

performed in the wilderness) are more obscure, and only some notes may be made here, offered with the caveat that the comparisons made are most speculative and are therefore offered even more tentatively. The topos of a wilderness journey for a set period of time followed by entrance into an area providing abundant food and drink is extant in a mythological setting in *KTU* 1.23, an Ugaritic text sometimes called 'the Birth of the Beautiful Gods'.

13. So following P.D. Hanson, Childs, *The Book of Exodus*, pp. 254-64.

14. For other typologies, see P. Buis, 'Les conflits entre Moïse et Israël dans Exode et Nombres', *VT* 28 (1978), pp. 257-70; Vervenne, 'The Protest Motif', pp. 257-71. For criticisms, see also van Seters, *The Life of Moses*, pp. 165-70.

15. Propp, *Water in the Wilderness*, pp. 59, 60.

16. Childs, *The Book of Exodus*, pp. 262-63.

17. See Noth, *A History of Pentateuchal Traditions*, p. 138.

Exod. 33–34.[18] If so, the priestly redaction inherited this view of the Sinai journey.) The water in the wilderness would be not only a source of testing of the people, as it is in the book of Numbers. Rather, it would also represent the divine blessing to the people in their pilgrimage journey (cf. Ps. 84.7).[19] The more positive tone in 15.22–16.35 might be due to the same cause. As noted below, the theme of pilgrimage informed the formation of chs. 19–24, and the older traditions of chs. 16 and 17 may have been construed accordingly.

2. Section B' i: Israel's First Covenant and the First Tablets (Chapters 19–31)

a. *Material Inherited by the Priestly Redaction in 19.2b–24.11*
The relationship of materials in this section represents a major critical problem discussed since the Middle Ages. Rashi, the great Jewish exegete of the twelfth century, observed that the section beginning with 24.1 was spoken before the Decalogue.[20] The following remarks do little more than point to the critical problems and discuss some of the proposed solutions in an effort to identify some of the priestly elements in 19.2b–24.11. The minimum consensus for chs. 19–40 assumes the original independence of the Ten Commandments in 20.1-17,[21] the Covenant Code[22] in 20.22–23.33,[23] and the instructions for the taber-

---

18. For more recent comparisons, see Cross, *Canaanite Myth*, pp. 191-94; Savran, '1 and 2 Kings', pp. 162-63; Zakovitch, *'And You Shall Tell Your Son . . . '*, pp. 70-72.

19. On the pilgrimage journey, see Chapter 1, section 1.

20. ‏ואל משה אמר פשרה נמרה קדם עצרת הדברים‎. For Rashi on Exod. 24.1, see Rosenbaum and Silbermann, *Pentateuch*, p. 128. Rashi also notes the narrative tensions between chs. 19 and 20 as well (see Rashi on Exod. 20.19 in Rosenbaum and Silbermann, *Pentateuch*, p. 106). See further Greenberg, 'Exodus', p. 1060.

21. For the Decalogue, see the essays of M. Weinfeld, A. Rofé, M. Weiss and M. Greenberg, in Segal (ed.), *The Ten Commandments*, pp. 1-119.

22. For the Covenant Code, see S. Paul, *Studies in the Book of the Covenant in the Light of Cuneiform and Biblical Law* (VTSup, 18; Leiden: Brill, 1970); L. Schwienhorst-Schönberger, *Das Bundesbuch (Ex 20, 22-23,33): Studien zu seiner Entstehung und Theologie* (BZAW, 188; Berlin: de Gruyter, 1990); Y. Osumi, *Die Kompositionsgeschichte des Bundesbuches Exodus 20.22b–23.33* (OBO, 105; Göttingen: Vandenhoeck & Ruprecht, 1991). McBride suggests that the Covenant Code 'may represent the tradition of covenantal law transmitted by the Shiloh circle of Mosaic priests' (McBride, 'Biblical Literature', p. 15). The reuse of the Covenant Code in the book of Deuteronomy would support the Levitical background of the

nacle in 25–31 (with the corresponding implementation in 35–40).[24] The Ten Commandments shows signs of priestly redaction, not only by virtue of the largely redactional context of Exodus 19–20, but also within their motivational clauses (e.g. Exod. 20.8-11).[25]

Commentators have argued that the narrative in 19.1–24.11 has been shaped in order to accomodate the secondary insertion of the legal sections. First, the journey to the mountain was linked to the Sinai legislation. It may be noted that the material of chs. 16–18 which refers to the mountain probably represents the core of material which went originally with the law (the decalogue?[26]), and the meal and vision in 24.9-11. These materials predate the priestly redaction; apart from this relative dating there is no further means presently available

Covenant Code (for the older view of E as the redactor of this law-code, see Alt, *Essays*, p. 124). Exod. 23.20 contains an apparent reference to the Levitical cities, noted at least as early as Rashi (for Rashi on 23.20, see Rosenbaum and Silbermann, *Pentateuch*, p. 110b). The redactional designation for the Covenant Code (*hammis-patîm*) in 24.3 implies that this section for the redactor begins at 21.1 and not 20.22 as most modern commentators have assumed.

23. Other separate materials may include Exod. 23.10-27. According to Ginsberg, this passage constitutes a ritual decalogue, a term customarily applied to Exod. 34.10-27, which Ginsberg argues is a post-Deuteronomic intrusion (*The Israelian Heritage*, pp. 46, 62-66) modelled on Exod. 23.10-27. The main problem with this view is that הדברים in Ginsberg's view refers to a decalogue as in Exod. 20.1, but this designation is absent from 23.10-27. For a synchronic approach to 23.10-27 and 24.10-27, see Brichto, *Toward a Grammar*, pp. 109-10, 119-21.

24. See the important studies of Hurowitz, 'The Priestly Account', pp. 21-30; *idem, I Have Built you an Exalted House*, pp. 110-13; also Kearney, 'Creation and Liturgy', p. 381. The specifics of the tabernacles material, which lies beyond the scope of this study, are very complex, as indicated not only by the differences be-tween the orders in 25–31 and their execution in 35–40, but also by the text-critical differences especially between the Hebrew and Greek texts. For discussion, see R.D. Nelson, 'Studies in the Development of the Tabernacle Account' (PhD disserta-tion, Harvard University, 1987); A. Aejmelaeus, 'Septuagintal Techniques—A Solu-tion to the Problem of the Tabernacle Account', in G.J. Brooke and B. Lindars (eds.), *Septuagint, Scrolls and Cognate Writings: Papers Presented to the Interna-tional Symposium on the Septuagint and its Relations to the Dead Sea Scrolls and Other Writings (Manchester, 1990)* (SBLSCS, 33; Atlanta: Scholars Press, 1992), pp. 381-402.

25. Knohl assigns v. 11 to HS (*The Sanctuary of Silence*, pp. 67, 104, 102 n. 144), but the connection between the Sabbath and desisting from work is made already in v. 10 which would suggest that the requirement of rest predates HS.

26. See below for further discussion.

to determine the antiquity of these elements. Through the itinerary notice in 19.1-2a, the priestly redaction split the older mountain materials between 15.22 through ch. 18 and 19.2b–24.11.

Secondly, many modern commentators would see the placement of 20.18-21 after the Decalogue as a secondary re-arrangement (originally belonging with ch. 19) in order to provide for the insertion of the Covenant Code.[27] Thirdly, Exod. 24.3 shows a redactional marker designed to include the Ten Commandments and the Covenant Code into the revelation to Moses.[28] For the E source in conventional source-critical discussions (the D redactor in the estimate of some more recent redactional critics), only the decalogue belongs to the tablets which Moses receives in Exod. 24.3 while v. 3 contains an interpolation designed to include both the decalogue (הדברים) and the Covenant Code (המשפטים) into the law which Moses receives on the mountain.

Although Exodus 19–24 shows rather marked redactional activity, these chapters' literary history has been an extremely difficult one to adjudicate. Exodus 19 contains a variety of material, some priestly, some not. Exod. 19.1-2a is generally accepted as priestly,[29] but consensus on Exod. 19.3-8 has not been reached. Three alternatives have

---

27. For discussion, see Childs, *The Book of Exodus*, pp. 350-51.
28. H.L. Ginsberg's comments on this chapter (beginning with ואת כל המשפטים 'and all the rules', in Exod. 24.3) are not atypical for a source-critical approach to this question.

> What is more important is that the phrase 'and all the rules' (*w't kl hmšptm*) which follows 'all the words of YHWH' at the end of v. 3 is an interpolation, since it is wanting after the other mentions of the said 'words' in 3b, 4, and 8 end. Its purpose is to include the 'rules' (*mišpaṭim*) of 21.1–23.9 in the covenant of 24.3-8; but that was not the orginal intention of this passage. For the E elements in 24.12-18; 31.18–34.28, which relate how Moses went up to the mountain of God for forty days and nights in order to receive 'the tablets of stone on which I have inscribed the teachings and commandments to instruct them', conclude by revealing that the tablets contained nothing other than 'the terms of the covenant, the Ten Words' (34.28), and this phrase can only refer to 'The First Ritual Decalogue', Exod. 23.10-27.

See Ginsberg, *The Israelian Heritage*, p. 46. So also McCarter, 'Exodus', p. 149; cf. Childs, *The Book of Exodus*, pp. 356, 500. Exod. 23 shows other links to Exod. 24 by including the cultic calendar which relates the times for pilgrimage to the sanctuary (vv. 14-17). Both of these treatments include the cultic experience of 'seeing' Yahweh: the cultic calendar in Exod. 23.15 mentions this experience in the summary of the three pilgrimage feasts (see below further on ch. 24) and Exod. 24.10 includes this experience as part of the complex of the meal on the mountain.
29. The priestly double itinerary notice in Num. 10.11-12 may be compared.

been considered. First, one might revert to the older source-critical view of attributing vv. 3-8 to E. Secondly, McCarthy suggests that Exod. 19.3-8 involves a pre-deuteronomic or proto-deuteronomic composition in order to explain the similarities and differences between this passage and Deuteronomy.[30] He comments: 'All this parallelism and unusual language is enough to make Yahweh's speech in 3b-6a a structured poetic whole'. The identification of the piece as poetic was made already by M. Noth and A.W. Jenks, and is followed by F.M. Cross who proposes that stripped of its prose particles Exod. 19.3-6 represents an older poetic piece secondarily incorporated into its present context.[31] Thirdly, some newer redactional critics assign this section largely to a deuteronomic redaction[32] or composition.[33] G. von Rad and M. Weinfeld reject attempts to assign material in 19.3-8 to D because in their view the passage lacks characteristically deuteronomic language.[34] Each item taken in support of deuteronomic redaction is addressed in turn:

1. 'You have seen' (אתם ראיתם) in 19.4a might seem deuteronomic given similar phrases in Deuteronomy. The phraseology is, however, slightly different: ראו עיניך (Deut. 4.9, 7.19, 10.21, 29.2); and הראות עיניכם (Deut. 3.21, 4.3, 11.7).[35] The variation, while apparently minor, may reflect modifications of deuteronomic language, a point evident with other expressions in 19.3-8.

2. The image of 'eagles' wings' in Exod. 19.4b appears also in Deut. 32.11, but the latter's context is poetic and its expression is quite different. An image such as this is hardly a characteristic deuteronomic expression or indicator of a deuteronomic redaction.

3 'If you obey my voice and keep my commandments' in 19.5a seems deuteronomic (cf. Deut. 11.13; 15.5; 28.1).[36]

---

30. D.J. McCarthy, *Treaty and Covenant: A Study in the Form in the Ancient Oriental Documents and in the Old Testament* (sec. ed. completely rewritten; AnBib, 21A; Rome: Biblical Institute Press, 2nd edn, 1978), pp. 270-72.

31. Noth, *Exodus*, pp. 157-59; Jenks, *The Elohist and North Israelite Traditions*, p. 48; Cross, 'The Epic Traditions of Early Israel', pp. 21-22.

32. See Dozeman, *God on the Mountain*, pp. 28, 39 n. 10.

33. So Blum, *Studien*, p. 170; *idem*, 'Israël à la montagne', p. 281.

34. Von Rad, *The Problem of the Hexateuch*, p. 40 n. 53; Weinfeld, *Deuteronomy 1–11*, p. 367; *idem*, Review of E.W. Nicholson, *God and His People*, *RB* 98 (1991), p. 435.

35. Weinfeld, *Deuteronomy 1–11*, p. 357 #11 and 11a.

36. Weinfeld, *Deuteronomy 1–11*, pp. 336-37 #17b.

4. A purportedly deuteronomic expression in Exod. 19.5a is 'to observe covenant', שמר* ברית (Deut. 29.8; cf. 1 Kgs 11.11).[37] The idiom occurs also in Pss. 78.10, 103.18 and 132.12 (cf. Ezek. 17.14), arguably reflections of deuteronomic usage. In Ps. 103.18 the phrase may represent an echo of earlier Pentateuchal language (cf. v. 8 with Exod. 34.6). Finally, the idiom also appears twice in Gen. 17.9-10, a well-known priestly context. It is possible to argue either that the priestly tradition used the idiom of its own accord or that it picked it up from the deuteronomic tradition. In either case, it may be attributed in Exod. 19.5a to a priestly redaction.

5. The term 'possession' (סגלה) is invoked as a deuteronomic term in Exod. 19.5b, since it occurs in Deut. 7.6, 14.2 and 26.18.[38] The term appears also in Mal. 3.17 and Ps. 135.4. While Malachi is a Levitical work,[39] the background of Ps. 135.4 is not as transparent. However, Psalm 135 shows one sign of a Levitical background upon comparison with Psalm 115.[40] Ps. 135.4 as well as Ps. 115.9-12 list those who

---

37. See Postma, Talstra and Vervenne, *Exodus*, p. 106. Deut. 7.9, 12 do not count since the subject is Yahweh and not the people. Deut. 33.9 attests to אמרה* שמר* and נצר ברית*.

38. Blum, *Studien*, p. 170; *idem*, 'Israël à la montagne de Dieu', p. 289; Dozeman, *God on the Mountain*, p. 39 n. 10, p. 83. On the second millennium background of $s^e gullâ$, see Weinfeld, Review of *God and His People*, by E.W. Nicholson, p. 434; Sarna, *Exodus*, p. 104; Dozeman, *God on the Mountain*, pp. 83-84 n. 89. For the origins of the term, see W.W. Hallo, *Origins: The Ancient Near Eastern Background of Some Modern Western Institutions* (Studies in the History and Culture of the Ancient Near East, 6; Leiden: Brill, 1996), p. 18.

39. Ginsberg, *The Israelian Heritage*, pp. 17-18; McBride, 'Biblical Literature', p. 23; P.D. Hanson, 'Israelite Religion in the Early Postexilic Period', in P.D. Miller, Jr, P.D. Hanson and S.D. McBride (eds.), *Ancient Israelite Religion: Essays in Honor of Frank Moore Cross* (Philadelphia: Fortress Press, 1987), p. 503. S.L. McKenzie and H.N. Wallace ('Covenant Themes in Malachi', *CBQ* 45 [1983], p. 559) comment: 'the reference to Yahweh's covenant with Levi implies that Yahweh has chosen Levi and his descendants from among their brethren to be his priests'. For a survey of the issues, see J.M. O'Brien, *Priest and Levite in Malachi* (SBLDS, 121; Atlanta: Scholars Press, 1990), pp. 24-26, 133-42, 143-46.

40. The two psalms have some important parallels. Ps. 135.6 is close to Ps. 115.3. Ps. 135.15-18 is virtually identical to Ps. 115.4-8 in its polemic against idols. Ps. 135.1-2 and 21 echo Ps. 134, the last psalm in the Songs of Ascent. On the basis of its parallels with Pss. 115 and 134, and the further fact that Ps. 135 does not belong to a particular collection of psalms, it might be suggested that it was molded specifically for this context (cf. G.H. Wilson, *The Editing of the Hebrew Psalter*

trust in or praise Yahweh. Both psalms list Israel, the house of Aaron, and those who fear Yahweh, but Ps. 135.10 adds 'the house of the Levite' (בית הלוי), possibly indicating the psalm's Levitical prove-nience.[41] Given the evidence of Malachi and Ps. 135.4, the term סגלה in Exod. 19.5 need not be attributed to a deuteronomic redaction, but to the deuteronomic tradition or Levitical 'tradition-stream'[42] to which 'E', Deuteronomy, Malachi and perhaps Psalm 135 belong.[43] It is to be noted that the declaration containing סגלה in Exod. 19.5 is, except for this word, identical with Jer. 7.22. The significance of the parallel is not simple to determine. It might be argued that the Jeremianic verse is deuteronomic, and therefore Exod. 19.5 is as well.[44] Or, both may be viewed as belonging to the stock Levitical language bearing on law-giving at Sinai.[45] Whether the term in Exod. 19.5b is to be regarded as specifically deuteronomic or more generally Levitical, it should be noted that its phrasing in Exod. 19.5b differs slightly from what is found in Deuteronomy which consistently uses 'people' (עם) with סגלה. This variation may be explained by a priestly redaction which took liberty with this seemingly deuteronomic term.

6. The phrase 'a kingdom of priests' (ממלכת כהנים) in 19.6a is enig-matic. It does not appear to comport with pre-exilic priestly material, since as many commentators on the priesthood suggest, the Aaronid priesthood to which the priestly material of Exodus and the Pentateuch more generally is to be assigned, arrogated to itself the privileges of priesthood (Num. 25.11-13), denying them even to the Levites who had traditional priestly claims (Josh. 18.7). Calling all Israel ממלכת כהנים would therefore not comport with traditional pre-exilic priestly (Aaronid) polemics against the Levites.[46] Whether one takes this ex-

[SBLDS, 76; Chico, CA: Scholars Press, 1985], p. 225).

41. See M.S. Smith, 'The Levitical Compilation of the Psalter', *ZAW* 103 (1991), pp. 258-63.

42. For this term, see H. Nasuti, *Tradition History and the Psalms of Asaph* (SBLDS, 88; Atlanta: Scholars Press, 1988).

43. Weinfeld, *Deuteronomy 1–11*, p. 367.

44. This is the general force of the observations made by R.P. Carroll, *Jeremiah: A Commentary* (OTL; Philadelphia: Westminster Press, 1986), pp. 214-18.

45. Some have related Jer. 7.21-22 to the larger issue of the formation of Sinaitic law. For a summary of opinions, see W.L. Holladay, *Jeremiah. 1. A Commentary on the Book of the Prophet Jeremiah. Chapters 1–25* (ed. P.D. Hanson; Hermeneia; Philadelphia: Fortress Press, 1986), pp. 261-62.

46. Blum, *Studien*, pp. 170-71.

pression as a pre-exilic Levitical notion or a post-exilic one,[47] its place in a document edited by an Aaronid redaction[48] points to a post-exilic time of adjudication between the priestly lines. (This view would suit Knohl's reconstruction of the Holiness School.[49]) This expression has been compared to Isa. 61.6a: 'While you shall be called "Priests of the Lord"' (NJPS).[50] While the oracles of 'Third Isaiah' are by no means a unified composition, they might derive from a Levitical group, judging from Isa. 66.21: '"And also some of them I will take as levitical priests" said the Lord'.[51] From the comparison with these verses from 'Third Isaiah', it might be concluded that ממלכת כהנים belongs to post-exilic Levitical language. (In view of this possibility, it is interesting to note that Dozeman attributes ממלכת כהנים to the P level of Exod. 19.3-6.) Accordingly, perhaps the priestly redaction picked up this expression from the Levitical tradition.

7. Von Rad and Weinfeld reject the claim that 'a holy nation' (קדוש גוי) in 19.6a is deuteronomic,[52] because Deut. 7.6, 14.2, 21 and 26.19 use the different phrase 'holy people' (עם קדוש). It may be noted that the priestly phrase 'great nation' (גוי גדול) occurs in Gen. 12.2, 17.20, and Num. 14.12. As a result, it may be suspected that the expression גוי קדוש represents a priestly conflation of the two expressions, עם קדוש

---

47. Blum, *Studien*, p. 170. To גוי קדוש Blum (*Studien*, p. 171) compares Isa. 62.12a: 'And they shall be called "The Holy People"', (NJPS). The first comparison may indicate not so much a date as a shared Levitical 'tradition-stream'. The second is complicated somewhat by the difference in terminology with גוי קדוש in Exod. 19.6.

48. Or at least a redaction with marked sympathy for the Aaronid priesthood. Friedman ('Torah', p. 618a) comments: 'The special relationship between the redactor and P is confirmed by the presence of passages that are similar to P but which are supplemental and which appear to come from a later period, viz. the era of the Second Temple'.

49. Knohl, *The Sanctuary of Silence*, pp. 197-98, 220-24.

50. So Blum, *Studien*, pp. 170-71.

51. My translation. RSV construes לכהנים and ללוים separately, but there is no conjunction *wᵉ*- demarcating them as two groups. NJPS correctly renders the two prepositional phrases: 'And from them likewise I will take some to be levitical priests, said the Lord'. NJPS is evidently reading the double prepositional phrases as appositional. The second term specifies the first to which it is in apposition. For another example, see Jer. 25.11.

52. Among others, Perlitt, Nicholson and Blum (*Studien*, p. 170; *idem*, 'Israël à la montagne', p. 289).

and גוי גדול.[53] Furthermore, Weinfeld argues for important theological distinctions between Exod. 19.5-6 and Deuteronomy. While the people's holy status in Exodus expresses 'the special merit and privilege of Israel', Deuteronomy 'developed the notion and turned it into the basis for duty to fulfill the obligations to YHWH'.[54]

8. The closing of 19.6b ('these are the words that you shall speak to the Israelites') sounds like Deut. 1.1 ('These are the words which Moses spoke to all Israel'). As a result, it might be argued that Exod. 19.6b is deuteronomic. The basis for comparison is notably slim, however. Indeed, Exod. 35.1b provides a priestly example of this formulation: 'These are the words which Yahweh commanded them to do'.

Given the variety of background among these expressions, neither an older source, whether it be 'E' or a poetic piece, nor a deuteronomic redaction seems a suffecent explanation.[55] A fourth alternative might be entertained. It would appear that the priestly redaction adopted and modified various expressions, some deuteronomic (or Levitical), in order to communicate its own notion of priestly life for the people of Israel.[56] The priestly redaction added the deuteronomic (Levitical) language in Exod. 19.3-6 (perhaps along the lines suggested by McCarthy and Cross), while in 19.7-8 the priestly redaction simply retained the old narrative which stands in tension with v. 9. If the priestly redaction of ch. 19 transpired in the post-exilic era, it would explain the juxtaposition of characteristically priestly, or more precisely Aaronid, material with Levitical sounding expressions in vv. 3-6.

A deuteronomistic redaction proposed for ch. 19 relies not only on alleged terminological parallels, but also on the order of the legal and narrative elements.[57] The influence of a deuteronomistic redaction to Exodus 19 has been supported by the order of elements in chs. 19–20, as van Seters's list of comparisons between Deuteronomy 4, 5 and

53. Following H. Cazelles, Ska sees the expression as priestly. See Ska, 'Quelques Remarques', p. 122.

54. Weinfeld, *Deuteronomy 1–11*, p. 367.

55. The cautionary remarks made by Zevit ('The Priestly Redaction', p. 198 n. 22) in commenting on another passage in Exodus may apply here as well: 'The fact that an extremely common term assumes theological significance in certain collocations in one source does not preclude a parallel development in another source.'

56. See the discussion of Exod. 24 below in this chapter and Chapter 8, section 3.

57. Dozeman, *God on the Mountain*, pp. 37-86. For a covenient summary, see Blenkinsopp, *The Pentateuch*, pp. 188-89.

Exodus 19–20 would seem to suggest.[58] The similar sequence of elements in this passages would imply deuteronomic influence on the formation of Exodus 19–20, but it is also possible to argue the dependence in the opposite direction. Indeed, Weinfeld has noted elements added in Deuteronomy lacking in the comparable Exodus account.[59] In sum, while some redactional touches might seem deuteronomistic, little more would be, and it would appear that a number of items which appear deuteronomistic could be priestly redactional modifications of earlier deuteronomistic language.

The material in Exod. 19.12-19 is equally difficult to assign. This section contains a prescription for purification and the three-fold distinction in purity.[60] The mention of Moses and Aaron, the priests and the people in this passage lends itself to the standard tri-partite priestly division of the population with respect to the holiness of the Temple.[61] This material has been subjected to minute analyses. Dozemann, for example, divides vv. 12-19 into old material, 'JE' in traditional source (vv. 12aα, 13b-15a, 16ab-17), a deuteronomic stratum (19.19) and a priestly stratum (19.12ab-13, 15b, 16aα, 18). A single verse hardly seems a substantive deuteronomic redaction, but in any case, the priestly redaction inherited and further adapted this material to suit its own view of the mountain as the holy site with priestly conventions. Indeed, vv. 20-25 which follow up this section are generally viewed as a secondary priestly expansion on vv. 12-13.[62] To summarize with respect to Exodus 19, commentators generally accept a final priestly redaction despite great variation in their views of the pre-priestly material. Out of prior material the priestly redaction creates a narrative experience of the divine mountain as sanctuary.

Like ch. 19, ch. 24 is a matter of some controversy. Verses 1-2 and

---

58. Van Seters, '"Comparing Scripture with Scripture"', pp. 116-17. For van Seters, these comparisons serve to show that a late Jahwist was dependent on Deuteronomy. See also Blum, 'Israël à la montagne', pp. 283-86.

59. Weinfeld, *Deuteronomy 1–11*, p. 66.

60. Sarna (*Exodus*, p. 105), citing Ramban.

61. See Jenks, *The Elohist and North Israelite Traditions*, p. 48; Moberly, *The Old Testament of the Old Testament*, p. 102. For this element of priestly theology, see Haran, *Temples and Temple Service*, pp. 158-74, 175-88. See also J. Milgrom, 'Israel's Sanctuary', pp. 390-99.

62. Childs, *The Book of Exodus*, pp. 361-64.

9-11 are generally regarded as older material.[63] Verses 9-11 represent
an independent tradition of theophany.[64] 'Seeing God' (v. 10) is the
standard expression for a liturgical audience with Yahweh in the Jerusalem Temple.[65] As noted in Chapter 2 (section 3), Exod. 23.15 as well
as 34.20 (also vv. 23-24) allude to 'seeing' Yahweh as the cultic culmination of the three pilgrimage feasts (ולא יראו פני ריקם). As argued in
Chapter 2, section 3, the sentence is not to be translated: 'and none
shall appear before me empty-handed'. Instead, it is to be rendered:
'and they shall not see my face empty-handed'. Although various texts
use 'to see Yahweh' as an expression for coming to the Temple at the
appointed times, the origins of the expression lie in a cultic experience
of Yahweh as suggested by Exod. 24.10. 'Seeing' Yahweh represents a
theophanic experience following the pilgrimage-journey (Ps. 42.3; cf.
Ps. 84.8).[66] Besides the experience of 'seeing' the deity, Exod. 24.9-11
mentions a vision of the heavenly abode,[67] which likewise reflects a

63. McCarthy, *Treaty and Covenant*, p. 265; Dozeman, *God on the Mountain*,
p. 28.

64. Following older commentators, Dozeman notes links between 24.9-11 and
the Baal Cycle (*KTU* 1.4 V-VII). See Dozeman, *God on the Mountain*, p. 114 n. 77.
For Mesopotamian background to the vision of Yahweh, see B. Scolnic, 'Bloom on
J on God: Upside-Down or Right-Side-Up?' *Conservative Judaism* 43.4 (1991),
p. 76.

65. For a greater de-anthropomorphic interpretation of Exod. 24.10, see LXX:
'and they saw the place where the God of Israel stood'. For discussion, Tournay,
Seeing and Hearing God, pp. 76-78; E. Tov, 'Theologically Motivated Exegesis
Embedded in the Septuagint', *Translation of Scripture: Proceedings of a Conference
at the Annenberg Research Institute May 15–16, 1989. A Jewish Quarterly Review
Supplement: 1990* (Philadelphia: Annenberg Research Institute, 1990), pp. 230-31.
De-anthropomorphic and 're-anthropomorphic' rabbinic views of this passage in
b. Ber. 7a and *Men.* 35b are discussed by G. Josipovici (*The Book of God* [New
Haven: Yale University Press, 1988], p. 304). For discussion of the expression 'to
see God', see Chapter 2, section 3.

66. See Smith, '"Seeing God"', pp. 177-78, 181. For the Near Eastern background of the language of 'seeing' the deity, see Smith, '"Seeing God"', p. 176;
idem, 'The Near Eastern Background of Solar Language for Yahweh', *JBL* 109
(1990), pp. 34-39. For the expression in the Pentateuch of the Septuagint and other
versions, see C.T. Fritsch, 'Greek Translations of Hebrew Verbs "To See", with
Deity as Subject or Object', *ErIsr* 16 (1982 = H.M. Orlinsky Volume), pp. 51-66;
A. Hanson, 'The Treatment in the LXX of the Theme of Seeing God', in Brooke and
Lindars (eds.), *Septuagint, Scrolls and Cognate Writings*, pp. 557-68.

67. See Smith, 'Biblical and Canaanite Notes', pp. 585-88.

larger cultic background. In sum, neither the vision of Yahweh nor
the meal on the mountain is cultic, but not especially priestly.

The background of 24.3-8 remains highly debated. Older theories
posited a number of sources. McCarthy suggests that like Exod. 19.3-8,
24.3-8 is a pre-deuteronomic independent unit, but closely related to the
tradition represented by E and D.[68] Newer treatments have proposed a
deuteronomic piece. Dozemann suggests a minimal amount of deuteronomic material in 24.3-4aa, 7, while Blenkinsopp proposes a larger
deuteronomic complex consisting of 24.3-8, 12-15a + 18b (followed
by 31.18–34.35).[69] The problem with these proposals is the lack of
specifically deuteronomic language in Exodus 24.[70] As with his suggestion for 19.3-6, McCarthy's suggestion for 24.3-8 remains attrac-
tive, because it accounts for both the similarities and differences with
Deuteronomy.

The connections noted between Exodus 19 and 24 and deuteronomic
literature have resulted in the positing of a general deuteronomic
redaction for chs. 19–24.[71] It might be argued that the genesis for this
view is to be traced to G. von Rad's argument that the pattern underlying 19.1–24.11 reflects the setting of a covenant festival based on
passages in the Deuteronomic History.[72] According to this reconstruction, the materials show a pattern of cultic materials involving exhor-
tation (Exod. 19.4-6), proclamation of the law (the Decalogue and the
Covenant Code), promise of blessing (Exod. 23.20-21) and covenant
ratification (Exod. 24). Following Mowinckel, von Rad noted this pat-

68. McCarthy, *Treaty and Covenant*, pp. 264-69. See also Hendel, 'Sacrifice as
a Cultural System', pp. 378-81.

69. Blenkinsopp, *The Pentateuch*, pp. 191-94. The deuteronomic argument,
perhaps for vv. 12-15a, but certainly for 31.18, depends on taking לוחת העדות in
31.18 and elsewhere as deuteronomic, a problematic assumption as noted above and
below.

70. Weinfeld (Review of *God and his People*, by E.W. Nicholson, p. 435)
argues that 24.3-7 lacks classic deuteronomic characteristics. That covenant is a
priori either late or deuteronomic in origin remains an unproven assumption. On this
point, see J.D. Levenson, Review of *God and his People*, by E.W. Nicholson,
CBQ 50 (1988), p. 307.

71. See Blum, *Studien*, p. 192. For a convenient summary, see Blenkinsopp,
The Pentateuch, pp. 191-94.

72. Von Rad, *The Problem of the Hexateuch*, pp. 26-40. See the summary and
criticisms in Moberly, *At the Mountain of God*, pp. 118-19.

tern in Psalms 50 and 81 and the book of Deuteronomy.[73] While the insights of Mowinckel and von Rad perhaps led toward the theory of a deuteronomic redaction, it remains to be noted that the work of these scholars has also led in another direction. A. Jepsen assigned Psalms 50 and 81 as well as the complex of 19.1–24.11 to Levitical tradition.[74] Based on the work of J. Jeremias,[75] H.J. Kraus categorizes Psalms 50 and 81 as 'Levitical sermons'.[76] According to M. Weinfeld, these two psalms represent a covenant renewal within the context of the pilgrimage feast of Weeks.[77] After Jepsen and others,[78] Weinfeld argues that both psalms quote the decalogue. The conjunction of covenant law and meal appears also in Psalms 81 and 132. Psalm 81 is an especially pertinent example as this collocation of covenant meal and law invokes the memory of the exodus and wilderness. As noted in Chapter 4 (section 2), the same conjunction also underlies two of the three parts of Isaiah 55. Verses 1-5 contain a call to a meal. H.C. Spykerboer has argued that this invocation is precisely for a pilgrimage meal in Jerusalem, 'the new, restored city of abundance where God reigns as King'.[79] The second part of Isaiah 55, vv. 6-11, present the divine word. The third part of the chapter, vv. 12-13, places this conjunction of meal and law as the end-point of a pilgrimage.[80]

73. See also Zimmerli, *I am Yahweh*, pp. 23-28; Levenson, *Sinai and Zion*, p. 80. There are two weaknesses in this approach. Von Rad's analysis accounts for a limited range of material in Exod. 19–24. Furthermore, as Moberly (*At the Mountain of God*, p. 139) notes, discerning such an ordering and comparing it with other biblical texts by no means indicates that the original setting of this ordering was particularly ritualist in character. Indeed, the order of materials in chs. 19.1–24.11 does not demonstrate that they originated in a covenant festival. Rather, the literary character of the chapters and the complex development underlying them would suggest rather that the cultic setting inspired their shaping.

74. Jepsen, 'Beiträge', p. 303. Zimmerli likewise views the statement of divine self-revelation in the Exodus decalogue and these psalms in terms broader than the deuteronomic tradition (Zimmerli, *I am Yahweh*, pp. 23-28, 104). For further discussion, see Kraus, *Psalms 1–59*, pp. 49-91.

75. Jeremias, *Kultprophetie*, pp. 125-27.

76. Kraus, *Psalms 1–59*, pp. 61, 490. See also Tournay, *Seeing and Hearing God*, pp. 170-75.

77. See Weinfeld, 'The Uniqueness of the Decalogue', pp. 21-27.

78. Jepsen, 'Beiträge', p. 303; Zimmerli, *I am Yahweh*, pp. 23-28.

79. Spykerboer, 'Isaiah 55.1-5', p. 357.

80. Anticipated by ריקם in v. 11, an echo of Exod. 3.21? For pilgrimage in ancient Israel, see Chapter 1.

The general complex and order of Exodus 19–20 appear to be pre-priestly with priestly additions. An overall deuteronomic redaction is lacking for Exodus 24 and even the similarities between Exodus 19–20 and Deuteronomy 4–5 noted by van Seters hardly indicate, at least by terminology, the former's dependence on deuteronomic tradition. Instead, this chapter used the old elements of the covenant meal associated with the law and covenant of pilgrimage feasts. Whatever the origins of the material of Exodus 19–20 and 24, it does not seem specifically deuteronomistic. Generally speaking, other deuteronomistic passages in Exodus involve entire blocks of material or relatively slight additions. It may be argued that using Levitical or deuteronomic elements as well as the Levitical or deuteronomic structure for chs. 19–20, a post-exilic Aaronid redactor arranged the structure of Exodus 19.1–24.11 as a preface to 24.12–31.18. Finally, it should be observed that however these issues are to be resolved, they do not alter the interpretation of the priestly arrangement of this section.

b. *The Priestly Redaction of Exodus 24.12–31.18*
The pilgrimage-covenant might be seen as concluding with Exod. 24.12-18. This section is usually said to close a section consisting of chs. 19–24 with the covenant ceremony, specifically with the reception of the tablets. This reading misses the literary, or more precisely redactional, function of Exod. 24.12-18, especially in its relation to 31.18. The unit did not end with ch. 24 for the priestly redaction. On the contrary, for this redaction the unit was complete with 31.18. This claim may be demonstrated first by examining Exod. 24.12-18. Exod. 24.12-18 introduces the concept of the 'tablets' for the first time in the book of Exodus. Because of the reference to writing in 24.7, readers are expected to identify the tablets in 24.12 with this writing. Exod. 24.12 identifies these 'stone tablets' as the medium for the previous 'teaching and commandments' of chs. 20–23. Exodus 24 does not close a narrative section. Rather, it leaves the narrative unconcluded, as Moses is with God and not with the people. Furthermore, the motif of the tablets is significant for determining the end of the unit within the priestly redaction. In 31.18 Moses finally receives the tablets. Exod. 31.18 ('And He [God] gave to Moses, when He was finished speaking with him on mount Sinai, the two tablets of the pact, stone tablets written with the finger of God') is a crucial verse because it signifies the conclusion of the giving of the law. Given the lack of context for

this verse, it is evidently redactional in character, and its function is to conclude the addition begun with Exod. 24.12-18.

Furthermore, in order to secure this bond between 19.1–24.11, the priestly redaction may have placed the vision of the divine abode in ch. 24 precisely to provide a secondary connection to the instructions for the tabernacle (משכן) beginning in ch. 25.[81] Indeed, 'seeing' (מראה) in Exod. 25.9 continues the vision of the heavenly abode gained in Exod. 24.10b.[82] This connection is in part designed to include chs. 25–31 as part of the revelation on the tablets, just as Exod. 24.3 serves a similar function for 'words' (דברים) and 'rules' (משפטים) of chs. 20–23. C. Cohen notes that the priestly redactional comments of Exod. 25.8-9, 40; 26.30; and 27.8b 'have been added to the original PI [priestly instruction] materials in Exod. 25–27 in order to connect it thematically with the narrative of Moses' ascent to Mount Sinai in Ex. 24.12-18'.[83] Cohen argues also that Exod. 25.1-7 'cannot be part of PI for stylistic and contextual reasons'. One reason is that PI [priestly instruction] does not use first person speech. The implication is that this passage has been created to provide a transition between the end of ch. 24 and the instructional material commencing in 25.10. This narrative transition extends to 25.8-9, as the first person speech in these verses also indicate their non-instructional character. While the legal material and some of the narrative material in chs. 19–24 existed prior to the priestly redaction, their present formation existed only as part of the priestly redactional schema of 19–31 and 32–40.

Moses' return to the Israelites and the completion of the first tablets in 31.18 close the section consisting of chs. 19–31.[84] According to some recent works, the motif of the tablets, the expression used for them and the redactional level involving this motif are deuteronomistic. However, there are indications that this is not the case. First, the

81. Dozeman, *God on the Mountain*, p. 115; Scolnic, 'Bloom on J on God', p. 76; Cohen, 'The Genre'.

82. For the vision of the תבנית in Exod. 25.9 and its Near Eastern parallels, see Levenson, *Sinai and Zion*, p. 140; Hurowitz, *I Have Built you an Exalted House*, pp. 168-70.

83. Cohen, 'The Genre'.

84. Exod. 32 may be viewed to a certain extent as a transition chapter, first because it contains so many structural parallels with section B′ i′, specifically Exod. 32–34 (see section B′ i′ for discussion), and, secondly because some of its details correspond to material in section B i′ (see Chapter 8).

tablets are introduced in 24.12-17, but this material shows no deuteronomistic characteristics. On the contrary, the feature of seven days in
24.16 would point to priestly material. Second, the language used to
designate the tablets is not deuteronomistic. As noted above, the tablets
bear two different designations in Exodus and Deuteronomy. Exod.
31.18, 32.15 and 34.29 calls them 'the tablets of the pact' (לוחת העדות).
In contrast, Deut. 9.9, 11, 15 refers to them as 'the tablets of the covenant' (לוחת הברית). The term עדות belongs to a group of priestly id-
ioms deriving ultimately from diplomatic terminology.[85] Cross comments: 'The Priestly tradent characteristically took up an archaic word
or expression and used it, often with a narrowed or technical meaning'.[86] The language associated with the tablets is priestly, which would

---

85. The 'tent of meeting' is commonly related to the West Semitic institution of
the divine council. See Cross, *Canaanite Myth*, pp. 37, 231 n. 52; R.J. Clifford,
'The Tent of El and the Israelite Tent of Meeting', *CBQ* 33 (1971), pp. 221-27. This
setting may provide a distant background to the לוחת העדות. Both nouns may echo
the West Semitic diplomatic terminology of the divine council to whom 'tablets' (*lḥt*)
are read by a 'delegation' (*t'dt*). So M.J. Dahood, 'Eblaite, Ugaritic, and Hebrew
Lexical Notes', *UF* 11 (1979 = C.F.A. Schaeffer Festschrift), p. 144; R.M. Good,
'Exodus 32.18', in J.H. Marks and R.M. Good (eds.), *Love and Death in the Ancient Near East: Essays in Honor of Marvin H. Pope* (Guilford, CT: Four Quarters,
1987), p. 140. For a defense of *lḥt* as 'tablets' in *KTU* 1.2 I, see J.C.L. Gibson,
Canaanite Myths and Legends (Edinburgh: T. & T. Clark, 2nd edn, 1978), p. 4 n. 7,
p. 41; A. Rainey, 'The Scribe at Ugarit: His Position and Influence', *Proceedings of
the Israel Academy of Sciences and Humanities* 3 (1969), pp. 141-42; Smith, *The
Ugaritic Baal Cycle*, pp. 304-305. Compare especially the usage of *lḥt* in *KTU*
2.72.14-16 (see D. Pardee, 'A New Ugaritic Letter', *BO* 34 [1977], p. 3). That this
terminology had long passed into religious literature may be seen in *KTU* 1.2 I which
employs *m'd* (ll. 14, 17, 20), *lḥt* (l. 26) and *t'dt* (ll. 22, 30). For a convenient
presentation of the text as well as a translation, see Gibson, *Canaanite Myths and
Legends*, pp. 40-42. The most recent analysis of the passage, also with text and
translation, appears in Smith, *The Ugaritic Baal Cycle*, pp. 260, 265-68, 282-307.
The language of the divine council attested in Ugaritic ultimately derives from the
human, royal council, and העדות may be placed in the sphere of the royal court.
2 Kgs 11.12 provides such a context. To this passage von Rad (*The Problem of the
Hexateuch*, pp. 224-25) compared Egyptian sources which speak of the divine
protocols (*nḫb.t*) given to the king. Some commentators have argued that the word is
an error. For further discussion, see Östborn, *Tora in the Old Testament*, p. 76;
B. Couroyer, '"*ēdût*: stipulation de traité ou enseignement?', *RB* 95 (1988), pp. 321-
31. NJPS translates *hāʿēdût* as 'the insignia' and remarks in a note that the 'Meaning
of Heb. uncertain'.

86. Cross, *Canaanite Myth*, p. 245.

suggest that it is in the priestly redaction[87] where the tablets exercise a redactional function. The motif of the tablets was perhaps deuteronomic, but the priestly expression for this motif would suggest that the priestly redaction picked up the motif, altered its language in favor of an expressly priestly phrasing and incorporated it into this section of Exodus.

This brief survey of the redactional markers and later literary history of chs. 19–40 suggests that these chapters changed their concept of law as successive stages of legal material were incorporated: first the Ten Commandments (20.2-17), then the Covenant Code (20.22–23.33) and later the instructions for the Tabernacle, etc. (Exod. 25–31). The Ten Commandments seem to constitute the original body of law, or at least the first extant one. The successive bodies of legal material are not presented as appendages to the Ten Commandments, but a full realization of the revelation.[88] The redactional addition of 24.12 to 31.18 altered the notion of this revelation. To anticipate the discussion of section B′ i′ (Exod. 32–40), all of the legal materials are identified jointly with the Ten Commandments in Exod. 34.28. Just as the redaction included the Covenant Code into the writing of the Ten Commandments in ch. 24, so also the rules for the Tabernacle have been included in the expanding legal corpus.

It has been customary to regard chs. 25–40 as a separate unit for the obvious reason that 25–31 + 35–40 clearly correspond: generally speaking, chs. 25–31 represent the instructions executed in chs. 35–40. The priestly chapters, Exodus 25–31, give a manifestly cultic character to the legislation. One feature of these chapters is the heightened role of Aaron and his sons in the administration of the tabernacle and cult in general. While Aaron holds no place in the legal order of Exodus 20–23, his sons and he hold a central place in 25–31. P.J. Kearney discusses the Levites in relation to the major role of Aaron in these chapters:

---

87. More specifically, the Holiness School redaction. See Knohl, *The Sanctuary of Silence*, p. 67 n. 21, p. 108.

88. This direction of incorporating diverse sections of legal material under the rubric of the Ten Commandments is most fully realized in the structuring of Deut. 12–26 after the order and content of the Ten Commandments. See S.A. Kaufman, 'The Structure of the Deuteronomic Law', *MAARAV* 1.2 (1978–79), pp. 105-58; and below in Chapter 12, section 5.

P alludes to them ('service of the Tent of Meeting', Ex 30 16) immediately after his extended treatment of Aaron in the first divine speech and later mentions them briefly (Exod. 38 21), just before his climactic description of Aaron's priestly garments. The Levites nearly disappear in the shadow of Aaron, to whom alone priestly ordination now belongs (Ex. 28 41 29 29).[89]

Exodus 24 reflects Moses' old role as a prophetic mediator[90] which in 25–31 is merged into the cultic leadership of Aaron and his sons. Not only the content, but the concept behind the redaction of chs. 25–31 is distinctly priestly.

Finally, Kearney argues that in the redactional ordering of material of Exodus 25–31, the seven speeches of God correspond to the seven days of creation in Gen. 1.1–2.3.[91] According to Kearney, the redactor has 'oriented the first speech to the first day of creation' by having Aaron cause light (מאור) to shine through the night, just as God brings light from darkness (Gen. 1.2-3). Kearney observes other correspondences between the other days of creation and divine instructions for the cultic apparatus in Exodus 25–31 culminating in the seventh day of divine cessation corresponding to the instructions for the Sabbath in Exod. 31.12-17.[92]

3. Section B′ i′: Israel's Second Covenant and the Second Tablets (Chapters 32–40)

As discussed in the previous section, the final formation of this section resulted from the secondary schematization by the priestly redaction.[93] The priestly redaction inherited Exodus 32–34 and framed these chapters by the divine commandments in chs. 25–31 and their implementation in chs. 35–40. For the priestly redaction, the two sections of 19–31 (B′ i) and 32–40 (B′ i′) address the important priestly issue of

89. See Kearney, 'Creation and Liturgy', pp. 381-84.

90. Childs, *The Book of Exodus*, p. 260. Childs (*The Book of Exodus*, pp. 173, 175) also notes especially stories in Exod. 33–34 and Num. 11–12; Cross (*Canaanite Myth*, p. 197) notes especially Exod. 33.7-11. Cf. Hos. 12.13.

91. Kearney, 'Creation and Liturgy', pp. 375-86.

92. To be noted in this connection is Moses' approaching God on the seventh day in the narrative introduction to this body of material in 24.16.

93. Kearney ('Creation and Liturgy', pp. 375-86) intimated this point in his reading of Exod. 25–40 as the thematic order of creation (Exod. 25–31), fall (32–33) and restoration (34–40).

divine proximity to the Israelites. Both the narrative and legal materials in these sections explore and contribute toward understanding the
paradox of divine–human interaction, given the limitations of sinning
Israel[94] and its holy deity.[95] The tabernacle and the priesthood that
services it offers a priestly solution to the problem of the interaction
between Israelites and Yahweh discussed in the pre-priestly Exodus
32–34.[96]

Apart from corresponding in terms of divine command and execution, sections B′ i and i′ show other relations.[97] It would appear that

94. I use this expression as a theological corrective to the older idea of a 'sinful'
(and its varied synonyms) Israel in anti-Jewish polemic.

95. For descriptions of the history of tradition in Exod. 32–34, see Childs, *The
Book of Exodus*, p. 610 as well as the discussions of Dozeman, Moberly and
Brichto. This formulation of the problem for Exod. 32–34 may be found in Moberly,
At the Mountain of God, pp. 62, 66, 79-80. See also J. Barr, 'Theophany and
Anthropomorphism in the Old Testament', in J. Emerton (ed.), *Congress Volume:
Oxford 1959* (VTSup, 7; Leiden: Brill, 1960), pp. 35-36.

96. For Exod. 32–34, see Kearney, 'Creation and Liturgy', pp. 381-84;
Moberly, *At the Mountain of God*; and Brichto, *Toward a Grammar*, pp. 88-121.
For further reasons given for the juxtaposition of their tabernacle material with the
Golden Calf incident, see A. Hurowitz, 'Ha‘egel wehammiškan', *Shnaton* 7 (1983–
84), pp. 51-59 (Heb.). Hurowitz notes that the building processes for the calf and
the tabernacle are in part parallel and that an episode of rebellion may interrupt
building of a palace or temple in ancient Near Eastern building accounts. The former
illustrates an element that may draw attention to the connection between the two; the
latter might be regarded as a bit forced, given the parallels and the apparent history of
composition here.

97. It might be argued that in sections B′ i and i′ the tabernacle materials are
preceded by a decalogue (20.2-14//34.10-28). Exod. 34.10-28 has not been uni-
formly understood as a decalogue, however. Johnstone (*Exodus*, p. 80) regards
34.17-26 'as a citation of the end of the Book of the Covenant'. The verbal contact
between 20.4 and 34.17 might indicate the parallel character of the two decalogues in
20 and 34 (Moberly, *At the Mountain of God*, p. 99), although this parallelism might
be regarded as superficial. The source of the second decalogue has been difficult to
establish. This question might be approached through the order of peoples listed in
34.11. M. Noth (*The Old Testament World* [trans. V.I. Gruhn; Philadelphia: Fortress Press, 1966], p. 77) argued that the Yahwist employed the term Canaanites, the
Elohist preferred the name Amorites, while the Priestly source made habitual use of
Hittites. T. Ishida ('The Structure and Historical Implications of the Lists of Pre-
Israelite Nations', *Bib* 60 [1979], p. 477) questions this hypothesis and argues that
usage reflects different periods. The initial position of Amorites reflects, in Ishida's
opinion, ninth- or eighth-century modifications of the tenth-century lists which begin

the priestly redaction inherited an older linkage of chs. 24 and 33–34, as both sections use cultic visionary language as a means of exploring Israel's relationship with its deity. Indeed, the pre-priestly sections, Exod. 33.17-23 and 34.6-8, may constitute a 'commentary' on the older text, Exod. 24.9-11. In order to delve into the problem of proximity and distance to the divine, Exod. 33.12-23 and 34.6-8 explore the meaning of the (relatively) static report of Exod. 24.10.[98] More specifically, Exod. 33.17-23 and 34.6-8 address the problematic statement about 'seeing God' in Exod. 24.9-11.[99] While 24.9-11 presents the visionary experience of Moses, Aaron and some of the elders in an unproblematic manner, Exod. 33.17-23 and 34.6-8 present the problematic dimensions of this experience. These thematic relations point to the literary character of Exodus 32–34. To echo M.Z. Brettler's insightful view of 2 Kings 17, the story of Moses on the mountain 'acted as a magnet, collecting an unusually large number of traditions and reflections'.[100]

In addition to relating back to Exodus 24, Exodus 32–34 shows internal structure of great theological importance, first between chs. 32 and 33–34 and then within 33–34 itself. As others have discussed these chapters at great length,[101] only a limited number of observations will be made here. First of all, there are some clear relations between the story of Exodus 32 and the theological reflection of chs. 33–34. Exod. 32.1-10 and 33.1-6 both involve the issue of leadership. In the first

with Canaanites. According to the analyses of either Noth and Ishida, the list in Exod. 34.11 would be early. Ishida ('The Structure', p. 478) notes the contrast of lists beginning with the Amorites as in Exod. 34.11 with lists of nations in deuteronomic literature (Josh. 3.10; Judg. 3.5; cf. Ezra 3.1; Neh. 9.8; 2 Chron. 8.7) which begin with Canaanites. Indeed, no list in the book of Exodus matches any list in deuteronomic literature according to Ishida's charts of lists (Ishida, 'The Structure', pp. 461-62, 471). If correct, this observation would point to a pre-deuteronomic origin for the second decalogue.

98. Commentators commonly note the resemblances between these two accounts. See Brichto, *Toward a Grammar*, pp. 94, 272 n. 8.

99. My friend James Ponet informs me that Michael Fishbane has made a suggestion of this sort, but I have been unable to locate Fishbane's discussion.

100. Brettler, *The Creation of History*, p. 133.

101. See for example Moberly, *At the Mountain of God*. Childs regards Exod. 32 as a separate unit and Exod. 32–34 as 'a superb, new literary composition' produced by redactional structuring (*The Book of Exodus*, p. 610; see also pp. 557-58). The following analysis accepts this view.

passage the people proclaim the calf as their leader, while in the second passage Yahweh dictates how an angel will lead the Israelites. The motifs of the people's 'stiff-necked' character and their ornaments appear in both of these sections as well. Furthermore, both Exod. 32.11-14 and 33.12-23 present Moses praying to Yahweh. The consequence of the people's sin in Exod. 32.1-10 leads Moses to pray for their welfare in Exod. 32.11-14, whereas the prospect of being led by an angel in Exod. 33.1-6 leads Moses to pray for further divine confirmation in 33.12-23. Finally, with Exod. 32.15-34 and 34.1-28 the tablets come into play. In the first passage the tablets are smashed as a result of the people's violation of the covenant. In the second passage the new set of tablets re-establishes the covenant. (It is within the second passage that the so-called 'second decalogue' of 34.11-25 has been secondarily inserted, framed by the references to the covenant in vv. 10 and 27-28.) Furthermore, 32.1-6 and 34.29-35 form an envelope around the entire narrative. According to Moberly, קרן*, literally 'to horn' (which refers to Moses' face as shining in the form of sun-rays in 34.29, 30, 35) suggests the legitimate authority of Moses designed to supplant the golden calf.[102]

The incident of the Golden Calf in ch. 32 uses the destruction of the first set of tablets to indicate that Yahweh cannot dwell in the midst of the people. Moses' dialogue with Yahweh and his subsequent experience of Yahweh in Exodus 33–34 address the problem of divine proximity to sinning Israelites.[103] The structure of these two chapters is hardly arbitrary or lacking in design. Instead, a series of envelopes frame Moses' central dialogue with Yahweh and the resultant liturgical experience, as illustrated by the following chiastic outline:

---

102. Moberly, *At the Mountain of God*, pp. 108-109. Although W.H. Propp's suggestion that Moses' face was disfigured by heat generated by the divine presence has not won favor, his survey of the history of interpretation of this passage is admirable (Propp, 'The Skin of Moses' Face—Transfigured or Disfigured?' *CBQ* 49 [1987], pp. 375-86; idem, 'Did Moses Have Horns?' *Bible Review* 4.1 [1988], pp. 30-37). For criticisms, see Blenkinsopp, *The Pentateuch*, p. 226 n. 101; Batto, *Slaying the Dragon*, p. 219 n. 40. As Rashi noted, the connection with קרן* in Hab. 3.4 points rather to the theophanic appearance of Moses' face. See Batto, *Slaying the Dragon*, p. 124.

103. See Mettinger, *The Dethronement of Sabaoth*, p. 119.

A   Exod. 33.1-11
> 1-6:   Yahweh will send an angel rather than his own Presence to accompany the Israelites
>
> 7-11:   Moses mediates between Yahweh and the people at the tent of meeting

  B   Exod. 33.12-17 Moses intercedes for the people for Yahweh
  to accompany them

    C   Exod. 33.18-23 Moses asks to see Yahweh
    C′ Exod. 34.1-8   Moses sees Yahweh

  B′ Exod. 34.8-9 Moses intercedes for the people for Yahweh
  to accompany them in their midst

A′ Exod. 34.10-35
> 10-28 Yahweh will accompany the Israelites thanks to the covenant
>
> 29-35 Moses' new condition in mediating between Yahweh and the people

The two units comprising the outer envelope, Exod. 33.1-6 (A) and 34.10-28 (A′), are parallel in that both present the divine decision regarding divine accompaniment to the land. In Exod. 33.1-6, because of the people being 'stiff-necked', Yahweh refuses to accompany the people to the land inhabited the various peoples so that the Divine Presence will not destroy them. Instead, an angel will serve the function of accompaniment. In Exod. 34.10-28 Yahweh describes how the Divine Presence will accompany the Israelites and how Yahweh will destroy the peoples in the land. The further addition in the second passage shows what enables this change of divine leadership. It is the covenant mentioned in v. 10, with its specifications spelled out in vv. 12-28. The newly written tablets will convey the record of Israel's commitments to its divine lord.

Exod. 33.7-11 and 34.29-35 seem also to be parallel. The first passage characterizes Moses' interaction with Yahweh before ascending to receive the second set of tablets and the special experience of Yahweh in 34.6-8. Moses would enter and exit the tent of meeting in order to speak with Yahweh and mediate for the people. The second text presents Moses after his experience of the divine presence and thereby heightens Moses' already special status. Moses' very person is now indelibly marked by the divine effulgence. This new condition allows Moses to mediate for the people and to instruct them.

Within the envelope structure of 33.1-11 and 34.10-28 stands
33.12–34.9. The outer parts of 33.12–34.9, namely 33.12-17 (B) and
34.8-9 (B′), frame the issue at hand of divine favor, mentioned explicitly in both sections. In 33.12-17 Moses gains Yahweh's concession
to 'go in the lead' before the Israelites. Moses asks Yahweh to re-
affirm his favor, and Yahweh complies. Moses answers by asking
Yahweh to be shown 'Your way(s)' (דרכך) in v. 13. This word is often
translated 'your ways' in accordance with the versions, with the exception of LXX, which uses 'yourself' (σεαυτον).[104] This translation may
suggest that the word does not mean 'your way'.[105] The LXX witness
may reflect an understanding quite divergent from the traditional
interpretation of MT. If Moses were seeking to see a manifestation of
divine 'power' or 'dominion', a meaning of *drkt* well known in
Ugaritic,[106] it would accord better with the other terms in this dialogue referring to various dimensions of divine manifestation.[107] The
matter is not this plain, however, given the context of the larger issue
of Moses' leading the people. Moberly suggests the possibility of a
double-entendre in Moses' request to know 'Your way' (דרכך): 'Moses
seeks to know the route by which Yahweh will go with his people'.[108]
There may well be word-play involved here, as divine power, divinely
approved behavior (cf. Ps. 27.11) and the divine plan of Israel's path
to the promised land come together in the expression, דרכך (cf. Exod.
18.20). Moses' request links the issues of his leadership, divine power
and the sin of the people who 'turned from the way' (מן הדרך סרו
מהר) in 32.8.[109] In v. 14, Yahweh responds by stating that 'my face'

104. For the textual evidence, see J.W. Wevers, *Exodus* (Septuaginta; Göttingen:
Vandenhoeck & Ruprecht, 1991), p. 370. I wish to thank Professor John Strugnell
for bringing this reading to my atttention.

105. J.W. Wevers comments:

> What Moses asks of God is that he reveal himself [*emphanismon moi seauton*]. Exod.
> maintains that understanding God's way must be based on his self-manifestation; only
> then [*gnostos eido se*], 'would I know you clearly'.

Wevers, *Notes on the Greek Text of Exodus* (SBLSCS, 30; Atlanta: Scholars Press,
1990), p. 548.

106. See *KTU* 1.2 IV 11, 13, 20; 1.4 VII 44; 1.14 I 42 (partially reconstructed);
1.16 VI 38; 1.108.7. For this meaning in Num. 16.5, *Ben Sira* 42.1 and rabbinic
sources, see Muffs, *Love and Joy*, pp. 113-20.

107. For this point in greater detail, see Smith, '"Seeing God"' pp. 182-83 n. 45.

108. Moberly, *At the Mountain of God*, p. 73.

109. Cf. Moberly, *At the Mountain of God*, p. 49.

(פָּנַי) will go (in the lead).[110] This term appears for divine presence in the psalms (e.g. Ps. 42.3). The important point is that Moses' pilgrimage experience of seeing Yahweh in 33.18–34.7 is ultimately paradigmatic for, related to, and literarily framed by, Moses' ultimate concern that Yahweh will accompany the Israelites. Here Moses exercises his role as cultic mediator to beg for the Divine Presence to accompany the Israelites.

Within this material lies Exod. 33.18–34.7. This section has two parts, the dialogue regarding Moses' request to see Yahweh in 33.18-23 (C), matched by the narrative describing this experience in 34.1-9 (C′). Exod. 33.18-23 begins this part of the dialogue by stating Moses' desire for divine confirmation in his capacity as the Israelites' leader. In v. 18 Moses asks Yahweh if he may 'behold your face'. Here again the issue of leadership is linked to Moses' privileged experience of the divine. In v. 19 Yahweh responds by offering to show Moses his 'goodness' (טוֹב), another divine characteristic used in a cultic context in the psalms (Ps. 27.4, 13), and in v. 20 Yahweh offers the rejoinder that humans cannot see the divine face and live, as known in the tradition (Gen. 32.31). Finally, in vv. 21-23 after Moses is stationed in the cleft of the rock, Yahweh proposes that when 'my effulgence (כְּבוֹדִי) passes by' Moses, Yahweh will shield him with his hand, and then 'you will see my back (אֲחֹרַי), but my face (פָּנַי) will not be seen'.[111] It is evident from the terms 'face', 'goodness' and 'glory' in the psalms that Exod. 33.12-23 draws on the theophanic experience known from Israelite cult, as discussed in Chapter 2, section 3.[112] Finally, the words declared by Yahweh as the divine back passes Moses (Exod. 34.6-8) likewise echo liturgical formulas. Y. Muffs has observed, for example, verbal connections between Exod. 34.7 and Ps. 99.8: נֹשֵׂא עָוֹן וָפֶשַׁע וְחַטָּאָה, 'forgiving iniquity, transgression, and sin' (Exod. 34.7; NJPS) and אֵל נֹשֵׂא הָיִיתָ לָהֶם, 'You were a forgiving God for them' (Ps. 99.8; NJPS); וְנַקֵּה לֹא יְנַקֶּה, 'He does not remit all punishment' (Exod. 34.7; NJPS) and וְנֹקֵם עַל עֲלִילוֹתָם, 'But you exacted retribution for their misdeeds' (Ps. 99.8; NJPS).[113] Muffs views the psalm as dependent on Exodus 34, but the relationship might be inversed. Just as likely, the

---

110. For this handling of the verb, see NJPS.

111. The word תְּמוּנָה is missing from this passage, but appears in Num. 12.8 (cf. Deut. 4.12; Ps. 17.15).

112. See Mettinger, *The Dethronement of Sabaoth*, p. 119.

113. Muffs, *Love and Joy*, pp. 22-23.

two texts may draw on a larger, shared liturgical background. Finally, the thematic contacts between Exod. 33.17-23, 34.6-8 and Elijah's journey to Mount Horeb in 1 Kgs 19.9-14[114] would also suggest that the account of Moses' experience of the deity reflects a tradition of pilgrimage culminating in a theophany. Indeed, Moses' experience reflects and evokes the epitome of the pilgrimage experience in the sanctuary.

Beyond the cultic language associated with pilgrimage, Exod. 33.17-23 and 34.6-8 show one unique feature. The divine 'face' is well-attested elsewhere for the human perception of the divine presence, but the divine 'back' in Exod. 33.23 is specific to this passage and represents a modification and expression of limitation on the human ability to experience the divine presence. This usage would point to a literary rendering aimed at modifying older cultic themes. It might be argued that the specific use of 'back' here might be a reversal of a non-cultic idiom for one person's refusal to pay attention to another. Jer. 18.17 reads עֹרֶף וְלֹא פָנִים אֶרְאֵם. Emended with the versions (with many commentators), this verse may be translated: '[My] neck but not [My] face will I show them'.[115] Exod. 33.23 modifies this idiom by giving it a positive spin. Exod. 33.23 would therefore seem to represent a literary expression incorporating both cultic and non-cultic elements. This view runs counter to von Rad's argument that the passage is a cult aetiology insofar as it legitimates the rite designed to produce a theophany or substitutes for that rite.[116] Accordingly, von Rad's description may be stood on its head. The passage is hardly a cult aetiology as von Rad argued. The passage instead uses the known pilgrimage idiom for the experience of the divine presence in the sanctuary and creates a new picture by recourse to a modification of a common idiom. Here there is no cult aetiology, but a literary picture using older tradition in order to reflect theologically on the possibility of divine presence in the midst of a sinning people. Moses receives a limited experience of seeing Yahweh and that experience, marked on

114. Cross, *Canaanite Myth*, pp. 192-93; Wilson, *Prophecy and Society*, pp. 196-99; Hendel, 'Sacrifice as a Cultural System', p. 376. On pilgrimage in 1 Kgs 19, see Axelsson, *The Lord Rose up from Seir*, pp. 62-63.

115. See NJPS, p. 811 n. e-e; Carroll, *Jeremiah*, p. 376; Holladay, *Jeremiah*, I, pp. 519, 526. See also Jer. 2.27; cf. Isa. 50.5b, 6b.

116. Von Rad, *Gesammelte Studien zum Alten Testament* (TBü, 8; Munich: Chr. Kaiser Verlag, 1961), p. 239; cited with qualified approval by Mettinger, *The Dethronement of Sabaoth*, p. 119.

Moses' own face before all the people, is a sign for them to recognize the divine presence in their midst. In a sense, when the Israelites see Moses' face, it is their mediated experience of seeing Yahweh. Through these modifications, Exodus 33–34 presents a brilliant new picture of the two-sided experience of Yahweh. The cult mediator can see Yahweh, but only in part, and the people can see Yahweh, but only through their leader. Moses' limited experience of Yahweh becomes the divine vehicle for fulfilling Moses' request for Yahweh to accompany the people.

Exodus 32–34 offers a new paradigm for Yahweh's accessibility to the people during the journey: Yahweh is indeed accessible, but not in a direct manner; it is one mediated by the leader, Moses. To date, these chapters have been regarded as pre-priestly and quite correctly so. The question here is whether the priestly redaction played any role in the structuring of these chapters apart from having inserted them into the larger context of Exodus 25–40. It is generally thought that Exodus 32–34 shows a larger literary character in its present form, and the chiastic structure outlined above would support this view. The issue is the creator of this structure. It might be thought that the deuteronomistic expansion proposed for Exod. 32.7-14 would point in the direction of a deuteromistic redaction for the chapters as a whole. Yet only one expansion is involved, and the theology of chs. 32–34 is not markedly deuteronomistic. As C.T. Begg concludes, the 'core narrative of Exod. 32–34 should not be called "Deuteronomistic"'.[117] As a result, it might be prudent to seek a solution in a different redactional level. Childs identifies the redactor of JE as the creator of the complex more or less in its present form.[118] Despite the larger priestly setting for Exodus 32–34, the priestly redaction was probably not responsible for the overall content of these chapters, but the theology was compatible with priestly concerns. In contrast to the deuteronomistic expansion of Exod. 32.9-14, it may be suspected that the bulk of the material is neither deuteronomistic nor priestly, but the organization is an open question.[119] As with Exodus 19 and 24, the priestly redaction of these passages may have incorporated non-priestly materials in

117. Begg, 'The Destruction of the Calf', p. 250.

118. Childs, *The Book of Exodus*, p. 610.

119. It may be noted also that according to Knohl, chiasm, the structure of these chapters, is favored by the Holiness School. Knohl, *The Sanctuary of Silence*, p. 61.

a new schema consistent with the priestly legislation involving the tabernacle in Exodus 25–31, 35–40.

In sum, the overall materials of chs. 32–34 are to be attributed to pre-priestly redactional activity, but this narrative is also linked to, and re-contextualized by, the priestly procedures outlined in chs. 35–40. The pre-priestly narrative and the priestly instructional materials jointly provide a new avenue for a sinning Israel and a holy Yahweh to dwell together. When the tabernacle is complete at the end of ch. 40, a new stage in Israel's relationship with Yahweh begins. It is a stage that now can accomodate both Yahweh's limits and Israel's within the mechanism of the holy priesthood and the holy space which it governs. With the completion of the tabernacle, the divine glory fills the new divine dwelling-place, in Kearney's words, 'a sign that the new "creation" has been achieved'.[120] The creation of Israel's life with Yahweh is finally completed, like the Sabbath at the end of the first week of the world in Gen. 1.1–2.4a.

EXCURSUS: THE PRIESTLY LINES AND THE PRODUCTION OF EXODUS

The priestly background of P over and against E and D in Exodus may be placed within the larger discussion of the lines of the Israelite priesthood especially in the post-exilic period. Important studies of the priesthood dating from the last century, such as the work of J. Wellhausen, and this century, represented in the investigations of A.H.J. Gunneweg, A. Cody, and F.M. Cross,[121] identified various lines of priesthood and placed a number of prophets and other biblical figures into these lines, specifically the priestly branches labelled the Aaronids ('the sons of Aaron'), the Zadokites ('the sons of Zadok') considered a subset of the Aaronids, and the Levites ('the sons of Levi', also called 'the house of Levi').[122] S.D. McBride, R.R. Wilson

120. Kearney, 'Creation and Liturgy', p. 381.

121. Wellhausen, *Prolegomena*, pp. 121-67; A.H.J. Gunneweg, *Leviten und Priester*; A. Cody, *A History of Old Testament Priesthood* (Rome: Pontifical Biblical Institute, 1969); Cross, *Canaanite Myth*, pp. 195-215. The background of the Zadokites and the date of their claim to Aaronid descent remain major subjects of disagreement. The lines are evidently in competition by the time of the exile; the main points of this excursus concern the later periods. For a serviceable summary in this regard, see Blenkinsopp, *Sage, Priest, Prophet*, pp. 66-114; see also Nelson, *Raising Up a Faithful Priest*, pp. 2-15.

122. For a detailed listing of terms for Levites, see M.D. Rehm, 'Levites and Priests', *ABD*, IV, p. 304. According to Rehm, the 'Levitical priests' refers to 'the keepers of the central sanctuary in the tribal league' (p. 305) as opposed to the Levites who served local sanctuaries during the monarchy. R.K. Duke doubts the

and P.D. Hanson invert the direction of argument by suggesting that the descriptions of the priesthood in biblical books provide a basis for attributing these works to various lines of the priesthood.[123] This sociological approach shifted the scholarly perspective from reconstructing priestly lines based on biblical texts to attributing biblical texts to priestly lines. McBride, Wilson and Hanson infer priestly authorship of various sorts from different textual indicators, including concern for priestly status and priestly language. There is an inherent difficulty with these criteria: concern expressed for different priestly lines or various sorts of priestly language is not tantamount to proof of priestly authorship. Nonetheless, while these criteria demonstrate only familarity with the priesthood[124] and are therefore insufficient in themselves, it stands to reason nonetheless that members of the priestly lines are precisely those members of Israelite society most familiar with, and expressive about, priestly concerns and language.

priestly status of the Levites in general ('The Portion of the Levite: Another Reading of Deuteronomy 18.6-8', *JBL* 106 [1987], pp. 193-201), but he ignores evidence such as Deut. 33.10b, Josh. 18.7, Isa. 66.21 and Jer. 33.18. Jer. 33.18 discusses Levitical priests explicitly in connection with the sacrificial cult. In order to maintain his thesis, Duke ('The Portion of the Levite', p. 199) assumes that Levites discussed in P, Chronicles and Ezra are non-priests. Yet this approach generally privileges the Aaronid view of the Levites. Distinctions offered between priests and Levites in material such as P, Jeremiah and Chronicles do not demonstrate that the Levites were not considered priests or potential priests, as Duke ('The Portion of the Levite', pp. 199-200) suggests. Rather, as McBride, Wilson and Hanson (see below) argue, they indicate that the Levites' claims to priestly functions were controverted and diminished by the Aaronid line. It would seem that the Levites' eventual secondary status within the Temple cult, including singing and policing the Temple precincts, are indications not necessarily of their non-priestly identity, but of their reduced status as priests. For a study of the Levites in the later periods, see R. Kugler, 'The Levi-Priestly Tradition: From Malachi to the Testament of Levi' (PhD dissertation, University of Notre Dame, 1994).

123. Wilson traces his work to McBride (see Wilson, *Prophecy and Society*, p. 18 n. 36). For this reason priority is here given to citations of McBride, 'Biblical Literature', pp. 14-26, although this publication postdates the cited works of Wilson or Hanson ('Israelite Religion in the Early Postexilic Period', p. 486). McBride, Wilson, Hanson and other scholars attribute other works to the Zadokites and Aaronids. The Zadokite background of Ezekiel has been recognized (McBride, 'Biblical Literature', p. 21; Wilson, *Prophecy and Society*, pp. 282-85; Hanson, 'Israelite Religion', p. 486; S.S. Tuell, *The Law of the Temple in Ezekiel 40–48* [HSM, 49; Atlanta: Scholars Press, 1992], esp. pp. 121-52). McBride ('Biblical Literature', p. 23) and Hanson ('Israelite Religion', pp. 494-95, 498, 501) describe Zechariah as Zadokite. For the Zadokite background of many intertestamental works, see P.D. Hanson, *The People Called: The Growth of Community in the Bible* (San Francisco: Harper & Row, 1986), pp. 358-72. Based on the priestly language in Second Isaiah, R.R. Wilson has suggested the view that this material was a priestly work, possibly Aaronid ('The Community of Second Isaiah', in C.R. Seitz [ed.], *Reading and Preaching the Book of Isaiah* [Philadelphia: Fortress Press, 1988], pp. 64-65). However, Third Isaiah might be Levitical (see Isa. 66.21; cf. the excursus to Chapter 10 below), which would seem to make an Aaronid attribution of Second Isaiah less likely. Some apocalyptic works of the post-exilic period have now been attributed to a priestly background. See S.L. Cook, *Prophecy and Apocalypticism: The Postexilic Social Setting* (Minneapolis: Fortress Press, 1996). Cook's book offers some important correctives to the current debate regarding the relationship between apocalyptic and the priesthood; he suggests that the two overlap in a number of post-exilic biblical works.

124. This issue is evident from the discussion of Exod. 19.5-6 in Chapter 10.

As E. Blum notes,[125] the interests of the different priestly lines are represented in Exodus. More specifically, material attributed to 'P' in traditional Pentateuchal studies reflects more precisely the Aaronid priesthood,[126] while 'E'[127] and deuteronomic material including the book of Deuteronomy and the redaction of the Deuteronomistic History manifest Levitical concerns.[128] The date and background of the priestly redaction represents a major question that defies a precise solution. For Blum, the book reflects an inner-Jewish program for reconstituting Judean society in the Persian period.[129] Furthermore, Knohl's analysis of the Exodus redaction by the 'Holiness School' would be consistent with positing an exilic and early post-exilic Aaronid priestly tradition that drew clearer delineations between priestly and Levitical roles.[130]

Dozemann argues that the figures named in Exod. 24.9-11 represent the redactional influences of different groups.[131] Moses constitutes an ideal for both the deuteronomic and priestly redactors. The seventy elders reflect deuteronomic editors of the exilic period while Aaron represents the priestly redaction. Because the only event in the Pentateuch besides Exod. 24.9-11 recalling Nadab and Abihu is a negative one (Lev. 10.1-2), Dozemann argues that these two figures represent the limits on the priesthood in public worship; they are foils to the positive priestly figures of Eleazar and Ithamar. Citing Ezekiel 8 as evidence of priestly competition during the Exile, Dozemann notes that priestly groups remained in conflict at this time and he concludes that the redaction of Exod. 24.9-11 is post-exilic. The character of the priestly redaction has been illuminated by Exod. 31.18. As noted in Chapters 7 and 10, the verse does not belong to either the preceding or following unit, and would appear to be redactional in character. The verse attests the specifically priestly expression, 'tablets of the Pact' (לוחת העדות).[132] The priestly ('Holiness School') redaction has incorporated deuteronomic material, not only in reflecting the notion of the tablets, but also in using and modifying the characteristic deuteronomic phrase, 'stone

---

125. Blum, *Studien*, p. 334.

126. See McBride, 'Biblical Literature', p. 20; Hanson, *The People Called*, pp. 231-32; *idem*, 'Israelite Religion', p. 486.

127. Wilson, *Prophecy and Society*, pp. 146-56.

128. Wilson, *Prophecy and Society*, pp. 156-225. Milgrom's attempt (*Leviticus 1–16*, pp. 29-34) to trace the P tradition to the Shilohite priesthood does not account for the distinctive Levitical character of that priesthood as opposed to the Aaronid character of 'P'. It is not the line of Aaron, but the line of Moses (Wilson's Levitical line) that is connected to the priesthood at Shiloh, as Cross has argued (see Cross, *Canaanite Myth*, p. 197). To connect the Aaronids to the priesthood of Shiloh, Milgrom relies on the genealogy of 1 Chron. 24.3 which makes Eli the priest at Shiloh in 1 Sam. 2 the son of Ithamar, the son of Aaron. It is unclear how much historical weight may be placed on this datum. Cross (*Canaanite Myth*, p. 207 n. 50) argues that it 'cannot be taken at face value'.

129. Blum, *Studien*, p. 358. See also Dozemann, *God on the Mountain*, pp. 180-92.

130. See Knohl, *The Sanctuary of Silence*, pp. 199-224. For discussion, see Chapter 5, section 3.

131. Dozeman, *God on the Mountain*, pp. 180-92.

132. For Knohl, the verse belongs to the 'Holiness School' redaction. See Knohl, *The Sanctuary of Silence*, p. 67 n. 21, p. 108.

tablets' (לוחת אבן). The fact that Exod. 31.18 contains this expression as well as Mount Sinai, as opposed to Mount Horeb, would point to a priestly redaction rather than a deuteronomic one.

This approach may be furthered by examining the book's descriptions of the priesthood. The narrative incorporates the priestly history in its references to Aaron and his sons, on the one hand, and to Moses and the Levites on the other. The institution of the Aaronid priesthood is given legitimacy in both narrative and legal material.[133] The kinship and roles manifested by Moses (and the Levites) on the one hand, and Aaron (and his sons), on the other hand, are represented synchronically as a grand order of a single unified priesthood, but regardless of whether one attributes pro-Levitical material to an E source or a D redaction, the book reflects non-Aaronid Levites incorporated and subordinated to the Aaronid priesthood. Aaron is presented as a Levite in Exod. 4.14,[134] and P extends this notion in the genealogy of 6.20. The material designated as E in the older source-critical analyses or deuteronomic in the newer redactional treatments shows a different view of the priesthood, however. The old Levitical traditions championed Moses and the Levites, mostly notably in the traditions surrounding Moses as covenant mediator, Jethro in chs. 2 and 18 as well as the story of the Golden Calf in ch. 32.[135]

The Aaronid priesthood both incorporated and displaced the Levitical traditions in elevating Aaron, his line and Aaronid legal material, but the book in the priestly redaction reflects a demarcation between priestly lines. The Aaronid redaction of the book has incorporated many Levitical themes in order to include the Levites, but also to give them a specific location within the religio-political order. This approach to the book would explain the story of Aaron's role in Israel's apostasy in Exodus 32. While the traditional Levitical version represented by Deut. 9.20 directly blames Aaron, Exodus 32 softens this criticism. An attempt at including Levites and their traditions is apparent from other details of the version in Exodus 32. The purifying role of the Levites in this story gives pride of place to them and not to Aaron. If the book of Exodus represented a polemical document aimed at excluding one line of the priesthood by another, then such episodes would have been omitted or altered further in a purely Aaronid redaction.

While priestly competition continued after the exile, there are some signs of accommodation during the post-exilic period that would fit the redaction of Exodus. The descriptions of the Aaronid and Levitical roles in the books of Chronicles reflect a place for the Levites within the Aaronid scheme of religious life. Furthermore, references to writing and reading material in Exodus (17.14; 24.4, 7, 12; 32.32-33)

133. Cross, *Canaanite Myth*, pp. 197, 205-206; Damrosch, *The Narrative Covenant*, p. 272.

134. Eissfeldt and Ginsberg render אחיך הלוי in 4.14 as 'your fellow Levite' (see Ginsberg, *The Israelian Heritage*, p. 85 n. 103). As confirmation Ginsberg cites Deut. 18.7 which contains the expression, ככל אחיו הלוים, translated 'like all his fellow Levites' (RSV). See also Friedman, 'Torah', p. 611b.

135. Exod. 32 has been used to posit the Levitical background of the Elohist. See Wilson, *Prophecy and Society*, pp. 17-18, 146-56; White, 'The Elohistic Depiction of Aaron', pp. 149-59. For the Levitical priesthood in poetic tradition, Cross and McBride cite Deut. 33.8-11 (see also Propp, *Water in the Wilderness*, pp. 53-55).

might also suggest these two phenomena as parts of the processes of the book's transmission, distribution and education. Both Aaronids and Levites functioned as scribes and teachers, but Levitical teaching extended beyond areas of traditional Aaronid teaching such as purity, feasts and sabbaths.[136] Deut. 17.18, 1 Chron. 24.6 and 2 Chron. 34.12-13 attest the Levitical scribal role. The Levitical tradition included a concern for the transmission of sacred writings. 4QTQahat, frg. 1, ll. 11-12 registers this concern (cf. 4Q'Amram^c, frg. 1, ll. 1-2):

> and they gave to Levi, my father, and Levi my father [gave] to me [
> all my books in testimony, so that you might be forewarned by them [[137]

Mal. 2.5-7, 3.22, *T. Levi* 19.2-3 and *T. Jud* 21.1-4 suggest a Levitical teaching role. It is no accident that references to writing *and reading* the text in Exod. 17.14, considered deuteronomistic,[138] and in 24.7, considered Elohist (in traditional source-critical terminology), belong to what has been considered the larger Levitical tradition. Their preservation in a document edited by an Aaronid redactor perhaps indicates a time of demarcation between the priestly lines. Exodus served not only to provide legitimacy for these Levitical roles, but it also delimited Levitical authority as well.

In sum, Exodus may be viewed as part of the foundational-story for rebuilding Judean society in the Persian period. It provides some guidelines for the establishment of theocratic authority. Given the priestly emphasis of Exodus, this document likely was the domain of the priesthood. As the document demarcating the different priestly lines, the Levites—with sanction from or directed by the Aaronids—likely stored, transmitted and taught to the people from this text. For this reason Exodus might be described as teaching, which as the following chapter discusses, lies at the heart of this biblical book's purpose.[139]

---

136. On this point, see Knohl, *The Sanctuary of Silence*, pp. 124-64. Cf. the presumably related Zadokite teaching of Ezek. 44.23-24. See Tuell, *The Law of the Temple*, p. 123.

137. J.A. Fitzmyer and D.J. Harrington, *A Manual of Palestinian Aramaic Texts (Second Century B.C.—Second Century A.D.)* (BibOr, 34; Rome: Biblical Institute Press, 1978), p. 97.

138. Childs, *The Book of Exodus*, p. 313.

139. The place of the Levites in Israelite society might profit from a cross-cultural comparison with other priestly groups which regard themselves as the custodians of sacred teaching enshrined in written forms. I am thinking in particular of D. Carpenter's description of the social location of Vedic authority. See Carpenter, 'Language, Ritual and Society: Reflections on the Authority of the Veda', *JAAR* 60 (1992), pp. 57-77. See also Carpenter, 'The Mastery of Speech: Canonicity and Control in the Vedas', in L.L. Patton (ed.), *Authority, Anxiety, and Canon: Essays in Vedic Interpretation* (ed. L.L. Patton; SUNY Series in Hindu Studies; Albany: State University of New York Press, 1994), pp. 19-34. For the role of the Levites in the formation of the canon, see the maximalist views of J.W. Miller, *The Origins of the Bible: Rethinking Canon History* (New York: Paulist Press, 1994).

Part III

LAW AND EXODUS IN CONTEXT

'I will make My entire goodness pass by your face...
you cannot see My face.'
Exodus 33.19, 20

'...you will see My back, but My face may not be seen.'
Exodus 33.23

Chapter 10

THEOLOGY AND LAW IN EXODUS

1. *The Theology of the Priestly Redaction Revisited*

The larger relations between the two halves of the book observed by earlier commentators are evident from the preceding chapters. The two halves of Exodus dramatize the foundational events of Israel's origins as a pilgrimage in a developed sense, namely as journey (A = Exodus 1–2; and A′ = Exod. 15.22–18.27), call and commission, and cultic experience of Yahweh (B i = Exod. 3.1–6.1 and i′ = Exod. 6.2–14.31; and B′ i = Exodus 19–31 and i′ = Exodus 32–40). It is the land of the divine mountain to which both Moses and Israel travel (A and A′). Their destinies unfold in the land of Midian. Moses and Israel receive their first experiences of the divine both by way of theophany and divine name (B and B′). Furthermore, the poem of Exodus 15, in its present context in the middle of the book of Exodus, presents the mountain of Sinai as the land of the holy sanctuary.

The sections of the book move Moses and the people toward the mountain of divine holiness. Pilgrimage to Sinai functions as the book's representation of earliest Israel and the pattern to be replicated throughout its history. The references to pilgrimage suggest this theme's importance for characterizing the life of Israel (3.18; 4.23; 5.1, 3, 8, 17; 8.27-29; 9.13; 10.8; 23.17, 34.23; cf. 15.22), but these reminders are less significant than the narrative presentation of the book as pilgrimage in a developed sense, noted in the previous chapter. The movement to Sinai is the movement toward identity and destiny. In J.D. Levenson's graceful formulation, 'Mount Sinai is the intersection of love and law, of gift and demand, the link between a past together and a future together'.[1] The pilgrimage expresses the ideal order of life

---

1. Levenson, *Sinai and Zion*, p. 136.

between Yahweh, Israel and the world.[2] Only Israel comes and stands at the mountain of Yahweh, and only Israel hears the voice of the Yahweh. Only Israel is the recipient of תורה, 'teaching', and only Israel's leaders see Yahweh. The pilgrimage to the mountain as well as the covenants made there suffuse the second part of Exodus with a cultic sensibility. This sense of cultic presence and power is by no means absent from the first part of the book. Moses' own experience of God on the mountain in Exodus 3 is a cultically charged description. Furthermore, the act of obeisance of 4.31, paralleled in 12.27,[3] gives a cultic cast to the people's relationship with Yahweh through Moses, and it anticipates the cultically charged meeting between Yahweh and the people through Moses at the mountain.

The priestly redaction used the building blocks of older ('JE') material as well as material from the priestly tradition. The priestly redaction's structure of additive parallels was crafted in both halves of the book, and thus invites further comparison between them. Just as the two calls and commissions to Moses in section B i and B′ are parallel, section B′ i′, consisting of the legal material in Exodus 35–40 and the narrative of chs. 32–34, may be viewed as parallel with section B′ i, comprising the legal material within Exodus 20–23 + 25–31 and the narrative of chs. 19, 24 and 31.18. The two experiences of 'seeing' the deity in sections B′ i and i′ parallel the two calls of Moses in sections B i and i′ and suggest an analogous relationship. Indeed, as noted above, Wellhausen recognized the highly theophanic character of the first call and the absence of a theophanic language from the second call. The same is evident in the experiences of 'seeing' the deity in sections B′ i and i′. The first relates the experience of 'seeing' the deity and provides details of the heavenly abode. In contrast, the second conveys the problematic character of the experience of 'seeing' the deity and omits any description of the divine palace. It might be possible to attribute this difference to historical developments governing cultic notions, but whatever diachronic features may be discerned, the two accounts in their present context parallel one another. Similarly,

2.   Cf. the remark of Zimmerli (*I am Yahweh*, p. 10) on the priestly perspective presented in Exod. 6.5 and Ezek. 20.5: 'this revelation calls the people... into a movement of recognition that is not a state of enraptured vision, but rather is life, activity, and movement toward a goal'.

3.   Rendtorff, *The Problem*, p. 186.

both sections B i′ and B′ i′ achieve a success in Moses' and Israel's missions lacking in sections B i and B′ i.

The parallels between the two halves draw a general contrast between Egypt and Israel. Both the Egyptians and the Israelites are the recipients of divine messages through Moses. The fate of Moses' first mission to the Egyptians (section B i) is a prelude to the manifestation of divine power in the second mission (section B i′). The first covenant embodied in the narrative by the first set of tablets (section B′ i) anticipates the divine mercy visited upon the Israelites by the resumption of the covenant with the second tablets (section B′ i′). This mercy is fully realized in the completion of the 'work of the tabernacle of the tent of meeting' (Exod. 32.32) and the indwelling of the divine effulgence (כבוד) in the tabernacle (Exod. 40.34-38). As noted above, Martin Buber and Franz Rosenzweig convincingly argued that this occasion consciously echoes the end of the priestly creation account (Exod. 39.43a//Gen. 1.31a; Exod. 39.32a//Gen. 2.1; Exod. 40.33b// Gen. 2.2a; and Exod. 39.43b// Gen. 2.3a).[4] Like Exod. 24.15–31.18, Exodus 35–40 is connected to the creation story of Genesis. While the account of Genesis marks the creation of the world, the creation language of Exodus 39–40 might be viewed as heralding the new creation of Israel's cultic life with its deity.

The use of Genesis 1 in the two halves of the book also highlights the deep contrast between Egypt and Israel in Exodus: the priestly redaction of the plague narrative in section B i′ echoes language from the creation account in Genesis in presenting a return to chaos in Egypt, while the priestly account detailing the execution of the tabernacle in section B′ i′ likewise evokes Genesis 1 in suggesting the new creation of the people of Israel in its relationship to Yahweh.[5] According to Z. Zevit, the priestly redaction of the plague stories show a reversal of the created order for Egypt and that the victory at the sea 'concludes the Egyptian period of Israelite history'.[6] In contrast, the creation language in the priestly redaction of Exodus 25–31 suggested by P.K. Kearney and especially in chs. 39–40 signals the new age of the Israelites' relationship with Yahweh. The major theme of creation clearly links the beginning and end of the book. In view of these clear echoes of the priestly creation story in those sections, Zevit and

---

4.   For discussion, see Blum, *Studien*, pp. 306-307.
5.   See section B′ i′.
6.   Zevit, 'The Priestly Redaction', p. 211.

Kearney's proposals gain in probability, and jointly the reverberations that they suggest both link and contrast the two halves of the book.

There are more specific correlations between parts of the two halves of Exodus. B i′ and B′ i′ correspond insofar as they both produce two successful conclusions, the first to the call of Moses in section B i′ and the second to the covenant of the people in section B′ i′. The second call and commission of section B i′ is successful with the divine intervention of the plagues, while the second section of law and covenant in section B′ i′, structurally presented in the narrative through the motif of the second set of tablets, successfully resolves the problem of divine access and presence in Israel. This feature may suggest further the theme of the Egyptians as a foil to the Israelites: in the first half of Exodus the Egyptians suffer the fate of divine intervention made on Israel's behalf, while in the second half of the book the Israelites avoid the Egyptians' fate and gain a second chance with Yahweh that at once avoids their own destruction and achieves their proper proximity to the divine.

The contrast between the Egyptians and the Israelites extends to some other thematic considerations. First, both Egyptian and Israel are sinning peoples, but the treatment that they receive at the hands of Yahweh could hardly differ more. As E.L. Greenstein has observed, Yahweh spares Israel's first-born who are about to be redeemed, but Egypt has no option of redemption.[7] Secondly, it has been noted that the book begins with an Egyptian construction project which enslaves the Israelites while the book ends with the Israelite construction project which brings them freedom through their relationship with their deity.[8] Finally, the priestly redaction shows theological reflection involving the contrast between Egypt and Israel. Exod. 29.1-42a,

---

7. Greenstein, 'The First-Born Plague', p. 566.

8. The plague narratives are a distinctive feature of section B i′ with the slight exception of 32.35 which stands in the narrative of section B′ i′ (Exod. 32–40). The ending to the Golden Calf story in Exod. 32.35 states that Yahweh 'struck' (ויגף) the people just as Yahweh struck the Egyptians with the plagues (נגף*, e.g., in 12.23). Given the brevity of 32.35, it might be considered that this notice was added in the priestly redaction, as 14 of the 15 Pentateuchal occurrences of this root are considered priestly by Friedman ('Torah', p. 610a); if so, Dr Benjamin Scolnic suggests (personal communication) that it may have been to associate the Golden Calf story with the refusal of Pharaoh to release the Israelites.

which discusses offerings to be made by Aaron and his sons at the
Tent of Meeting, is followed by a priestly gloss in vv. 42b-46 that uses
as its point of departure the phrase 'Tent of Meeting' in v. 42a:

> For there *I will meet* (נועדתי) with you, and there I will speak with you,
> and there I will meet with the Israelites, and it shall be sanctified by My
> Presence. I will sanctify the Tent of Meeting and the altar, and I will
> consecrate Aaron and his sons to serve Me as priests. I will abide among
> the Israelites, and I will be their god. And they shall know that I the Lord
> am their God, who brought them out from the land of Egypt *that I might
> abide among them*, I the Lord their God. [9]

The contrast made in this gloss between Egypt and Sinai is foundational for the priestly redaction. According to this gloss, the purpose of
the exodus for the priestly redaction was to create the mechanism to
enable Israel's deity 'to dwell among them' (see also Lev. 22.32-33;
Num. 15.41). The freedom from the Egyptians was made complete
only by the Sinai legislation.[10] Freedom fulfilled was the freedom
obtained through law. This understanding stems not only from the specific gloss of Exod. 29.46, but also from the correspondences between
the two halves of the book.

The priestly gloss of Exod. 25.22 also uses the otherwise rare form
of נועדתי. The first passage gives the instruction for the building of the
ark and adds the reflection:

> There I will meet (נועדתי) with you, and I will impart to you—from above
> the cover, from between the two cherubs that are on top of the Ark of the
> Pact—all that I will command you concerning the Israelite people.

Perhaps punning on אהל מועד ('tent of meeting') and נועדתי, both passages describe how the Tent of Meeting will be the meeting-place between Yahweh and Israel from this point forward. These two passages
may also echo the first call of Moses (Exod. 6.2). In Moses' call, he
learns from Yahweh: 'but I did not make myself known (נודעתי) to

---

9. My italics. For Knohl (*The Sanctuary of Silence*, pp. 65, 95 n. 120, 104
127, 129), Exod. 29.42 is Holiness School, but 25.22 is Priestly School. Knohl cites
נועדתי as an example of the fact that the only anthropomorphic language in Priestly
Theology (as opposed to the Holiness School) is interpersonal contact between
Yahweh and Moses (*The Sanctuary of Silence*, p. 129). This verb is in fact quite
unusual for such contact, and the point of using this verb may lie in the paranomasia
which it creates with the phrase אהל מועד.

10. So see Levenson, 'Liberation Theology', pp. 30-36; Levenson, *The Hebrew
Bible*, pp. 127-59, esp. pp. 144-48.

them by my name Yhwh'. The priestly glossator perhaps extends the word-play between נועדתי and the אהל מועד with נודעתי in order to mark two stages in the history of communication between Yahweh and Israel, the period of Egypt and the period of Israel at Sinai.

In closing, the priestly redaction not only contrasts Egypt and Israel or makes a general statement about Israel's relationship with Yahweh. The priestly redaction of the book used additive parallels of B i and i′ and B′ i and i′ to dramatize Israel's origins and thereby make a foundational statement about Israel's identity. This identity may be appreciated not only from the structure of the book created by the priestly redaction. Rather, the priestly redaction continued and extended an essential linkage between story and law and instructional literature in order to teach Israel's religious and social order. This linkage may be appreciated better by examining the treatment of law in Exodus.

2. *Terms for Law in Exodus*

In traditional Christian usage, 'the Law' has conjured up a kind of legalistic mindset. However, Exodus as a book of the Law shows a variety of materials that is not strictly legal. The word תורה ('instruction, teaching') shows a range of usage and association with other terms. In the book of Exodus, תורה covers the Ten Commandments, legal cases such as are found in the Covenant Code, priestly instructional literature, the cultic calendar and many other priestly matters. In other words, תורה includes law in the legal sense, but it also extends to non-legal materials. Indeed, the term covers such a wide variety of materials that 'law', insofar as this word evokes a purely legal sensibility, is an insufficent translation for תורה. Instead, as noted at the outset of this book, its more precise etymological and contextual sense outside of the Pentateuch is 'teaching'.

The word תורה is used in different ways in Exodus. Different levels of the book of Exodus use the term תורה for an instruction. Older material uses תורות, 'instructions', with מצות, 'commandments' (16.28) and תורות with חקים, 'statutes' (18.16, 20). In the priestly material in 24.12, תורה is used collectively for the laws of chs. 19.1–24.11. The priestly section of 24.12-18 includes the rationale for the priestly teacher. A contribution of the Holiness School,[11] Exod. 24.12 informs

---

11. Knohl, *The Sanctuary of Silence*, pp. 62-63, 66, 104.

Moses that he is to be given the tablets written with 'the law and the commandment' (והמצוה והתורה), in order 'to teach them' (להורתם).[12] G. Östborn remarks on this verse:

> The fact that תורה has come to denote 'the law' is conceivably due. . .to the dominating position acquired by *torot* as constituting part of 'the law'. It will be recalled that they occupy a relatively prominent place in the Sinai pericope. In my opinion, however, the basic cause, as previously maintained, is to be sought in the fact that the entire substance of the covenant, the 'book of the covenant', 'the law', came to be used as a foundation for teaching. The process is best illustrated by Deuteronomy. But it is also illuminating to refer to Exod. 24: 12. When Yahweh here writes the law and gives it to Moses, the underlying purpose is to 'teach', תורה the same.[13]

The deuteronomic material may presuppose this notion in using תורה in Exod. 13.9 and 16.4, and the later notion that Exodus as a whole constitutes תורה may derive from this tradition and is reflected in its position within the Pentateuch.[14]

Besides the use of תורה and תורות, the divine commandments are called הדברים האלה, 'these words' (Exod. 19.6-7). This text borrows this phrase from the older usage in 20.1, perhaps to signal a bracket with כל דברי יהוה ('all the words of Yahweh') in 23.3-4 and האלה הדברים in 24.8 around the Ten Commandments and the Covenant Code. 'The words' (הדברים) remains a standard term for the words on the two tablets in Exod. 34.1, 27-28. In Exod. 34.28, these words are identified for the first time, explicitly as the Ten Commandments. Yet in 35.1, הדברים האלה refer to the commandments regarding the tabernacle and the priestly cult in chs. 35–40. Perhaps as a characterization of the combination of the Ten Commandments and the Covenant Code, Exod. 24.3 uses the expression, כל דברי יהוה המשפטים, 'all the words

---

12. The nouns are collectives which, as the waw preceding התורה suggests, stand · in an epexegetical relationship to the preceding את לחת האבן to explain their content. The nouns והתורה והמצוה do not constitute a hendiadys, as the pronominal suffix on the infinitive indicates. The old material in Exod. 4.14-15 preserves this model of teaching in its presentation of Moses and Aaron. Characterized in 4.14 as Levites, Moses and Aaron are the recipients of the divine word (Exod. 4.15b): 'I will be with your mouth and with his mouth.'

13. Östborn, *Tora in the Old Testament*, p. 53.

14. See Weinfeld, *Deuteronomy 1–11*, pp. 17-18. The priestly tradition in Exodus approaches this usage (12.49).

of Yahweh and the ordinances'. These different terms for legal material tell only part of the story involving the larger historical development in the notion of תורה. In its most basic sense, this word begins as a term for 'instruction' or 'directive' and it ends up as Torah, the normative Jewish term for the first five books of the Bible.

3. *Different Concepts of Law in Exodus*

The narrative in Exodus 19–40 shows a number of different concepts of teaching. The first is the communication conveyed directly by God to Moses and the people. The people heard 'the words' (הדברים) beginning in 20.1 directly from God. These laws are accorded a special status, not only because they appear first in the narrative and not only because they are accompanied by a theophany. The text also emphasizes that these are the only words that the people heard directly from Yahweh. According to 20.19 the people ask Moses: 'you, speak with us (דבר אתה עמנו) that we may hear'. This request is made because the divine appearance on the mountain is too frightening (v. 18). The narrative shows a second model of the relationship between Yahweh, Moses and the people at the mountain. From this point onwards Moses mediates between Yahweh and the people. Yahweh is to speak to Moses who in turn is to convey the divine word to the people. Originally given to both Moses and the people, now the law is mediated to the people.[15] In sum, Exodus 19–24 shows two basic pictures of the giving of the law. Law begins as a body of material originally heard by the people, and then it becomes mediated by Moses.

The two views of law-giving might be traced to the influence of different historical settings. The representation of Moses and the people hearing the law directly from Yahweh might be derived from teaching

---

15. Cf. Childs's comment:

> In the E form of the tradition Moses functioned as the covenant mediator and sealed the covenant with Israel on the basis of the laws which he communicated to the people (24.ff.) But in the J form there is no place for a covenant ceremony. Rather, Moses functions as continual vehicle for the will of God in his office before the tent of meeting. His is a continuous medium of revelation. The covenant is based solely on the Ten Commandments, but understood in the context of Moses' ongoing role as recipient of the living will of the covenant God.

Childs, *The Book of Exodus*, p. 356. For Wilson, both E and the depiction of Moses as covenant mediator more generally stand in the Ephraimite or levitical tradition. See Wilson, *Prophecy and Society*, pp. 146-66.

in the name of Yahweh.[16] As Chapter 9 notes, both Psalms 50 and 81 contain the sequence of theophany, divine self-revelation and citation of the decalogue which many scholars compare with the Sinai revelation and legislation. This picture is known likewise from Psalm 95 (discussed in Chapter 2, section 2). In these psalms a cultic mediator[17] quotes the divine word to exhort the congregation to obedience. These psalms rely on either a citation of the Ten Commandments or references to the old Pentateuchal moments.

In contrast, the figure of Moses as mediator might be imputed to prophetic teaching of Torah (with no oracular context). Moses' mediation on Sinai between Yahweh and the people is explicitly cited as the model for the ideal prophet in Deut. 18.18-22. This mediator role may derive from Levitical circles as opposed to priestly (i.e. Aaronid) ones, first, because both Psalms 50 and 81 are attributed to Asaph, who is traditionally considered a Levite,[18] and secondly, because chs. 19 and 24 show Levitical terms (such as סגלה, 'possession'). (In contrast, Aaronid teaching might be expected to allude to issues of holiness or other cultic concerns such as feasts and sabbaths.[19]) This sort of cultic preaching on the part of a mediator citing the divine words apparently lies behind this side of Moses' role as mediator between Yahweh and the people known from Exodus 19–24.[20] The teaching given in the first person in Psalm 78 and the book of Deuteronomy might be compared.[21] Whether or not this delineation is correct, the two roles involving giving the law were incorporated into the priestly redaction

---

16. Levenson ('The Sources of Torah', p. 564) notes this meditative sort of divine teaching à propos of Ps. 119.26-29. See below for further discussion.

17. Zimmerli, *I am Yahweh*, p. 27.

18. See Nasuti, *Tradition History*; Tournay, *Seeing and Hearing God*, pp. 170-75.

19. Ezekiel 18's religious-ethical obligations include cultic-ritual concerns in v. 6 (see Weinfeld, 'The Uniqueness of the Decalogue', pp. 16-17). See also the teaching of Ezek. 44.23-24 (Tuell, *The Law of the Temple*, p. 123).

20. Östborn, *Tora in the Old Testament*, p. 86; von Rad, *The Problem of the Hexateuch*, p. 30.

21. See the remarks of E.L. Greenstein, 'Mixing Memory and Design: Reading Psalm 78', *Prooftexts* 10 (1990), p. 201. Also note the final sentence on p. 209: 'The psalmist does not ruminate on the past; he addresses the present and, like a prophet, seeks to transform the future'.

of Exodus, and as a result, Exodus 19–24 places these two pictures in a dialectical relationship.[22]

The narrative linkage of these two models results in making the law at once permanent and additive. By virtue of its narrative placement with the decalogue in ch. 20, the following Covenant Code becomes part of the original legislation of 'the words' (הדברים). In the narrative the Covenant Code is not regarded as a secondary addition. Rather, it constitutes part of the original deposit of divine instruction. This shift incorporates all the legal material positioned following the Ten Commandments. G. Sheppard remarks: 'The laws, regardless of what we may say about their original historical settings, refer in this context to a revealed Torah rather than to law codes that reflect merely compromises to the experiences of life at various times in the land'.[23]

The media for law also show a shift. The communication of the Ten Commandments first appears oral, with law as a body of text that Moses mediates in an ongoing manner after the giving of the Ten Commandments.[24] With Exod. 24.4, this body of law is characterized for the first time as written in character. At the conclusion of the legal material, Moses recounts all the words of Yahweh and all the judgments (את כל דברי יהוה ואת כל המשפטים) in 24.3a. The people assent to this recounting (24.3b), Moses writes down the law (24.4b), and Moses and the elders join in a meal and enjoy a partial vision of the heavenly palace and deity (24.9-11). The written character of instruction allows it to become unmediated again, but not in the sense of being able to dispense with legal authority. Rather, divine teaching is unmediated in that it is visibly present. Whereas the people heard the law of the decalogue directly from Yahweh and then had law mediated by Moses, now they have law directly in written form.

The status of law is changed by virtue of its written character

---

22. The book of Deuteronomy likewise presents the narrative joining of the two models of law-giving, one issued directly from Yahweh and one mediated orally by Moses, as a matter of temporal sequence. G.T. Sheppard ('Canonical Criticism', *ABD*, I, p. 864) comments:

> In the context of the Mosaic Torah, the laws found in Exodus, Leviticus and Numbers belong to the legislation as given to Moses in the region of Sinai, while the laws presented in Deuteronomy belong to Moses' subsequent 'interpretation' of them on the plains of Moab to the next generation (Deut. 1.5).

23. Sheppard, 'Canonical Criticism', *ABD*, I, p. 864.
24. McCarthy, *Treaty and Covenant*, p. 256.

because writing changes the potential range of the audience. In Exodus instruction is written not only for the generation that receives it; in fact, this generation will largely pass away in the wilderness. Rather, this law-giving is designed also for later audiences who receive it in the acts of reading it or hearing it read. J. Culler's reflections on writing apply to this dimension of law: 'The physical representation of a text gives it a stability... Writing has something of the character of an inscription, a mark offered to the world and promising by its solidity and apparent autonomy, meaning which is momentarily deferred.'[25] This presentation of law in the Pentateuch as a whole enshrines concepts of oral and written law. Exodus does not simply manifest a sequential ordering of heard and written law. Instead, as noted above, the final form of Exodus presents the oral and written laws as two different modes of divine communication inextricably joined as a single body of material.

Oral תורה as received tradition may have been known in the pre-exilic period.[26] Different notions of תורה besides the five books of Moses appear in Second Temple Judaism as well. According to J. Levenson, Psalm 119 recognizes these different sources of תורה. Verses 26-29 acknowledge unmediated divine teaching, while verses 99-100 recognize received tradition, transmitted by teachers and perhaps including some biblical books.[27] Like Psalm 119, Exodus shows oral תורה paralleling written תורה, but with the important difference that the Sinai legislation is the referent of these categories.[28] This presentation likewise enshrined within Exodus anticipates one aspect of the rabbinic idea of the Torah (*b. Yoma* 28b).[29] While the first five books of the

---

25. Culler, *Structuralist Poetics* (Ithaca, NY: Cornell University Press, 1975), pp. 131, 134.

26. See Östborn, *Tora in the Old Testament*, pp. 119-20, 138-39, 141-42.

27. So Levenson, 'The Sources of Torah', pp. 564, 570. For the defense of the objects as visionary rather than literary, see Levenson, 'The Sources of the Torah', p. 573 n. 35. Levenson notes that the verb '*hibbît* ('to look at') can denote prophetic vision (e.g., Num. 12.8 of Moses), it is never used in connection with reading a document'. Levenson ('The Sources of Torah', p. 569) also notes cosmic or natural law in vv. 89-91.

28. So stressed by Levenson, 'The Sources of Torah', p. 566.

29. While Levenson ('The Sources of Torah', p. 571) does not discuss the formation of the book of Exodus in this connection, his comments on oral תורה in Second Temple Judaism bear note (Levensons's italics):

Bible constitute the written Torah (תורה שבכתב, literally 'law which is in writing') and the Talmud represents the oral Torah (תורה שעל פה, literally 'law which is upon the mouth'),[30] together the two bodies of texts constitute a single, divine Torah given to the Jewish people through Moses at Mount Sinai and handed down through the ages (*Pirqe Ab.* 1.1). Despite their considerable differences, both the rabbinic tradition and the text of Exodus involve oral and written law which constitute a single body of revelation transmitted in written form. Historically both works involve the secondary addition of bodies of law which the tradition identified as the original revelation. This aspect of oral תורה is sometimes traced through the prophets and the Writings,[31] but it is reflected also in the formation and presentation of Sinai law in Exodus.[32]

Exodus 24.12–31.18 presents some further alterations in the depiction of Sinai law-giving. Like the presentation in 24.1-11, this law is written in character, but rather than Moses being the writer as in 24.4 (cf. 34.28b), now Yahweh becomes the writer of law (24.12; 31.18; 32.16; 34.1; cf. 32.32). Now law comes directly from Yahweh to the

The Sadducaic limitation of Toraitic authority to the Pentateuch is no less an innovation than the Pharasaic doctrine of non-Pentateuchal Torah. There is no evidence whatsoever for a period in which the Pentateuch (or any other parts of the Hebrew Bible) alone held the allegiance of *all* Jewish groups, to the exclusion of contemporary prophecy, inspired wisdom, the enactments of legal authorities, and the like, including ultimately the Oral Torah of the rabbis and the gospel of the Church.

While this claim is based largely on an argument from silence, it is consistent with the presently known evidence.

30. See M.D. Herr, 'Oral Law', *EncJud*, XII, pp. 1439-41; J. Neusner, *The Oral Torah. The Sacred Books of Judaism: An Introduction* (San Francisco: Harper & Row, 1987), pp. 45-87; E.P. Sanders, 'Law in Judaism', *ABD*, IV, pp. 259a-60b. For some of the complexities of the rabbinic notion, see M.I. Gruber, 'The Mishnah as Oral Torah: A Reconsideration', *JSJ* 15 (1984), pp. 112-22. According to recent authors, this concept of the oral Torah was not operative in the period of the New Testament authors and the two should not be compared. The concept is disputed even for the Mishnah. Legal material privileged through the later rabbinic concept of the oral Torah was understood in the New Testament period as 'traditions' (see Mk 7.3; Josephus, *Ant.* 13.16.2 #408; discussed by Sanders, 'Law in Judaism', p. 259a).

31. See Herr, 'Oral Law', p. 1440; Levenson, 'The Sources of Torah', p. 560.

32. The decisions of legal authorities apart from the laws of Deuteronomy are sanctioned by Deut. 17.8-11. Herr ('Oral Law', pp. 1440-41) makes this passage a basis for the Oral Torah.

people, and Moses is only the transporter and not the writer of the divinely written law. Accordingly, this writing is given a medium for the first time in the Sinai legislation, namely in 'the tablets of stone' (24.12). This motif ends the directions in 31.18, and becomes the rhetorical and redactional means of adding another section to the original legislation begun in ch. 20. Exodus 20–31 now constitutes the original law which for the first time in the book in 34.28 is called 'the ten words', traditionally understood as the Ten Commandments (עצרת הדברים). While this expression refers to the decalogue, for the narrative this rubric encompasses all the Sinai legislation presented in Exodus. Furthermore, the book of Exodus presents this law as designed for present and future generations (24.12).

Finally, Exodus manifests yet another concept of תורה, namely as visionary experience. According to Exod. 25.9 (also 26.30, 27.8, 35.9, 40), the Israelites are to do all that 'I am showing you' (אותך אני מראה; cf. Num. 8–9) with respect to the construction of the taber-nacle.[33] This visionary presentation of תורה may reflect the influence of visionary prophecy. Östborn rightly argues that תורה is not used for prophetic vision,[34] but the content of תורה in Isa. 30.9 may refer,

---

33. For a discussion of the character of this visionary experience, see Hurowitz, *I Have Built you an Exalted House*, pp. 168-70.

34. Östborn, *Tora in the Old Testament*, p. 128. According to him, both priests and prophets had visionary experiences labelled as דבר (as a synonym of תורה). His further point, that דבר 'is used synonymously with' חזון, 'vision', is perhaps mis-leading since only a general sense of דבר (not a more specific sense synonymous with תורה) obtains in these contexts. As further support that the priests and prophets alike engaged in visions, Östborn cites 'Jer. 18.18 with Ezek. 7.26', but these verses intimate only that תורה is the proper domain of the priests while vision belongs to the prophets (so, too, Lam. 2.6). Similarly, the wisdom voice of Prov. 29.18 casts חזון and תורה in comparable terms relative to the social order, but this passage does not indicate the character of the two terms. The use of תורה in the legal sense in Ezek. 43.11-12 or 44.5 shows only the Aaronid background which this book shares with the priestly tradition of most legislation in Leviticus and Numbers (see the excursus to the previous chapter above). Östborn holds that prophetic use of תורה derived sec-ondarily from the priesthood. For a prophetic call to obey divine תורה, see Isa. 1.10; 5.24; the precise sense of תורה in this type of case is unknown. BDB, pp. 435-36 cites a number of cases of תורה in prophetic texts where it is unclear whether the term refers to priestly or prophetic teaching (Isa. 42.21, 24; 51.7; Jer. 9.12; 16.11; 26.4; 44.10, 23; Hos. 8.12; Amos 2.4; Hab. 1.4; Zech. 7.12; cf. Pss. 37.31; 40.9), but this difficulty applies as well to Isa. 1.10 and 5.24. If the second term of 'the Torah and the Words' (את התורה את הדברים) in Zech. 7.12 were understood as legal

at least in part, to the content of prophetic visions. Similarly, the תורה transmitted in Isa. 8.16 may include prophetic teaching obtained through visionary means. In sum, some law in Exodus, in this case priestly instructions for the tabernacle, is conveyed in visionary as well as in oral and written forms to Moses. As the different sets of legal collections were accumulated, they involved four concepts of how to give and convey torah. Torah was ultimately the rubric for all of the varied forms of divine teaching. Prophecy, oral and written teaching and even divine oracles became transmuted into a single teaching given context and identity in Exodus.

4. *The Linkage of Law and Narrative*

The book of Exodus does not represent simply a late combination of 'legal sections' and 'narrative sections'. Rather, the linkage of legal and narrative materials under the genre of covenant was probably an old one that partially governed the evolution of Exodus 19–40. This point might be suggested from Psalms 50 and 81, which may show the old cultic setting of Sinai law and narrative.[35] The connection of material in Exodus 19–40 to material in Exodus 1–18 at different levels of the tradition perhaps suggests that teaching served as the basic rubric which subsumed the highly variegated genres within the book.[36] The book of Exodus extends the integration of law and narrative through many loose verbal connections. The parallel wording in the Ten Commandments in 20.6 and the divine declaration during the manifestation

---

material, then the prophets would be understood as teachers of legal material (see D.L. Petersen, *Haggai and Zechariah 1–8* [OTL; Philadelphia: Westminster Press, 1984], p. 292). The second term may refer, however, to prophetic texts, according to some commentators (see C.L. and E.M. Meyers, *Haggai, Zechariah 1–8* [AB, 25B; New York: Doubleday, 1987], p. 402). Cf. Dan. 9.10-13. These issues are difficult and beyond the scope of this study.

35. See the previous section as well as Chapter 9, section 2.

36. For helpful discussions of the combination of genres in biblical literature, see Damrosch, *The Narrative Covenant*, pp. 41-43; F.W. Dobbs-Allsopp, *Weep, O Daughter of Zion: A Study in the City-Lament Genre in the Hebrew Bible* (BibOr, 44; Rome: Pontifical Biblical Institute, 1993), pp. 15, 97-98. For a historical assessment for the linkage of narrative and law, see J.D. Watts, 'Rhetorical Strategy in the Composition of the Pentateuch', *JSOT* 68 (1995), pp. 3-22; *idem*, 'Public Readings and Pentateuchal Law', *VT* 45 (1995), pp. 540-57.

to Moses in 34.6[37] predates the priestly redaction. The priestly redaction also shows the same phrases in both narrative and legal material. The beginning-point for priestly narrative and law is the self-revelation of Yahweh through this name. The basic expression 'I am Yahweh' opens and closes the initial section of the priestly commission of Moses (Exod. 6.2, 8). These words also open the Ten Commandments in 20.2. The phrase recurs elsewhere in the priestly editorial composition of Exod. 6.5, 7, 29, 7.5 as well as in the priestly gloss of 29.37 and the priestly composition of 31.14. Similarly, the expression, 'as Yahweh commanded', echoes in both narrative (7.10, 20) and legal sections (35.29; 36.1; 38.22; 39.1, 5, 7, 21, 26, 29, 31, 32, 42, 43; 40.16, 19, 21, 23, 25, 27, 29, 32; cf. 29.35; 31.6, 11; 35.4). Exod. 4.28 uses the expression כל דברי יהוה, 'all the words of Yahweh', a phrase also in 23.3-4 which with אלה הדברים ('These are the words') in 19.6 forms a bracket around the Ten Commandments and the Covenant Code (see also 'the words', הדברים, in Exod. 34.1, 27-28; 35.1). The content of these phrases provides a common basis for both the narrative of Exodus and the instructions for the cult, and thereby creates a fundamental unity between them.

Furthermore, law and priestly instructional literature penetrate narrative, and narrative penetrates law and instructional literature. In Exodus narrative extends into law in different ways. Legal texts commonly make the exodus event the basis or rationale for law. The beginning of the decalogue in Exod. 20.2 cites the exodus event as the basis for the legal relationship between Israel and Yahweh. Exod. 20.2 has the effect of connecting the exodus event with legal material.[38] The first words from Yahweh identify this deity as the deity of the Exodus, and the legal sections that follow this identification are predicated on the exodus event. In this sense, law is related to narrative. The Covenant Code in Exod. 23.15 likewise relates the law of pilgrimage at Passover with the exodus.

In a rather different manner, the priestly gloss to the legal material in Exodus 29 relates the narrative of the exodus to the law of the Tent of Meeting. As part of a gloss to Exodus 29 (noted at the end of the last chapter), Exod. 29.46 states that the Tent of Meeting and the accompanying cultic assemblage function so that Yahweh will dwell among the Israelites. By this means of relationship the Israelites will

---

37. Moberly, *At the Mountain of God*, p. 97.
38. For 20.2, see Childs, *Introduction*, p. 174.

know that Yahweh brought them out of Egypt 'that I might abide among them'. The Exodus event was the necessary requisite for the consummation of the legal relationship between Israel and its deity. These glosses show priestly connections made between law and narrative.[39]

Law penetrates narrative as well. One instance of this phenomenon involves the many connections between the Covenant Code and Exodus 1–15. D. Daube argues that many usages in the Exodus story are based on known social practices reflected in legal material, including the Covenant Code.[40] Some examples may illustrate Daube's claim. First, the root יצא*, 'to depart', appears in the laws of redemption in the seventh year in Exod. 21.2, 7, 11 as well as thirty-five times for the Israelites' departure from Egypt.[41] Daube suggests that the legal language in the Covenant Code served as the model for the Exodus presentation of Israel's departure from Egypt. Secondly, the root שלח* for 'sending' the Israelites from Egypt occurs about forty times in sections B and C. According to Daube this language derives from social usage as attested in Exod. 21.26, that a master who mistreats his slaves by dislodging their eye or tooth must release the slaves (שלח*).[42] Thirdly, in Daube's view Pharaoh's 'afflicting' (ענה* 'to afflict [a dependent]') of the Israelites in Exod. 1.11-12 and the Israelites' cry to Yahweh to 2.23 is related to material in the Covenant Code (22.21-24).[43] Pharaoh has 'afflicted' (ענה) the Israelites in Exod. 1.11-12 and therefore Yahweh hears their cry (2.23; 3.7, 9; 14.10, 15).[44] According to the Covenant Code, Yahweh will hear the

39. See Watts, 'Rhetorical Strategy', p. 21.

40. Daube, *The Exodus Pattern*. Daube also studied the influence of the 'exodus pattern' beyond the book of Exodus. In this vein, see more recently Zakovitch, *'And You Shall Tell Your* Son . . . , pp. 46-98. See also Blenkinsopp, *The Pentateuch*, p. 143.

41. Daube, *The Exodus Pattern*, p. 31.

42. Daube, *The Exodus Pattern*, p. 29.

43. Daube, *The Exodus Pattern*, pp. 26-27. They also cry to Pharaoh 5.8, 15 (J).

44. Perhaps the P amplifications in 1.13-14 and 2.23-25 are designed to heighten the presentation of 'affliction'. Fretheim ('The Plagues', p. 394) notes further that as punishment for causing the Israelites to cry, the Egyptians cry as well (11.6; 12.30). Levenson (*The Hebrew Bible*, p. 171) notes that Lev. 25.43, 46, and 53 forbid that a Hebrew slave be worked בפרך, 'ruthlessly', the word which Exod. 1.13-14 uses

cry of the dependent who is afflicted wrongly. It should be noted that
the various narrative texts apparently utilizing the legal practices appear in different 'sources' or 'redactions' in Exodus 1–14.[45]

Taken cumulatively, Daube argues, material in the Covenant Code
served as the legal justification for the Israelites' release. For Daube[46]
these examples indicate that P used various legal practices as a model
for the departure from Egypt. Daube comments: 'Obviously P accepts
fully the construction of the exodus on legal lines. Such proclamations
should not, as is commonly done, be dismissed as mere rhetoric: they
testify to a profound influence of that basic view of the event.'[47] Furthermore, P gives these correspondences a general interpretation by
applying the word שׁפטים, '(acts of) judgment', in 6.6, 7.4 and 12.12 to
the divine response to Pharaoh.[48] By labelling these actions as שׁפטים,
the divine actions are presented as standing in accordance with משׁפטים,
'(legal) judgments' (Exod. 21.1). This connection lies more in the realm
of paranomasia (based on different meanings of the same root) than in
proximate meanings, as שׁפטים refers to miraculous acts while משׁפטים
are legal judgments.[49]

to describe Egypt's treatment of Israel. Levenson regards the usages in both the law
and narrative as one theology.

45. Daube, *The Exodus Pattern*, p. 38.

46. Daube (*The Exodus Pattern*, p. 26) relates the status of Israel as גֵר in
Gen. 47.4 to Exod. 22.20 and 23.9. Daube (*The Exodus Pattern*, pp. 61, 87) and
U. Cassuto (*A Commentary on the Book of Exodus* [trans. I. Abrahams; Jerusalem:
Magnes, 1967], p. 44) relate the despoliation of Egyptians (Exod. 3.21-22, J; 11.2-
3, E; 12.35-36, J) to rules concerning the dismissal of the slave with 'openhandness'
(Deut. 15.13). This motif appears also in in the language of Holy War (e.g. 1 Sam.
6.3; 2 Sam. 1.22; Jer. 50.9; see B. Couroyer, 'Note sur II Sam., I, 22 et Is., LV,
10-11', *RB* 88 [1981], p. 505-14). Similarly, the appearance of Israelites at times
of pilgrimage before Yahweh 'not empty-handed' (ריקם לֹא; Exod. 23.15; 34.20;
Deut. 16.16) may be dependent on the usage in Holy War in signifying the bringing
of tribute to the divine king. The other aspects of Holy War language noted by
Wilson ('The Hardening of Pharaoh's Heart', pp. 33-34) would appear to militate in
this direction for ריקם in Exod. 3.21.

47. Daube, *The Exodus Pattern*, p. 36.

48. Daube, *The Exodus Pattern*, p. 37.

49. Daube, *The Exodus Pattern*, p. 37. It should be noted that the Samaritan
Pentateuch reads משׁפטים for שׁפטים at Exod. 7.4. Cf. the readings of this word in
Exod. 6.6 in 4QGen–Exodᵃ, frg. 25, col. ii, l. 4 in E. Ulrich *et al.*, *Qumran Cave 4*,
pp. 25-26. That these readings are indicative of some perceived thematic relationship
between these two etymologically related words is unclear.

While Daube sees P's deliberate hand behind these connections, it may be preferable to view these associations in terms of a fundamental insight which M. Noth discusses at the end of his monumental work, *A History of Pentateuchal Traditions*:

> The question still remains as to whether the combination of the sources— even though the purpose of this was simply to augment the tradition- material through addition—actually did not give rise to something new, which transcended the individual sources and their particular content and put them in a peculiar light, beyond the conscious intentions of the redac- tors. The question is whether this combination has not resulted, perhaps unintentionally, in unexpected narrative connections and theological in- sights, and hence whether in the final analysis the whole has not become greater than merely the sum of the parts. . . Therefore, it also the task of scholarship to take into its purview this totality in the form in which it has been transmitted.[50]

Daube's connections may be viewed in terms of Noth's 'unexpected narrative connections' which cumulatively result in a legal interpreta- tion of the exodus event. On the synchronic level these correspon- dences link the exodus narrative in section B (Exod. 3–14) with legal materials in section B' (Exod. 19–40).

H. Nasuti offers some astute theological observations about these kinds of narrative connections in Exodus law.[51] As Israelite readers identify with their ancestors mentioned in so-called motive clauses ('do x because you were sojourners in the land of Egypt', for instance in Exod. 22.20, 23.9), they not only identify themselves with their ancestors, but recognize that their freedom is the fulfillment of Yahweh's work in Egypt and Sinai. Moreover, commands to rest on the Sabbath, which invoke as a motive Yahweh's own behavior such as resting on the seventh day of creation (Exod. 20.8-11), express a di- vine ideal of holiness for the community. On the one side is an iden- tification with the past experience of freedom by Yahweh and on the other is an imitation of divine action and attributes. Nasuti remarks: 'The Pentateuchal laws work to preserve both identities. Put in another way, the laws work to define Israel's present identity in terms of its past status and its future goal.'[52] Overall the interpenetration of

---

50. Noth, *A History of Pentateuchal Traditions*, p. 250.

51. Nasuti, 'Identity, Identification, and Imitation: The Narrative Hermeneutics of Biblical Law', *The Journal of Law and Religion* 4 (1986), pp. 9-23, esp. pp. 15-19.

52. Nasuti, 'Identity, Idenitification, and Imitation', p. 18.

Exodus narrative and Exodus law and instructional literature produces a cohesion between sections of materials that are otherwise disparate in genre and historical background and development. This interpenetration is not restricted to Exodus 1–15 and the Covenant Code, but extends to the book as a whole and it effects a statement of Israel's identity. Law and narrative together provide a context and possibility for the real freedom gained through the community's relationship with Yahweh. This deeper interpenetration of narrative and law produces a more extensive form of instruction for shaping Israelite moral identity.[53] The community's participation in learning the story and the law together shapes identity.

This insight is indeed a theological one, but it hardly belongs only to people with theological interests. Here I would like to refer to the impact that this revolution in viewing narrative and law has made in legal studies. In an article in the *Harvard Law Review* in 1983, the lamented Robert Cover made a case for the understanding of law which has deeply affected the legal community in the United States:

> In this normative world, law and narrative are inseparably related. Every prescription is insistent in its demand to be located in discourse—to be supplied with history and destiny, beginning and end, explanation and purpose. And every narrative is insistent in its demand for its prescriptive point, its moral. History and literature cannot escape their location in a normative universe, nor can prescription, even when embodied in a legal text, escape its origin and its end in experience, in the narratives that are the trajectories plotted upon material reality by our imaginations.[54]

Cover's article reflects centuries of Jewish tradition contemplating the intersection and interaction between law and story, and the roots of this intellectual and spiritual dynamic lie in Exodus and the other books of the Pentateuch. Exodus is precisely the book of Israel's origins: as an enslaved people now free, its law calls it to understand and grasp its destiny in covenantal relationship with Yahweh. In reading

---

53. Cf. Sir. 24.24 (RSV).

54. Cover, 'The Supreme Court, 1982 Term–Forward: *Nomos* and Narrative', *Harvard Law Review* 97.1 (1983), p. 5; quoted and discussed in G. Tucker, 'The Sayings of the Wise are Like Goads: An Appreciation of the Works of Robert Cover', *Conservative Judaism* 45.3 (1993), p. 22. Tucker describes Cover's work: 'Cover sought to effect a revolution in how people would see the legal universe. Rules and the narratives in which they are embedded would henceforth have to be treated with parity, as equal partners in the creation of a normative universe' (p. 21).

Exodus, past and future intersect in the moment of the community's present. In encountering this book, Israelites in every generation identify their own origins and destiny, in conjunction with their ancestors and descendents. In sum, the linkage of law and story led to the notion of Exodus as תורה, 'teaching'. While this claim is not found in Exodus, this final stage in the community's understanding of it is inferred from its place in the Jewish and Christian canons.

Exodus presents the foundational teaching of Israel's ancient heritage, and it does so in a cultically suffused way that displays Israel's ongoing experience of its deity. The book expresses a vision of holinesss for all Israel *in toto*, resulting in a delimitation of outer boundaries. The purpose of Exodus's teaching involves a delimitation of inner boundaries as well. (This may be the reason for the presentation of so many specifically priestly matters to all of Israel.) While Israel should understand itself in terms of the priestly understanding of holiness, various groups of Israeites should also understand their different places within the divine plan of holiness. Moses so represents Yahweh's view of this religious delineation in Lev. 10.3 (NJPS):

> Then Moses said to Aaron: 'This is what the Lord meant when He said:
> Through those near to Me I show Myself holy,
> And gain glory before all the people'.[55]

The total result of the priestly materials and redaction in Exodus is not simply information for Israelites about the priesthood, but a reformulation of Israel's primary identity: thanks to their sacred institutions, Israel is to be transformed into a fundamentally special and sacred, even priestly, people (Exod. 19.5-6) which belongs no longer to Pharaoh, but to Yahweh.[56] S.D. McBride remarks on the priestly vision for Israel: 'When, under the close supervision of Moses and Aaron, Israel carries out the divine instructions, it is transformed from

---

55. If NJPS has correctly rendered the force of this verse, then it shows yet another aspect of Law, that Law is not transparent but requires interpretation. While the subsequent traditions have also presupposed this point as a fact of life, it is rarely explicitly acknowledged in the biblical text. However, the referent of the divine citation is unclear and the verb rendered by NJPS as 'meant' (דבר) has been understood in other ways (on both points see Milgrom, *Leviticus 1–16*, p. 600). In either case, the verse constitutes an interesting instance of citation of the divine word to apply to a situation presented in narrative.

56. So see Levenson, 'Liberation Theology', pp. 30-36. See also Levenson, *The Hebrew Bible*, pp. 127-59.

a tribal assembly into an articulated cultic community, a human temple as it were, both serving and sustained by the sovereign God who tabernacles in their midst'.[57] The book of Exodus as rendered by the priestly redaction taught Israelites that the cultic institutions and events presented in the book reflect not only their ancestors' ancient passage from the slavery of Egypt to the freedom of Sinai lived through תורה. Rather, the book teaches their own passage as well, and 'throughout their generations' (Exod. 31.16).

57. McBride, 'Biblical Literature', p. 23. See also Sarna, *Exodus*, pp. xiii, xv. On the theology of covenant in Exodus, see Levenson, Review of *God and his People*, by E.W. Nicholson, p. 307.

Chapter 11

EPILOGUE: EXODUS IN THE PENTATEUCH

The significance of Exodus is not restricted to its own boundaries. Within the Pentateuch Exodus holds wider ramifications. The priestly itinerary notices in Exodus and Numbers (discussed above in Chapter 6) point to the larger architecture produced by the priestly redaction of the whole Pentateuch. This chapter proceeds in five parts: (1) introduction to current proposals as to the structural relations between Exodus and Numbers and preliminary considerations; (2) analysis of geographical markers in these two books; (3) examination of chronological markers in these books; (4) further reflections on the relationship between Exodus and Numbers; and (5) some broader implications of the markers for the formation and form of the Pentateuch.

1. Current Proposals

The structure of Genesis–Deuteronomy has emerged as a significant line of research after many decades devoted to studying their sources, redactions and other aspects. Current proposals for the literary structure of the Pentateuch tend to focus on the symmetry displayed especially between Exodus and Numbers.[1] J. Milgrom, for example, argues for the general chiastic arrangement of features in Exodus

---

1. D.J.A. Clines is to be noted for raising the question of the Pentateuch as a whole in his *The Theme of the Pentateuch* (JSOTSup, 10; Sheffield: JSOT Press, 1978). Clines's agenda is generally synchronic and thematic in its concerns. R.N. Whybray also broaches the issue of synchronic study of the Pentateuch as a whole, but the agenda is pursued on the level of theme. Whybray regards the Pentateuch ultimately as the product of a single author who intended it to serve as the preface to the Deuteronomistic History. This view assumes the importance of deuteronomistic material in the Pentateuch, but does not come fully to grips with the final priestly redaction of the Pentateuch. See Whybray, *The Making of the Pentateuch*, pp. 221-42; *idem, Introduction to the Pentateuch*, pp. 133-43.

through Numbers, with the Sinai material of Exodus 19 through Numbers 10 standing as the middle and obviously major element.[2] Similarly, A. Schart has proposed a 'Ringstruktur' surrounding the Sinai legislation[3]:

A	Exod. 15.22-25		Wasserumwandlung ('transformation of the water' from bitter to sweet)
	B	17.1-7	Wasser aus dem Felsen ('water from the rock')
		C 17.8-16	Krieg: Amalek–Israel ('Amalekite–Israelite war')
		D 18	Entlastung des Mose (leadership 'relief for Moses')
		E 18.27	der Midianiter Jitro (חתן משה) ('the Midianite Hobab' who is 'Moses' father-in-law')
		F 19.1-2	Ankunft am Sinai ('arrival at Sinai')

SINAI

		F´ Num. 10.11-23	Aufbruch vom Sinai ('departure from Sinai')
		E´ 10.29-32	der Midianiter Hobab (חתן משה) . . . ('the Midianite Hobab' who is 'Moses' father-in-law')
		D´ 11	Entlastung des Mose (leadership 'relief for Moses')
		C´ 14.39-45	Krieg: Israel–Amalek ('Amalekite–Israelite war')
	B´	20.1-13	Wasser aus dem Felsen ('water from the rock')
A´	21.16-18		Brunnen ('the spring')

The general thrust of this arrangement may be discerned by comparing some of its correspondences. The positive tone of the murmuring stories in Exod. 15.22–17.7 relative to the more negative accents in the murmuring narratives in Numbers 11 and 20 would suggest that the material after Sinai in Numbers is, at least in part, the negative image of the material before Sinai in Exodus.[4] As noted in Chapter 9, the selection and general tone in the first three stories in Exod. 15.22–17.7 may be due in part to the purposes of the priestly redaction. The question is why the priestly redaction left the positive tone relatively intact. It may be suggested tentatively that the priestly redaction may have interpreted the Exodus passages as the people's pilgrimage to the mountain. In contrast, Numbers might be regarded as depicting a pilgrimage

---

2. See Milgrom, *The JPS Torah Commentary. Numbers* במדבר, pp. xvii-xviii (henceforth *Numbers*).

3. Schart, *Mose und Israel im Konflikt*, p. 52.

4. Milgrom argues that in the Exodus murmuring stories the Israelites had not yet accepted the Sinai revelation and therefore were not yet subject to divine punishment. The degree to which this view is anachronistic is debatable. See Milgrom, *Numbers*, p. xvi.

journey from the mountain to the sanctuary-land, but not in a manner precisely parallel to Exodus. Numbers manifests a dialectic between the anti-pilgrimage of the older generation which departs Sinai and sins, on the one hand, and on the other hand, the pilgrimage of the new generation born in the wilderness and prepared to reach the promised land. In Exodus, the water in the wilderness is a source of divine blessing to the people in their pilgrimage journey (described in Chapter 1), but it is a source of testing the people in the book of Numbers.

The more positive tone set in Exod. 15.22–16.35 may be attributed to the positive view of the Exodus journey. The theme of pilgrimage informed the formation of chs. 19–24, and the older traditions of chs. 16 and 17 may have been construed accordingly. The treatment of the Amalekites in Exod. 17.8-16 and Num. 14.39-43 follows suit: the first passage witnesses the Israelites' utter defeat of the Amalekites while the second mentions the Amalekites as victors over the Israelites. Schart also observes that the Israelites' testing (נסה*) Yahweh 'these ten times' (זה עשׂר פעמים) in Num. 14.22 corresponds to the number of the plagues in the priestly redaction of Exodus.[5] In short, the narrative material in the book of Numbers shows an inverse relationship with the narrative in Exodus, a notion that was not lost on later tradition: '...the Lord, who once for all saved a people out of the land of Egypt, afterward destroyed those who did not believe' (Jude 5). Besides the positive-negative mirror images of Israel reflected in the pre- and post-Sinai material, a further notion of import for understanding the priestly redaction of Exodus and Numbers might be suggested: the Egyptians destroyed in the book of Exodus serve both as foil to the saved Israelites in the book of Exodus and perhaps as a foreshadowing to the same generation of Israelites who perish in the wilderness in the book of Numbers.

To these observations may be added some relevant points made by J.H. Sailhammer.[6] He notes a general correspondence between the figures of Pharaoh and Balak in opposing the Israelites. More specifically, Israel is 'a mighty nation' (Exod. 1.9) against whom Pharaoh's heart is 'hard' (כבד*). Similarly, Israel is called 'a mighty nation' (Num. 22.3, 6) and Balaam is 'honored' (כבד*). In both the plagues narratives

---

5. Schart, personal communication. Num. 14.14 likewise echoes the dialogue in Exod. 33 and Num. 14.18 echoes (or cites?) Exod. 34.6-8.

6. J.H. Sailhammer, *The Pentateuch as Narrative: A Biblical–Theological Commentary* (Grand Rapids: Eerdmans, 1992), pp. 42-44

and the Balaam narratives, the root כבד* functions as a key word (Exod. 7.14; 8.11, 28; 9.7, 34; 10.1; 14.4; Num. 22.17, 37; 24.11). Sailhammer's analysis perhaps sheds light on the placement of the poems of Exodus 15 and Numbers 22–24, which demarcate the books to which they belong and thereby balance one another in function. These insights will play a role in the analysis offered below. Sailhammer's points highlight an overall balance between the first part of Exodus and the final section of Number in that both involve holy war.

These studies[7] into the structure of Exodus and Numbers may be extended by examining the significance of geography and chronology in these books. Indeed, within the geographical and chronological markers of the priestly redaction, Schart's contributions will receive further definition and focus. Two caveats should be noted at the outset. This analysis is premised on the general consensus reached on the priestly material and redaction of Exodus and Numbers (discussed in Chapter 5, section 4). Exodus and Numbers show a number of priestly glosses and compositions, which point to major priestly redactional activity in these books. This redaction is part of a long priestly tradition which made several contributions to the Pentateuch and its formation, including geographical and temporal markers indicating the major blocks of material. Indeed, as commentators have noted, such markers are a staple of the priestly organization of Pentateuchal material.

Furthermore, Leviticus is not examined in this chapter because it contains none of these chronological markers. From the chronological discrepancy between Exodus 40 and Numbers 1, it might be inferred that the redaction of Exodus–Leviticus–Numbers allows a few weeks for the events of the book of Leviticus at Mount Sinai. So B.A. Levine comments: 'all of the activities prescribed in the Torah between Exodus 40 and Numbers 7 occurred within only a few weeks. Although no dates are given in the book of Leviticus for any events, the entire context of Leviticus belongs, as well, to the beginning of the wilderness period, according to the priestly chronology.'[8]

---

7.   For another proposal for the structure of Numbers, see M. Douglas, *In the Wilderness: The Doctrine of Defilement in the Book of Numbers* (JSOTSup, 158; Sheffield: JSOT Press, 1994). For some trenchant criticisms, see R. Gnuse, Review of *In the Wilderness*, by M. Douglas, *CBQ* 57 (1995), pp. 124-25.

8.   B.A. Levine, *Numbers 1–20* (AB, 4; New York: Doubleday, 1993), p. 253. See also Milgrom, *Numbers*, pp. 4, 364.

2. *Geography in Exodus and Numbers*

In the most general terms, Exodus through Numbers exhibits a basic geographical symmetry: Egypt–Sinai–Wilderness/Transjordan. The Israelites travel from Egypt to Sinai, sojourn at Sinai, and then travel from Sinai through the wilderness. The itinerary notices in Exodus and Numbers largely balance one another: six notices chart the Israelites' journey from Egypt to Rephidim, the station before Sinai (Exod. 12.37a; 13.20; 14.1-2; 15.22a; 16.1; 17.1) and six notices follow the Israelites from Sinai to the plains of Moab in Numbers (Exod. 19.2; Num. 10.12; 20.1, 22; 21.10-11; 22.1).[9] 'Thus Exodus and Numbers, at least in their wilderness narratives, reveal the same redactional hand.'[10] These notices mark not only smaller units; within the priestly redaction they indicate the boundaries of the major middle sections of the books. Through the notices the priestly redaction indicates balance and correspondence between the two journeys to and from Sinai, as suggested by the following schema:

Exodus	*Numbers*
1.1–15.21 in Egypt	1.1–10.10 at Mount Sinai
15.22—ch. 18 in the wilderness	10.11—ch. 21 in the wilderness
19–40 at Mount Sinai	22–36 in Transjordan

In general, the priestly arrangement of Exodus and Numbers presents the geographical progression in the book of Numbers in part as an inversion of the progression in Exodus. The Sinai legislation places Exodus 19–40 and Num. 1.1–10.10 at Mount Sinai. Both sections focus on the tabernacle and the creation of sacred space in and around it. For the final block of Exodus, it is the creation of the tabernacle itself. For the first major block of Numbers, the concern is the arrangement of the camp personnel around the tabernacle and the materials for the tabernacle.

As noted above, Exodus and Numbers use itinerary notices to mark a major middle wilderness section. The itinerary notices demarcate Num. 10.11–21.35 as a major unit. Furthermore, Num. 10.11–21.35 makes frequent mention of the wilderness (by different names) in 10.12, 20.1, 21.11, 13, 18, 23. It is pertinent to note at this point that

9.   So Cross, *Canaanite Myth*, pp. 310-17; Milgrom, *Numbers*, p. xvii.
10.   Milgrom, *Numbers*, p. xvii.

Schart's observation of 'Ringstruktur' around the Sinai material assumes that ch. 21 ends the second major block in Numbers. The new
geographical marker ('in the plains of Moab beyond the Jordan at
Jericho') at 22.1 delimits the third major section as chs. 22–36. This
division follows Childs' proposal (following R. de Vaux) to see 10.11–
21.35 as a unit, which is based on the content of Numbers 21, specifically the defeat of the Amorite kings in this chapter, and not on
any redactional markers.[11] Childs notes the geographical itinerary for
chs. 10–36, but his analysis focuses on the contents, and his considerations do not include the schema the redaction seems to give to the
contents of the narrative. To be sure, Childs's reading is not limited to
a specific redactional schema, but in either case his view would appear
supported by the important geographical marker in 22.1.[12] Finally,
Egypt in Exodus 1–15 and Transjordan in Numbers 27–34 correspond
in the schema of Exodus and Numbers. Egypt is the beginning point
and Transjordan brings the Israelites to the brink of their final destination.

3. *Chronology in Exodus and Numbers*

Exodus
The chronological markers in Exodus through Numbers have received
less attention than geographical markers, in part because they are scattered and the priestly tradition does not provide a helpful summary of

---

11. Childs, *Introduction*, pp. 194-99.

12. At this juncture it is interesting to note how at odds the suggestions of Childs
and Olson are here. Both base their claims on content which each scholar views as
important. Without redactional markers to serve as guides, it would be difficult, if
not impossible, to adjudicate between these claims. See Olson, *The Death of the Old*,
p. 83. The scholarly discrepancy between Childs and Olson is discussed by
R. Knierim, *The Task of Old Testament Theology: Method and Cases* (Grand
Rapids: Eerdmans, 1995), p. 381. Knierim regards Numbers at its highest structural
level as the saga of a campaign and therefore consists of only two parts, the organization and execution of the campaign. See *The Task of Old Testament Theology*,
p. 384. This is a valuable insight and is indeed supported by some comparable ancient
Near Eastern itineraries (see Davies, 'The Wilderness Itineraries: A Comparative
Study', p. 80). In view of Numbers' relations with Exodus, this view is not an ex-
haustive indication of overall structure. To his credit, Knierim recognizes the importance of chronological and geographical markers; for him these stand at a lower
structural level. See below in section 3 for further discussion.

them, as is found for the itinerary notices in Numbers 33. Yet given
the importance of time exhibited in priestly legislation, the chronological markers in Exodus and Numbers may hold some helpful information for the priestly arrangement of these books.

The chronological markers in Exodus present the better part of a
year, as indicated in the following list:

Year 1, Month 1, Days 14–21 = Passover/Unleavened Bread
Exod. 12.2:   'This month shall mark for you the beginning of the
                      months; it shall be the first of the months of the year
                      for you' (see also 12.17-18).
Exod. 12.41:   'at the end of the four hundred and thirtieth year, to
                      the very day, all the ranks of the Lord departed from
                      the land of Egypt' (cf. Num. 33.3 = exodus from
                      Egypt on the fifteenth day of the first month).

Month 3, Day 1 = Weeks
Exod. 19.1:   'On the third new moon after the Israelites had gone
                      forth from the land of Egypt, on that very day, they
                      entered the wilderness of Sinai'.
Exod. 19.16 (19.11)   = day 3 (divine appearance)

Year 2, Month 1, Day 1 = New Year's
Exod. 40.17:   'On the first month of the second year, on the first of
                      the month, the Tabernacle was set up'. Cf. 40.2.

The chronological markers in Exodus 12 begin a new temporal reckon-
ing. While time is counted by years from Genesis 1 through Exodus 11,
Exodus 12 initiates a counting of time that is focused on the cycle of
the year. This chapter signals the first pilgrimage feast as the appropriate time for the departure from Egypt. The relationship between the
feast of Passover/Unleavened Bread and the exodus story is generally
regarded as pre-exilic. The ancient connection between Passover and
the exodus was inherited by the priestly tradition which made it serve
as the cornerstone of Pentateuchal chronology in the life of the people
of Israel from their departure from Egypt onwards. The chronological
scheme was not extended backwards. Rather, it was extended only forward.

The chronological marker given in Exod. 19.1 signals the feast of
Weeks although the feast is not explicitly celebrated in Exodus 19 as
with Passover in Exodus 12–13. It is sometimes assumed that the
attachment of the theme of Sinai to the feast of Weeks is a rabbinic
invention, despite the unlikelihood of a pure rabbinic fiction in the

liturgical calendar. Yet the marker in Exod. 19.1 is hardly made casually. The verse clearly associates Sinai with Weeks. R. Hendel makes
the point: 'In the Priestly chronological framework of Exodus it is
clear that the ceremony in Ex 24,3-8 occurs during the spring festival
of Shabuot (Ex 19,1)'.[13] As noted above in Chapter 1 on pilgrimage
feasts, the connection between Weeks and Sinai is a late biblical priestly development. It is difficult to pin down the date for the connection
any further, but the evidence of Exod. 19.1 cannot be dismissed out of
hand.[14] Exod. 19.1 itself represents probably a late (biblical period)
chronological marker that makes the connection. Indeed, Exod. 19.1-2a
shows the style of the priestly tradition, and its temporal marker
should be generally regarded in the same light as the other priestly
chronological markers. With the description of Passover in Exodus
12–13, the priestly redaction had inherited the connection between pilgrimage feast and Pentateuchal event. This type of connection was extended to the Sinai covenant and the feast of Weeks secondarily by the
chronological marker in Exod. 19.1.

The chronological markers in Exod. 40.2, 17 mark the turn of the
year. The chronological marker refers to New Year (Rosh Hashanah).[15]
Although it might be supposed that Exod. 40.2, 17 refers to the time
of Booths (Sukkot), as this feast occurs at 'the end of the year' (Exod.
23.16) or 'the turn of the year' (Exod. 34.22), priestly calendars such as
Numbers 28–29 distinguish the two feasts and clearly assign to the first
day of the year to New Year's and not Booths. New Year's in Exod.
40.1 evokes the new creation of Israel's relationship with Yahweh
through the creation of the tabernacle and thereby hearkens back to
the priestly creation of the world in Genesis 1. In sum, the chronological markers in the book of Exodus suggest a year arranged primarily
according to two of three pilgrimage feasts: Passover begins the series
with the exodus from Egypt, the Israelites arrive at Sinai on the feast

13. See Hendel, 'Sacrifice as a Cultural System', p. 373.

14. B. Bäntsch and other older commentators regarded this marker as a late redactional means to relate the feast of Weeks with the Sinai covenant. See B. Bäntsch,
Exodus–Leviticus–Numeri (HAT; Göttingen: Vandenhoeck & Ruprecht, 1903), pp.
169-70, 171. Childs criticizes Bäntsch's further supposition that either the original
date had fallen out or was probably removed intentionally. See Childs, *The Book of
Exodus*, p. 342.

15. Milgrom, *The JPS Torah Commentary. Exodus* שמות (Philadelphia: The
Jewish Publication Society, 1991), p. 235.

of Weeks, and the tabernacle (מִשְׁכָּן) is completed around the New Year. A full year will not elapse, however, until Numbers 9–10.

Numbers
In general, the structure of the book of Numbers is very difficult to gauge. As M. Noth commented, 'within these various strata it is difficult to discern any definite lines of continuity'.[16] Chronology is hardly exceptional in this regard; it is considerably more complicated in the book of Numbers than in the book of Exodus. The main reason involves the tradition of the forty-year journey in the wilderness. So J. Milgrom comments:

> The tradition that Israel spent forty years in the wilderness following its Exodus from Egypt is demonstrably old (Deut. 1.46; Amos 2.10; 5.25). Yet the chronology within that forty-year period is marred by two major problems. The events of 1.1–10.11 cover nineteen days from the first to the nineteenth of the second month of the second year. Those of the final chapters 21.10–36.13 occur within five months of the fortieth year (see 20.28 = 33.38; 20.29; Deut. 1.3). The material in between, 10.12–21.9, is undated but must fall in the intervening thirty-eight years... All that can be said is that the wilderness traditions survived, in the main without fixed dates, and they were clustered at the beginning and at the end of the wilderness sojourn.[17]

As summarized by Milgrom, the book of Numbers, like the book of Exodus, contains chronological markers designed to provide some structure to the book:

Year 2, Month 2, Day 1
Num. 1.1:   'On the first day of the second month, in the second year following the exodus from the land of Egypt...'

Year 2, Month 1, Day 1 = Exod. 40.9-11 and Lev. 8.10 (older chronology?)
Num. 7.1:   'On the day that Moses finished setting up the Tabernacle...'

Year 2, Month 2, Day 14 = Passover
Num. 9.1:   'The Lord spoke to Moses in the wilderness of Sinai, on the first month of the second year following the exodus from the land of Egypt'.

---

16. Noth, *Numbers: A Commentary* (ET; London: SCM Press, 1968), p. 4. See the survey of P material discussed on pp. 4-11.

17. Milgrom, *Numbers*, p. xi.

Year 2, Month 2, Day 20 = end of Passover
Num. 10.11-12:   'In the second year, on the twentieth day of the
                        second month, the cloud lifted from the Tabernacle of
                        the Pact, and the Israelites set out on their journeys
                        from the wilderness of Sinai'.

Year 40, Month 1
Num. 20.1:   'The Israelites arrived in a body at the wilderness of
                        Zin on the first month'.

The book of Numbers works with two sets of chronological markers. The first set of markers in Num. 1.1, 7.1, 9.1, and 10.11 relates
to the chronology of Exodus and Leviticus. These markers chronologically mirror the beginning of the journey from Egypt. Clearly Num.
9.1 is a problem relative to the chronology of Num. 1.1. B.A. Levine
suggests a redactional explanation to the problem with this verse:
'There is a simple way of resolving this discrepancy. Most likely the
caption of Num. 9.1 already appeared in the text of Numbers before
the opening caption of the book was added, and may take us back to
Exod. 40.2.'[18] Milgrom prefers a literary solution to the problem; he
regards the chronological notice as 'a flashback'.[19] Did the incongruity
arise from some redactional reason, but the resultant redactor(s) read
the discrepancy in some manner akin to Milgrom's proposal? In any
case, the purpose of this temporal notation is to present the beginning
of the journey from Sinai in a way that echoes the exodus from Egypt
at Passover. With the return to Passover in Numbers 9–10, the cycle
of the year which began with the exodus from Egypt comes full circle
with the departure from Mount Sinai in Numbers 9–10. Prior to and
after Exodus 12 through Numbers 10, the time is counted in years,
but the special events within these chapters are marked according to
the liturgical calendar.[20] These events therefore are placed within the
compass of sacred time unlike the events preceding or following them.
In short, the year from departure to departure marks one liturgical
year which celebrates Passover at either end.

18. Levine, *Numbers 1–20*, p. 295.
19. Milgrom, *Numbers*, p. 67.
20. The shift with Exod. 12 was noted by Wellhausen, *Prolegomena*, p. 351.
For some of these liturgical connections, see in a different vein, J. van Goudoever,
'The Celebration of the Torah in the Second Isaiah', in Vermeylen (ed.), *The Book of
Isaiah*, pp. 313-17.

The second set of markers, specifically Num. 20.1, is connected to the forty-year sojourn (cf. Exod. 16.35). Despite the discrepancies between these two sets of markers, they are hardly unconnected. For despite the constraints placed on the priestly redaction by the tradition of the forty-year journey, the marker of Num. 20.1 returns to the beginning of the year just like Num. 1.1. While the chronological picture presented in the book of Numbers hardly reflects the sort of unified, coherent pattern apparent in the book of Exodus, nonetheless chronological markers provide indicators of structure for the different sections of Numbers. Because of the partial character of the notices in 7.1 and 20.1, Childs claims that 'it is highly unlikely that these notices form a structure for the book'.[21] However, such formal discrepancies hardly preclude the possibility that these markers bear some importance (which Childs does not address), and indeed the differences in form may not have affected the understanding of the temporal referents in 7.1 and 20.1. However, in agreement with Childs, chronological markers do not form the only basis for overall structure in Numbers, much less Exodus; rather, geography determines larger units. Geography supersedes chronology as the markers for major sections as shown by 7.1 and 9.11. It would seem that when the two types of coincide, for example, Exod. 19.1-2, chronology reinforces geography. However, as noted above, the chronological markers serve a variety of other functions, such as to structure and link the two departures from Egypt and Sinai.

The three sections in Numbers require some elaboration in light of the chronological markers. Apart from 1.1, the first block of material, 1.1–10.10, contains two chronological markers. The chronological marker in 7.1 may have been retained by the redaction in order to mark a transition between 1.1–6.27 and 7.1–10.10. The first section of 1–6 delineates personnel preparations for departure while the second section of 7.1–10.10 describes material preparations. The poetic priestly blessing in Num. 6.24-26 may serve as a transition between the two sections. The chronological marker in 9.1 is geared to refer back to the Exodus from Egypt and therefore to mark the final block of material in the first major section of Numbers.

The second section of material in 10.11–21.35 is striking for its absence of chronological markers apart from the notice in 10.11.

---

21. Childs, *Introduction*, p. 195.

Chronologically, this verse closes the first part of the book, but its geographical marker serves to delimit the middle section of the book. This section is devoted to two interrrelated themes: the sins of the old generation described in 11–16 and the related failure of the leaders to take the land in ch. 13. Chapters 17–19, though largely quite separate originally from 11–16, have been secondarily related by the connections forged between ch. 17 and the rebellion in ch. 16. In their present context, chs. 17–19 serve to make provisions for the kinds of sins experienced in chs. 11–16.[22] The successive stories and 'priestly concern' (to use Childs's phrase) in 10.11–21.35 set the stage for the separation of the old generation from the emerging one in the third and final section of Numbers. Accordingly, the chronological notice in 20.1 functions to mark the narrative as approaching the end of the old generation and entering the final stage in Transjordan. Indeed, the deaths of Miriam and Aaron in Numbers 20 reinforce the point that this chapter is marking the end of the old generation within the framework of the second major block of material. In sum, the overarching theme of the second major section of Numbers is the sin of the old generation and its failure to enter the land, in contrast with the third block's stress of the emergence of the new generation graced with the prospect of entering the land. The sins described in 11–16 prepare for the passing of the old generation which begins in ch. 20.

The final block of material, 22.1–36.13, resembles the second section in having a geographical notice standing at its head. The third block is devoted to two themes, both of which set it in relation to the second block. The second block in ch. 20 begins the theme of the death of the old generation with the deaths of Miriam and Aaron. The census in the third block, in ch. 26, located now in Transjordan, signals the emergence of the new generation. This conclusion holds major repercussions for Olson's theory regarding the place of the two census lists as the major indicators of structure in the book: 'The census lists in Numbers 1 and 26 serve to divide the book of Numbers into two separate generations of God's holy people on the march'.[23] Olson highlights the temporal and geographical markers in ch. 26, but their significance in relation to other clearly priestly markers is insufficiently

22. See Childs, *Introduction*, p. 198.
23. Olson, *The Death of the Old*, p. 83. Olson's division is followed by K.D. Sakenfeld, *Numbers: Journeying with God* (International Theological Commentary; Grand Rapids: Eerdmans; Edinburgh: Handsell, 1995), pp. 7-8.

explained. Olson stresses the change in geographical locale in Num.
26.3 ('in the plains of Moab by the Jordan at Jericho') compared to
Num. 1.1 ('in the wilderness of Sinai'), but Olson leaves unnoted the
geographical change in Num. 20.1 ('at the wilderness of Zin') or the
arrival to Transjordan noted in Num. 22.1 ('Then the Israelites set
out, and camped in the plains of Moab beyond the Jordan at Jericho').
In contrast, 'after the plague', in 26.1 is hardly a significant chronological marker in the priestly style. The chronological marker of Num.
20.1 ('The Israelites arrived in a body at the wilderness of Zin on the
first month') refers to year 40[24] and therefore delimits this section
from the preceding in a way wholly unlike the chronological marker
in 26.1 ('after the plague'), which marks only an immediate transition.
It is undoubtedly true, as Olson emphasizes, that the death of the old
generation and the birth of the new are central developments in the
book of Numbers, but this theme appears already in ch. 20. This chapter, with the geographical and chronological markers mentioned above,
begins the passing of the old generation with its description of the
deaths of Miriam (v. 1) and Aaron (vv. 28-29).[25] The end of the unit
marked by these deaths was at one time—before the inclusion of the
book of Deuteronomy—the death of Moses recounted now in Deuteronomy 34. The death of the old and the birth of the new constitutes
the major theme of chs. 20–36.

A further division within the third block can be proposed, one that
depends on anticipating the comparison of Exodus with Numbers in
the following section. As Sailhammer observes, the poems in Numbers
22–24 stand at the head of Number's final block just as Exodus 15.1-
21 mark the end of the first block in Exodus. The poems have a
delimiting function, described in greater detail below. If correct, then
Numbers 25–36 require explanation. Chapters 25–31 may constitute a
section here. Chapter 31 refers back not only to Balaam (v. 8), but
explicitly back to ch. 25 (v. 16). Chapters 25–31 would form a section
linked to and following 22–24. While Numbers 25–31 contains a diversity of materials, they mark the final turning point in the death of
the old generation in ch. 25, the emergence of the new generation
marked by the new census in 26 and the commission of Joshua in
27.12-23. Chapters 32–36 mark a shift to issues which involve preparation for the land: the assignment of Transjordan (32); Israel's

24. So most commentators, including NJPS, p. 241 n. a, citing Num. 33.36-38.
25. So Levine, *Numbers 1–20*, p. 483.

itinerary (33); the boundaries of the land (33); the Levitical cities and cities of refuge in the land (35); and the principle of keeping the family land intact in the land (36). While these materials are diverse in origin, within the book they stand together as shifting the perspective from the past journeys to the present moment, with the people poised and prepared to enter the land.

4. Relations between Exodus and Numbers

The preceding discussion makes clear that Num. 1.1–10.10, 10.11–21.35 and 22.1–36.13 are the three main units recognized by the priestly redaction. Furthermore, it is evident that these three sections stand in inverse relationship to the main three sections of Exodus, namely 1.1–15.21, 15.22–18.27 and 19.1–40.38. The inverse relationship between Exodus and Numbers was discussed at the outset of this chapter, in noting the proposals of Milgrom and Schart. The question is whether any further specific relations can be proposed on the basis of the book's specific geographical and chronological markers. Despite the apparent lack of 'formal literary markers' in Exodus,[26] the following structure, may be useful for determining further points of contact between Exodus and Numbers:

Exodus	*Numbers*
Egypt: The opposition of Pharaoh 1.1–15.21	*Transjordan*: The opposition of Balak and other nations 22.1–36.13
1–2 The emergence of Moses	
Moses' two calls and confrontations:	Preparations for the land:
3.1–6.1 Moses' first call and confrontation with Pharaoh	25–31 Preparation of new generation for the land
6.2–14.31 Moses' second call and Yahweh's confrontation with Pharaoh	32–36 Final preparations for the land
+ 15.1-21 *End-Poem*	22–24 *Preface Poems* +

26. The assessment belongs to Childs, *Introduction*, pp. 170-71. However, the following proposal accounts for the units and themes which Childs deems important to mention. I agree wholeheartedly with Childs's further judgment that 'the whole of Exodus is far greater than the sum of its parts' (*Introduction*, p. 173). For full discussion, see above Chapters 7 through 11.

Wilderness (Exodus)	*Wilderness (Numbers)*
15.22–18.27: solicitous care of Yahweh murmuring stories:	10.11–21.35: passing of the old, sinning generation murmuring stories.
16 manna and quail	11 manna and quail
17.1-7 water at Massah and Meribah	20.1-13 water at Meribah
17.8-16 battle with Amalek	14.39-45 battle with Amalek
18 help for Moses	11 help for Moses
18 Moses' father-in-law	10.29-32 Moses' father-in-law
Sinai (and tabernacle)	*Sinai* (and tabernacle)
19–31 first tablets, tabernacle commanded	1–6 personnel preparation around the tabernacle
32–40 second tablets, tabernacle executed	7.1–10.11 material preparation for tabernacle

In the redactional plan of Exodus and Numbers, the blocks of the books stand in inverse relation. The two books both divide generally into two major parts due to geography, Egypt and Sinai in Exodus, Sinai and Wilderness–Transjordan in Numbers. Chronology also serves to delimit each book into two major stages. The time in Egypt up to the exodus (Exod. 1–11) runs in the chronology of years until Passover marks its specific ending (Exod. 12–13), and the time at Sinai (Exod. 19–40) runs from Booths to New Year's. The time at Sinai in Numbers runs up to Passover (Num. 10.10), and then the wilderness journey (Num. 10.11–36.13) returns to a schema in terms of years, ending with forty years as the organizational principle.

Exodus and Numbers share some further thematic points. First, as noted above, the Sinai material in both books focuses on the creation of sacred space centered around the tabernacle. For the final block of Exodus, it is the creation of the tabernacle itself. For the first major block of Numbers, the arrangement of the camp personnel around the tabernacle and the materials for the tabernacle are the concern. Therefore, while the Sinai covenant is the subject of the whole section running from Exod. 19.1 through Num. 10.10, it is evident that for the priestly redaction, this material was reconfigured and interpreted along the lines that now assume the shape of the five books of the Torah. Secondly, both books describe how the leaders first journey toward the geographical goal, and later accompany the people's movement toward the same goal. In Exodus Moses travels from Egypt to Sinai, only later to move with the whole people to that holy mountain. In the book of

Numbers, Joshua, Caleb and the other leaders travel to the promised land to scout it out, only to accompany the whole people in their progress toward the land through the remainder of the book. Thirdly, both books use poems to signal both the past and the future. While Exodus 15.1-12 refers back to the escape from Egypt, 15.13-18 looks forward to God's holy mountain, which in the priestly redaction signals the journey to Mount Sinai. Similarly, the oracles of Balaam in Numbers 23–24 review Israel's character as a people set apart (Num. 23.9), empowered by God and freed from Egypt (23.21-24) as well as its future conquests (Num. 24.8) and promise in the land (Num. 24.17-19).[27] Although the priestly redaction of the poems was constrained by their traditional positions in the pre-priestly narrative, the poems form a transition between major blocks, the first at the end of the first block in Exodus, the second at the beginning of the final block in Numbers. In both books, the poems could still fulfill similar functions for the priestly redaction, namely looking both backward and forward in the narrative. Both sets of poems proclaim God's victoriousness on behalf of Israel and mark the prospects of Israel led under the power of God.

Both books show the preference of the priestly redaction for stages occurring in pairs. In the first block in Exodus, the initial audience with Pharaoh fails, followed by the successful confrontation. In the final block of Exodus, the first set of tablets is smashed, to be replaced by a second set. In the second block of Numbers, the leaders of the new generation try to begin the conquest of the land from the wilderness, which is unsuccessful due to the old generation's response, but then followed by successful campaigns in the Transjordan. The purpose of this redactional strategy is to highlight the fact that Israel's only hope and success lie purely with Yahweh; otherwise, Israel on its own falls into idolatry and failure.

Finally, both books are infused with 'a sacerdotal perspective',[28] not only in the expressly priestly sections, but also in the arrangement between holy and unholy practices and people. Both books juxtapose incidents of human sin with the descriptions of the tabernacle and its holiness. Both are concerned with the holy tabernacle and the divine presence connected to it and the unholy people whose behaviors re-

27. Note what Childs (*Introduction*, p. 200) calls 'the strong, eschatological note which was sounded in the final oracle of Balaam'.
28. The expression is Childs's. See Childs, *Introduction*, p. 198.

peatedly threaten the possibility of divine presence among them and therefore any hope for them. Furthermore, Exodus is the book of divine promise and provision and Numbers the book of human failure. Despite this general tendency in the two books, Exodus uses the golden calf story to highlight the people's sinning behavior which will play itself out more fully in Numbers, and Numbers offers a glimpse of hope in the faithful figures of Joshua, Caleb and the emerging generation ready to inherit the land. In sum, the chronological and geographical structures of the priestly redaction of Exodus and Numbers bring the two books into relation with one another as studies of sin and sanctity, as Yahweh and Israel live together through the sacred events of Passover and Booths and through the fundamental spaces in Egypt, Sinai and the wilderness. These would serve as the definitive and defining foundational moments in the religious imagination of ancient Israel and the Jewish people, and in their Christian transformations for the Church as well.

5. *Toward the Formation and the Form of the Pentateuch*

The general importance of the chronological markers is that they mark all five books of the Pentateuch as separate units in the priestly redaction.[29] The disjunction signalled by Exod. 1.1 involves the movement from a family to a new people. As noted above, Exodus 40 concludes with a chronological marker marking the end of the year and a disjunction in the present arrangement of the Pentateuch. Numbers begins with a new chronological marker, which suggests a new beginning. The result is a separate book of Leviticus, although this book is lacking in chronological markers. The materials from Exodus 25 through 40, Leviticus 8–10 and perhaps Numbers 7 originally may have been all of a piece treating the standard building procedures for a sanctuary,[30] but in their current form, these materials have been re-ordered due to the insertion of additional materials, such as Leviticus 1–7. Although the description of the cloud of the divine presence in Exod. 40.34-37 parallels that of Num. 9.15-23, this parallel no longer functions as a structural indicator due to the insertion of Numbers 1–7 and the chronological markers contained in these chapters. The chronological

29. A point emphasized by my friend, Rabbi James Ponet.
30. See Hurowitz, 'The Priestly Account', pp. 21-30; *idem, I Have Built you an Exalted House*, pp. 267-68.

marker in 1.1 marks the beginning of this book, and it ends with a
summary statement in Num. 36.13. As a recapitulation of the events in
Exodus through Numbers, the book of Deuteronomy reflects in genre
and contents a different sort of unit.[31] From the comparisons drawn
above between Exodus and Numbers, a cumulative priestly arrangement for the Pentateuch may be suggested, with the added caveat that
this proposal offers only a very broad picture, with little attention devoted to the internal structures of Genesis, Leviticus and Deuteronomy. The issues pertaining to these books would require full studies
of their own, which is beyond the scope of this volume. Despite these
limitations, Exodus and Numbers represent a balance of two books,
with Leviticus in the middle. J. D. Watts's comments on the arrangement of Exodus through Numbers correctly capture the priestly combination of story and legal material ('list'): 'The close relationship
between P's narratives and lists suggests that the priestly writers and
editors worked with the larger context in mind and intentionally structured the whole to highlight Levitical legislation as the central lists in
the Pentateuch's rhetoric'.[32]

The book of Genesis seems to divide into two blocks of material in
Genesis, the primeval history in chs. 1–11 and the patriarchal history
in chs. 12–50.[33] In Genesis 1–11, the priestly genealogies reckon ten
generations from Adam to Noah and ten more from Noah to Abraham.
It would seem, then, that for the priestly redaction, Genesis 1–11 represents a major section with two sub-units. In priestly narrative mat-

31. Dr Benjamin Scolnic also points out to me that all of the five Pentateuchal
books but Leviticus end on a theme related to the land which is the goal of the Pentateuch as a whole: Genesis ends on Joseph's promise to bring the bones of his father
back to the land; Exodus ends the description of the Israelites' journeys with the
tabernacle and divine presence in its midst; Number's final verse places the Israelites
'on the steppes of Moab, at the Jordan near Jericho' (NJPS); and Deuteronomy's final
chapter describes Moses' viewing of the land and his burial near Beth-Peor. Leviticus
ends with rules on the redemption of land; so perhaps this book is not exempt from
Dr Scolnic's observation.

32. Watts, 'Rhetorical Strategy', p. 21.

33. For a considerably fuller discussion, see Cross, *Canaanite Myth*, pp. 301-
307. On Gen. 1–11, see most recently J. Blenkinsopp, 'P and J in Genesis 1.1–
11.26: An Alternative Hypothesis', in A.B. Beck *et al.* (eds.), *Fortunate the Eyes
That See: Essays in Honor of David Noel Freedman in Celebration of his Seventieth
Birthday* (Grand Rapids: Eerdmans, 1995), pp. 1-15.

erial Noah and Abraham both enter into an 'eternal covenant' (עולם
ברית) with God in Genesis 9 and 17, respectively, which are to anticipate and build toward the eternal covenant made at mount Sinai in the
book of Exodus (see Exod. 31.18). Insofar as these priestly covenants
anticipate the Sinai covenant,[34] Genesis seems to function in the capacity of prologue for the priestly tradition.[35] Indeed, the life of each
patriarch foreshadows the lives of his descendants. With slightly different variations echoing one another, Abraham, Jacob-Israel and
Joseph all journey in the land and then to Egypt. For Abraham Egypt
represents only a single incident in his life; for Jacob-Israel, it is the
end of a bitter life; and for Joseph it is the salvation of his people
thanks to unforeseen divine providence.[36] All three figures are initially
subject to the authority of Egypt (for Jacob-Israel, it is because of his
own son!), all three are subsequently exalted, and finally all three recognize that Egypt is not the final destination for himself or for the
destiny of his family. Abraham travels to Egypt, is exalted by Pharaoh
and returns from Egypt in Genesis 12. Jacob-Israel and Joseph both
travel to Egypt, and on their death-beds these two patriarchs instruct
their surviving family to bury their bones in the promised land (Gen.
49.29-32; 50.24-25). Encapsulated in the experience of the patriarchs
is the experience of the Israelites as a people in Exodus 1–15: after
they are subject to Egyptian authority, they are later exalted by God,
and then they depart for the land promised to their ancestors. This
proleptic function is not restricted to the patriarchal narratives for the
priestly redaction, however. Genesis 1, too, serves as prologue[37] in
sounding the divine plan of creation which Israel enters with the book
of Exodus.

Deuteronomy was added into the Pentateuch, apparently by the
priestly redaction. This rearrangement was achieved by moving the old

34. So many scholars, for example, Cross, *Canaanite Myth*, pp. 295-98.

35. See Wellhausen, *Prolegomena*, pp. 315, 339-40; Levenson, *The Death and
Resurrection*, pp. 82-86.

36. These comments assume an Abraham cycle (Gen. 12–25), a Jacob-Israel
cycle (Gen. 26–36) and a Joseph cycle (Gen. 37–50). There is no longer a separate
Isaac cycle; Isaac appears toward the beginning of his life as Abraham's son and as
the aged father of Jacob. For specific verbal connections between the Abraham cycle
(Gen. 12–25) and Exodus, see the links noted very nicely by Levenson, *The Death
and Resurrection*, pp. 85-88.

37. So van Seters, *The Life of Moses*, p. 1.

story of Moses' death from the end of the old material in Numbers (thereby ending finally the old generation in Numbers) to the end of Deuteronomy.[38] Deuteronomy was basically inherited by the priestly redaction and incorporated into the Pentateuch. While smaller subsections and long additions are apparent in Deuteronomy, overall the book shows three major blocks of material.[39] Two introductions have been detected in 1.1–11.32, namely in 1.1–4.40 and 4.44–11.32. In their present configuration they function as a single introduction. The principle of arrangement of material within the second block in Deuteronomy has been discussed at great length by S.A. Kaufman.[40] Kaufman's basic hypothesis (following W. Schultz in 1859 and H. Schulz in 1966), that Deuteronomy 12–26 is arranged according to the order and topics of the Ten Commandments, illustrates how principles based on earlier legal material provided order for very diverse materials. Deuteronomy 27–34 covers last things: blessings and curses in 27–30; the commissioning of Joshua, the writing of the Torah, its future use and its deposition in 31.1–32.47; and finally, the episode of the death of Moses in 32.48–34.12. It would seem that the book functions within the priestly work as a separate recapitulation. If that is correct, then Deuteronomy may function also to balance the book of Genesis.

The book of Leviticus is delimited by the tabernacle in the final block of Exodus and the camp arrangement in the initial block of Numbers. The center of the Pentateuch corresponds to the center of the holy, liturgical life attached to the tabernacle. B.A. Levine suggests the division 1–16 and 17–27 for the book.[41] The priestly redaction incorporated the earlier priestly materials in Leviticus 1–16 and the Holiness Code in 17–27.[42] No doubt other subdivisions such as 1–9,

---

38. So, following many commentators, Weinfeld, *Deuteronomy 1–11*, p. 10.

39. The comments here have little bearing on the historical relations between Deuteronomy and earlier tradition. On this issue, see Weinfeld, *Deuteronomy 1–11*, pp. 19-24. For the historical relations between Deuteronomy and the priestly tradition, see in addition to observations made above in Chapters 5 and 10, Weinfeld, *Deuteronomy 1–11*, pp. 25-37.

40. Kaufman, 'The Structure of the Deuteronomic Law', pp. 105-58.

41. Levine, *The JPS Torah Commentary. Leviticus*, p. xvi.

42. On the Holiness Code and its relations to the priestly tradition, see the important studies of I. Knohl, 'The Priestly Torah', pp. 65-117; and *Silence in the Sanctuary* (Minneapolis: Fortress Press, 1995); and Milgrom, *Leviticus 1–16*, pp. 13-42.

10–16 and 17–27 may be proposed,[43] but it is perhaps more important here to stress the central position which the whole book occupies within the Pentateuch.[44]

These observations provide some basis for offering a basic proposal for the priestly arrangement of the Torah.[45] The discussion thus far would point to the following chiastic outline:

A. *Book of Genesis* as Prologue
  1–11 First things: the primeval history
  12–50 Patriarchal history

 B. *Book of Exodus*
  1.1–15.21 *Egypt*
   1–2 The emergence of Moses
   3.1–6.1, 6.2–14.31 Moses' two calls and confrontations:
   + 15.1-21 End-poem

  15.22–18.27 *Wilderness*
   Solicitous care of Yahweh; murmuring stories:
   16 Manna and quail
   17.1-7 Water at Massah and Meribah
   17.8-16 Battle with Amalek
   18 Help for Moses
   18 Moses' father-in-law

  19–40 *Sinai* (and tabernacle)
   Two sets of tablets, tabernacle commanded and constructed

  C. *The Book of Leviticus* Sanctuary life in the center
   1–16 The manual of practices for the priesthood
   17–27 The manual of practices for the people

Milgrom holds to a priestly redactor ('P$_3$') who postdates 'H'. See above Chapter 5, section 3.

43. See the discussion of Milgrom, *Leviticus 1–16*, pp. 61-63.

44. For a synchronic reading of the structure of Leviticus, see M. Douglas, 'Poetic Structure in Leviticus', in Wright, Freedman and Hurvitz (eds.), *Pomegranates and Golden Bells*, pp. 239-56. See also C.R. Smith, 'The Literary Structure of Leviticus', *JSOT* 70 (1996), pp. 17-32.

45. For a very different view of the arrangement of the Pentateuch which addresses in part the points thus far, see Knierim, *The Task of Old Testament Theology*, pp. 351-79. Knierim makes several helpful methodological points. For example, for Knierim the Pentateuch is not simply Torah in general but the Torah of Moses and in some sense the biography of Moses.

B'. *Book of Numbers*
    1.1–10.10 *Sinai* (and tabernacle)
        1–6 Personnel preparation around the tabernacle
        7.1–10.10 Material preparation for tabernacle

    10.11–21.35 *Wilderness*
    Passing of the old, sinning generation; murmuring stories:
    11 Manna and quail
    20.1-13 Water at Meribah
    14.39-45 Battle with Amalek
    11 Help for Moses
    10.29-32 Moses' father-in-law

    22.1–36.13 *Transjordan*
    22–24 Preface poems
    25–31, 32–36 Two sets of preparations for the land

A'. *Book of Deuteronomy* as Recapitulation
    1.1–11.32 Narrative recapitulated in two introductions in 1.1–4.40,
        4.44–11.32
    12–26 The Torah recapitulated
    27–34 Last things

The final product or literary architecture moves slowly toward the mountain of God and sets the norms for life after the mountain, as the people progress toward the land. Mount Sinai is the goal of the book of Exodus and it serves as the defining basis for all following standards in the book of Numbers. It is a gross understatement to say Sinai occupies a central place in the priestly theology of the Pentateuch. As noted in Chapter 8, Sinai became the Mount Everest of priestly theology which looms larger than subsequent cultic sites such as Jerusalem. For the priestly tradition Sinai would represent the site of the definitive covenant and model for cultic recollection in the land. In short, this mountain defines life inside and outside of the land. Sacred space is therefore highlighted in the priestly materials and redaction in Exodus and Numbers.

Sacred time likewise moves in stages, likewise arranged chiastically around the book of Leviticus. Genesis 1 through Exodus 12 and Numbers 10 through Deuteronomy 34 are reckoned by years. Exodus 12–Numbers 10 is counted by months and evokes the liturgical year as a whole. Passover in Exodus 12–13 and Numbers 9, as well as the feast of Weeks in Exod. 19.1, are used to anchor the two great events dominating Exodus through Numbers, namely the exodus and the Sinai covenant.[46] In the book of Leviticus time is hardly reckoned at all, slowing to a virtual standstill. In Lev. 9.1 seven days have lapsed in order for the ritual of priestly consecration to be completed (8.33). Lev. 16.1 assumes some lapse of time when it refers back to ch. 10 when Yahweh had killed Aaron's sons, Nadab and Abihu, due to their presumedly illicit use of 'strange fire'.[47] Otherwise, the passing of time is hardly noticeable. While the chronology of Num. 1.1 signals that about three weeks have passed in Leviticus, this book provides little or no sense of time, with its virtual absence of time indicators or narrative apart from introductions to divine instructions (and even fewer narrative executions of those commands). Exodus 12–Numbers 10, but especially the book of Leviticus, creates an increasing density of sacred events within an extremely short compass, a kind of compacted time at Mount Sinai, unlike and beyond the normal passage of time. The time at Mount Sinai virtually stops, perhaps signalling that the events at the mountain of God are timeless. Those instructions given in that timeless moment were intended to serve for all time.

This study may end where the Introduction began, namely with the impact of the priestly liturgical sensibility on the book of Exodus. As the study of Exodus and Numbers in this chapter suggests, the priestly redaction of the Pentateuch shows liturgical influence in its geographical and chronological markers. It is argued above that Passover and Weeks were evoked in the liturgical year represented by Exodus 12 through Numbers 10. The correlation between pilgrimage feasts and the shape of the Pentateuch did not end with Numbers 10. The final shape of Exodus–Numbers resulted in a broader correlation between the great pilgrimage feasts and the three great themes of Exodus through Numbers. The three feasts taken together recapitulated the

46. In contrast, Booths plays no explicit role in the chronological markers in Exodus or Numbers. The reason for this apparent absence is evident: in the priestly tradition Booths evoked the entire forty-year sojourn in the wilderness, not only the period after the Sinai legislation (Lev. 23.39-43, esp. v. 43). However, while Booths was not immediately malleable to schematization along the lines of Passover and Weeks, it should be noted that the priestly chronological markers caused this sojourn to be weighted heavily to the period after Sinai and not before. New Year's, however, does have a place in the post-exilic schema of the year. While New Year's is absent from the pilgrimage cycle of the older calendars in Exod. 23.14-17 and 34.12-13 and Deut 16.16 (see Chapter 1), priestly tradition (Lev. 23.23; Num. 29) gives it a place in the plan of sacred events of the year in Exod. 12 through Num. 10.

47. See Milgrom, *Leviticus 1–16*, p. 1061.

central old, foundational events known in post-exilic liturgical memory. In celebrating the exodus from Egypt, Passover begins the chain of events with the departure from Egypt. Weeks continues by celebrating the divine gift of the Torah at Mount Sinai. Booths ends the series by recalling the forty years in the wilderness following the departure from Sinai. The pilgrimage festivals and their liturgical practices played a decisive role in the priestly formation of the Pentateuch, to which dedicated readers have since returned in the cycles of their years.

BIBLIOGRAPHY

Abbott, W.M. (ed.), *Dei Verbum in the Documents of Vatican II* (New York: America Press, 1966).

Abou-Assaf, A., P. Bordreuil and A.R. Millard, *La statue de Tell Fekherye et son inscription bilingue assyro-araméenne* (Etudes Assyriologiques; Paris: Editions recherche sur les civilisations, 1982).

—*Der Tempel von 'Ain Dara* (Damaszener Forschungen, 3; Mainz: Philip von Zabern, 1990).

Aejmelaeus, A., 'Septuagintal Techniques: A Solution to the Problem of the Tabernacle Account', in Brooke and Lindars (eds.), *Septuagint, Scrolls and Cognate Writings*, pp. 381-402.

Ahlström, G.W., *Psalm 89: Eine Liturgie aus dem Ritual des leidenden Königs* (Lund: Gleerup, 1959).

—*Aspects of Syncretism in Israelite Religion* (Horae Soederblomianae, 5; Lund: Gleerup, 1963).

Albertz, R., *Persönliche Frömmigkeit und offizielle Religion* (Stuttgart: Calwer Verlag, 1978).

—*A History of Israelite Religion in the Old Testament Period. I. From the Beginnings to the End of the Monarchy* (trans. J. Bowden; OTL; Louisville, KY: Westminster/ John Knox Press, 1994).

Albright, W.F., 'Jethro, Hobab and Reuel in Early Hebrew Tradition', *CBQ* 25 (1963), pp. 1-11.

—'What Were the Cherubim?', *BA* 1 (1938), pp. 1-3.

Alt, A., *Essays on Old Testament History and Religion* (trans. R.A. Wilson; Garden City, NY: Doubleday, 1968).

Alter, R., *The Art of Biblical Poetry* (New York: Basic Books, 1985).

—*The Art of Biblical Narrative* (New York: Basic Books, 1981).

Alter R., and F. Kermode (eds.), *The Literary Guide to the Bible* (Cambridge, MA: The Belknap Press of the Harvard University Press, 1987).

Amiet, P., *Art of the Ancient Near East* (trans. J. Shepley and C. Choquet; New York: Abrams, 1980).

Andersen, F.T., and D.N. Freedman, *Hosea* (AB, 24; Garden City, NY: Doubleday, 1980).

Anderson, A.A., *The Book of Psalms. II. Psalms 73–150* (NCB; Grand Rapids: Eerdmans; London: Marshall, Morgan & Scott, 1972).

Anderson, G.A., *Sacrifices and Offerings in Ancient Israel: Studies in their Social and Political Importance* (HSM, 41; Atlanta: Scholars Press, 1987).

—'The Cosmic Mountain: Eden and its Early Interpreters in Syriac Christianity', in G.A. Robbins (ed.), *Genesis 1–3 in the History of Exegesis: Intrigue in the Garden* (Studies in Women and Religion, 27; Lewiston, NY: Edwin Mellen, 1988), pp. 187-224.

—*A Time to Mourn, A Time to Dance: The Expression of Grief and Joy in Israelite Religion* (University Park, PA: Pennsylvania State University Press, 1991).

Auffret, P., 'Essai sur la structure littéraire du Psaume XV', *VT* 31 (1981), pp. 383-99.

Aufrecht, W.E., *A Corpus of Ammonite Inscriptions* (Lewiston, NY: Edwin Mellen, 1989).

Avishur, Y., '*RWM (RMM)–BNY* in Ugaritic and the Bible', *Leš* 45 (1981), pp. 270-79.

Axelsson, L.E., *The Lord Rose up from Seir: Studies in the History and Traditions of the Negev and Southern Judah* (ConBOT, 25; Stockholm: Almqvist & Wiksell, 1987), p. 61.

Balentine, S.E., *The Hiding of the Face of God in the Old Testament* (New York and Oxford: Oxford University Press, 1983).

Bäntsch, B., *Exodus–Leviticus–Numeri* (HAT; Göttingen: Vandenhoeck & Ruprecht, 1903).

Barnett, R.D., *Ancient Ivories in the Middle East* (Qedem, 14; Jerusalem: Institute of Archaeology of the Hebrew University, 1982).

Barr, J., 'Theophany and Anthropomorphism in the Old Testament', in J. Emerton (ed.), *Congress Volume: Oxford 1959* (VTSup, 7; Leiden: Brill, 1960), pp. 31-38.

—*The Bible in the Modern World* (New York: Harper, 1973).

—*The Scope and Authority of the Bible* (Philadelphia: Westminster Press, 1980).

Barré, M.L., 'An Unrecognized Precative Particle in Phoenician and Hebrew', *Bib* 64 (1983), pp. 411-22.

—'Recovering the Literary Structure of Psalm XV', *VT* 34 (1984), pp. 207-11.

—' "My Strength and My Song" in Exodus 15.2', *CBQ* 54 (1992), pp. 623-37.

Barré, M.L., and J.S. Kselman, 'New Exodus, Covenant, and Restoration in Psalm 23', in C.L. Meyers and M. O'Connor (eds.), *The Word of the Lord Shall Go Forth: Essays in Honor of David Noel Freedman in Celebration of his Sixtieth Birthday* (ASOR Special Volume Series, 1; Philadelphia: ASOR, 1983), pp. 97-127.

Barrelet, M.T., 'Une peinture de la cour 106 du palais de Mari', *Studia Mariana* 4 (1950), pp. 9-15.

Barstad, H., *The Religious Polemics of Amos: Studies in the Preaching of Am. ii 7B-8, iv 1-13, v 1-27, vi 4-7, viii 14* (VTSup, 34; Leiden: Brill, 1984).

Barton, J., *Reading the Old Testament: Method in Biblical Study* (Philadelphia: Westminster Press, 1984).

Batto, B., *Slaying the Dragon in the Biblical Tradition* (Louisville, KY: Westminster/ John Knox Press, 1992).

Beck, A.B., *et al.* (eds.), *Fortunate the Eyes that See: Essays in Honor of David Noel Freedman in Celebration of his Seventieth Birthday* (Grand Rapids: Eerdmans, 1995).

Beck, P., 'The Drawings from Horvat Teiman (Kuntillet 'Ajrud)', *TA* 9 (1982), pp. 56-58.

Beek, F.J. van, SJ, *Loving Torah More than God? Toward a Catholic Appreciation of Judaism* (Chicago: Loyola Press, 1989).

Begg, C.T., 'The Destruction of the Calf (Exod. 32,20/Deut. 9,21)', in N. Lohfink (ed.), *Das Deuteronomium: Entstehung, Gestalt und Botschaft* (BETL, 68; Leuven: Leuven University Press/Peeters, 1985), pp. 208-51.

Berge, K., *Die Zeit des Jahwisten: Ein Beitrag zur Datierung jahwistischer Vätertexte* (BZAW, 186; Berlin: de Gruyter, 1990).

Berlin, A., *The Dynamics of Biblical Parallelism* (Bloomington: Indiana University Press, 1985).

Beyer, K., 'The Ammonite Tell Siran Bottle Inscription Reconsidered', in Z. Zerit, S. Gitin and M. Sokoloff (eds.), חיים ליונה *Solving Riddles and Untying Knots:*

Biblical, Epigraphic, and Semitic Studies in Honor of Jonas C. Greenfield (Winona Lake, IN: Eisenbrauns, 1995), pp. 389-91.

Beyerlin, W., *Origins and History of the Oldest Sinaitic Traditions* (trans. S. Rudman; Oxford: Basil Blackwell, 1965).

Bird, P.A., '"Male and Female he Created them", Gen. 1.27b in the Context of the Priestly Account of Creation', *HTR* 74 (1981), pp. 129-59.

Blenkinsopp, J., 'The Structure of P', *CBQ* 38 (1976), pp. 275-92.

—'Old Testament Theology and the Jewish–Christian Connection', *JSOT* 28 (1984), pp. 3-15.

—Review of *Studien zur Komposition des Pentateuch*, by E. Blum, *CBQ* 54 (1992), pp. 312-13.

—*The Pentateuch: An Introduction to the First Five Books of the Bible* (ABRL; Garden City, NY: Doubleday, 1992).

—'P and J in Genesis 1.1–11.26: An Alternative Hypothesis', in Beck *et al.* (eds.), *Fortunate the Eyes that See*, pp. 1-15.

—*Sage, Priest, Prophet: Religious and Intellectual Leadership in Ancient Israel* (Louisville, KY: Westmnister/John Knox, 1995).

Bloch-Smith, E.M. '"Who is the King of Glory?" Solomon's Temple and its Symbolism', in M.D. Coogan, J.C. Exum and L.E. Stager (eds.), *Scripture and Other Artifacts: Essays on the Bible and Archaeology in Honor of Philip J. King* (Louisville, KY: Westminster/John Knox Press, 1994), pp. 18-31.

—'The Cult of the Dead in Judah: Interpreting the Material Remains', *JBL* 111 (1992), pp. 213-24.

—*Judahite Burial Practices and Beliefs about the Dead* (JSOTSup, 123; Sheffield: JSOT Press, 1992).

—'Solomon's Temple: The Politics of Ritual Space' (paper delivered at the national meeting of the American Schools of Oriental Research in November, 1995).

Bloom, H., *The Anxiety of Influence: A Theory of Poetry* (London: Oxford University Press, 1975).

—*The Book of J* (New York: Grove Weidenfeld, 1990).

Blum, E., *Die Komposition der Väter Geschichte* (WMANT, 57; Neukirchen–Vluyn: Neukirchener Verlag, 1984).

—'Israël à la montagne de Dieu: Remarques sur Ex 19–24; 32–34 et sur le contexte littéraire et historique de sa composition', in de Pury (ed.), *Le Pentateuque en question*, pp. 211-95.

—*Studien zur Komposition des Pentateuch* (BZAW, 189; Berlin: de Gruyter, 1990).

Blum, E., C. Macholz and E.K. Stegemann (eds.), *Die hebräische Bibel und ihre zweifache Nachgeschichte: Festschrift für Rolf Rendtorff zum 65. Geburtstag* (Neukirchen-Vluyn: Neukirchener Verlag, 1990).

Bokser, B., 'Unleavened Bread and Passover, Feasts of', *ABD*, VI, pp. 755-65.

Bordreuil, P., 'Recherches ougaritiques', *Sem* 40 (1991), pp. 17-30.

Bordreuil, P., and D. Pardee, 'Le combat de *Ba'lu* avec *Yammu* d'après les textes ougaritiques', *MARI* 7 (1993), pp. 63-70.

Borowski, O., 'Agriculture', *ABD*, I, pp. 95-98.

—'Harvests, Harvesting', *ABD*, III, pp. 63-64.

—*Agriculture in Iron Age Israel* (Winona Lake, IN: Eisenbrauns, 1987).

Boyarin, D., 'The Eye in the Torah: Oracular Desire in Midrashic Hermeneutic', *Critical Inquiry* 16 (1990), pp. 532-50.

Brenner, M.L., *The Song of the Sea: Ex 15.1-21* (BZAW, 195; Berlin: de Gruyter, 1991).

Brettler, M.Z., *God is King: Understanding an Israelite Metaphor* (JSOTSup, 76; Sheffield: JSOT Press, 1989).

—*The Creation of History in Ancient Israel* (New York: Routledge, 1995).

Brichto, H.C., *Toward a Grammar of Biblical Poetics: Tales of the Prophets* (New York and Oxford: Oxford University Press, 1992).

Briggs, C., and E. Briggs, *A Critical and Exegetical Commentary on the Book of Psalms* (2 vols.; ICC; Edinburgh: T. & T. Clark, 1907).

Brooke, G.J., and B. Lindars (eds.), *Septuagint, Scrolls and Cognate Writings: Papers Presented to the International Symposium in the Septuagint and its Relations to the Dead Sea Scrolls and Other Writings (Manchester, 1990)* (SBLSCS, 33; Atlanta: Scholars Press, 1992).

Brooks, R., *The Spirit of the Ten Commandments: Shattering the Myth of Rabbinic Legalism* (San Francisco: Harper & Row, 1990).

Brooks, R., and J.J. Collins (eds.), *Hebrew Bible or Old Testament? Studying the Bible in Judaism and Christianity* (Christianity and Judaism in Antiquity, 5; Notre Dame: University of Notre Dame Press, 1980).

Brown, W.P., *Structure, Role, and Ideology in the Hebrew and Greek Texts of Genesis 1.1–2.3* (SBLDS, 132; Atlanta: Scholars Press, 1993).

Brueggemann, W., 'Pharaoh as Vassal: A Study of a Political Metaphor', *CBQ* 57 (1995), pp. 27-51.

Buis, P., 'Les conflits entre Moïse et Israël dans Exode et Nombres', *VT* 28 (1978), pp. 257-70.

Buchanan, B., and P.R.S. Moorey, *Catalogue of Ancient Near Eastern Seals in the Ashmolean Museum. III. The Iron Age Stamp Seals* (Oxford: Clarendon Press, 1993

Busink, T.A., *Der Tempel von Jerusalem von Salomo bis Herod. I. Der Tempel Salomos* (Leiden: Brill, 1970).

Campbell, A.F., and M.A. O'Brien, *Sources for the Pentateuch: Texts, Introductions, Annotations* (Minneapolis: Fortress Press, 1993).

Canby, J., 'The Walters Gallery Cappadocian Tablet and the Sphinx in Anatolia in the Second Millennium BCE', *JNES* 34 (1975), pp. 225-48.

Caquot, A., 'Les énigmes d'un hémistique biblique', *Dieu et l'Etre* (Paris: Etudes augustiniennes, 1978), pp. 17-26.

Carpenter, D., 'Language, Ritual and Society: Reflections on the Authority of the Veda', *JAAR* 60 (1992), pp. 57-77.

—'The Mastery of Speech: Canonicity and Control in the Vedas', in L.L. Patton (ed.), *Authority, Anxiety, and Canon: Essays in Vedic Interpretation* (SUNY Series in Hindu Studies; Albany: State University of New York Press, 1994), pp. 19-34.

Carroll, R.P., *Jeremiah: A Commentary* (OTL; Philadelphia: Westminster Press, 1986).

Cassuto, U., *A Commentary on the Book of Exodus* (trans. I. Abrahams; Jerusalem: Magnes, 1967).

Catling, H.W., *Cypriot Bronzework in the Mycenean World* (Oxford: Clarendon Press, 1964).

Causse, A., *La vision de la nouvelle Jérusalem (Esaie LX) et la signification sociologique des assemblées de fête et des pèlerinages dans l'Orient sémitique* (Paris: Geuthner, 1939).

Childs, B.S., 'A Traditio-Historical Study of the Reed Sea Tradition', *VT* 20 (1970), pp. 406-18.

—*The Book of Exodus* (OTL; Philadelphia: Westminster Press, 1974).

—*Introduction to the Old Testament as Sacred Scripture* (Philadelphia: Fortress Press, 1979).

—*Biblical Theology of the Old and New Testaments: Theological Reflection on the Christian Bible* (Minneapolis: Fortress Press, 1992).

Christiansen, E.J., *The Covenant in Judaism and Paul: A Study of Ritual Boundaries as Identity Markers* (AGJU, 27; Leiden: Brill, 1995).

Clifford, R.J., 'Exodus', *NJBC*, I, pp. 44-60.

—'The Tent of El and the Israelite Tent of Meeting', *CBQ* 33 (1971), pp. 221-27.

—*The Cosmic Mountain in Canaan and the Old Testament* (HSM, 4; Cambridge, MA: Harvard University Press, 1972).

—*Creation Accounts in the Ancient Near East and in the Bible* (CBQMS, 26; Washington: Catholic Biblical Association, 1994).

Clines, D.J.A., *The Theme of the Pentateuch* (JSOTSup, 10; Sheffield: JSOT Press, 1978).

Coats, G.W., 'The Song of the Sea', *CBQ* 31 (1969), pp. 1-17.

—'The Traditio-Historical Character of the Reed Sea Motif', *VT* 17 (1967), pp. 253-65.

Cody, A., *A History of Old Testament Priesthood* (Rome: Pontifical Biblical Institute, 1969).

Cohen, C., 'The Genre of Priestly Instructions in the Torah and the Isolation of a New Torah Source—PI' (unpublished paper).

—'Was the Document Secret?', *JANESCU* 1.2 (1969), pp. 39-44.

Collins, J.J., 'The "Historical Character" of the Old Testament in Recent Biblical Theology', *CBQ* 44 (1979), pp. 185-204.

—'Is a Critical Biblical Theology Possible?', in W.H. Propp, B. Halpern and D.N. Freedman (eds.), *The Hebrew Bible and its Interpreters* (Winona Lake, IN: Eisenbrauns, 1990), pp. 1-17.

Collon, D., *The Alalakh Cylinder Seals: A New Catalogue of the Actual Seals Excavated by Sir Leonard Woolley at Tell Atchana, and from Neighboring Sites on the Syrian–Turkish Border* (BAR International Series, 132; Oxford: British Archaeological Reports, 1987).

—*First Impressions: Cylinder Seals in the Ancient Near East* (Chicago: University of Chicago Press, 1987).

Cook, E.M. (ed.), *MAARAV* 5–6 (1990) = *Sopher Mahir: Northwest Semitic Studies Presented to Stanislav Segert* (Santa Monica, CA: Western Academic Press, 1990).

Cook, S.L., *Prophecy and Apocalypticism: The Postexilic Social Setting* (Minneapolis: Fortress Press, 1996).

Cooper, A., 'Structure, Midrash and Meaning: The Case of Psalm 23', in *Proceedings of the World Congress of Jewish Studies: Jerusalem, August 4–12, 1985. Division A. The Period of the Bible* (Jerusalem: World Union of Jewish Studies, 1986), pp. 107-14.

Cooper, A., and B.R. Goldstein, 'Exodus and *Maṣṣôt* in History and Tradition', *MAARAV* 8 (1992), pp. 15-37.

—'The Cult of the Dead and the Theme of Entry into the Land', *BI* 1 (1993), pp. 285-303.

Coote, R.B, *Amos Among the Prophets: Composition and Theology* (Philadelphia: Fortress Press, 1981).

—*The Elohist: In Defense of First History* (Minneapolis: Fortress Press, 1991).

Coote, R.B. (ed.), *Elijah and Elisha in Socioliterary Perspective* (Semeia, 22; Atlanta: Scholars Press, 1992).

Coote, R.B., and D.R. Ord, *The Bible's First History* (Philadelphia: Fortress Press, 1989).

Cormie, L., 'Revolutions in Reading the Bible', in D. Jobling, P.L. Day and G.T. Sheppard (eds.), *The Bible and the Politics of Exegesis: Essays in Honor of Norman K. Gottwald on his Sixty-Fifth Birthday* (Cleveland: Pilgrim Press, 1991).

Couroyer, B., 'Note sur II Sam., I, 22 et Is., LV, 10-11', *RB* 88 (1981), pp. 505-14.

—'*ēdût*: stipulation de traité ou enseignement?' *RB* 95 (1988), pp. 321-31.

—'L'Exode et la bataille de Qadesh', *RB* 97 (1990), pp. 321-58.

Cover, R., 'The Supreme Court, 1982 Term—Forward: *Nomos* and Narrative', *Harvard Law Review* 97.1 (1983), pp. 4-68.

Craigie, P.C., 'Psalm XXIX in the Hebrew Poetic Tradition', *VT* 22 (1972), pp. 143-51.

Cross, F.M., *Canaanite Myth and Hebrew Epic: Essays in the History of the Religion of Israel* (Cambridge, MA: Harvard University Press, 1973).

—'The Epic Traditions of Early Israel: Epic Narrative and the Reconstruction of Early Israelite Tradition', in R.E. Freedman (ed.), *The Poet and the Historian: Essays in Literary and Historical Biblical Criticism* (HSS, 26; Chico, CA: Scholars Press, 1983), pp. 13-39.

—'Reuben, First-Born of Jacob', *ZAW* 100 (1988), pp. 57-63.

Cross, F.M., and D.N. Freedman, 'The Song of Miriam', *JNES* 14 (1955), pp. 237-50.

Crowly, P., 'An Ancient Catholic: An Interview with Richard Rodriguez', *America* 173.8 (September 23, 1995).

Crüsemann, F., *Die Tora: Theologie und Sozialgeschichte des alttestamentlichen Gesetzes* (Munich: Chr. Kaiser Verlag, 1992).

Culler, J., *Structuralist Poetics* (Ithaca, NY: Cornell University Press, 1975).

Dahood, M.J., *Psalms. I. 1–50* (AB, 16; Garden City, NY: Doubleday, 1965).

—*Psalms. II. 51–100* (AB, 17; Garden City, NY: Doubleday, 1968).

—'Eblaite, Ugaritic, and Hebrew Lexical Notes', *UF* 11 (1979 = C.F.A. Schaeffer Festschrift), pp. 141-46.

Damrosch, D., *The Narrative Covenant: Transformations of Genre in the Growth of Biblical Literature* (San Francisco: Harper & Row, 1987).

Danby, H., *The Mishnah* (Oxford: Oxford University Press, 1974).

Daniels, D.R., 'The Creed of Deuteronomy XXVI Revisited', in Emerton (ed.), *Studies in the Pentateuch*, pp. 231-42.

Daube, D., *The Exodus Pattern in the Bible* (All Souls Studies, 2; London: Faber & Faber, 1963).

Davies, G.F., *Israel in Egypt: A Reading of Exodus 1–2* (JSOTSup, 135; Sheffield: JSOT Press, 1992).

Davies, G.I., 'The Wilderness Itineraries: A Comparative Study', *TynBul* 25 (1974), pp. 46-81.

—*The Way of the Wilderness: A Geographical Study of the Wilderness Itineraries in the Old Testament* (SOTSMS, 5; Cambridge: Cambridge University Press, 1979).

—'The Wilderness Itineraries and the Composition of the Pentateuch', *VT* 23 (1983), pp. 1-13.

—'The Wilderness Itineraries and Recent Archaeological Research', in Emerton (ed.), *Studies in the Pentateuch*, pp. 161-75.

Day, J., *God's Conflict with the Dragon and the Sea: Echoes of a Canaanite Myth in the Old Testament* (Cambridge: Cambridge University Press, 1985).

Delcor, M., 'Rites pour l'obtention de la pluie', *RHR* 178 (1970), pp. 117-32.

Dessenne, A., *Le Sphinx: Étude iconographique*. I. *Des origines à la fin du second millénnaire* (Bibliothèque des écoles françaises d'Athènes et de Rome, 186; Paris: Boccard, 1957).

Dobbs-Allsopp, F.W., *Weep, O Daughter of Zion: A Study in the City-Lament Genre in the Hebrew Bible* (BibOr, 44; Rome: Pontifical Biblical Institute, 1993).

Donaldson, J., *The Apostolic Constitutions* (Ante-Nicene Christian Library, 17; Edinburgh: T. & T. Clark, 1870).

Dorsey, D.A., *The Roads and Highways of Ancient Israel* (Baltimore: The Johns Hopkins University Press, 1991).

Douglas, M., *Natural Symbols: Explorations in Cosmology* (New York: Vintage Books, 1973).

—*In the Wilderness: The Doctrine of Defilement in the Book of Numbers* (JSOTSup, 158; Sheffield: JSOT Press, 1994).

—'Poetic Structure in Leviticus', in Wright, Freedman and Hurvitz (eds.), *Pomegranates and Golden Bells*, pp. 239-56.

Dozeman, T., *God on the Mountain: A Study of Redaction, Theology and Canon in Exodus 19–24* (SBLMS, 37; Atlanta: Scholars Press, 1989).

—'The Tradition-Historical Development of the Song of the Sea' (paper presented at the Old Testament Theology group, Catholic Biblical Association, August, 1993).

Drazin, I., *Targum Onkelos to Exodus: An English Translation of the Text with Analysis and Commentary (Based on the A. Sperber and A. Berliner Editions)* (n.p.: Ktav/ Center for Judaic Studies University of Denver/Society for Targumic Studies, 1990).

Driver, S.R., *The Book of Exodus* (CB; Cambridge: Cambridge University Press, 1911).

—*An Introduction to the Literature of the Old Testament* (Gloucester, MA: Peter Smith, 1972).

Duhm, B., *Die Psalmen* (KHAT, 14; Tübingen: Mohr–Siebeck, 1899).

Duke, R.K., 'The Portion of the Levite: Another Reading of Deuteronomy 18.6-8', *JBL* 106 (1987), pp. 193-201.

Dumortier, J.-B., 'Un rituel d'intronisation: Le Ps. LXXXIX 2-38', *VT* 22 (1972), pp. 76-96.

Durand, J.M., 'Le mythologème du combat entre le dieu de l'orage et la mer en Mésopotamie', *MARI* 7 (1993), pp. 41-61.

Eagleton, T., *Literary Theory: An Introduction* (Minneapolis: University of Minnesota Press, 1983).

Eaton, J.H., *Kingship and the Psalms* (Biblical Seminar, 3; Sheffield: JSOT Press, 2nd edn, 1986).

Eissfeldt, O., *The Old Testament: An Introduction* (trans. P.R. Ackroyd; New York: Harper & Row, 1965).

Ellis, E.E., *The Old Testament in Early Christianity: Canon and Interpretation in the Light of Modern Research* (WUNT, 54; Tübingen: Mohr–Siebeck, 1991).

Emerton, J.A. (ed.), *Studies in the Pentateuch* (VTSup, 41; Leiden: Brill, 1990).

Finkelstein, I., 'Seilun, Khirbet', *ABD* 5 (1992), pp. 1069-72.

—*The Archaeology of the Israelite Settlement* (Jerusalem: Israel Exploration Society, 1988).

Fish, S., *Is There a Text in this Class? The Authority of Interpretive Communities* (Cambridge, MA: Harvard University Press, 1980).

Fishbane, M., *Text and Texture: Close Readings of Selected Biblical Texts* (New York: Schocken Books, 1979).

—*Biblical Interpretation in Ancient Israel* (Oxford: Clarendon Press, 1986).

Fishbane, M., and E. Tov with W.W. Fields (eds.), *'Sha'arei Talmon': Studies in the Bible, Qumran, and the Ancient Near East Presented to Shemaryahu Talmon* (Winona Lake, IN: Eisenbrauns, 1992).

Fisher, E.J., and L. Klenicki (eds.), *In Our Time: The Flowering of the Jewish–Catholic Dialogue* (New York: Paulist Press, 1990).

Fitzmyer, J.A., 'The Qumran Scrolls, the Ebionites and their Literature', in *idem, Essays on the Semitic Background of the New Testament* (SBLSBS 5; Missoula, MT: Society of Biblical Literature/Scholars Press, 1974).

—*The Gospel according to Luke X–XXIV* (AB, 28A; Garden City, NY: Doubleday, 1985).

—*According to Paul: Studies in the Theology of the Apostle* (Mahwah, NJ: Paulist Press, 1993).

Fitzmyer, J.A., and D.J. Harrington, *A Manual of Palestinian Aramaic Texts (Second Century B.C.—Second Century A.D.)* (BibOr, 34; Rome: Biblical Institute Press, 1978).

Fokkelman, J.P., 'Exodus', in Alter and Kermode (eds.), *The Literary Guide to the Bible*, pp. 56-65.

Ford, J.M., 'The New Covenant, Jesus, and Canonization', in Brooks and Collins (eds.), *Hebrew Bible or Old Testament?*.

Foster, B.R., *Before the Muses: An Anthology of Akkadian Literature* (2 vols.; Bethesda, MD: CDL Press, 1993).

Fraden, R., 'Response to Professor Carolyn Porter', *New Literary Criticism* 21.2 (1990), pp. 273-78.

Frank, R.W., Jr, 'Pilgrimage and Secret Power', in B.N. Sargent-Baur (ed.), *Journeys Toward God: Pilgrimage and Crusade* (JMC, 30; Medieval Institute Publications; Kalamazoo, MI: Western Michigan University Press, 1992), pp. 31-43.

Frankfort, H., *Cylinder Seals: A Documentary Essay on the Art and Religion of the Ancient Near East* (London: Macmillan, 1939).

—*The Pelican History of Art: The Art and Architecture of the Ancient Orient* (Harmondsworth: Penguin Books, 4th edn, 1970).

Freedman, D.N., 'Archaic Forms in Early Hebrew Poetry', *ZAW* 72 (1960), pp. 101-107.

—*Pottery, Poetry and Prophecy* (Winona Lake, IN: Eisenbrauns, 1980).

—'The Twenty-Third Psalm', in L. Orlin (ed.), *Michigan Studies in Honor of George G. Cameron* (Ann Arbor: University of Michigan Press, 1976), pp. 139-66.

Fretheim, T., 'The Plagues as Ecological Signs of Historical Disaster', *JBL* 110 (1991), pp. 385-96.

Friedman, R.E., 'Torah (Pentateuch)', *ABD*, VI (1992), pp. 609-14.

—'The Biblical Expression *mastîr pānîm*', *HAR* 1 (1977), pp. 139-47.

—*Who Wrote the Bible?* (New York: Summit Books, 1987).

—'Scholar, Heal Thyself; Or How Everybody Got to be an Expert on the Bible', in *The Iowa Review* 21.3 (1991), pp. 33-47.

—'The Deuteronomistic School', in Beck *et al.* (eds.), *Fortunate the Eyes that See*, pp. 70-80.

Fritsch, C.T., 'Greek Translations of Hebrew Verbs "To See", with Deity as Subject or Object', *ErIsr* 16 (1982 = H.M. Orlinsky Volume), pp. 51-66.

Fritz, V., 'Temple Archaeology: What Can Archaeology Tell us about Solomon's Temple?' *BARev* 13 (1987), pp. 38-49.

Fuss, M., *Die deuteronomische Pentateuchredaktion in Exodus 1–17* (BZAW, 126; Berlin: de Gruyter, 1972).

Futato, M., 'A Meteorological Analysis of Psalms 104, 65, and 29' (PhD dissertation, The Catholic University of America, 1984).

Gaál, E., 'Tuthmosis III as Storm-God?', *Studia Aegyptiaca* 3 (1977), pp. 29-38.

García Martínez, F., *The Dead Sea Scrolls Translated: The Qumran Texts in English* (Leiden: Brill, 1994).

Garr, W.R., 'The Grammar and Interpretation of Exodus 6.3', *JBL* 111 (1992), pp. 385-408.

Gese, H., 'The Law', in *Essays on Biblical Theology* (trans. K. Crim; Minneapolis: Augsburg, 1981).

—*Alttestamentliche Studien* (Tübingen: Mohr [Paul Siebeck], 1991).

Gibson, J.C.L., *Canaanite Myths and Legends* (Edinburgh: T. & T. Clark, 2nd edn, 1978).

Ginsberg, H.L., 'A Strand in the Cord of Hebrew Psalmody', *ErIsr* 9 (1969 = W.F. Albright volume), pp. 45-50.

—*The Israelian Heritage of Judaism* (New York: The Jewish Theological Seminary of America, 1982).

Gitin, S., 'Tel Miqne-Ekron in the 7th Century BCE: The Impact of Economic Innovation and Foreign Cultural Influences on a Neo-Assyrian Vassal City-State', in S. Gitin (ed.), *Recent Excavations in Israel: A View to the West. Reports on Kabri, Nami, Miqne-Ekron, Dor and Ashkelon* (Colloquia and Conference Papers, 1; Boston: Archaeological Institute of America, 1995), pp. 57-79.

Gnuse, R., Review of *In the Wilderness*, by M. Douglas, CBQ 57 (1995), pp. 124-25.

Goldin, J., *The Song at the Sea: Being a Commentary on a Commentary in Two Parts* (New Haven: Yale University Press, 1971).

Goldstein, B.R., and A. Cooper, 'The Festivals of Israel and Judah and the Literary History of the Pentateuch', *JAOS* 110 (1990), pp. 19-31.

Good, R.M., 'Metaphorical Gleanings from Ugarit', *JJS* 33 (1982 = Essays in Honor of Yigael Yadin), pp. 55-59.

—'Exodus 32.18', in Marks and Good (eds.), *Love and Death in the Ancient Near East*, pp. 137-42.

Gothóni, R., 'Pilgrimage = Transformation Journey', in T. Ahlbäck (ed.), *The Problem of Ritual: Based on Papers Read at the Symposium on Religious Rites Held at Åbo, Finland on the 13th–16th of August 1991* (Scripta Instituti Donneriani Aboensis, 15; Stockholm: Almqvist & Wiksell, 1993), pp. 101-15.

Gottstein, M.H., 'Afterthought and the Syntax of Relative Clauses in Biblical Hebrew', *JBL* 68 (1949), pp. 42-47.

Goudoever, J. van, 'The Celebration of the Torah in the Second Isaiah', in Vermeylen (ed.), *The Book of Isaiah*, pp. 313-17.

Gray, J., *The Biblical Doctrine of the Reign of God* (Edinburgh: T. & T. Clark, 1979).

Grayson, A.K., 'Akkadian Myths and Epics', in *ANET*, pp. 501-18.

Greenberg, M., 'Exodus', *EncJud*, VI, p. 1054.

—*Understanding Exodus* (New York: Behrman, 1969).

Greenfield, J.C., 'The "Cluster" in Biblical Poetry', in Cook (ed.), *Sopher Mahir*, pp. 159-68.

Greenstein, E.L., 'Aspects of Biblical Poetry', *Jewish Book Annual* 44 (1986–87), pp. 33-42.

—'Mixing Memory and Design: Reading Psalm 78', *Prooftexts* 10 (1990), pp. 197-218.

—'The Formation of the Biblical Narrative Corpus', *AJS Review* 15 (1990), pp. 151-78.

—'Beyond the Sovereign Self', in *The Jerusalem Report* (February 9, 1995), p. 45.

—'The First-Born Plague and the Reading Process', in Wright, Freedman and Hurvitz (eds.), *Pomegranates and Golden Bells*, pp. 555-68.

Gropp, D.M., and T.J. Lewis, 'Notes on Some Problems in the Aramaic Text of the Hadd-Yith'i Bilingual', *BASOR* 259 (1985), pp. 45-61.

Gruber, M.I., 'Ten Dance-Derived Expressions in the Hebrew Bible', *Bib* 62 (1981), pp. 328-46.

Gruber, M.I., *Aspects of Nonverbal Communication in the Ancient Near East* (2 vols.; Studia Pohl, 12; Rome: Pontifical Biblical Institute, 1980).

—'The Mishnah as Oral Torah: A Reconsideration', *JSJ* 15 (1984), pp. 112-22.

Gunkel, H., *Genesis übersetzt und erklärt* (HKAT; Göttingen: Vandenhoek & Ruprecht, 1901).

—*The Legends of Genesis: The Biblical Saga and History* (New York: Schocken Books, 1964).

Gunneweg, A.H.J., *Leviten und Priester* (FRLANT, 89; Göttingen: Vandenhoek & Ruprecht, 1965).

Hallo, W.W., 'The First Purim', *BA* 46 (1983), pp. 19-29.

—*The Book of the People* (BJS, 225; Atlanta: Scholars Press, 1991).

—*Origins: The Ancient Near Eastern Background of Some Modern Western Institutions* (Studies in the History and Culture of the Ancient Near East, 6; Leiden: Brill, 1996).

Halpern, B., *The Emergence of Israel in Canaan* (SBLMS, 29; Chico, CA: Scholars Press, 1983).

—' "Brisker Pipes than Poetry": The Development of Israelite Monotheism', in J. Neusner, B.A. Levine and E.S. Frerichs (eds.), *Judaic Perspectives on Ancient Israel* (Philadelphia: Fortress Press, 1987), pp. 77-115.

—'Jerusalem and the Lineages in the Seventh Century BCE: Kinship and the Rise of Individual Moral Liability', in B. Halpern and D.W. Hobson (eds.), *Law and Ideology in Monarchic Israel* (JSOTSup, 124; Sheffield: JSOT Press, 1991), pp. 11-107.

—'Shiloh', *ABD*, V, pp. 1213-15.

Hanson, A., 'The Treatment in the LXX of the Theme of Seeing God', in Brooke and Lindars (eds.), *Septuagint, Scrolls and Cognate Writings*, pp. 557-68.

Hanson, P.D., *The People Called: The Growth of Community in the Bible* (San Francisco: Harper & Row, 1986).

—'Israelite Religion in the Early Postexilic Period', in P.D. Miller, Jr, P.D. Hanson and S.D. McBride (eds.), *Ancient Israelite Religion: Essays in Honor of Frank Moore Cross* (Philadelphia: Fortress Press, 1987), pp. 485-508.

Haran, M., 'The Law-Code of Ezekiel XL–XLVIII and its Relation to the Priestly School', *HUCA* 50 (1979), pp. 45-71.

—'The Character of the Priestly Source', *Proceedings of the Eighth World Congress of Jewish Studies: Jerusalem, August 16–21, 1981* (Jerusalem: World Union of Jewish Studies, 1983), pp. 131-38.

—*Temples and Temple-Service in Ancient Israel: An Inquiry into Biblical Cult Phenomena and the Historical Setting of the Priestly School* (Oxford: Clarendon Press, 1978; repr. Winona Lake, IN: Eisenbrauns, 1985).

Hartmann, L., and A.A. Di Lella, *The Book of Daniel* (AB, 23; Garden City, NY: Doubleday, 1978).

Haudebert, P. (ed.), *Le Pentateuque: Débats et recherches: Quatorzième congrès de l'ACFEB, Angers (1991)* (LD, 151; Paris: Cerf, 1992).

Haupt, P., 'Moses' Song of Triumph', *AJSL* 20 (1904), pp. 149-72.

Hauser, A.J., 'Two Songs of Victory: A Comparison of Exodus 15 and Judges 5', in E.R. Follis (ed.), *Directions in Biblical Hebrew Poetry* (JSOTSup, 40; Sheffield: JSOT Press, 1987), pp. 265-84.

Hayes, J.H. 'The Traditions of Zion's Inviolability', *JBL* 82 (1963), pp. 419-26.

Hendel, R., *The Epic of the Patriarch: The Jacob Cycle and the Narrative Traditions of Canaan and Israel* (HSM, 42; Atlanta: Scholars Press, 1987).

—'Biblical Literature in its Historical Context: The Old Testament', *Harper's Bible Commentary* (ed. J.L. Mays; San Francisco: Harper & Row, 1988), pp. 14-26.

—'Sacrifice as a Cultural System', *ZAW* 101 (1989), pp. 366-90.

Hermisson, H.J., 'Einheit und Komplexität Deuterojesajas: Probleme der Redaktionsgeschichte von Jes. 40–55', in Vermeylen (ed.), *The Book of Isaiah*, pp. 287-312.

Herr, M.D., 'Oral Law', *EncJud* 12, pp. 1439-45.

Hesselink, I.J., *Calvin's Concept of the Law* (Allison Park, PA: Pickwick Publications, 1992).

Hiebert, 'Theophany in the OT', *ABD*, VI, pp. 505-11.

Hoffman, Y., 'A North Israelite Typological Myth and Judaean Historical Tradition', *VT* 39 (1989), pp. 169-82.

Hoffmeier, J.K., 'Egypt, Plagues in', *ABD*, II, pp. 374-78.

Holladay, W.L., *Jeremiah. 1. A Commentary on the Book of the Prophet Jeremiah. Chapters 1–25* (ed. P.D. Hanson; Hermeneia; Philadelphia: Fortress Press, 1986).

—*The Psalms through Three Thousand Years: Prayerbook of a Cloud of Witnesses* (Minneapolis: Fortress Press, 1993).

Hollenbach, D., SJ, 'The Catholic University and the Common Good', *Current Issues in Catholic Higher Education* 16.1 (1995), pp. 3-15.

Holstein, J.A., 'How Not To Read the Hebrew Bible', *The Iowa Review* 21.3 (1991), pp. 48-59.

Houston, W., *Purity and Monotheism: Clean and Unclean Animals in Biblical Law* (JSOTSup, 140; Sheffield: JSOT Press, 1993).

Howell, M., 'A Song of Salvation; Exodus 15, 1b-18' (Doctoral dissertation, Katholieke Universiteit Leuven, 1986).

Hübner, H., *Das Gesetz bei Paulus: Ein Beitrag zum Werden der paulinischen Theologie* (FRLANT, 119; Göttingen: Vandenhoeck & Ruprecht, 1978).

Huehnergard, J., 'The Early Hebrew Prefix Conjugations', *Hebrew Studies* 29 (1988), pp. 19-23.

Hurowitz, A., 'Ha'egel wehammiškan', *Shnaton* 7 (1983–84), pp. 51-59 (Heb.).

—'The Priestly Account of Building the Tabernacle', *JAOS* 105 (1985), pp. 21-30.

Hurowitz, A.(V.), *I Have Built you an Exalted House: Temple Building in the Bible in Light of Mesopotamian and Northwest Semitic Writings* (JSOTSup, 115; ASOR Monograph Series, 5; Sheffield: JSOT Press, 1992).

Hurvitz, A., 'The Evidence of Language in Dating the Priestly Code', *RB* 81 (1974), pp. 24-56.

—*A Linguistic Study of the Relationship between the Priestly Source and the Book of Ezekiel* (CahRB, 20; Paris: Gabalda, 1982).

—'The Language of the Priestly Source and its Historical Setting: The Case for an Early Date', *Proceedings of the Eighth World Congress of Jewish Studies 1981* (Jerusalem: World Union of Jewish Studies, 1983), V, pp. 83-94.

—'Dating the Priestly Source in Light of the Historical Study of Biblical Hebrew a Century after Wellhausen', *ZAW* 100 supplement (1988), pp. 88-99.

Hyatt, J.P., *Exodus* (NCB; London: Oliphants, 1971).

Irmscher, J., 'The Pseudo-Clementines', in E. Hennecke, *New Testament Apocrypha* (ed. W. Schneemelcher; trans. R.M. Wilson; 2 vols.; Philadelphia: Westminster Press, 1965).

Ishida, T., 'The Structure and Historical Implications of the Lists of Pre-Israelite Nations', *Bib* 60 (1979), pp. 461-90.

Jacob, B., *The Second Book of the Bible: Exodus* (trans. W. Jacob with Y. Elman; Hoboken, NJ: Ktav, 1992).

Jacobs, L., 'Shavuot', *EncJud* 14, pp. 1319-22.

Jacobsen, T., *The Harps that once. . . Sumerian Poetry in Translation* (New Haven: Yale University Press, 1987).

Jaki, S.L., *Genesis 1 through the Ages* (London: Thomas More, 1992).

Janowski, B., 'Tempel und Schöpfung. Schöpfungstheologische Aspekte der priester-schriftlichen Heiligtumskonzeption', *Jahrbuch für Biblische Theologie* 5 (1990), pp. 37-69.

—'Herrschaft über die Terre: Gen. 1, 26-28 und die Semantik von רדה', in G. Braulik, W. Gross and S. McEvenue (eds.), *Biblische Theologie und gesellschaftlicher Wandel. Für Norbert Lohfink SJ* (Freiburg: Herder, 1993), pp. 183-98.

Janzen, J.G., 'On the Moral Nature of God's Power: Yahweh and the Sea in Job and Deutero-Isaiah', *CBQ* 56 (1994), pp. 458-78.

Jenks, A.W., *The Elohist and North Israelite Traditions* (SBLMS, 22; Missoula, MT: Scholars Press, 1977).

—'Elohist', *ABD*, II, pp. 478-82.

Jensen, J., *The Use of Tôrâ by Isaiah: His Debate with the Wisdom Literature* (CBQMS, 3; Washington: Catholic Biblical Association, 1973).

Jensen, J., and W.H. Irwin, 'Isaiah 1-39', *NJBC*, I, pp. 229-48.

Jepsen, A., 'Beiträge zur Auslegung und Geschichte des Dekalogs', *ZAW* 79 (1967), pp. 277-304.

Jeremias, J., *Kultprophetie und Gerichtsverkündigung in der späten Königszeit Israel* (WMANT, 35; Neukirchen-Vluyn: Neukirchener Verlag, 1970).

—*Das Königtum Gottes in den Psalmen: Israels Begegnung mit dem kanaanäischen Mythos in den Jahwe-König-Psalmen* (FRLANT, 141; Göttingen: Vandenhoeck & Ruprecht, 1987).

Jervell, J., 'The Law in Luke–Acts', in idem, *Luke and the People of God: A New Look at Luke–Acts* (Minneapolis: Augsburg, 1972), pp. 133-51.

Johnstone, W., 'Reactivating the Chronicles Analogy in Pentateuchal Studies, with Special Reference to the Sinai Pericope in Exodus', *ZAW* 99 (1987), pp. 16-37.

—'The Decalogue and the Redaction of the Sinai Pericope in Exodus', *ZAW* 100 (1988), pp. 361-85.

—*Exodus* (OTG; Sheffield: JSOT Press, 1990).

Jones, F.S., *An Ancient Jewish Christian Source on the History of Christianity: Pseudo-Clementine Recognitions 1.27-71* (Atlanta: Scholars Press, 1994).

Josipovici, G., *The Book of God* (New Haven: Yale University Press, 1988).

Kaiser, O., 'The Law as the Center of the Hebrew Bible', in Fishbane and Tov with W.W. Fields (eds.), *'Sha'arei Talmon'*, pp. 93-103.

Kalimi, I., 'The Land of Moriah, Mount Moriah, and the Site of Solomon's Temple in Biblical Historiography', *HTR* 83 (1990), pp. 345-62.

Kaufman, S.A., 'The Structure of the Deuteronomic Law', *MAARAV* 1.2 (1978–79), pp. 105-58.

Kaufman, Y., *The Religion of Israel: From its Beginnings to the Babylonian Exile* (trans. and abridged M. Greenberg; New York: Schocken Books, 1972).

Kearney, P.J., 'Creation and Liturgy: The P Redaction of Ex. 25-40', *ZAW* 89 (1977), pp. 375-86.

Keel, O., *Jahwe-Visionen und Siegelkunst: Eine neue Deutung der Majestätschilderungen in Jes 6, Ez 1 und Sach 4* (Stüttgarter Bibelstudien, 84/85; Stuttgart: Katholisches Bibelwerk, 1977).

Keel, O., and C. Uehlinger, *Göttinnen, Götter und Gottessymbole: Neue Erkenntnisse zur Religionsgeschichte Kanaans und Israels aufgrund bislang unerschlossener ikonographischer Quellen* (Quaestiones Disputatae, 134; Freiburg: Herder, 1992).

Kepinski, *L'arbre stylisé en Asie Occidentale au 2e millénaire avant J.-C.*, I–III (Bibliothèque de la délégation archéologique Française en Iraq, 1; Centre de recherche d'archéologie Orientale, Université de Paris, 1.1; Editions recherche sur les civilisations, 7; Paris: Editions recherches sur les civilisations, 1982).

Kikawada, I.M., 'Literary Conventions of the Primeval History', *Annual of the Japanese Biblical Institute* 1 (1975), pp. 13-18.

Kirkpatrick, A.F., *The Book of Psalms* (Cambridge: Camridge University Press, 1957).

Kitchen, K., 'Exodus, The', *ABD*, II, pp. 700-708.

Kiuchi, N., *The Purification Offering in the Priestly Literature: Its Meaning and Function* (JSOTSup, 56; Sheffield: JSOT Press, 1987).

Kloos, C., *Yhwh's Combat with the Sea: A Canaanite Tradition in the Religion of Ancient Israel* (Amsterdam: van Oorschot; Leiden: Brill, 1986).

Knierim, R., *The Task of Old Testament Theology: Method and Cases* (Grand Rapids: Eerdmans, 1995).

Knight, D.A., 'The Pentateuch', in D.A. Knight and G.M. Tucker (eds.), *The Hebrew Bible and its Modern Interpreters* (Philadelphia: Fortress Press; Decatur, GA: Scholars Press, 1985), pp. 263-96.

Knohl, I., 'The Priestly Torah versus the Holiness School: Sabbath and the Festivals', *HUCA* 58 (1987), pp. 65-117.

—*The Sanctuary of Silence: The Priestly Torah and the Holiness School* (Minneapolis: Fortress Press, 1995).

—*Silence in the Sanctuary* (Minneapolis: Fortress Press, 1995).

Koch, K., 'P—Kein Redaktor! Erinnerung an zwei Eckdaten der Quellenscheidung', *VT* 37 (1987), pp. 446-67.

Koehler, L., 'Vom hebräischen Lexikon', *OTS* 8 (1950), pp. 1-19.

Kraus, H.J., *Worship in Israel: A Cultic History of the Old Testament* (trans. G. Buswell; Richmond, VA: John Knox, 1965).

—*Psalms 1–59: A Commentary* (trans. H.C. Oswald); Minneapolis: Augsburg, 1988).

—*Psalms 60–150: A Commentary* (trans. H.C. Oswald, Minneapolis: Augsburg, 1989).

Krebernik, M., '*ḥbrk b'l* in den phön. Karatepe-Inschriften und *'à-ba-ra-gú in Ebla*', *WO* 15 (1984), pp. 89-92.

Kruger, P.A., 'Nonverbal Communication and Symbolic Gestures in the Psalms', *BT* 45 (1994), p. 219.

Kugler, R., 'The Levi-Priestly Tradition: From Malachi to the Testament of Levi' (PhD dissertation, University of Notre Dame, 1994).

Küng, H., 'Jewish Christianity and its Significance for Ecumenism Today', in Beck *et al.* (eds.), *Fortunate the Eyes that See*, pp. 584-600.

Kutsch, E., 'Sukkot', *EncJud*, XV, pp. 495-502.

Kutscher, E.Y., *A History of the Hebrew Language* (ed. R. Kutscher; Jerusalem: Magnes; Leiden: Brill, 1982).

Laato, T., *Paul and Judaism: An Anthropological Approach* (Atlanta: Scholars Press, 1995).

Lane, E.W., *An Arabic–English Lexicon* (London: Williams & Norgate, 1963–93; repr. Beirut: Librairie du Liban, 1968).

Layton, B. (ed.), *The Gnostic Scriptures* (Garden City, NY: Doubleday, 1987).

Levenson, C., 'Liberation Theology and the Exodus', *Mainstream* 35.7 (1989), pp. 30-36.

Levenson, J.D., *Theology of the Program of Restoration of Ezekiel 40–48* (HSM, 10; Missoula, MT: Scholars Press, 1976).

—'The Theologies of Commandment in Biblical Times', *HTR* 73 (1980), pp. 17-33.

—*Sinai and Zion: An Entry into the Jewish Bible* (San Francisco: Harper & Row, 1985).

—'The Sources of Torah: Psalm 119 and the Modes of Revelation in Second Temple Judaism', in Miller, Hanson and McBride (eds.), *Ancient Israelite Religion*, pp. 559-74.

—Review of *God and his People*, by E.W. Nicholson, *CBQ* 50 (1988), pp. 306-308.

—*Creation and the Persistence of Evil: The Drama of Divine Omnipotence* (San Francisco: Harper & Row, 1988).

—'Theological Consensus or Historicist Evasion? Jews and Christians in Biblical Studies', in Brooks and Collins (eds.), *Hebrew Bible or Old Testament?*, pp. 109-45.

—*The Hebrew Bible, the Old Testament, and Historical Criticism: Jews and Christians in Biblical Studies* (Louisville, KY: Westminster/John Knox Press, 1993).

—*The Death and Resurrection of the Beloved Son: The Transformation of Child Sacrifice in Judaism and Christianity* (New Haven: Yale University Press, 1993).

Levine, B.A., *In the Presence of the Lord: A Study of Cult and Some Cultic Terms in Ancient Israel* (Leiden: Brill, 1974).

—'Late Language in the Priestly Source: Some Literary and Historical Observations', *Proceedings of the Eighth-World Congress of Jewish Studies 1981* (Jerusalem: World Union of Jewish Studies, 1983), V, pp. 69-82.

—*The JPS Torah Commentary. Leviticus* ויקרא: *The Traditional Hebrew Text with the New JPS Translation* (Philadelphia: The Jewish Publication Society, 1989).

—'*Lpny YHWH*—Phenomenology of the Open-Air Altar in Biblical Israel', *Biblical Archaeology Today 1990: Proceedings of the Second International Congress on Biblical Archaeology* (Jerusalem: Israel Exploration Society, 1992), pp. 196-205.

—*Numbers 1–20* (AB, 4; New York: Doubleday, 1993).

—Review of *Leviticus 1–16*, by J. Milgrom, *Bib* 74 (1993), pp. 280-85.

Levine, H.J., *Sing unto God a New Song: A Contemporary Reading of the Psalms* (Indiana Studies in Biblical Literature; Bloomington: Indiana University Press, 1995).

Levinson, S., *Constitutional Faith* (Princeton, NJ: Princeton University Press, 1988).

Lewis, T.J., *The Cults of the Dead in Ancient Israel and Ugarit* (HSM, 39; Atlanta: Scholars Press, 1989).

—'The Ancestral Estate (נחלת אלהים) in 2 Samuel 14.16', *JBL* 110 (1991), pp. 599-612.

Lichtheim, M., *Ancient Egyptian Literature. I. The Old and Middle Kingdoms* (Berkeley: University of California Press, 1973).

—*Ancient Egyptian Literature*. III. *The Late Period* (Berkeley: University of California Press, 1980).

Lipiński, E., *Le poème royal du Psaume LXXXIX 1.5.20-38* (CahRB 6; Paris: Gabalda, 1967).

—'Shemesh', *DDD*, p. 1445-52.

Livingstone, A., *Mystical and Mythological Explanatory Works of Assyrian and Babylonian Scholars* (Oxford: Clarendon Press, 1986).

Loewenstamm, S.E., *The Evolution of the Exodus Tradition* (trans. B.J. Schwartz; Jerusalem: Magnes, 1992).

Lohfink, N., *Das Jüdische am Christentum: Die verlorene Dimension* (Freiburg: Herder, 1987).

—*The Inerrancy of Scripture and Other Essays* (Berkeley, CA: Bibal, 1992).

Löhr, M., *Der Priesterkodex in der Genesis* (BZAW, 38; Berlin: de Gruyter, 1924).

Long, D.S., *Living the Discipline: United Methodist Theological Reflections on War, Civilization, and Holiness* (Grand Rapid: Eerdmans, 1992).

Loretz, O., 'Marziḫu im ugaritischen und biblischen Ahnenkult; Zu Ps. 23; 133; Am. 6. 1-7 und Jer. 16.5-8', in M. Dietrich and O. Loretz (eds.), *Mesopotamia–Ugaritica–Biblica: Festschrift für Kurt Bergerhof zur Vollendung seines 70. Lebensjahres am 7. Mai 1992* (AOAT, 232; Kevelaer: Butzon & Bercker; Neukirchen–Vluyn: Neukirchener Verlag, 1993), pp. 94-144.

Lustiger, J.M., 'The Absence of God? The Presence of God? A Meditation in Three Parts on Night', *America* (November 19, 1988), pp. 402-406.

McBride, S.D., 'Biblical Literature in its Historical Context: The Old Testament', *Harper's Bible Commentary* (ed. J.L. Mays; San Francisco: Harper & Row, 1988), pp. 14-26.

McCarter, P.K., 'Exodus', *Harper's Bible Commentary* (ed. J.L. Mays; San Francisco: Harper & Row, 1988), pp. 129-56.

McCarthy, D.J., *Treaty and Covenant: A Study in the Form in the Ancient Oriental Documents and in the Old Testament* (AnBib, 21A; Rome: Biblical Institute Press, 2nd edn, 1978).

McEvenue, S.E., *The Narrative Style of the Priestly Writer* (AnBib, 50; Rome: Pontifical Biblical Institute, 1971).

McKenzie, S.L., and H.N. Wallace, 'Covenant Themes in Malachi', *CBQ* 45 (1983), pp. 549-63.

Malamat, A., *Mari and the Early Israelite Experience* (The Schweich Lectures of the British Academy, 1984; Oxford: Oxford University Press, 1989).

Marcus, D., Review of *New Year with Israelites and Canaanites*, by J.C. de Moor, *JAOS* 93 (1973), pp. 589-91.

Marks, J.H., and R.M. Good (eds.), *Love and Death in the Ancient Near East: Essays in Honor of Marvin H. Pope* (Guilford, CT: Four Quarters, 1987).

Marshall, I.H. 'The Significance of Pentecost', *SJT* 30 (1977), pp. 347-69.

Martin, B.L., *Christ and the Law in Paul* (NovTSup, 62; Leiden: Brill, 1989).

Mays, H.G., 'Some Cosmic Connotations of *Mayim Rabbîm "Many Waters"*', *JBL* 74 (1955), pp. 9-21.

Meier, J.P., *A Marginal Jew: Rethinking the Historical Jesus* (ABRL; New York: Doubleday, 1991).

—*A Marginal Jew*. II. *Rethinking the Historical Jesus: Mentor, Message, and Miracles* (ABRL; New York: Doubleday, 1995).

Mendenhall, G.E., *The Tenth Generation: The Origins of the Biblical Tradition* (Baltimore: The Johns Hopkins University Press, 1973).

Mettinger, T.N.D., 'The Veto on Images and the Aniconic God in Ancient Israel', in H. Biezais (ed.), *Religious Symbols and their Functions* (Scripta Instituti Donnerians Aboensis, 10; Stockholm: Almqvist & Wiksell, 1979), pp. 15-29.

—*The Dethronement of Sabaoth: Studies in the Shem and Kabod Theologies* (ConBOT, 18; Lund: Gleerup, 1982).

—*Its Ancient Near Eastern Context* (ConBOT, 42; Stockholm: Almqvist & Wiksell, 1995).

—*No Graven Image? Israelite Aniconism in Its Ancient Near Eastern Context* (ConBOT, 42; Stockholm: Almqvist & Wiksell, 1995).

—'Cherubim', DDD, pp. 362-67.

Meyers C.L., 'Was There a Seven-Branched Lampstand in Solomon's Temple?' *BARev* 5.5 (1979), pp. 46-57.

—'Jachin and Boaz', *ABD*, III, pp. 597-98.

—'Lampstand', *ABD*, IV, pp. 141-43.

—'Sea, Molten', *ABD*, V, pp. 1061-62.

—'Temple, Jerusalem', *ABD*, VI, pp. 350-69.

Meyers, C.L., and E.M. Meyers, *Haggai, Zechariah 1–8* (AB, 25B; New York: Doubleday, 1987).

Milgrom, J., 'Israel's Sanctuary: The Priestly "Picture of Dorian Gray"', *RB* 83 (1976), pp. 390-99 [reprinted in *Studies in Cultic Theology and Terminology* [Leiden: Brill, 1983], pp. 75-84).

—*The JPS Torah Commentary. Numbers* במדבר (Philadelphia: The Jewish Publication Society, 1990)

—*Leviticus 1–16* (AB, 3; New York: Doubleday, 1991).

—*The JPS Torah Commentary. Exodus* שמות (Philadelphia: The Jewish Publication Society, 1991).

—'Priestly ("P") Source', *ABD*, V, pp. 454-62.

Milik, J.W., *Ten Years of Discovery in the Wilderness of Judaea* (trans. J. Strugnell; SBT, 26; Naperville, IL: Allenson, 1959).

—'*Milkî-ṣedeq* et *Milkî-reša'* dans les ancien écrit juifs et chrétiens', *JJS* 23 (1972), pp. 95-144.

Miller, J.W., *The Origins of the Bible: Rethinking Canon History* (New York: Paulist Press, 1994).

Miller, P.D., 'Poetic Ambiguity and Balance in Psalm XV', *VT* 29 (1979), pp. 416-24.

Miller, P.D., Jr, P.D. Hanson and S.D. McBride (eds.), *Ancient Israelite Religion: Essays in Honor of Frank Moore Cross* (Philadelphia: Fortress Press, 1989).

Moberly, R.W.L., *At the Mountain of God: Story and Theology in Exodus 32–34* (JSOTSup, 22; Sheffield: JSOT Press, 1983).

—*The Old Testament of the Old Testament: Patriarchal Narratives and Mosaic Yahwism* (Overtures to Biblical Theology; Minneapolis: Fortress Press, 1992).

Moor, J.C. de, *The Seasonal Pattern in the Ugaritic Myth of Ba'lu according to the Version of Ilimilku* (AOAT, 16; Kevelaer: Butzon & Bercker; Neukirchen–Vluyn: Neukirchener Verlag, 1971).

—*New Year with Canaanites and Israelites* (Kampen: Kok, 1972).

Moore, M., Review of *Studien zur Priestschrift*, by Schmidt, *CBQ* 56 (1994), pp. 778-90.

Moran, W.L., 'The Hebrew Language in its Northwest Semitic Background', in G.E.

Wright (ed.), *The Bible and the Ancient Near East: Essays in Honor of William Foxwell Albright* (Garden City, NY: Doubleday, 1965), pp. 59-84.

Morgenstern, J., *Rites of Birth, Marriage, Death and Kindred Occasions among the Semites* (Cincinnati: Hebrew Union College Press, 1966).

Mosca, P., 'Once Again the Heavenly Witness of Ps 89:38', *JBL* 105 (1986), pp. 27-37.

—'Ugarit and Daniel 7: A Missing Link', *Bib* 67 (1986), pp. 509-12.

Mowinckel, S., 'Der Ursprung der Bil'amsage', *ZAW* 48 (1930), pp. 233-71.

—*The Psalms in Israel's Worship* (trans. D.R. Ap-Thomas; Biblical Seminar, 14; 2 vols.; Sheffield: JSOT Press, 1992 [1962]).

Muffs, Y., *Love and Joy: Law, Language and Religion in Ancient Israel* (New York: Jewish Theological Seminary, 1992).

Muilenberg, J., 'A Liturgy on the Triumphs of Yahweh', *Studia Biblica et Semitica: Theodoro Christiano Vriezen* (Wageningen: Veenman & Zonen, 1966), pp. 233-51.

Muraoka, T., 'Much Ado About Nothing? A Sore Point or Two of Hebrew Grammarians', *JEOL* 32 (1991–92), pp. 131-40.

Murphy, R.E., 'Old Testament/*Tanakh*—Canon and Interpretation', in Brooks and Collins (eds.), *Hebrew Bible or Old Testament?*, pp. 11-29.

Nasuti, H., 'Identity, Identification and Imitation: The Narrative Hermeneutics of Biblical Law', *The Journal of Law and Religion* 4 (1986), pp. 9-23.

—*Tradition History and the Psalms of Asaph* (SBLDS, 88; Atlanta: Scholars Press, 1988).

National Conference of Catholic Bishops, *Economic Justice for All: Pastoral Letter on Catholic Social Teaching and the US Economy* (Washington, DC: United States Catholic Conference, 1986).

Nelson, R.D., 'Studies in the Development of the Tabernacle Account' (PhD dissertation, Harvard University, 1987).

—*Raising Up a Faithful Priest: Community and Priesthood in Biblical Theology* (Louis-ville, KY: Westminster/John Knox Press, 1993).

Neusner, J., *The Oral Torah. The Sacred Books of Judaism: An Introduction* (San Fran-cisco: Harper & Row, 1987).

Nicholson, E.W., *God and His People: Covenant and Theology in the Old Testament* (Oxford: Clarendon Press, 1986).

—'The Pentateuch in Recent Research: A Time for Caution', in J.A. Emerton, *Congress Volume: Leuven 1989* (VTSup, 43; Leiden: Brill, 1991), pp. 10-21.

Norin, S.I.L., *Er spaltete das Meer: Die Auszugsüberlieferung in Psalmen und Kult des Alten Testament* (ConBOT, 9; Lund: Gleerup, 1977).

North, C.R., 'Pentateuchal Criticism', in H.H. Rowley (ed.), *The Old Testament and Modern Study: A Generation of Discovery and Research* (Oxford Paperbacks; Oxford: Clarendon Press, 1961), pp. 48-83.

Noth, M., *Exodus: A Commentary* (trans. J.S. Bowden; OTL; Philadelphia: Westminster Press, 1962).

—*The Old Testament World* (trans. V.I. Gruhn; Philadelphia: Fortress Press, 1966).

—*A History of Pentateuchal Traditions* (trans. with introduction by B.W. Anderson; Atlanta: Scholars, 1981 [1972]).

—*Numbers: A Commentary* (ET; London: SCM Press, 1968).

O'Brien, J.M., *Priest and Levite in Malachi* (SBLDS, 121; Atlanta: Scholars Press, 1990).

O'Connor, C., 'The Structure of Psalm 23', *Louvain Studies* 10.3 (1984), pp. 206-30.

Oates, J., *Babylon* (London: Thames & Hudson, rev. edn, 1986), pp. 169-74.

Oesterly, W.O.E., *The Psalms* (London: SPCK, 1962).

326   *The Pilgrimage Pattern in Exodus*

Ollenburger, B., *Zion the City of the Great King: A Theological Symbol of the Jerusalem Cult* (JSOTSup, 41; Sheffield: JSOT Press, 1987).

Olson, D., *The Death of the Old and the Birth of the New: The Framework of the Book of Numbers and the Pentateuch* (BJS, 71; Chico, CA: Scholars Press, 1985).

—'Numbers', *Harper's Bible Commentary* (ed. J.L. Mays; San Francisco: Harper & Row, 1988), pp. 182-83.

Olson, M.J., 'Pentecost', *ABD*, V, pp. 222-23.

Olyan, S., *Asherah and the Cult of Yahweh in Israel* (SBLMS, 34; Atlanta: Scholars Press, 1988).

Östborn, G., *Tora in the Old Testament: A Semantic Study* (Lund: Håkan Ohlssons Boktryckeri, 1945).

Osten-Sacken, P. von der, *Die Heiligkeit der Tora: Studien zum Gesetz bei Paulus* (Munich: Chr. Kaiser Verlag, 1989).

Osumi, Y., *Die Kompositionsgeschichte des Bundesbuches Exodus 20.22b–23.33* (OBO, 105; Göttingen: Vandenhoeck & Ruprecht, 1991).

Ottosson, M., *Temples and Cult Places in Palestine* (Boreas, Uppsala Studies in Ancient Mediterranean and Near Eastern Civilizations, 12; Uppsala: Uppsala University Press, 1980).

Outler, A.C. (ed.), *The Work of John Wesley* (Nashville: Abingdon Press, 1984–87).

Pardee, D., 'A New Ugaritic Letter', *BO* 34 (1977), pp. 3-20.

—'A Further Note on *PRU* V, No. 60', *UF* 13 (1981), pp. 152-56.

—'Structure and Meaning in Hebrew Poetry: The Example of Psalm 23', in Cook (ed.), *Sopher Mahir*, pp. 275-80.

Parker, S.B., 'Exodus XV 2', *VT* 20 (1970), pp. 358-59.

Parrot, A., *Mission archéologique de Mari. II. Le palais: Peintures murales* (Institut Français d'Archéologie de Beyrouth; Bibliothèque archéologique et historique, 59; Paris: Geuthner, 1958).

Paul, S., *Studies in the Book of the Covenant in the Light of Cuneiform and Biblical Law* (VTSup, 18; Leiden: Brill, 1970).

Paul, S., and W. Dever, *Biblical Archaeology* (Jerusalem: Keter Publishing House, 1973).

Pedersen, S. (ed.), 'Legalism and Salvation by the Law', *Die paulinische Literatur und Theologie. Skandinavische Beiträge* (Teologiske Studier, 7; Göttingen: Vandenhoeck & Ruprecht, 1980) (reprinted in *The Torah and Christ: Essays in German and English on the Problem of the Law in Early Christianity* [Publications of the Finnish Exegetical Society, 45; Helsinki: Finnish Exegetical Society, 1986]).

Perlitt, L., *Bundestheologie im Alten Testament* (WMANT, 36; Neukirchen–Vluyn: Neukirchener Verlag, 1969).

Petersen, D.L., *Haggai and Zechariah 1–8* (OTL; Philadelphia: Westminster Press, 1984).

Pleins, J.D., 'Murderous Fathers, Manipulative Mothers, and Rivalrous Siblings: Re-thinking the Architecture of Genesis–Kings', in Beck *et al.* (eds.), *Fortunate the Eyes that See*, pp. 121-36.

Pope, M.H., *Song of Songs* (AB, 7; Garden City, NY: Doubleday, 1977), pp. 599-600.

—'The Timing of the Snagging of the Ram, Genesis 22.13', *BA* 49 (1986), pp. 114-17; reprinted in *idem*, *Probative Pontificating in Ugaritic and Biblical Literature: Collected Essays* (ed. M.S. Smith; Ugaritisch-Biblische Literatur, 10; Münster: Ugarit-Verlag, 1994), pp. 305-10.

Porada, E., *Mesopotamian Art in Cylinder Seals of the Pierpont Morgan Library* (New York: Pierpont Morgan Library, 1947).

Porter, B.N., *Images, Power, and Politics: Figurative Aspects of Esarhaddon's Babylonian Policy* (Memoirs of the American Philosophical Society held at Philadelphia for Promoting Useful Knowledge, 208; Philadelphia: American Philosophical Society, 1993).

Porter, C., 'History and Literature: "After the New Historicism"', *New Literary History* 21.2 (1990), pp. 253-72.

Porter, C., 'Response to Rena Fraden', *New Literary Criticism* 21.2 (1990), pp. 279-81.

Postgate, J.N., 'In Search of the First Empires', *BASOR* 293 (1994), pp. 1-13.

Postma, F., E. Talstra, and M. Vervenne, *Exodus: Materials in Automatic Text Processing. I. Morphological, Syntactical and Literary Case Studies* (Instrumental Biblica, 1.1; Amsterdam: Turnhout; Brepols: Vu Boekhandel, 1983), pp. 98-108.

Propp, W.H., 'The Skin of Moses' Face—Transfigured or Disfigured?', *CBQ* 49 (1987), pp. 375-86.

—*Water in the Wilderness: A Biblical Motif and its Mythological Background* (HSM, 40; Atlanta: Scholars Press, 1987).

—'Did Moses Have Horns?', *Bible Review* 4.1 (1988), pp. 30-37.

Pury, A. de (ed.), *Le Pentateuque en question: Les origines et la composition des cinq premiers livres de la Bible à la lumière de recherches récentes* (MDB, 19; Geneva: Labor et Fides, 2nd edn, 1989).

Quintens, 'La vie du roi dans le Psaume 21', *Bib* 59 (1978), pp. 516-41.

Rabin, C., 'Etymological Miscellanea', *Scripta Hierosolymitana* 8 (1961), pp. 384-400.

Rad, G. von, *The Problem of the Hexateuch and Other Essays* (trans. E.W.T. Dicken; New York: McGraw–Hill, 1966).

—*Die Priesterschrift in Hexateuch* (BWANT, 4; Berlin/Stuttgart: n.p., 1934).

—*Old Testament Theology. I. The Theology of Israel's Historical Traditions* (trans. D.M.G. Stalker; New York: Harper & Brothers, 1962).

—*Gesammelt Studien zum Alten Testament* (TBü, 8; Munich: Chr. Kaiser Verlag, 1961).

Rainey, A.F, 'The Scribe at Ugarit: His Position and Influence', *Proceedings of the Israel Academy of Sciences and Humanities* 3 (1969), pp. 126-47.

—'The Hebrew Prefix Conjugation in the Light of Amarnah Canaanite', *Hebrew Studies* 27 (1986), pp. 4-19.

Räisänen, H., 'Paul's Theological Difficulties with the Law', *JSNT* 3 (1980), pp. 301-20.

—'Legalism and Salvation by the Law', in S. Pedersen (ed.), *Die paulinische Literatur und Theologie. Skandinavische Beiträge* (Teologiske Studier, 7; Göttingen: Vandenhoek & Ruprecht, 1980), pp. 63-83.

—*Paul and the Law* (WUNT 29; Tübingen: Mohr (Siebeck), 1983).

—*The Torah and Christ: Essays in German and English on the Problem of the Law in Early Christianity* (Publications of the Finnish Exegetical Society, 45; Helsinki: Finnish Exegetical Society, 1986).

Reeves, E.B., *The Hidden Government: Ritual, Clientalism, and Legitimation in Northern Egypt* (Salt Lake City: University of Utah Press, 1990).

Rehm, M.D., 'Levites and Priests', *ABD*, IV, pp. 297-310.

Renaud, B., *La théophanie du Sinaï, Exod. 19–24: Exégèse et théologie* (CahRB, 30; Paris: Gabalda, 1991).

Rendsburg, G., 'Late Biblical Hebrew and the Date of "P"', *JANESCU* 12 (1980), pp. 65-80.

—*The Redaction of Genesis* (Winona Lake, IN: Eisenbrauns, 1986).

—*Linguistic Evidence for the Northern Origin of Selected Psalms* (SBLMS, 43; Atlanta: Scholars Press, 1990).

Rendtorff, R., *The Problem of the Process of Transmission in the Pentateuch* (trans. J.J. Scullion; JSOTSup, 89; Sheffield: JSOT Press, 1990 [BZAW, 147; Berlin: de Gruyter, 1976]).

—'Old Testament Theology, Tanakh Theology, or Biblical Theology? Reflections in an Ecumenical Context', *Bib* 73 (1992), p. 451.

—'The Image of Postexilic Israel in German Bible Scholarship', in Fishbane and Tov with Fields (eds.), *'Sha'arei Talmon'*, pp. 165-73.

—'The Paradigm is Changing: Hopes—and Fears', *BI Sample Issue* (1922), pp. 6-12.

Richardson, M.E.J., 'Ugaritic Place-Names with Final -*y*', *JSS* 23 (1978), pp. 298-315.

Richardson, P., and S. Westerholm, *Law in Religious Communities in the Roman Period: The Debate over* Torah *and* nomos *in Post-Biblical Judaism and Early Christianity* (Studies in Christianity and Judaism, 4; Waterloo, ON: Wilfred Laurier University Press, 1991).

Roberts, J.J.M., 'The Religio-Political Setting of Psalm 47', *BASOR* 220 (1975), pp. 129-32.

Robertson, D.A., *Linguistic Dating in Dating Early Hebrew Poetry* (Missoula, MT: Scholars Press, 1972).

Rochberg-Halton, F., 'Astrology in the Ancient Near East', *ABD*, I, pp. 504-507.

Rofé, A., *The Prophetical Stories. The Narratives about the Prophets in the Hebrew Bible: Their Literary Types and History* (Jerusalem: Magnes, 1988).

Rogerson, J.W., *W.M.L. de Wette. Founder of Modern Biblical Criticism: An Intellectual Biography* (JSOTSup, 126; Sheffield: JSOT Press, 1992).

Rooker, M.F., *Biblical Hebrew in Transition: The Language of the Book of Ezekiel* (JSOTSup, 90; Sheffield: JSOT Press, 1990).

Rosenbaum, M., and A.M. Silbermann, *Pentateuch with Targum Onkelos, Haphtaroth and Rashi's Commentary: Exodus* (Jerusalem: The Silbermann Family, 1930).

Roth, M.S., 'Introduction', *New Literary History* 21.2 (1990), pp. 239-51.

Rowley, H.H., 'Moses and the Decalogue', *BJRL* 34 (1951), pp. 81-118.

Rudolph, W., *Der 'Elohist' von Exodus bis Joshua* (BZAW, 68; Giessen: Töpelmann, 1983).

Rummel, S., 'Narrative Structures in the Ugaritic Texts and Hebrew Bible', in S. Rummel (ed.), *Ras Shamra Parallels III: the Texts from Ugarit and the Hebrew Bible* (AnOr, 51; Rome: Pontifical Biblical Institute, 1981), pp. 234-77.

Safrai, S., *Die Wallfahrt im Zeitalter des zweiten Tempels* (Neukirchen–Vluyn: Neukirchener Verlag, 1981).

—'Religion in Everyday Life', in S. Safrai and M. Stern (eds.), *The Jewish People in the First Century: Historical Geography, Political History, Social, Cultural and Religious Life and Institutions.* II (CRINT, 1; Assen: Van Gorcum; Philadelphia: Fortress Press, 1987), pp. 793-833.

—'The Temple', in S. Safrai and M. Stern (eds.), *The Jewish People in the First Century: Historical Geography, Political History, Social, Cultural and Religious Life and Institutions.* II (CRINT, 1; Assen: Van Gorcum; Philadelphia: Fortress Press, 1987), pp. 865-907.

Sailhammer, J.H., *The Pentateuch as Narrative: A Biblical–Theological Commentary* (Grand Rapids: Eerdmans, 1992).

Sakenfeld, K.D., *Numbers: Journeying with God* (International Theological Commentary; Grand Rapids: Eerdmans; Edinburgh: Handsell, 1995).

Sanders, E.P., *Paul, the Law and the Jewish People* (Philadelphia: Fortress Press, 1983).

—*The Jewish Law from Jesus to the Mishnah* (London: SCM; Philadelphia: Trinity, 1990).

—'Law in Judaism of the New Testament Period', *ABD*, IV, p. 254-65.

Sargent-Baur, B.N. (ed.), *Journeys toward God: Pilgrimage and Crusade* (SMC, 30; Medieval Institute Publications; Kalamazoo, MI: Western Michigan University Press, 1992).

Sarna, N., *Exodus: The Traditional Hebrew Text with the New JPS Translation* (Philadelphia: The Jewish Publication Society, 1991).

—*Songs of the Heart: An Introduction to the Book of Psalms* (New York: Schocken Books, 1993).

—'Exodus, Book of', *ABD*, II, pp. 689-700.

Sasson, J.M., 'Time. . . To Begin', in Fishbane and Tov with Fields (eds.), *'Sha'arei Talmon': Studies in the Bible, Qumran, and the Ancient Near East Presented to Shemaryahu Talmon*, pp. 183-94.

Savran, G., '1 and 2 Kings', in Alter and Kermode (eds.), *The Literary Guide to the Bible*, pp. 146-64.

Schaeffer, C.F.A., 'Nouveaux témoignages du culte de El et de Baal à Ras Shamra et ailleurs en Syrie Palestine', *Syria* 43 (1966), pp. 1-19.

Schaeffer-Forrer, C.F.A., *Corpus des cylindres-sceaux de Ras-Shamra-Ugarit et d'Enkomi-Alaasia*, 1 (Éditions recherche sur les civilizations, 13; Paris: Association pour la Diffusion de la Pensée Française, 1983).

Schart, A., *Mose und Israel im Konflikt: Eine redaktionsgeschichtliche Studie zu den Wüstenerzählung* (OBO, 98; Freiburg: Universitätsverlag; Göttingen: Vandenhoeck & Ruprecht, 1990).

Schmid, H., *Der sogenannte Jahwist: Beobachtungen und Fragen zur Pentateuch-forschung* (Zürich: Theologischer Verlag, 1976).

—*Die Gestalt des Mose: Probleme alttestamentlicher Forschung unter Berücksichtigung der Pentateuchkrise* (Erträge der Forschung, 237; Darmstadt: Wissenschaftliche Buchgesellschaft, 1986).

Schmidt, B., *Israel's Beneficent Dead: Ancestor Cult and Necromancy in Ancient Israelite Religion and Tradition* (repr. Winona Lake, IN: Eisenbrauns, 1995).

Schmidt, B.B., 'Moon', *DDD*, pp. 1098-1113.

Schmidt, L., *Studien zur Priestschrift* (BZAW, 214; Berlin: de Gruyter, 1993).

Schmidt, W.H., *Exodus, Sinai und Mose* (Erträge der Forschung, 191; Darmstadt: Wissen-schaftliche Buchgesellschaft, 1983).

Schmitt, H.C., 'Das sogenannte vorprophetie Berufungsschema. Zur "geistigen Heimat" des Berufungsformulars von Exod. 3,9-12; Jdc 6,11-24 und I Sam. 9,1-10,16', *ZAW* 104 (1992), pp. 202-16.

Schroer, S., 'Die Göttin auf den Stempelsiegeln aus Palästina/Israel', in O. Keel, H. Keel-Lev and S. Schroer (eds.), *Studien zu den Stempelsiegeln aus Palästina/ Israel*. II. *Die Frühe Eisenzeit, ein Workshop* (OBO, 20; Freiburg: Universitätsverlag; Göttingen: Vandenhoeck & Ruprecht, 1989).

Schunck, K.D., 'Benjamin', *ABD*, I, pp. 671-73.

Schwienhorst-Schönberger, L., *Das Bundesbuch (Ex 20, 22-23,33): Studien zu seiner Entstehung und Theologie* (BZAW, 188; Berlin: de Gruyter, 1990).

Scolnic, B., 'Theme and Context in Biblical Lists' (PhD dissertation, The Jewish Theological Seminary of America, 1987).

—'Bloom on J on God: Upside-Down or Right-Side-Up?', *Conservative Judaism* 43.4 (1991), pp. 73-79.

—'Strangers in the PaRDeS: Conservative Judaism and the Torah', in E.S. Schoenberg (ed.), *Study Guide to the Discovery* (New York: Jewish Theological Seminary, n.d.).

Segal, A.F., '*Torah* and *nomos* in Recently Scholarly Discussion', *Studies in Religion/ Sciences Religieuses* 13 (1984) (reprinted in Segal, *The Other Judaisms of Late Antiquity* [BJS, 127; Atlanta: Scholars Press, 1987]).

—*Paul the Convert: The Apostolate and Apostasy of Saul the Pharisee* (New Haven: Yale University Press, 1990).

Segal, B.-Z. (ed.), *The Ten Commandments in History and Tradition* (trans. G. Levi; Jerusalem: The Hebrew University, 1987).

Seitz, C., 'The Divine Council: Temporal Transition and New Prophecy in the Book of Isaiah', *JBL* 109 (1990), pp. 229-46.

Seitz, C.R., *Zion's Final Destiny: The Development of the Book of Isaiah. A Reassessment of Isaiah 36–39* (Minneapolis: Fortress Press, 1991).

Seow, C.L., 'Ark of the Covenant', *ABD*, I, pp. 386-93.

—'Face', *DDD*, pp. 607-13.

Setel, D.O., 'Exodus', in C.A. Newsom and S.H. Ringe (eds.), *The Women's Bible Commentary* (London: SPCK; Louisville, KY: Westminster/John Knox Press, 1992), p. 28.

Seters, J. van, 'The So-Called Deuteronomistic Redaction of the Pentateuch', in J.A. Emerton (ed.), *Congress Volume: Leuven 1989* (VTSup, 43; Leiden: Brill, 1991), pp. 58-77; Blum, *Studien*, p. 103.

Sheppard, G.T., 'Canonical Criticism', *ABD*, I, pp. 861-66.

Shuval, M., 'A Catalogue of Early Iron Stamp Seals from Israel', in O. Keel, M. Shuval and C. Uehlinger (eds.) *Studien zu den Stempelsiegeln aus Palästina/Israel. III. Die Frühe Eisenzeit, Ein Workshop* (OBO, 100; Freiburg: Universitätsverlag; Göttingen: Vandenhoeck & Ruprecht, 1990).

Silberman, L.H., 'Wellhausen and Judaism', in D. Knight (ed.), *Julius Wellhausen and his Prolegomena to the History of Israel* (Semeia, 25; Chico, CA: Scholars Press, 1983), pp. 75-82.

Simkins, R.A., *Creator and Creation: Nature in the Worldview of Ancient Israel* (Peabody, MA: Hendrickson, 1994).

Ska, J.L., 'Quelques remarques sur P^g et la dernière rédaction du Pentateuque', in de Pury (ed.), *Le Pentateuque en question,* pp. 95-125.

Skehan, P.W., E. Ulrich and J.E. Sanderson, *Qumran Cave 4. IV. Palaeo-Hebrew and Greek Biblical Manuscripts* (DJD, 9; Oxford: Clarendon Press, 1992).

Smith, C.R., 'The Literary Structure of Leviticus', *JSOT* 70 (1996), pp. 17-32.

Smith, M., 'Helios in Palestine', *ErIsr* 16 (1982), pp. 199-214.

—'Divine Travel as a Token of Divine Rank', *UF* 16 (1984), p. 397.

Smith, M.S., 'Biblical and Canaanite Notes to the Songs of the Sabbath Sacrifice from Qumran', *RevQ* 48 (1987), pp. 585-87.

—*Psalms: The Divine Journey* (Mahwah, NJ: Paulist Press, 1987).

—'Divine Form and Size in Ugaritic and Pre-Exilic Israelite Religion', *ZAW* 100 (1988), pp. 424-27.

—'"Seeing God in the Psalms": The Background to the Beatific Vision in the Hebrew Bible', *CBQ* 50 (1988), pp. 171-83.

—'Setting and Rhetoric in Psalm 23', *JSOT* 41 (1988), pp. 61-66.

—'The Near Eastern Background of Solar Language for Yahweh', *JBL* 109 (1990), pp. 34-39.

—'The Levitical Compilation of the Psalter', *ZAW* 103 (1991), pp. 258-63.

—*The Early History of God: Yahweh and the Other Deities of Ancient Israel* (San Francisco: Harper & Row, 1991).

—'The Psalms as a Book for Pilgrims', *Int* 46 (1992), pp. 156-66.

—'The Invocation of Deceased Ancestors in Psalm 49.12c', *JBL* 112 (1993), pp. 105-107.

—'Mythology and Myth-Making in Ugaritic and Israelite Literatures', in G.J. Brooke, A.H.W. Curtis and J.F. Healey (eds.), *Ugarit and the Bible: Proceedings of the International Symposium on Ugarit and the Bible. Manchester, September 1992* (Ugaritisch-Biblische Literatur, 11; Münster: Ugarit-Verlag, 1994), pp. 309-21.

—*The Ugaritic Baal Cycle*. I. *Introduction with Text, Translation and Commentary of the First Two Tablets (KTU 1.1–1.2)* (VTSup, 55; Leiden: Brill, 1994).

Speiser, E.A. (ed.), 'Leviticus and the Critics', in M. Haran, *Yehezkel Kaufman Jubilee Volume* (Jerusalem: Magnes, 1960), pp. 29-45.

Spieckermann, H., *Juda unter Assur in der Sargonidenzeit* (FRLANT, 129; Göttingen: Vandenhoeck & Ruprecht, 1982).

—*Heilsgegenwart: Eine Theologie der Psalmen* (FRLANT, 148; Göttingen: Vandenhoeck & Ruprecht, 1989).

Spronk, K., *Beatific Afterlife in Ancient Israel and in the Ancient Near East* (AOAT, 219; Kevelaer: Butzon & Bercker; Neukirchen–Vluyn: Neukirchener Verlag, 1986).

Spykerboer, H.C., 'Isaiah 55.1-5: The Climax of Deutero-Isaiah; An Invitation to Come to the New Jerusalem', in Vermeylen (ed.), *The Book of Isaiah*, pp. 357-59.

Stager, L.E., 'The Archaeology of the Family', *BASOR* 260 (1985), pp. 1-35.

Steck, O.H., 'Tritijesaja im Jesajabuch', in Vermeylen (ed.), *The Book of Isaiah* (BETL, 81; Leuven), pp. 361-406.

Strange, J., 'The Idea of Afterlife in Ancient Israel: Some Remarks on the Iconography in Solomon's Temple', *PEQ* 117 (1985), pp. 35-40.

Stuhlmueller, C., 'Psalms', in *Harper's Bible Commentary* (ed. J.L. Mays; San Francisco: Harper & Row, 1988), pp. 433-94.

Tabori, J., *Jewish Festivals in the Time of the Mishna and Talmud* (Jerusalem: Magnes, 1995) (Hebrew).

Taylor, J.G., *Yahweh and the Sun: Biblical and Archaeological Evidence for Sun Worship in Ancient Israel* (JSOTSup, 111; Sheffield: JSOT Press, 1993).

Tengström, S., *Die Toledotformel und die literarische Struktur der priestlichen Erweiterungsschicht im Pentateuch* (ConBOT, 17; Lund: Gleerup, 1971).

Tessier, B., *Ancient Near Eastern Cylinder Seals from the Marcopoli Collection* (Berkeley: University of California Press; Beverly Hills, CA: Summa Publications, 1984).

Thielman, F., *From Plight to Solution: A Jewish Framework for Understanding Paul's View of the Law in Galatians and Romans* (NovTSup, 61; Leiden: Brill, 1989).

Thompson, T.L., *The Origin Tradition of Ancient Israel*. I. *The Literary Formation of Genesis and Exodus 1–23* (JSOTSup, 55; Sheffield: JSOT Press, 1988).

Tigay, J.H., 'On Some Aspects of Prayer in the Bible', *American Jewish Studies Review* 1 (1976), pp. 363-79.

—'Conflation as a Redactional Technique', in Tigay (ed.), *Empirical Models*, pp. 53-95.

—'The Evolution of the Pentateuchal Narratives in Light of the Evaluation of the *Gilgamesh Epic*', in Tigay (ed.), *Empirical Models*, pp. 21-52.

Tigay, J.H. (ed.), *Empirical Models for Biblical Criticism* (Philadelphia: University of Pennsylvania, 1985).

Tomson, P.J., *Paul and the Jewish Law: Halakha and the Letters of the Apostle to the Gentiles* (CRINT, 3; Jewish Traditions in Early Christian Literature I; Assen: Van Gorcum; Philadelphia: Fortress Press, 1990).

Toorn, K. van der, 'The Babylonian New Year Festival: New Insights from the Cuneiform Texts and their Bearing on Old Testament Study', *Congress Volume: Leuven 1989* (ed. J.A. Emerton; VTSup, 43; Leiden: Brill, 1991), pp. 331-44.

—*From her Cradle to her Grave: The Role of Religion in the Life of the Israelite and the Babylonian Woman* (trans. S.J. Denning-Bolle; Biblical Seminar, 23; Sheffield: JSOT Press, 1994).

—'Migration and the Spread of Local Cults', in K. van Lerberghe and A. Schoors (eds.), *Immigration and Emigration within the Ancient Near East: Festschrift E. Lipiński* (OLA, 65; Leuven: Peeters, 1995), pp. 365-77.

—'Ritual Resistance and Self-Assertion: The Rechabites in Early Israelite Religion', in J. Platvoet and K. van der Toorn (eds.) *Pluralism and Identity: Studies in Ritual Behavior* (Leiden: Brill, 1995), pp. 244-48.

—*Family Religion in Babylonia, Syria and Israel: Continuity and Change in the Forms of Religious Life* (Studies in the History and Culture of the Ancient Near East, 7; Leiden: Brill, 1996).

Tournay, R.J., 'Chronologie des Psaumes', *RB* 65 (1958), pp. 340-57.

—*Seeing and Hearing God with the Psalms: The Prophetic Liturgy of the Second Temple in Jerusalem* (trans. J.E. Crowley; JSOTSup, 118; Sheffield: JSOT Press, 1991).

Tov, E., 'Theologically Motivated Exegesis Embedded in the Septuagint', *Translation of Scripture, Proceedings of a Conference at the Annenberg Research Institute May 15–16, 1989, A Jewish Quarterly Review Supplement: 1990* (Philadelphia: Annenberg Research Institute, 1990), pp. 215-33.

Trible, P., 'The Bible in Bloom', *The Iowa Review* 21.3 (1991), pp. 19-32.

Tromp, N.J., *Primitive Conceptions of Death and the Nether World in the Old Testament* (BibOr, 21; Rome: Pontifical Biblical Institute, 1969).

Tucker, G., 'The Sayings of the Wise are Like Goads: An Appreciation of the Works of Robert Cover', *Conservative Judaism* 45.3 (1993), pp. 17-39.

Tuell, S.S., *The Law of the Temple in Ezekiel 40–48* (HSM, 49; Atlanta: Scholars Press, 1992).

Turner, V., 'Pilgrimages as Social Processes', in *idem, Drama, Fields, and Metaphors: Symbolic Action in Human Society* (Ithaca, NY: Cornell University Press, 1974), pp. 166-230.

Turner, V., and E. Turner, *Image and Pilgrimage in Christian Culture: Anthropological Perspectives* (New York: Columbia University Press, 1978).

Uchelen, N.A. van, 'Psalm xxiii. Some Regulative Linguistic Evidence', *OTS* 25 (1989), pp. 156-62.

Ulrich E., *et al.*, *Qumran Cave 4. VII. Genesis to Numbers* (DJD, 12; Oxford: Clarendon Press, 1994).

Van Buren, E.D., *Symbols of the Gods in Mesopotamian Art* (AnOr, 23; Rome: Pontifical Biblical Institute, 1945).

Van Seters, J., *Abraham in History and Tradition* (Yale Near Eastern Researches; New Haven: Yale University Press, 1975).

—' "Comparing Scripture with Scripture": Some Observations on the Sinai Pericope of Exodus 19–24', in G.M. Tucker, D.L. Petersen and R.R. Wilson (eds.), *Canon, Theology and Old Testament Interpretation* (Philadelphia: Fortress Press, 1988), pp. 111-30.

—*Prologue to History: The Yahwist as Historian in Genesis* (Louisville, KY: Westminster/John Knox Press, 1992).

—*The Life of Moses: The Yahwist as Historian in Exodus–Numbers* (Louisville, KY: Westminster/John Knox Press, 1994).

—'A Contest of Magicians? The Plague Stories in P', in Wright, Freedman and Hurvitz (eds.), *Pomegranates and Golden Bells*, pp. 569-80.

—'The So-Called Deuteronomic Redaction of the Pentateuch', in J.A. Emerton (ed.), *Congress Volume: Leuven 1989* (VTSup, 43; Leiden: Brill, 1991), pp. 58-77.

Vanderkam, J.C., 'Ahikar/Ahiqar', *ABD*, I, pp. 113-15.

Vaux, R. de, *Ancient Israel* (2 vols; New York: McGraw–Hill, 1965).

—'Sur l'origine kénite ou midianite du Yahvisme', *ErIsr* 9 (1969 = W.F. Albright Festschrift), pp. 28-30.

Vermeylen, J. (ed.), *The Book of Isaiah: Le livre d'Isaïe: Les oracles et leur relectures: Unité et complexité de l'ouvrage* (BETL, 81; Leuven: Leuven University Press/ Peeters, 1989).

Vervenne, M., 'The Protest Motif in the Sea Narrative (Exod. 14.11-12): Form and Structure of a Pentateuchal Pattern', *ETL* 63 (1987), pp. 257-71.

—'The "P" Tradition in the Pentateuch: Document and/or Redaction? The "Sea Narrative" (Exod. 13,17–14,31) as a Test Case', in C. Brekelmans and J. Lust (eds.), *Pentateuchal and Deuteromistic Studies: Papers Read at the XIIIth IOSOT Congress, Leuven 1989* (BETL, 94; Leuven: Leuven University Press/Peeters, 1990), pp. 67-90.

Viviano, B., 'Matthew', *NJBC*, II, p. 641.

Vollenweider, M.L., *Catalogue raisonné des sceaux cylindres et intailles*, I (Geneva: Musée d'art et d'histoire Genève, 1967).

Volz, P., *Neujahrsfest Jahwes* (Tübingen: Mohr, 1912).

Volz, P., and W. Rudolph, *Der Elohist als Erzähler ein Irrweg der Pentateuchkritik?* (BZAW, 63; Giessen: Töpelmann, 1933).

Vriezen, T.H., 'Exodusstudien Exodus 1', *VT* 17 (1967), pp. 334-53.

Waldman, N.M., 'A Comparative Note on Exodus 15.14-16', *JQR* 66 (1978), pp. 189-92.

Wallace, H.N., *The Eden Narrative* (HSM, 32; Chico, CA: Scholars Press, 1985).

Waltke, B.K., and M.P. O'Connor, *An Introduction to Biblical Hebrew Syntax* (Winona Lake, IN: Eisenbrauns, 1990).

Watts, J.D., 'Public Readings and Pentateuchal Law', *VT* 45 (1995), pp. 540-57.

—'Rhetorical Strategy in the Composition of the Pentateuch', *JSOT* 68 (1995), pp. 3-22.

Watts, J.D.W., 'The Song of the Sea—Ex. XV', *VT* 7 (1957), pp. 371-80.

Watts, J.W., *Psalm and Story: Inset Hymns in Hebrew Narrative* (JSOTSup, 139; Sheffield: JSOT Press, 1992), pp. 41-62.

Wei, T.F., 'Pithom', *ABD*, V, pp. 376-77.

Weimar, P., *Die Berufung des Mose: Literaturwissenschaftliche Analyse von Exodus 2,23–5,5* (OBO, 32; Freiburg: Universitätsverlag; Göttingen: Vandenhoeck & Ruprecht, 1980).

Weinfeld, M., Review of *God and His People*, by E.W. Nicholson, *RB* 98 (1991), p. 435.
—*Deuteronomy and the Deuteronomic School* (Oxford: Oxford University Press, 1972).
—'Literary Creativity', in A. Malamat and I. Eph'al, (eds.), *World History of the Jewish People. First Series: Ancient Times. IV.2 The Age of the Monarchies: Culture and Society* (Jerusalem: Masada, 1979), pp. 28-33.
—'Sabbath, Temple and the Enthronement of the Lord—The Problem of the Sitz im Leben of Genesis 1.1–2.3', in A. Caquot and M. Delcor (eds.), *Mélanges bibliques et orientaux en l'honneur de M. Henri Cazelles* (AOAT, 212; Kevelaer: Butzon & Bercker; Neukirchen-Vluyn: Neukirchener Verlag, 1981), pp. 501-12.
—'Instructions for Temple Visitors in the Bible and Ancient Egypt', in S. Israelit-Groll (ed.), *Egyptological Studies Scripta Hierosolymitana XXVIII* (Jerusalem: Magnes, 1982), pp. 224-50.
—'Zion and Jerusalem as Religious and Political Capital: Ideology and Utopia', in R.E. Friedman (ed.), *The Poet and the Historian: Essays in Literary and Historical Biblical Criticism* (HSS, 26; Chico, CA: Scholars Press, 1983), pp. 75-115.
—'The Uniqueness of the Decalogue and its Place in Jewish Tradition', in B.-Z. Segal (ed.), *The Ten Commandments*, pp. 21-27.
—*Deuteronomy 1–11* (AB, 5; New York: Doubleday, 1991).
Weisman, Z., 'Societal Divergences in the Patriarchal Narratives', *Henoch* 17 (1995), pp. 11-27.
Weiss, M. 'Psalm 23: The Psalmist on God's Care', in Fishbane and Tov with Fields (eds.), *'Sha'arei Talmon'*, pp. 31-41.
Wellhausen, *Prolegomena to the History of Ancient Israel* (Gloucester, MA: Peter Smith, 1973).
Westbrook, R., *Property and the Law in Biblical Law* (JSOTSup, 113; Sheffield: JSOT Press, 1991).
Westermann, C., *Creation* (trans. J.J. Scullion; Philadelphia: Fortress Press, 1974).
Wevers, J.W., *Notes on the Greek Text of Exodus* (SBLSCS, 30; Atlanta: Scholars Press, 1990).
—*Exodus* (Septuaginta; Göttingen: Vandenhoeck & Ruprecht, 1991).
White, M., 'The Elohistic Depiction of Aaron: A Study in the Levite–Zadokite Controversy', in Emerton (ed.), *Studies in the Pentateuch*, pp. 149-59.
Whybray, R.N., *The Making of the Pentateuch: A Methodological Study* (JSOTSup, 53; Sheffield: JSOT Press, 1987).
—*Introduction to the Pentateuch* (Grand Rapids: Eerdmans, 1995).
Wills, L.M., *The Jew in the Court of the Foreign King: Ancient Jewish Court Legends* (HDR, 26; Minneapolis: Fortress Press, 1990).
Wilson, G.H., *The Editing of the Hebrew Psalter* (SBLDS, 76; Chico, CA: Scholars Press, 1985).
Wilson, R.R., 'The Hardening of Pharaoh's Heart', *CBQ* 41 (1979), pp. 18-36.
—*Prophecy and Society in Ancient Israel* (Philadelphia: Fortress Press, 1980).
—'The Death of the King of Tyre: The Editorial History of Ezekiel 28', in Marks and Good (eds.), *Love and Death*, pp. 211-18.
—'The Community of Second Isaiah', in C.R. Seitz, (ed.), *Reading and Preaching the Book of Isaiah* (Philadelphia: Fortress Press, 1988), pp. 53-70.
Wilson, S.G., *Luke and the Law* (Cambridge: Cambridge University Press, 1983).
Wimmer, J.F., 'Tradition Reinterpreted in Ex. 6.2-7.7', *Augustianum* 7 (1967), pp. 405-18.

Winnett, F.V., 'Re-Examining the Foundations', *JBL* 84 (1965), pp. 1-19.

Wright, D.P., D.N. Freedman, and A. Hurvitz (eds.), *Pomegranates and Golden Bells: Studies in Biblical, Jewish, and Near Eastern Ritual, Law, and Literature in Honor of Jacob Milgrom* (Winona Lake, IN: Eisenbrauns, 1995).

Wright, G.E., 'Solomon's Temple Resurrected', *BA* 4 (1941), pp. 17-31.

Wyatt, N., 'Of Calves and Kings: The Canaanite Dimension in the Religion of Israel', *SJOT* 6 (1992), pp. 77-83.

Yee, G.A., *Jewish Feasts and the Gospel of John* (Zacchaeus Studies: New Testament; Wilmington, DE: Michael Glazier, 1989).

Zakovitch, , *'And You Shall Tell Your Son . . .' The Concept of the Exodus in the Bible* (Jerusalem: Magnes, 1991).

Zalcman, L., 'Pleiades', *DDD*, pp. 1240-42.

Zatelli, I., 'Astrology and the Worship of the Stars in the Bible', *ZAW* 103 (1990), pp. 92-93.

Zatelli, , 'Constellations', *DDD*, pp. 386-91.

Zenger, E., 'Tradition and Interpretation in Exodus XV 1-21', *Congress Volume: Vienna 1980* (ed. J.A. Emerton; VTSup, 32; Leiden: Brill, 1981), pp. 452-83.

Zevit, Z., 'The Priestly Redaction and the Interpretation of the Plague Narrative in Exodus', *JQR* 66 (1976), pp. 194-205.

—'Converging Lines of Evidence Bearing on the Date of P', *ZAW* 92 (1982), pp. 481-511.

—'Philology, Archaeology, and a *Terminus a Quo* for P's *ḥaṭṭā't* Legislation', in Wright, Freedman and Hurvitz (eds.) *Pomegranates and Golden Bells*, pp. 29-38.

Zimmerli, W., *I am Yahweh* (ed. W. Brueggemann; trans. D.W. Stott; Atlanta: John Knox, 1982).

INDEXES

INDEX OF REFERENCES

OLD TESTAMENT

INDEX OF AUTHORS

JOURNAL FOR THE STUDY OF THE OLD TESTAMENT
SUPPLEMENT SERIES